D0640856

YOUR MEMORY

YOUR
MEMORY

How It Works

&

How to Improve It

SECOND EDITION

KENNETH L. HIGBEE, PHD.

Marlowe & Company
New York

First Marlowe & Company edition, 1996

Published by
Marlowe & Company
841 Broadway, Fourth Floor
New York, NY 10003

Copyright ©. 1977, 1988 and 1996 by Kenneth L. Higbee

Manufactured in the United States of America

Library of Congress Cataloging-in-Publication Data

Higbee, Kenneth L., 1941-
 Your memory : how it works and how to improve it / Kenneth L.
 Higbee. —2nd ed.
  p. cm.
 Originally published : New York : Prentice Hall, c1988.
 Includes bibliographical reference and index.
 ISBN 1-56924-801-X
 1. Mnemonics. 2. Memory. I. Title
 BF385.H48 1996
 153. 1'4—dc20   95-49468
                     CIP

To Dawn, Janelle, Loren, and Lana, who have accepted their roles as children of a memory researcher and willingly (?) tried many of the techniques in this book.

Contents

Introduction:
What Can You Expect from
This Book?

What is memory? Why do you remember some things and forget others? How can you remember more? Does it depend on what you learn? Does it depend on how you learn? Were you born with a good or a bad memory? Can a bad memory be improved? Can you develop a photographic memory? How can you study more effectively? What are mnemonics?* Can mnemonics improve your memory in everyday life? How can you set up and use your own mental filing system? Can mnemonics help you to remember people's names, to overcome absent-mindedness, and to succeed in school? These are just a few of the questions that will be answered in this book.

WHY DID I WRITE IT?

My interest in questions such as the ones above began when I first read a book on memory improvement as a student in high school. I was amazed at the things I could do with my memory by using mnemonic techniques. Through the years I have continued to add memory books to my personal library, and to learn and use new memory systems and techniques. My reading of popular books on memory improvement has supplemented my academic research and professional training as a psychologist, giving me a balanced perspective between the popularized treatments of memory training and the scientific research on learning and memory. That balance is reflected in this book. I am a university

---

*Mnemonics are defined and discussed in chapter 7. However, since the word *mnemonic* is used frequently in the first six chapters, a brief definition is also given here. The term *mnemonic* means "aiding the memory." Thus, a mnemonic system or technique is literally any system or technique that aids the memory. Typically, however, the term *mnemonic* refers to rather unusual, artificial memory aids.

professor of psychology who has a serious teaching and research interest in memory improvement: I am not primarily a memory performer or a self-proclaimed expert with "the greatest memory in the world." (There are already plenty of those "experts" around!)

Since 1971 I have given hundreds of lectures and conducted seminars and workshops throughout the United States and in a half dozen other countries. I have taught memory improvement and reported my memory research to diverse audiences, including psychologists and memory researchers, business groups, professional groups, students, children, and the elderly. During this period, I have also taught a college course on memory improvement.

My teaching and research experiences have given me an idea of what people want to know and need to know about memory. In fact, the main reason I wrote the first edition of this book in 1976 was my inability to find any one textbook that covered all these areas for my memory course. More than a decade later, most books on memory still tend to fall into one of two categories: college textbooks on learning and memory and popular books on mnemonics and memory training.

This book provides a reasonable balance between the textbooks and the popular books. I like to think of it as the thinking person's memory book. Methods, principles, and systems are related to relevant research literature in such a way as to make the book accurate (so that it will be valid to psychologists) but also understandable (so that it will be useful to the layman). Feedback on the first edition indicates that this attempt to combine scholarly accuracy with readability was successful.

Even though the original impetus for this book arose from my desire to provide a textbook for students in my memory course, I have written the book so that it can be used by anyone who is interested in improving memory. This consideration has determined my choice of what subjects to cover, what to say about them, and in what order to cover them. The book is a practical, self-contained guide that you can study on your own to understand and improve your memory.

WHY SHOULD YOU READ IT?

Comments made by students in my memory course suggest some of the ways in which the contents of this book can aid you. Some representative remarks selected from hundreds of comments written by students who finished the book and the course follow.

By applying mnemonics I find myself to be more effective and more organized, and to have a considerable amount of self-confidence that I had not experienced before.

If I could have learned these things early in my college career, I would have saved many hours and probably had a higher grade point average.

I honestly did not think any of this memory business would be of help to me now that I am out of school, but it really has.

The systems make learning seem more like a game than work. I almost feel guilty it's so fun.

Truthfully, I had always been skeptical of mnemonic devices, especially in regards to my ability to use them. Yet now I find them to be useful as well as fun.

I am now aware of some of the capabilities of the human mind (mine specifically) which I previously thought were out of reach.

When you finish studying this book you, too, will have a better under-standing of what your memory is and what it can do; you will be aware of basic principles to guide you in improving your memory; and you will have an extensive repertoire of learning strategies and mnemonic systems that will enable you to use some of the capabilities of your mind that you may have thought previously were "out of reach." Specifically, this book has five characteristics that should help you achieve these results:

It is more practical than textbooks on learning and memory. Memory textbooks are oriented generally toward an academic understanding of memory theories and research, and contain little information on improving memory. Mnemonic techniques are not discussed or are touched on only in passing as interesting oddities that are of little practical value. This book avoids discussion of many theories and side issues that are of interest to the academician and researcher but are not as important to the layman. I have discovered through my teaching experiences that most people are more concerned with improving their memories than they are with understanding how their memories work.

This book is intended to be a practical guide to understanding and improving your memory; therefore, the emphasis is more on how to do it than on academic and theoretical issues of memory. Thus, only the first three chapters are primarily devoted to understanding memory (the "how it works" part), and they cover only what is necessary to be able to use the other chapters (the "how to improve it" part).

It is less technical than textbooks on learning and memory. Besides being academically oriented in content, most memory textbooks tend to be written in a style that is too technical to be interesting and understand-able to people without a background in psychology. These readers almost need a psychologist to explain the book to them. This book was written for the intelligent student and layman who does not have a background in psychological research on learning and memory, and it is intended to bridge the communication gap that sometimes exists between scientists and laymen. Thus, the technical terms and professional jargon used in many textbooks are avoided as much as possible, and such terms are explained whenever they are used.

It is more technical than popular books on memory training. This book is intended primarily to instruct, not to entertain (although I have nothing against entertaining, and I try to combine the two whenever possible). Thus, it is intended to be studied, not to be read like a novel or a magazine article. It is intended more for people who are serious about wanting to improve their memories than for people who want to do some light reading.

In addition, although the primary emphasis of this book is on improving your memory, some attention is also given to understanding your memory. The serious reader not only learns how to use memory techniques but gains an understanding of how and why they work; this approach is not found in most popular books on the subject.

It is more objective than popular books on memory training. Many popular books on memory training tend to be sensationalistic and some-what unrealistic in their claims. For example, they give the reader the impression that the mnemonic techniques discussed will help in every possible learning task (with little or no effort), and that if you use the right techniques you will never forget anything again. In addition, they give the impression that mnemonic techniques are all-powerful and have no limitations. Many books are sprinkled with such sensationalistic terms as "super-power memory," "computer mind," and "amazing mental powers." This book presents a more realistic perspective.

Mnemonics can make a significant contribution to memory in many situations, but different principles and methods (discussed in this book) can be applied in other situations. In addition, although mnemonic techniques are very powerful for many kinds of learning, they do have limitations. This book presents both the strengths and limitations of mnemonics. I cannot promise you that after reading this book (or any other book) you will be able to learn everything the first time you see or hear it, and that you will never forget anything you learn. However, I can promise you that if you apply the methods described in this book, your memory will improve significantly, and you will be able to do things with your memory that you could not do before reading this book.

It is based on recent research evidence. Most popular books on memory training do not present any sound evidence that the techniques really work. As a result, many people get the impression that mnemonics and some other techniques are just gimmicks associated with showmanship, or that they are not practical, or that they are not worth the effort. After reading such a book, people may say, "Well, that was interesting," and go on their way unchanged because they don't plan to give memory demonstrations onstage. This book presents research evidence that illustrates the strengths and weaknesses of the principles, techniques, and systems discussed. Thus, what has actually been found to work is discussed, rather than what someone says should work, or what seems as if it should work. This approach should help you realize that the techniques are based on sound scientific principles of learning: They can make a significant contribution to practical memory tasks in everyday life.

The research evidence in this book is recent, not what was known about memory a decade or more ago. More than three-fourths of the research references are dated after the first edition of this book was published in 1977, with two-thirds of these new references dated during the last five years.

WHAT WILL YOU FIND IN IT?

A lot has happened in the area of memory training since 1977. At least two memory-training books that were originally published more than 25 years ago were reprinted in the 1980s. In addition, more than a dozen new books have been published; two of these were written for general audiences by psychologists and memory researchers, and another half dozen were targeted at specific audiences—business executives, elderly people, students. (And these are only the books I have read. Undoubtedly, there are others that I'm not even aware of!)

During the past decade, memory researchers and psychologists have also shown an increased interest in mnemonics and other practical aspects of memory (e.g., schoolwork, names and faces, everyday experiences, absentmindedness, eyewitness testimony). This increased research interest was reflected in the first international conference on practical aspects of memory in 1978; the second was held in 1987. (I participated in both.) The appearance of several new journals that publish primarily research on the practical aspects of memory and the publication of several books dealing with research on mnemonics and other practical aspects of memory underscore this redirected interest. What all this means is that in 1988 there is at least as much, if not more, interest in the topics that this book covers as there was when the first edition was published in 1977.

Chapter 1 clarifies some memory myths—misconceptions that many people have about what they can expect from their memories. Chapters 2 and 3 give a basic understanding of the nature of memory and answer some questions you may have about your memory. The first three chapters serve as a foundation for understanding and using the rest of the book. Chapters 4 and 5 discuss some principles on which effective memory strategies (including most mnemonics) are based. Chapter 6 describes learning strategies that can help you learn material that may not be especially suited for mnemonics. Chapters 7 and 8 give an introduction to mnemonics, including the strengths and limitations of mnemonic techniques and systems. Chapters 9 through 12 explain the nature and uses of specific mnemonic systems as mental filing systems. Chapters 13 and 14 suggest additional practical uses of mnemonics in three areas of everyday life: remembering people's names, overcoming absentmindedness, and doing schoolwork.

As a result of a decade of experience with the first edition, I have made many minor changes in content and organization to make the second edition even more beneficial. Many of the topics covered in the first edition have been expanded in the second edition, and many new topics have been included. Some of these new topics are scattered throughout the book, such as examples of how my memory students have used mnemonics and the relevance of some memory aids to special populations like the elderly, young children, students, and the learning disabled. Other new topics have been added in specific sections: additional memory myths (chapter 1), the serial position effect and the strategy of "thinking around it" (chapter 4), the effects of anxiety and context on memory (chapter 5), the problem of maintaining newly learned memory skills (chapter 8), and the role of mnemonics and memory in education (chapter 14).

Another major change in the second edition is the updating of the research references so that the book still reflects the most recent findings. Most of the hundreds of hours I spent on the second edition were spent finding and reading the relevant research published since 1976. I read about the same number of articles and books for the second as I did for the first edition (700–800); however, fewer than half of them are included in the book.

The research activity on understanding and improving memory has accelerated during the time since the first edition was written. Literally thousands of research articles and scholarly books are relevant to the topics covered in this book. (Indeed, whole books have been written on topics that constitute only one section of a chapter in this book.) To cite all of the relevant research would be unduly burdensome (both to me and to you), so I have used two strategies to limit the number of references. First, when several studies are relevant to a certain point, one or two of the most recent studies have usually been cited. Second, articles or books that review a number of studies have frequently been cited, rather than the original studies.

YOUR
MEMORY

1

What Can You Expect from Your Memory? Ten Myths

You, too, can have a photographic memory! With this new miracle memory system, you will never again forget anything. It requires no work or willpower, and anyone can use it immediately. Once you learn this secret of a super-power memory you will be able to learn everything perfectly and effortlessly!

For years, claims like these have been made in advertisements for memory-training books and courses. In fact, these claims come from actual advertisements I have read. If you think such claims sound too good to be true, you are right. Yet they continue to attract people because they are consistent with myths that many people believe about what is involved in improving memory.

This chapter discusses some memory myths to give you a realistic idea of what you can expect and what you cannot expect from your memory. In some ways people expect too much from their memories; in other ways they expect too little. At one extreme are people who believe the fantastic claims like those in the advertisement above; at the other extreme are people who believe they are stuck forever with a "bad" memory, and there is nothing they can do about it. A realistic understanding of what the potential is for your memory can help you achieve that potential.

As you read the following myths, keep in mind that some of them may have a grain of truth. However, all the myths are false enough to be misleading. Let's look at some memory myths that can affect what you expect from your memory.

1

MYTH 1: MEMORY IS A THING

People often talk about their memories as if a memory were some *thing* that they possess. They talk about having a good memory or a bad memory like they talk about having good teeth or a bad heart; or they speak of strong and weak memories like muscles (see myth 7); or they say their memory is failing like their eyes are failing. Memory does not exist in the sense of some thing (object, organ, gland, etc.) that can be seen, touched, weighed, or X-rayed. We can't cut open a person's head and say, "That's a good, healthy-looking memory" or "That memory looks bad, it must come out" or "This person definitely needs a memory transplant."

The word *memory* is merely an abstraction that refers to a process rather than a structure. As one experienced memory researcher wrote recently, "Over the past 10 years my ideas have moved progressively away from a view of memory as a structural system—a 'thing in the head'—and towards the viewpoint . . . of *remembering* as an activity."[1] Not only is memory not an identifiable structure but the process cannot even be located at an identifiable place in the brain: There is no one particular part of the brain where all remembering occurs. (Researchers do not even fully understand exactly *what* occurs when we remember, let alone *where* it occurs.)

Thus, memory is more appropriately viewed as an abstract process rather than as a tangible thing. Actually, however, memory may not even be a single process, but rather a number of different processes (activities, skills, attributes, etc.). Recent approaches to memory are organized around the idea of separate subsystems.[2] There appear to be at least three memory systems—sensory, short-term, and long-term—and many psychologists believe that long-term memory is composed of several different types of remembering (see chapter 2).

Even a specific memory of a specific object may consist of a number of different attributes or categories.[3] For example, you may remember a particular chair in terms of its class (furniture), its characteristics (large), its function (sitting), and its location (living room). Memories can also be stored in different senses. There is a difference between remembering what things look like, what they sound like, what they feel like, and what they taste or smell like. Even within the same sense there can be differences; for example, a person may be able to repeat a conversation he has heard but not be able to reproduce a simple melody. There are also motor memories that are not even stored in the conscious levels of the brain (try to describe how you tie a shoelace, or where certain keys are located on a typewriter).

In light of the complexity of your memory it should not be too surprising that psychologists must measure several features when they try to diagnose memory. For example, the most widely used memory scale, the Wechsler Memory Scale, consists of seven different subtests that are added together to give a summary score of memory functioning. However, psychologists do not always agree on what features to measure: One analysis of 9 memory scales found that they measured a total of 18 different memory features and no single scale measured more than 10 of the features.[4]

Thus, when we talk about improving "memory," we are not talking about some thing that we are making stronger or bigger. We have seen that there are two misconceptions involved in the myth that memory is a thing. One is that memory is a *thing* (a tangible structure rather than an abstract process) and the other is that memory is *a* thing (one memory rather than many memories). This myth underlies several others.

MYTH 2: THERE IS A SECRET TO A GOOD MEMORY

One of the most common questions people ask about memory improvement is, "What is the secret of a good memory?" Some people who read a book or take a course on memory training expect to find *the* secret of memory improvement—the one key that will enable them to master their memories completely. They hope that if they can just do that one thing, they will never again forget anything they see or hear. This is an unrealistic expectation.

Suppose you show to people in a carpentry class a tool that you call a "hammer." You demonstrate the amazing things it can do that cannot be done with the unaided hand. Someone says, "Yes, but how do you saw a board with it?" You explain, "This tool isn't intended to saw boards. There is another tool for sawing boards; it's called a *saw*. What a hammer does, it does very powerfully, but it is not supposed to do everything." Wouldn't it seem unrealistic of people to expect one tool to do all carpentry jobs?

Similarly, there is no single tool that will handle all memory jobs; there is no single "secret" to a good memory. Many techniques and systems can serve as tools to build an effective memory and enable us to do amazing things that cannot be done with the unaided memory. What these memory tools do, they do very powerfully, but no tool does the whole job by itself. You cannot build a complete memory with a single memory tool any more than you can build a complete building with a single carpentry tool.

Well, if there is no single memory method that will do everything, is there a *best* one? This question is analogous to asking: Is there a best golf club to use? The answer is: It varies with the circumstances. Many circumstances determine what memory method is best to use to learn material. For example:

1. Who is doing the learning? A chemistry professor and a beginning chemistry student may use different methods to study a new chemistry book.
2. What is to be learned? Different methods may be used for learning word lists, nonsense syllables, numbers, poems, speeches, and book chapters.
3. How will remembering be measured? Preparing for a recognition task may require a different method than preparing for a recall task.
4. What kind of remembering is required? Rote rememering of facts may require a different method than understanding and applying the facts, and word-for-word memorizing may require a different method than remembering ideas and concepts.
5. How long will remembering be required? Preparing to recall material immediately after learning it may require a different method than preparing to recall it a week later.

The practical implication of this consideration is that when a person asks how he can improve his memory, he cannot expect a useful answer until he makes his question more specific.[5] What kind of material does he want to remember? In what way? Under what circumstances? For how long? There are methods and principles in this book that apply to almost any kind of learning situation, but none applies to all situations.

Not only is there no single secret to mastering your memory but most memory techniques are not even "secrets." Many memory-training authors and lecturers give the impression that they are letting you in on their own secret memory techniques; however, the techniques are secret only in the sense that many people are not aware of them. They are not secret in the sense of being someone's own discovery or invention, or of anyone having a patent on them or having the right to control who gets to learn them or use them. One widely used memory system (discussed in chapter 10) is about 2,500 years old, and many others are more than 300 years old (see chapters 11 and 12).

MYTH 3: THERE IS AN EASY WAY TO MEMORIZE

This myth goes hand in hand with myth 2. Many people not only hope to find the one key to a good memory but expect that key to take the work out of memorizing. In fact, that is why they are looking for the secret. However, remembering is hard work, and memory techiques do not necessarily make it easy, they just make it more effective. You still have to work at it, but you get more out of your efforts. Some people talk about memory "tricks" as if they were used in the place of "real" memorization, but memory techniques do not *replace* the basic psychological principles of learning (such as those discussed in chapters 4 and 5), they *use* them (see chapter 7).

Some people believe that an intelligent person (one with a high IQ) will naturally remember more easily than a person with a lower IQ. It is true that some relationship exists between intelligence and memory ability. If memory tests were given to two groups of people who had no formal memory training, one group with high IQs and one group with low IQs, most of the high-IQ people would score better on the test. One reason for this is that intelligent people may be more likely to learn and use effective memory techniques and methods on their own. (Research has found that in school good students show more initiative in using memory aids and learning strategies on their own than do poor students.)[6] However, if a group of people with high IQs who had not learned effective memory techniques were compared on a memory test with people with average IQs who had learned effective memory techniques, the average-IQ people would perform better. Remembering is a learned skill.

Because remembering is a learned skill, improving memory is like developing any other skill. You must work at it by learning the appropriate techniques and practicing them. Suppose you want to be good at golf, math, speed-reading, or anything else. Would you expect to learn just one secret and have the skill mastered without further effort? No. You would expect to learn principles and techniques, apply them, practice them, and thus gradually develop the skill.

Unfortunately, many people do not think this way when it comes to memory; they don't want to work at it. Some authors purposely appeal to such people; for example, at least two memory-training books published in the 1980s have the word *easy* in the title. When such people find out that improving memory takes effort, they often decide they can get along well enough with their present memories. Plan to expend some effort if you really want to benefit from the principles and systems discussed in this book. (Research on learning strategies used by students in school supports this idea: Improved study effectiveness and school performance do not come easy, but depend on extensive training and practice with study skills and learning strategies.)[7]

My experiences and observations suggest that laziness may play a role in the inability of many adults to learn and remember as well as they say they would like to. They are not used to investing the mental effort necessary to learn as they had to do when they were in school. They have gotten out of the habit of studying and are not willing to put in the work it takes to remember effectively. Research has shown that number of years of schooling and currently being in school were both positively related to memory ability and use of memory techniques in middle-aged women, and that adults who remain mentally active by maintaining reading and studying habits are able to remember what they read better than adults who do not stay mentally active.[8]

MYTH 4: SOME PEOPLE ARE STUCK WITH BAD MEMORIES

"I have a bad memory." Have you ever heard that statement? Have you ever made it? In the first place, you do not even have a memory (see myth 1). But even if we view memory as an ability or skill rather than a thing, this myth still applies. If people mean that they have not learned the memory skills that others have learned when they say "I have a bad memory," then this statement would not be a myth. But what people usually mean when they say they have a bad memory is "There is something innately inferior about my memory ability." This statement implies that nothing can be done to improve memory.

Remembering is a basic psychological process that is common to all people, barring brain damage or severe mental or psychological disturbances. Some popular books on memory training even go so far as to suggest that there is no such thing as a good memory or a bad memory: There are only trained memories or untrained memories. Although there may be some truth to this statement, it is not completely accurate. There are probably some differences among people in innate memory abilities; in this sense, there may be such a thing as a good memory and a bad memory. However, the important point is that even if there are such innate differences in memory, except for a few extreme cases these innate differences are not nearly as important in the ability to remember as are differences in learned memory skills.

The capacity of your memory is a function of the memory techniques you use more than a function of any innate differences in memory ability. Thus, improving your techniques improves your capacity. To illustrate this point, let us compare a large cardboard box to a small 3″ × 5″ file box. Which one has more "capacity" in terms of how much it can hold? The cardboard box does. But suppose that one person writes notes on 3″ × 5″ cards and throws them in the cardboard box. A second person writes his notes on 3″ × 5″ cards and files them alphabetically in the small file box. Now, suppose each person later wants to find a specific card. Which one will be able to find it more easily? Even though the cardboard box can hold more cards, the file box actually has a larger usable capacity because the cards are stored in such a way that they can be found when needed. Similarly, the usable capacity of your memory depends more on how you store information than it does on any innate "capacity." (In fact, we will see in chapter 2 that your long-term memory has a virtually unlimited capacity.) Unfortunately, most people use their memories like the big cardboard box—they just throw the information in and hope that they will be able to find it when they need it.

We saw in myth 1 that memory consists of a number of different activities. This means that there is no single standard by which to judge a "good" or "bad" memory. For example, a person who claims to have a good memory may mean that he can do any one of a number of very different things: Read a book and tell you everything that is in it; read a paragraph and recite it word for word; tell you anything you want to know about a given topic; recall many experiences from his early childhood; never forget anniversaries and appointments; or still be able to do something, like play chess or speak a foreign language, that he has not done for years.[9] Many people would have a good memory for some of these memory tasks and a bad memory for others.

MYTH 5: SOME PEOPLE ARE BLESSED WITH PHOTOGRAPHIC MEMORIES

Wouldn't it be great to have a photographic memory that works like a camera taking a snapshot? You could take a quick picture of a scene or a page of print, and then describe it in complete detail at any time by conjuring up the whole snapshot in your mind. Are there people who can do this? Would it solve all your memory problems if you could do this? Most psychologists do not believe in this popular notion of a photographic memory, although there is a valid phenomenon called *eidetic imagery* that is somewhat similar to this notion (see chapter 3).

As a teacher of memory improvement, I am concerned that the popular notion of photographic memory leads people to believe that a person who remembers well has some *thing* that others do not (see myth 1). Whenever they see someone perform an amazing memory feat they may throw it under the vague heading of "photographic memory" because they do not know how else to explain it. After seeing a person perform a fantastic memory feat, they shrug their shoulders and say, "He has a photographic memory. I don't. That's why I could never do that." The fact that this person has a photographic memory seems to give them a convenient excuse for not being able to remember as well as he can.

In a sense, the photographic memory myth is just the flip side of the bad memory myth. Both lead people to emphasize innate differences in memory ability rather than learned memory skills. There may possibly be such a thing as photographic memory. I cannot completely discount the possibility of its existence, because of rare examples of truly exceptional memories like those described in chapter 3. However, when people with amazing memories are tested in controlled research settings it is usually found that what most people would attribute to photographic memory is not something innate, but is merely the skillful application of powerful memory techniques like those discussed in this book that virtually anyone can use if he or she really wants to learn the techniques and practice them.

I have done a demonstration several times that illustrates the difference between a photographic memory and the application of powerful memory techniques. The demonstration consists of memorizing a 50-page magazine completely enough to be able to answer such questions as: What is on page 32? On what page is the article about communication? What is on the page opposite the picture of a tower? How many pictures are on page 46? How many people are in the lower left picture on page 9, and what are they doing? Who wrote the article about tolerance? What is the name of the main character in the story that begins on page 17, and what happened to her on page 19? I can answer almost any question people may ask.

When I finish such a demonstration, someone almost always asks if I have a photographic memory. I explain that I possess no such power, but merely use the powerful mnemonic techniques explained in this book. (Incidentally, my daughter performed this same demonstration when she was thirteen years old.) There is nothing magical or effortless about my memorizing a 50-page magazine so that I know what is on every page, where it is on the page, who wrote everything and took all the photographs, and what is in every picture and article. It takes me about three hours of study to memorize a magazine to that extent. The fact that I do not have a photographic memory is shown by an occasional question that I cannot answer, such as: How many of the people in the picture on page 21 are wearing glasses? Or, what is the third word on page 42? If I did not consciously record such information when studying the magazine in the first place, I cannot answer the question. On the other hand, if I had a photographic memory I could merely conjure up in my mind a picture of page 21 or page 42 and count how many people are wearing glasses, or read the third word.

MYTH 6: SOME PEOPLE ARE TOO OLD/YOUNG TO IMPROVE THEIR MEMORIES

You have probably heard the saying that you can't teach an old dog new tricks. Actually, there is another saying that is probably more accurate, but is not quite as well known: "The quickest way to become an old dog is to quit learning new tricks." There has been a lot of recent research interest in memory of the elderly. The number of published studies on adult development and aging doubled from the mid-1970s to the mid-1980s, reaching more than 1,000 articles a year; about two-thirds of that research is on memory and there were at least 17 review articles published on the subject in just the first half of the 1980s.[10]

Not too surprisingly, most research has shown that elderly adults do not learn as efficiently or remember as well as young adults do. However, research since the 1970s has been less negative in this respect than earlier research, indicating in general that declines in mental abilities occur later in life, and in fewer abilities, than was thought earlier.

Several significant considerations should be kept in mind regarding the apparent memory decline in the elderly.

1. The term *elderly* generally refers to people in their mid-sixties through their seventies (a few people in their eighties and a few in their early sixties may be included); typically, they are compared with young adults in their twenties. Not much memory research has been done on adults in their thirties through fifties.

2. The amount of decline in memory performance with age is not as great as is popularly believed; middle-aged and elderly people particularly often have exaggerated beliefs about their own mental inadequacies. Memory difficulties that occur in people of all ages may be emphasized in the elderly and attributed to age, which causes less confidence in their abilities and more reporting of memory problems.

3. All memory skills do not decline equally; for example, visual and spatial skills typically decline in most adults from their twenties through their sixties, but verbal skills (such as memory for names, stories, words, and numbers) show very little, if any, decline.

4. A fourth consideration is suggested by a saying I once read: The error of youth is to think that intelligence is a substitute for experience, while the error of age is to think that experience is a substitute for intelligence. Although neither intelligence nor experience may completely substitute for the other, research indicates that a rich experience and knowledge base helps many old adults perform some mental tasks at the same or higher levels as young adults, even though they might not be able to learn as quickly. Such "practical intelligence" can compensate for many negative effects of aging.[11]

5. Researchers do not agree on the causes of a decline of memory skills in old age. Most researchers do agree that there is probably no single process that accounts for age differences in memory. Some of the aging effects may be due to physiological causes (e.g., cell loss or central nervous system dysfunction), but many of the effects are probably due to psychological causes or other causes that may be amenable to change. Examples of such causes suggested by research include motivation, distractibility, response speed, motor skills, lazy mental habits, interest, depression, health, education, and anxiety in research settings that are new or involve time pressure. Notice that many of these factors have nothing to do directly with mental ability: This has led some researchers to make a distinction between *competence* and *performance* in remembering and other mental skills in the elderly.

Regardless of the reasons why many elderly adults remember less than young adults, a more important question is whether the elderly can improve their memory abilities. That is, for an elderly person the question, "Can you remember as well as a twenty-year-old?" may not be as important as the question, "Can you remember better than you do now?" The answer to the latter question is yes! Much research has shown that elderly people can learn and use the memory techniques in this book to remember better, and my own experiences in teaching elderly students also support this claim.[12]

At the other end of the age scale from the very old are the very young. There has also been a great amount of research done on learning and memory in young children.[13] Most children younger than the early teens would probably have a hard time reading and understanding a book such as this one well enough to use the memory techniques effectively on their own. However, a lot of research shows that with the help of adults, children as young as ages seven or eight can use most of the techniques and systems in this book; even preschool children can be taught to use some of the techniques. I have taught memory courses to children as young as age eight, and I taught the Peg system to two of my own children when they were ages three and four (see chapter 11). Experimental research has even been done on memory in infants, although, obviously, they cannot be taught the techniques in this book.

MYTH 7: MEMORY, LIKE A MUSCLE, BENEFITS FROM EXERCISE

Some popular books on memory training suggest that memory is like a muscle. If you want a muscle to become stronger, you exercise it.

Similarly, they say that if you want your memory to become stronger, all you have to do is exercise it—practice memorizing. In fact, some people believe that practice is one of the simple "keys" to memory improvement (see myth 2): All you have to do is practice memorizing things and your memory will become stronger. For example, in one book, a chapter titled, "How to Cash in on Your Unused Brainpower," advocates "Iso-mental exercises" (patterned after isometric exercises for the body) as "the secret of learning faster and remembering more." A chapter in another book on learning is titled "Strengthening Your Mental Muscle," and tells us, "In one sense, the mind is like a set of muscles. And those muscles never gain tone—usability—until they're properly exercised." This mental exercise is proposed as the answer to the question of how we can unlock the "other 80 or 90 percent" of our mental powers (see myth 10).[14]

In the late 1800s, William James, often referred to as the father of American psychology, tested whether he could improve his memory by exercising it. He memorized some of Victor Hugo's works, and then practiced memorizing Milton for 38 days. After this practice, he memorized more from Hugo, and found that he actually memorized a bit slower than he had previously; he reported similar results for several other people who tried the same task. Similarly, twelve-year-old girls practiced memorizing poetry, scientific formulas, and geographical distances for 30 minutes a day, 4 days a week, for 6 weeks. The practice did not result in any improvement in their ability to memorize. A more recent study found that after practicing several hours a week for 20 months, a college student was able to increase his short-term memory span for digits from 7 to 80 digits. However, he showed no increased ability in other kinds of memory tasks, including short-term memory for letters or words: He improved his memory for digits because he had learned to apply a mnemonic technique to the digits, not because of any actual increase in the capacity of his short-term memory.[15]

There is no substantial evidence that practice alone makes a signifi-cant difference in improving memory. It is true that practicing memoriz-ing can help improve memory, but what you *do* during practice is more important than the *amount* of practice. One classic study (discussed in chapter 6) found that 3 hours of practicing memorizing did not improve long-term memory, but that 3 hours of practicing using certain tech-niques did improve long-term memory.

The memory–muscle myth has been expressed in the field of education as mental discipline. The "doctrine of formal discipline" says that the mind can be strengthened through exercise. This notion was prevalent in education around the turn of the century, and was used as an argument for teaching subjects such as Greek and Latin in school. It was argued that the study of such subjects exercised and disciplined the mind, so that the student would do better in his other subjects, and it was observed that students who studied these difficult subjects did tend to do better in their other school subjects. However, studies done on thousands of high school students during the first half of this century found that the reason students who studied Greek, for example, did better in school than students who did not study Greek was that it was the brighter students who took Greek. It was not the Greek that made them brighter. Some educators still adhere to the concept of mental discipline, even though it is not supported by research evidence.[16]

MYTH 8: A TRAINED MEMORY NEVER FORGETS

People who know that I have written a book and teach a course on memory improvement are often surprised when they find out that I have forgotten something. (When I do not remember something I try to say "I don't know" instead of "I don't remember"; this way, most people do not make the connection and accuse me of being a charlatan for forgetting.) One well-known memory expert and performer similarly has noted that people sometimes come up to him and ask, for example, "Did you read the newspaper this morning?" When he says yes, they ask, "Well, what is on page 6, line 4?" and he cannot tell them. Or after speaking with him for a few minutes, they ask him to repeat the conversation word for word, and he cannot do it. Why not? Because he did not read the newspaper for the purpose of memorizing it, and he did not engage in conversation for the purpose of memorizing it.[17]

Many people do not realize that a person who has a trained memory does not necessarily remember everything. As I mentioned in myth 2, they expect that once they learn the secret of a good memory, they will never again forget anything. But the advantage of a well-trained memory is that you can remember what you *want* to remember, and you don't necessarily want to remember everything. Realistically, even with a trained memory, you are still likely to forget even some of the things you want to remember. You just won't forget as much as most people do, or as much as you used to forget.

Actually, there is some truth in the contention that we never really "forget" anything in the sense that it is recorded in our brains—for untrained as well as trained memories. However, when we talk about "remembering," our practical interest is usually in getting the information out of our brains when we want it. It doesn't do us much good to know that the information we need is in there someplace if we cannot get it out at will. Memory training helps you store information in your brain in such a way that you are more likely to be able to find it and get it out when you want it (as *during* the exam or the speech rather than just after you have finished).

MYTH 9: REMEMBERING TOO MUCH CAN CLUTTER YOUR MIND

People sometimes think of this myth when they see someone who gives memory demonstrations—feats that involve memorizing vast amounts of information that may or may not be useful. They think that the person's mind will get cluttered with useless information, which will get in the way of remembering what he needs to remember.

Actually, to say that remembering too much can clutter your mind is an ironic memory myth, because most people's minds are already cluttered—and they don't remember enough! Your ability to remember something depends less on *how much* material you have stored in your memory than it does on *how* you learned it (see "organization" in chapter 4). Recall the example in myth 4 of the large unorganized cardboard box and the small organized file box. The person with the small organized file box can find needed information better than the person with the large unorganized box. But it is the disorganization, *not* the amount of material in the large box, that hinders memory. A large organized file box would be very efficient, and a small file box would be very inefficient if the material were filed haphazardly.

In some ways, the more you learn about something the more it may actually *help* memory. We will see in chapter 4 that the more you learn about a particular topic the easier it is to learn new things about that topic. We will also see in later chapters that most mnemonic systems actually add to the amount you need to remember, but they do so in a way that increases your memory ability.

Another aspect of the "cluttered mind" myth can be illustrated by pursuing the file-box analogy a little further. Suppose you just keep throwing material into the cardboard box. Soon it will fill up. Filing any more material would mean stuffing it in, and something would have to fall out of the other end of the box to make room for it. This is how some people view the memory that has stored vast amounts of material. Not only will the material clutter the memory, but it will take up valuable storage space that you may want to use later for more important information. This is not completely valid, because the storage capacity of your memory is virtually unlimited (see chapter 2). Thus, remembering too much does not necessarily either clutter your mind or fill up your memory.

MYTH 10: PEOPLE ONLY USE 10 PERCENT OF THEIR MENTAL POTENTIAL

The claim is often made that we use only about 10 percent of our potential brainpower in remembering and in other mental activities. Here are just three examples from published sources: "Most of us, psychologists say, don't use more than 10 percent of our native ability to remember." "You've probably heard that we use only 10 or 20 percent of our mental powers. How can that be? Is there some secret to unlocking the other 80 to 90 percent?" "If you're like most people, you're using only about 10 percent of your brainpower."[18]

Although the claimed amount of potential used is generally around 10 percent, some authors have claimed even smaller percentages. One author observed that it used to be an oft-quoted statistic that we use only 10 percent of our potential brainpower, but that the more psychologists have learned in the past ten years, the less likely they are to dare to attempt to quantify our brain potential. So far, so good, but then he went on to draw the following amazing conclusion: "The only consistent conclusion is that the proportion of our potential brainpower is probably nearer 4 percent than 10 percent. Most of us, then, appear to let 96 percent of our mental potential lie unused." Why stop at 4 percent? Another author wrote that "the commonly heard statement that on the average we use only 1 percent of our brain may well be wrong, because it now seems that we use even less than 1 percent."[19]

Whether the claimed percentage of used brainpower is 1 percent or 10 percent, the inference usually drawn from this claim is that it is easy to make miraculous improvements in mental ability because they require very small increases in brain usage. For example, if you are operating at only 10 percent of your potential you need to use only 2 percent of the remaining potential, and you have increased your performance by 20 percent (200 percent for the 1-percent claim). One book observed that the average IQ is 100, the genius level is 160, and the average human being probably uses 4 percent of his potential brainpower, and then asked, "If that average human could learn to use not 4 percent of his brain but a still minimal 7 percent of his brain, could he attain genius level?" The implication, of course, is that a 75-percent improvement (from 4 percent to 7 percent) corresponds with a 75-percent improvement in IQ—from 100 to 175.[20]

Another book gives the illusion of scientific precision by working out this reasoning in a mathematical formula using a "Mental Performance Ratio (MPR), the percentage of your total mental capacity that you are putting to use." Suppose a person who uses the typical 10 percent of his brainpower has an IQ of 140; his "Learning Power" would be 14.0

(140 IQ × .10 MPR). Now suppose a second person with an IQ of 120 (about the average of most college graduates) could increase the use of his brainpower by only one-fifth (from 10 percent to 12 percent); his Learning Power would now be higher than that of the person with the IQ of 140 (120 IQ × .12 MPR = 14.4 Learning Power).[21]

What is wrong with the 10-percent claim and the reasoning that underlies the complex calculations above? The main problem is that none of these authors (or any others I have ever read) presents any evidence to support the 10-percent figure. In fact, I have never found any actual research evidence anywhere for the 10-percent claim, nor have I ever seen the claim made by any brain researchers (and I probably have used more than 10 percent of my potential searching ability looking for such evidence). I have even challenged my memory students, many of whom have heard the 10-percent claim, to find evidence for me, and no one has yet been able to do so—even for extra credit!

It is possible that there may be some research evidence to support the 10-percent claim, but I doubt it for several reasons. First, I doubt that researchers could agree on a definition of what "mental potential" or "potential brainpower" really means. Second, even if researchers could define mental potential, I doubt that they could measure it to determine what constitutes a person's total potential. Third, even if they could define and measure mental potential, I doubt that researchers could define what it means to "use" our mental potential, and that there would be any way to measure what percentage of the total we use.

My own belief is that we do have more potential mental ability than we use. That is why I wrote this book: to help you come closer to achieving the full potential of your learning and memory abilities. However, I do not think we can quantify how much our potential is, or determine whether the percentage of potential that we use is 1 percent, 10 percent, 50 percent, or 99 percent.

2

Meet Your Memory: What Is It?

People can learn an amazing number of different things. We can learn to walk, dance, and swim. We can learn to type, repair watches, and program computers. We can learn to drive cars, ride bikes, and fly airplanes. We can learn languages, chemical formulas, and mathematical proofs. We can learn to read road maps, make out income tax returns, and balance checkbooks. The list of things we can learn to do could be continued almost indefinitely.

Of course, all this learning would be useless if we could not remember. Without memory we would have to respond to every situation as if we had never experienced it. The value of memory is also shown by the fact that we reason and make judgments with remembered facts. In addition, we are able to deal with time, relating the present to the past and making predictions about the future, because of what is stored in our memories. Even our own self-perceptions depend on our memories of our past.

The uses and the capacity of the human memory are indeed amazing. You can store billions of items of information in your memory. Your two-pound brain can store more than today's most advanced computers.[1] But people also forget. We forget things we would like to remember. We forget names, anniversaries, birthdays, and appointments. We forget what we learned for an exam in school (usually within a short time after the exam, and sometimes before the exam).

What is your memory? How does your memory work? Chapters 2 and 3 try to answer these two closely related questions. The aspects of memory that I have selected to discuss in these two chapters are those that will give you an understanding of your memory sufficient to make the rest of this book meaningful. Some understanding of the theories underlying memory techniques can help in using the techniques more effectively and also in being motivated to use them.[2] Thus, chapters 2 and 3 provide a basic foundation for understanding and using the principles, methods, and systems discussed in the rest of this book. For the reader who wants a more complete understanding of the nature of memory, more comprehensive (and more technical) coverage is given in a number of recent memory textbooks in which you can read more about most of the topics in chapters 2 and 3, plus additional topics.[3]

WHAT ARE THE STAGES AND PROCESSES OF MEMORY?

Remembering is generally viewed as consisting of three stages:

1. *Acquisition* or *encoding* is learning the material in the first place.
2. *Storage* is keeping the material until it is needed.
3. *Retrieval* is finding the material and getting it back out when it is needed.

To help remember these three stages, we can refer to them as the "Three Rs of Remembering": Recording (acquisition), Retaining (storage), and Retrieving (retrieval). Another way to remember the three stages of memory is by referring to the "Three Fs of Forgetting" (or, more accurately, the three Fs of *not* forgetting). Corresponding with Recording, Retaining, and Retrieving are, respectively, Fixating, Filing, and Finding.

The three stages of memory can be illustrated by comparing the memory to a file cabinet. You first type the desired information on a piece of paper (Recording). Then you put it in a file cabinet drawer under the appropriate heading (Retaining). Later you go to the file cabinet, find the information, and get it back out (Retrieving).

Sometimes when a person cannot locate what he wants in a file cabinet it may be because the information was never recorded; sometimes it may be because the recorded information was never put in the cabinet; but often it is because the information was not put in the cabinet in such a way as to be easy to find. Suppose a person using the file cabinet throws letters and documents haphazardly into the drawers. A few months later he goes to the cabinet to retrieve a specific document. He would likely have a problem getting it. Why? Because it was not recorded? No, the document had been typed. Because it was not retained? No, the document had been put in the cabinet. *How* the document was stored is the problem.

Similarly, most problems in remembering come at the retrieval stage rather than the storage stage. We are all very aware that memory is limited more in getting things out than in getting them in. More can be stored in memory than can be retrieved. There is not much we can do to improve retrieval directly, but retrieval is a function of how the material is recorded and retained. Therefore, improved methods of recording and retaining will improve retrieval, both from a file cabinet and from your memory. The principles and methods discussed in this book will help you record and retain information in such a way as to be able to retrieve it more effectively.

It is useful to distinguish between material in memory that is *accessible* and material that is *available*. This distinction can be illustrated by the boy who asks his father, "Dad, is something lost when you know where it is?" His father replies, "No, son." Clearly relieved, the boy responds, "Good, your car keys are at the bottom of the well." The keys were available but they were not accessible. Similarly, material that is misplaced in a file cabinet is available because it is stored, but it is not accessible because it cannot be retrieved. However, if the material is not even in the file cabinet then it is neither accessible nor available. Likewise, material that is recorded and retained in your memory may not be accessible even if it is available; you know it is in there somewhere, but you just cannot find it. In this situation, the answer to the boy's question may be, "Yes, something can be lost even when you know where it is."

In addition to the three stages of memory there appear to be at least two different processes involved in memory—*short-term memory* (also called *primary memory* and *working memory*) and *long-term memory* (also called *secondary memory*). The distinction between short-term memory and long-term memory is more than just a semantic distinction between remembering for a short time and remembering for a long time. Most psychologists view short-term memory and long-term memory as being two separate storage mechanisms that differ in several ways, although some psychologists have suggested that they are not really different mechanisms but merely different manifestations of the same mechanism (such as different levels of processing). I will avoid this theoretical issue and merely follow the conventional approach of viewing them as two different processes.

WHAT IS SHORT-TERM MEMORY?

Short-term memory refers to how many items can be perceived at one time—how much a person can consciously pay attention to at once. It is similar to the older concept of "attention span." Short-term memory has a rapid forgetting rate. Information stored in short-term memory is forgotten in less than 30 seconds, and sometimes the forgetting rate can be much faster. (People who don't expect a memory test can rarely recall three consonants correctly after only 2 seconds of distraction.)[4] The usual way of combating this rapid forgetting rate is rehearsal, which consists of repeating the information over and over again. Rehearsing can serve two functions: It can keep the information in short-term memory, and it can help you transfer the information into long-term memory by giving you time to code it. These two functions apply to remembering pictures and images (mental pictures) as well as to remembering verbal material.[5]

The rapid forgetting rate of short-term memory is shown in an experience that may be familiar to you. Have you ever looked up a telephone number and forgotten it before you got to the phone to dial it? Or perhaps you remembered it (by rehearsing it) long enough to dial it, but you received a busy signal. A few seconds or a few minutes later, you had to look up the number again to dial it. The ease with which short-term memory can be disrupted is shown if someone asks you a question such as, "What time is it?" right after you look up a number. You answer the question, and find you have to go back to the phone book. One study found that this disruption can be caused just by an operator saying, "Have a nice day," right after telling you a phone number.[6]

Besides having a rapid forgetting rate and being easily disrupted, short-term memory also has a limited capacity, around seven items for most people. (This capacity has been found to be about the same for elderly adults as for young adults, and for people in oriental cultures as for people in western cultures.)[7] You can demonstrate the limited capacity of short-term memory by having someone read to you a list of digits one at a time at the rate of about one digit per second. Then you repeat them. Start with a list of 4 digits (for example, 8293). Next try a list of 5 digits (for example, 27136). Add 1 digit each time, building up to a list of 12 digits (for example, 382749562860).

Most people find that when they get above seven digits they cannot remember all of them long enough to repeat them. It seems as if they must lose the first few digits to "make room" for the last few. A few people can remember 10 or 11 digits, but very few people can remember more than 11 digits. This demonstration can also be used to illustrate the rapid forgetting rate of short-term memory. Instead of repeating the digits as soon as they are read to you, wait for 5 to 10 seconds to repeat them. If you do not rehearse the digits during this delay, you will find that the number of digits you can remember decreases considerably.

Chunking

We can increase the limited capacity of short-term memory by a process that is referred to as "chunking." Chunking consists of grouping separate bits of information into larger chunks. For example, a person can remember the following eight letters, c-o-m-p-l-e-t-e, by chunking them into one word, *complete*. Numbers are also easier to remember if they are grouped into chunks of two or three. A number such as 376315374264 can be remembered as 12 separate digits, but it is easier to remember as four chunks of 3 digits each—376-315-374-264. Similarly, a phone number can be remembered better as 601-394-1217 than as 6013941217, and a social security number of 513-63-2748 is easier to remember than 513632748. Of course, chunking takes time; if the items are presented too fast (for example, 1 digit per second) then chunking is less effective than if they are presented more slowly (for example, 1 digit every 5 seconds).

Short-term memory can be compared to a purse that can hold seven coins. If the coins are pennies, then the capacity of the purse is only 7 cents. But if the coins are nickles (each representing a "chunk" of 5 pennies), then the capacity is 35 cents. If they are dimes, the capacity is increased to 70 cents. Similarly, a short-term memory may be able to hold only about seven items, but we can increase the amount of information contained in these items by grouping the separate bits of information into larger chunks. For example, the capacity of short-term memory is about 8.0 for separate digits, about 7.3 for consonants, about 5.8 for concrete nouns, and about 1.8 for 6-word sentences; assuming that the nouns contain an average of 4 letters each, we increase the capacity from 7.3 letters using only consonants, to about 23 letters using concrete nouns, and to more than 40 letters using sentences.[8]

Chunking is also illustrated by an interesting phenomenon in chess. An excellent chess player can look for 5 seconds at the board of a chess game in progress and then look away and recall the position of every piece. This suggests that chess masters have unusual memories. However, if the chess pieces are placed randomly on the board, rather than in the positions one would find in an ongoing game, the chess master cannot remember the positions of any more pieces than can the beginning chess player. What makes the difference? One possible explanation is that the chess master makes use of his vast chess experience to recognize familiar visual patterns and interrelations among the pieces. Rather than remembering the position of each separate piece, he remembers groups (chunks) of pieces. He can only remember about seven chunks, but each of his chunks consists of several pieces.[9]

What Good Is Short-term Memory?

Because short-term memory has such a limited capacity and items in it are forgotten so rapidly, you might wonder why such a process is part of our memory system at all. Short-term memory has several uses.

1. The rapid forgetting in short-term memory is not necessarily undesirable. Imagine how cluttered and jumbled your mind would be if you were consciously aware of every little bit of information your mind recorded. It would be almost impossible to concentrate on one thing or to select useful information. For example, add the following numbers mentally: 1,8,4,6,3,5. In doing this problem, something like the following probably went through your mind: "1 plus 8 is 9, plus 4 is 13, plus 6 is 19, plus 3 is 22, plus 5 is 27." Of all the numbers that went through your mind the only one that is necessary to remember for any length of time is 27. All the others needed to be remembered only long enough to use them. Imagine how difficult it would be to keep track of your addition if each subtotal did not disappear as soon as you reached the next one.

Thus, short-term memory can serve as a sort of temporary scratch pad, allowing us to retain intermediate results while we think and solve problems. Short-term memory is used not only in numerical problems but also in the whole range of complex problems we face regularly.[10] When a chess master is planning the next move, for example, he or she develops in short-term memory a temporary, imaginary picture of critical parts of the chessboard as they will appear after several future moves and countermoves. And think about how hard it would be for waiters or waitresses to keep track of what they were doing if they did not forget each order as soon as it had been filled.

2. Short-term memory helps us maintain our current picture of the world around us—indicating what objects are out there and where they are located. By constructing and maintaining these world frames, short-term memory keeps our visual perceptions stable. Our process of visual perception actually skitters here and there about a scene, taking about five retinal images, or "snapshots," per second. Yet we do not discard an old image every fifth of a second and construct a new scene of our surroundings. Rather, we integrate information from all the "snapshots" into one sustained image, or model, of the scene around us. As we notice small changes, we update this model, deleting old objects, adding new ones, and changing the relative location of objects. Short-term memory enables us to do this.

3. Short-term memory holds whatever goals or plans we are following at the moment. By keeping our intentions in active memory, we are able to guide our behavior toward those goals.

4. Short-term memory keeps track of the topics and referents that have been recently mentioned in conversation. If I mention my friend John, I can later refer to him as "he" or "my friend" and you will know who I am talking about; the idea of John is still in your active memory: You can figure out that I mean John and not Scott or David.

After noting the above uses of short-term memory, a recent psychology textbook made the following interesting observation:

Perhaps because short-term memories are so very useful, nearly every computer system for storing information is designed with a kind of short-term memory, located within its central processing unit (CPU). The CPU of a computer system receives data, stores it in memory, retrieves it, performs a variety of calculations, and either stores the result, displays it on a screen, or prints it. These functions are remarkably similar to the functions of our short-term memory. In fact, the parallels are so close that many cognitive psychologists view the computer's CPU as a useful metaphorical model of human short-term memory. [11]

WHAT IS LONG-TERM MEMORY?

Long-term memory is what most people mean when they talk about memory, and what most memory-improvement techniques are aimed at improving. Many psychologists believe that long-term memory is composed of several different types. For example, one common view divides long-term memory into three types.

1. *Procedural* memory involves remembering how to do something (skills such as typing or solving a quadratic equation).
2. *Semantic* memory involves remembering factual information (such as math equations or word meanings) with no connection to time or place; we don't remember when or where we learned the information.

3. *Episodic* memory involves remembering personal events (such as your first date or where you learned a particular equation).[12]

Long-term memory differs from short-term memory in several ways:

1. The nerve changes that take place in the brain may be different for short-term memory and long-term memory.
2. Short-term memory is an active, ongoing process that is easily disrupted by other activities; long-term memory is not as easily disrupted.
3. Short-term memory has a limited capacity; the capacity of long-term memory is virtually unlimited.
4. Retrieval from short-term memory is an automatic, dumping-out process; retrieval problems come in long-term memory.
5. Some drugs and diseases can affect short-term memory without affecting long-term memory, and vice versa.

There is evidence that more is stored in our memories, and that memories are more permanently recorded in our brains, than we might assume. Long-term memory is relatively permanent, and has a virtually unlimited capacity. When you really try to remember a specific event, you sometimes find that you can recall more than you thought possible. On repeated recall attempts, people can recall more material than they did on the first recall attempt, without having the material presented again. Recall of "forgotten" information (such as early childhood experiences) under drugs or hypnosis also illustrates the large capacity and permanent nature of long-term memory.

Electrical stimulation of the brain provides some of the most striking evidence for the large capacity and relatively permanent nature of long-term memory. When surgeons prepare patients for brain surgery, they may touch parts of the brain with an electric probe. The patient is conscious and can report what he experiences as different parts of the brain are electrically stimulated. Under such conditions, patients have reported reliving a previous event, complete with all the sensations experienced at that earlier time. These memories are much more vivid than ordinary memories, as if the electric probe started a film strip or a tape recording on which the details of the event were registered. One man saw himself in his childhood home laughing and talking with his cousins. A woman reported that she heard a song playing that she had not heard since her youth; and she believed that there was a phonograph in the room playing the song. These people are not just reminded of the event: Their memory of the event seems very real, even though they know that they are on the operating table; it is as if they are experiencing a double-consciousness. The experience stops when the probe is removed, and may be repeated if the probe is replaced. [13]

Evidence that nerve changes in the brain may be different for short-term memory and long-term memory is provided by brain-damaged patients. One patient (K. F.) had a defective short-term memory with a normal long-term memory. His retention of events in everyday life was not impaired, indicating that his long-term learning ability was normal. However, K. F. could not repeat number sequences of more than two digits. Another patient (H. M.) could not form new long-term memory traces, although his short-term memory and his existing long-term memory appeared to be normal. He performed well on tests involving knowledge acquired before his brain damage, and had no apparent personality changes as a result of the brain damage. However, he could not remember any new information for very long. H. M. read the same magazines over and over and worked the same jigsaw puzzles without realizing he had seen them before. As long as information was held in short-term memory he behaved normally, but the contents of his short-term memory were lost when his attention was distracted. The connecting link between short-term memory and long-term memory seemed to have been broken; H. M. could not transfer information from short-term memory into long-term memory. [14]

Relationship of Long-term Memory to Short-term Memory

Earlier I compared memory to a file cabinet. We can now refine the analogy. Short-term memory is like the in-basket on an office desk. Long-term memory is like the large file cabinets in an office. The in-basket has a limited capacity; it can hold only so much information before it must be emptied to make room for more. Some of what is removed is thrown away, and some is put into the file cabinets; however, nothing is put into the file cabinets without first sorting through the in-basket.

Similarly, information goes through short-term memory to reach long-term memory. This makes short-term memory the bottleneck in storing information. Not only does short-term memory have a limited capacity but information in short-term memory must be coded in some way to be transferred into long-term memory. This coding takes time, which limits the amount of information that can be sent into long-term memory in a given period. Getting information out of short-term memory is not too hard; everything is dumped out at once. Problems arise in retrieving information from long-term memory. Some kind of systematic search is necessary. We have seen that the information will be hard to find if it is not stored in some orderly way. The principles and methods discussed in later chapters provide ways to code and categorize information so that it can be efficiently transferred from short-term memory to long-term memory.

A workroom analogy can be used to shed light on the relationship between long-term memory and short-term memory.[15] Suppose a carpenter is building a cabinet. All his materials are neatly organized on shelves around the walls of his workroom. He gets the materials that he is currently using (tools, boards ready to put in place, etc.) from the shelves and places them on the workbench, leaving space on the bench to work. When the bench gets too messy, he may stack material in piles so that he can get more on the bench. If the number of stacks gets too large, some may fall off, or the carpenter may put some of the materials on a shelf.

We can think of the shelves as long-term memory (holding the large amount of material available for the carpenter to use), and of the bench as short-term memory (divided into the work space and a limited-capacity storage area). The carpenter's operations are like the work that goes on in short-term memory. Stacking things to make more space and get more material on the workbench is like chunking. Things that fall off the bench are like items forgotten from short-term memory, and getting things from the shelves and putting them back is like transferring information from and to long-term memory. Materials that the carpenter may need that are not on the shelves are like information that is unavailable; materials on the shelves that the carpenter cannot locate are like information that is inaccessible.

The following diagram summarizes many of the points discussed so far in this chapter. It pictorially illustrates the relationship between short-term memory and long-term memory.

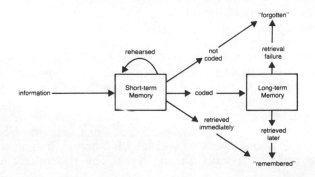

WHAT ARE THE MEASURES OF MEMORY?

How we measure memory affects our definition of what memory is. There are three main ways to measure how much a person remembers, and each can give a different picture of memory. We can ask him to tell us everything he remembers; we can ask him to pick out the items he remembers from a group of items; or we can see how easily he learns the material a second time. These three approaches are referred to, respectively, as recall, recognition, and relearning.[16]

Recall

Most people are thinking of recall when they talk about remembering. Recall requires producing information by searching the memory for it. In school, recall is the task you are given in test questions such as: "Name the first five presidents of the United States," or "Name the capital of Argentina," or "Recite the Gettysburg Address." When most people say they do not remember something, what they mean is that they do not recall it.

A person who is unable to recall something may be able to recall it if he is given some cues. This is called *aided recall*. For example, we will see in chapter 7 that giving people the first letters of words they have learned improves their recall of the words. If you are unable to recall the names of the first five presidents, try again, using the first letters of the last names of the presidents as cues: *W, A, J, M, M.*

There are several different methods that psychologists use to study recall. In the *free-recall* method a person is presented a list of words one at a time and required to learn the list so that he can recall as many words as possible in any order. Examples of free recall in everyday life are remembering the items on a shopping list and remembering what movies are playing in town. In the *serial learning* method the person is presented a list of words one at a time and is required to learn the list so that he can recall the words in the same order they were presented. Serial learning differs from free recall in that the order of recall is important, and each word serves as the cue for the next word. Examples of serial learning in everyday life are learning the alphabet and learning a speech. A third method for studying recall is the *paired-associate* method. In this method pairs of words are shown, and the person is required to associate them so that when he is given the first word he will recall the second word. Examples of paired-associate learning in everyday life are learning the capitals of states and learning a foreign language vocabulary.

The Link system discussed in chapter 9 is especially appropriate for improving memory in serial learning tasks. The systems discussed in chapters 10, 11, and 12 also involve paired-associate learning. All the systems can help in free-recall tasks.

Recognition

A person may be unable to recall something even when given cues, but may still show evidence of remembering if recognition is used as the measure of memory. When we recognize something, we acknowledge that it is familiar, that we have met it before (the word *recognition* means literally "to know again"). In recognition the test is, "Is this the item?"; in recall the test is, "What is the item?" An example of a recognition task in school is a multiple-choice question such as: Which of the following is the capital of Argentina? (a) Lima (b) Rio de Janéiro (c) Santiago (d) Buenos Aires.

Recognition is usually easier than recall because we do not have to search for the information; it is given to us and all we have to do is be able to identify it as something we learned. The high sensitivity of recognition as a measure of memory was demonstrated by showing people 600 pairs of items (words, sentences, pictures). Later the people were shown some of these items paired with new items and were asked to indicate which member of the pair was the one they had seen previously. The average correct recognition score was about 88 percent for sentences, 90 percent for words, and 98 percent for pictures. Although most elderly adults do not perform as well as most young adults in free-recall tasks, they do perform as well in recognition or cued-recall tasks.[17]

Long after people can no longer recall most of the students in their high school graduating class, they can still recognize their yearbook pictures and names from sets of pictures and names.[18] Most people remember other people's faces better than their names. (Do you often hear people say, "Your name is familiar but I don't remember your face"?) One reason is that remembering a face is usually a recognition task and remembering a name is usually a recall task. Other possible reasons why we remember faces better than names are discussed in chapter 13.

Relearning

A person may be unable to recall something, to recall it with cues, or even to recognize it, but may still show evidence of remembering by the third measure—relearning or savings.[19] Suppose you measure how long it takes you to learn something the first time. Later you measure how long it takes you to learn it again. If you learn it faster the second time (there is a savings in learning time), that is evidence that you still have some memory of the material. For example, college professors showed evidence of memory for former students' names when the measure of relearning was used but not when picture-cued recall was used. [20]

Relearning may be illustrated by the common experience of a person who studies a foreign language that he learned many years ago. He may not be able to recall any of it. He may recognize very little. But when he starts studying it, he may find that it comes back to him rather easily. Similarly, you may not be able to recite the Gettysburg Address, or the Declaration of Independence, or something else that you learned in school, but you could probably relearn them faster than someone who has never seen them before could learn them.

An interesting study that a psychologist conducted on his own son shows that relearning is a very sensitive measure of memory, and also that relearning may show evidence of memory even when the material was not fully learned originally. The psychologist read passages of Greek to his son from the age of fifteen months to three years. He later tested the boy for retention at ages eight, fourteen, and eighteen by having him memorize the original passages and some comparable new passages. At age eight it took the boy 27 percent fewer trials to memorize the original passages than the new passages, suggesting a considerable savings in relearning effort as a result of retention of the earlier learning. The methods of recall and recognition would likely have shown no evidence of remembering. The savings decreased from 27 percent at age eight, to 8 percent at age fourteen, and to only 1 percent at age eighteen. [21]

Thus, it is not accurate to say that you do not remember something merely because you do not recall it. Information that is available in memory may be inaccessible by recall but may be accessible by recognition or relearning. Recognition is generally a more sensitive measure of memory than is recall in the sense of detecting retention where recall does not. (Surprisingly, however, some studies have found conditions in which some words can be recalled after failure to recognize them.) [22] Likewise, relearning is more sensitive than recognition. If you can recognize something or can relearn it faster than you learned it the first time, you have some memory of it even though you cannot recall it. This is one answer to the person who says that it does not do any good for him to read something because he cannot "remember" (recall) it anyway.

Similarly, students who criticize school exams because they forget most of what they learn soon after the exam are basing their complaint solely on recall. It is interesting to note that some of these same students may complain that a certain course is a waste of time because they have had the same material in another course. This suggests that they have not forgotten the material because they can still recognize it.

Of course, practically speaking, we are more concerned with recall than with recognition or relearning because most of us have the greatest problem with recall. One way in which the mnemonic systems discussed in chapters 9 through 12 help recall is to change recall to aided recall by providing you with cues that you can use to cue yourself.

With respect to measuring memory, a method that is frequently used to study memory should be noted. One of the problems in studying memory is that people have different degrees of familiarity with different words. Thus, if one person learns a list of words faster than another person, it might be because he has seen those words more often. To control for this difference in familiarity, much research on learning has used *nonsense syllables* that are unfamiliar to virtually everyone who participates in the study. A nonsense syllable is a meaningless three-letter "word" such as CEJ, ZUL, or ZIB.

WHAT IS THE TIP-OF-THE-TONGUE PHENOMENON?

Have you ever had the experience of almost being able to recall a specific word but not quite being able to get it? You are sure you know the word but are unable to recall it. You may have had this experience when trying to recall a name. Perhaps you could tell what letter the name started with, what it rhymed with, or maybe even how many syllables it had, but could not quite get the name itself. It is from such a situation that we get the expression, "It's on the tip of my tongue," and most people have had this kind of experience.[23]

I had this experience when trying to recall the last name of a person I knew many years ago. I could picture him in my mind but couldn't think of his name. In searching my mind for the name I thought of Scotland and of hillbillies. It seemed that the name had two syllables and was rather short. Finally it came to me. The name was "McCoy." The associations were obvious: The Scottish association came from the "Mc" prefix (McDuff, McDougall, etc.); the hillbilly association came from an old television show about hillbillies—"The Real McCoys."

Psychologists have tried to study this interesting, widespread phenomenon.[24] The first experimental studies on the tip-of-the-tongue phenomenon (and the closely related feeling-of-knowing phenomenon) were published in the mid-1960s, although it had been observed and analyzed much earlier. Several studies published during the 1970s duplicated the initial findings and investigated possible theoretical explanations and implications of the phenomenon.

One way to study the tip-of-the-tongue phenomenon has been to read to people definitions of words that are infrequently used (for example, *sextant, nepotism, sampan*). The people were asked to tell what the word was. If they could not think of the exact word, they were to tell everything they could about the word. Some people could give other words with a similar meaning or similar sounds (sound being more frequent than meaning), tell the first or last letter of the word, and even tell how many syllables it had, but could not quite tell the word itself. For example, when trying to remember sampan (a small Chinese boat), they thought of such words as *Saipan, Siam,* and *sarong;* they also thought of words similar in meaning, such as *barge* and *junk*. The phenomenon has also been studied in memory for people's names, for poetry, and even for odors (where it was called the "tip-of-the-nose" phenomenon).[25]

Another way to study the phenomenon has been to ask people questions of general information. Some people could not recall the answers, but still felt they knew them. Later recognition tests showed that they were right. Other research has studied naturally occurring tip-of-the-tongue experiences by having people keep diaries recording such experiences. Research on elderly adults has found that they do not differ from young adults in their feeling of knowing experiences or in their accuracy of estimating how well they could remember something that was on the tip of their tongue. A recent diary study found that over the period of one month elderly adults reported about twice as many tip-of-the-tongue experiences as young adults, but were able to resolve them as well as the young adults did.[26]

The tip-of-the-tongue phenomenon has at least four implications for understanding what memory is:

1. Memory is not an all-or-none process. Memory is a matter of degree; it is a continuum, not a dichotomy. We do not necessarily remember something either completely or not at all. Rather, we can remember a part of something without remembering all of it.

2. Most memory is generative, not duplicative. Memory is not an automatic picture-taking process. Most memories do not appear as full-blown, exact duplicates of the information learned, but are generated through a process of reconstruction.

3. Words may be stored in memory in more than one way. They may be stored in auditory terms (how many syllables and how they are pronounced), in visual terms (the first and last letters of the word), and in terms of meaning (cross-referenced with other words of similar meaning).

4. There is a difference between availability and accessibility of information. The availability of information is shown by the fact that you know when you know the answer to a question, or that you can produce part of the word you are trying to recall. But although the information is available, it is not completely accessible by unaided recall.

3

Meet Your Memory: How Does It Work?

PATIENT: "Doc, I need help with a memory problem. I'll be talking to someone, and right in the middle of the conversation I'll forget what I am talking about." PSYCHIATRIST: "How long have you had this problem?" PATIENT: "What problem?"

WIFE: "Oh-oh, I forgot to unplug the iron." HUSBAND: "Don't worry, the house won't burn down. I forgot to turn off the water in the tub."

There are three signs that you are getting senile. The first one is that you begin to lose your memory . . . and I can't remember the other two.

These are just a few examples of memory jokes and cartoons which I have collected. It has been said that we make jokes about things that bother or concern us the most to help us deal with those things, and that this may be one reason why there are so many jokes dealing with sex, money, and weight. This may also be one reason why there are many jokes about memory. Although memory jokes are not nearly as numerous as are jokes about the other three topics, remembering and forgetting is still the topic of much humor. We are concerned with how our memories work, especially when they do not work. How do we remember? More important, how and why do we forget? This chapter continues toward the goal of chapter 2 to help you understand your memory by answering a few questions that will help you better understand how your memory works.

HOW AND WHY DO WE FORGET?

In discussing short-term memory it was noted that forgetting is not all bad. If you didn't forget, your mind would be cluttered with so many trivial things that it would be impossible to select the useful and relevant items you need for decisions. Thus, it is not desirable to clutter your mind with unimportant things. Forgetting the unimportant may help you to remember the important. The trick is, of course, to be able to forget the unimportant, not the important.

You probably do not have to be told that forgetting is easier than remembering. But why is it? One way of answering this question is to consider again the "Three Rs of Remembering" in chapter 2. To forget something you only have to fail at any one of the three stages—recording, retaining, or retrieving—but to remember something you have to succeed at all three of these stages. It is as if there is only one chance to remember versus three chances to forget. Psychologists have suggested several theories to explain why we forget. Let us consider briefly five of the most common explanations (see reference 3, chapter 2):

Decay. This explanation suggests that memories cause some kind of a physical "trace" in the brain that gradually decays or fades away with time, such as a pathway across a meadow will become overgrown if not used. The basis of forgetting is disuse. This is one of the oldest and most widespread explanations of forgetting.

Repression. This explanation was suggested by the work of Sigmund Freud on the unconscious mind. According to Freud, unpleasant or unacceptable memories may be forgotten intentionally. They are pushed into the unconscious on purpose so that the person will not have to live with them. Although some of the details of Freud's elaborate theories are not widely accepted, most psychologists do believe that such motivated forgetting can occur.

Distortion. Memories may be affected by our values and interests, so that we remember some things the way we *want* to remember them. This explanation suggests that we change our memories to fit what we want them to be or how we feel they should be. To demonstrate such distortion, read the following list of words aloud to someone: bed, rest, awake, tired, dream, wake, night, eat, comfort, sound, slumber, snore. Now ask the person to list as many of the words as he can remember. Usually, at least half of the lists include the word *sleep*. Why? Because most of the words are related to sleep, so it seems like "sleep" *should* be on the list.[1]

Distortion has some interesting implications for courtroom practices and eyewitness investigations. For example, by asking leading questions, a questioner can cause a person to "remember" an event that never occurred: "What color was the victim's coat?" may cause a person to remember a coat that did not exist. Similarly, statements that only imply a conclusion may cause a person to remember the conclusion as if it had happened. Such inferences are also exploited in advertising. For example, the ad "Get through this winter without colds. Take Eradicold pills" does not actually say that Eradicold pills prevent winter colds, but 85 percent of people tested for memory of such an ad remembered it that way.[2]

Interference. Forgetting may not be affected so much by how much time passes (as is suggested by the delay explanation) as it is by what happens during that time. Much forgetting is likely due to interference by other learning. Interference does not imply a limited memory capacity, where new information that is stuffed into our heads pushes the old information out. It is not so much the *amount* we learn as it is *what* we learn that determines forgetting by interference.

Information you have learned in the past may interfere with your memory for something you have learned recently. Psychologists refer to this as *proactive inhibition.* It is "proactive" because the interference is in a forward direction; learned material affects memory for material learned later. It is "inhibition" because the effect is to inhibit or hinder memory for the later material. Likewise, information you have learned recently may interfere with your memory for something you learned in the past. This is called *retroactive inhibition,* because the interference is in a backward direction. Suppose that you met a number of people at a business meeting last week and then met some more people at a party last night. If you try to recall the names of the people at the party, you might find that the names from the business meeting get in the way. This is proactive inhibition. If you try to recall the names of the people at the business meeting, you may find that the names of the party-goers get in the way. This is retroactive inhibition.

Cue dependency. A fifth explanation of forgetting is more recent than the first four that have been discussed. It attributes forgetting to failure in retrieval (versus recording or retaining). The memory does not fade away; it is not interfered with by other information; rather, it is merely dependent on your finding the right cue to get it. This explanation is thus referred to as "cue-dependent forgetting." If you can find the right cue, you can retrieve a desired item from memory; if you "forget" the item it is because you have not found the right cue. You have probably found yourself unable to remember something, and then recalled it later when you saw or heard something that "jogged" your memory.

Your Memory Attic

To illustrate these five explanations of forgetting, let's compare your memory to the attic of a house.[3] You store things in your memory and in your attic. Suppose you go to the attic to find a specific item. The decay explanation of forgetting would be like a "deteriorating room"; you cannot find your item because it has been left in the attic so long that it has deteriorated and disappeared. The repression explanation would be like a "walled-up room"; part of the attic is blocked off, so you cannot get into it to find the item. The distortion explanation would be somewhat like a "rearranged room"; objects in the attic are all mixed up so you cannot find your item because things are not arranged as you thought you left them. The interference explanation would be like a "cluttered room"; the room has become cluttered with other things that get in the way when you try to find your item. The cue-dependency explanation would be like a "locked room" where the items in the room are locked in chests, drawers, and treasure boxes; you must find the right key (retrieval cue) to unlock the one that contains your item.

No single explanation is adequate to account for all forgetting, so each of these five explanations has its place. However, this book does not deal much with the first three explanations of forgetting. Decay is not well substantiated by research. It may apply to short-term memory but probably not to long-term memory. Repression, although fairly well substantiated by clinical experiences, involves primarily memories of traumatic, unpleasant, personal experiences. These kinds of memories are not of central concern in this book. Distortion is substantiated by some research evidence, but there is not a lot we can do about it except perhaps to be aware of it and guard against it. Research evidence indicates that interference is responsible for much of our forgetting, and there is even more research support for cue-dependent forgetting. Subsequent chapters discuss ways in which you can reduce interference and cue yourself in searching your memory for information.

HOW FAST DO WE FORGET?

Research on memory indicates that we do not forget at a constant rate but that most forgetting occurs soon after learning; the rate of forgetting then slows down and levels off as time passes. Thus, most of what we forget about something will occur shortly after we have learned it. For example, after learning a list of nonsense syllables you would probably forget almost half of them within 20 minutes, and more than two-thirds after two days; a month later your memory would not be much lower than it was at two days. Similarly, people who studied Spanish in high school or college forgot most of what they had learned (about 60 percent) within 3 years, but very little more (about 5 percent) through 50 years. The decreasing rate of forgetting as time passes helps us understand why drugs that can affect memory are most effective when given shortly after learning, and why in retrograde amnesia recent memories are more susceptible to interruption than older memories.[4]

Of course, not all learning follows this pattern of a decreasing forgetting rate with time. Material that is learned very thoroughly or that is very important to us may be retained all our lives. Also, we remember the gist, or general idea, of what we learn much longer than we remember specific details.[5]

Is there a difference between slow learners and faster learners in their forgetting rates? Will a slow learner forget more rapidly than a fast learner? Contrary to the belief of many people, the answer to this question appears to be no. An analogy illustrates why this is so.[6] Let's compare the learning process to the pumping of water into a pyramid-shaped beaker (see the diagram). Learning is represented by the level of water. Forgetting is represented by evaporation. As the level of water rises, the surface area decreases, so there is less evaporation. Fast input (beaker A) represents the fast learner; his beaker fills up faster. However, in time the slow input (beaker B) will fill the beaker just as full.

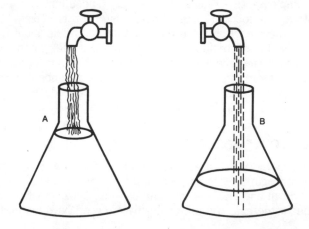

If we run water into each beaker the same amount of time, less evaporation will occur from beaker A because it will be fuller and thus have less surface area. But if we let the water continue to run into B until it reaches the same level as A, then there will be no difference between the two in the rate of evaporation.

Similarly, if a slow learner is allowed enough time to study something so that he can reproduce it as readily as a fast learner, he will score just as high as the fast learner in later tests of remembering. The ultimate *degree* of learning (how well you learn it) rather than the *rate* of learning (how fast you learn it) is the critical factor in the rate of forgetting; this has been found for poetry as well as for word lists and in Nigeria as well as in the United States. Research has also found that although young adults generally learn faster than elderly adults, when the original learning levels are equated there are no age differences in forgetting rates.[7]

The beaker analogy has implications for students in school. A bright student may do better on an examination than a dull one because he has learned the material more effectively, not because he has a better memory. If both students study a lesson for an hour, the bright student will master the lesson more fully: He will have filled his beaker to a higher level. But if the dull student fills his beaker to the same level by studying for 2 or 3 hours, then he is likely to do equally well on the examination. Thus, students of average learning ability can do as well in school as students with greater learning ability by spending more time studying.

The beaker analogy can also illustrate the rate of forgetting for meaningful versus meaningless material. Let beaker A represent the meaningful material and beaker B represent the meaningless material. The more meaningful the material is, the faster it is learned. Does this mean that it is remembered longer? Not necessarily. If the less meaningful material is studied until it is learned as well as the meaningful material, then there will be no significant difference in how fast the two are forgotten. Again, the rate of forgetting is determined more by how well the material is learned than by how fast it is learned.

HOW DO WE REMEMBER PICTURES VERSUS WORDS?

Information can be recorded either in visual form (pictures, scenes, faces) or in verbal form (words, numbers, names). For example, you can see in your mind's eye a visual image (a mental picture) of a chair, or you can think of the word *chair*. These two types of recording processes may be referred to, respectively, as an *imagery process* and a *verbal process.* Research shows that there are several ways in which visual material is remembered differently from verbal material.

The imagery process appears to be best suited for representing concrete events, objects, and words, whereas the verbal process may be best suited for representing abstract verbal information. One reason for this is that concrete nouns are better able to produce mental images than are abstract nouns. The following four words illustrate the difference between concrete and abstract nouns: *Apple* is more concrete than *fruit*, *fruit* is more concrete than *food*, and *food* is more concrete than *nourishment*. It is easier to picture an apple in your mind than it is to picture nourishment.

There is some evidence that concrete words are processed in the memory differently from abstract words. Concrete words and their associated images may be processed by the visual system, whereas abstract words may be processed by the verbal system. Not only may visual and verbal memories be different *processes* but they may also occur in different *places*. Evidence exists that visual memory and verbal memory are located in different parts of the brain. The right half of the brain seems to play the predominant role in the visual imagery process; the left half seems to predominate in the verbal process.[8] (However, differences between the right brain and the left brain are not nearly as great as are the similarities, or as the popular press would have us believe; the recent fad in education and business of training people to use the right halves of their brains goes way beyond the research data.)[9]

Further evidence for a difference between verbal memory and visual memory is suggested by the finding that verbal and visual memory processes may operate at different speeds. The average person can generate the 26 letters of the alphabet (speaking to himself) in about 4 seconds, but it takes about 13 seconds to generate visual images of the 26 letters. Also, it takes longer to name a picture of an object than to read the printed name of the object.[10]

The capacity of memory for pictures may be almost unlimited. We saw in chapter 2 that recognition memory for 600 pictures was very high. Another study illustrates this fact even more strikingly. People were shown 2,560 different pictures over a period of several days. They were later shown 280 pairs of pictures. One of each pair was a picture the person had seen before and the other was not. The people were asked to indicate which of the two pictures they had seen before. In this recognition task they correctly identified about 90 percent of the pictures. Other research has found equally striking results with as many as 10,000 pictures, and that picture memory exceeds word memory when measured by recall as well as by recognition. In addition, pictures were remembered with surprising accuracy as long as three months after seeing them just once.[11]

The saying that "one picture is worth a thousand words" is usually applied to the effectiveness of a picture in communicating an idea that would take many words to express; it may also apply to the effectiveness of a picture in remembering what was communicated. For example, including pictures in a textbook can help the reader remember the written text (see chapter 6). Also, many studies have found that pictures of objects are remembered better than verbal descriptions of the objects, and better than the names of the objects, by young children, adults, and elderly adults.[12] Similarly, one reason why visual imagery (mental pictures) may be a powerful aid in recalling verbal material is because images are apparently more memorable than words alone.[13]

Another reason why imagery may help in recalling verbal material is that imagery may be processed in two different parts of the brain—a nonverbal location and a verbal location.[14] This means that a word that can be visualized may be processed both in a verbal location and a visual location. Concrete words may be recalled better than abstract terms that are only verbal because of this dual representation (verbal and visual); any information that is represented in two ways is more likely to be recalled than if it is represented in only one way. You are more likely to remember words plus images better than words alone for the same reason that it is better to leave two notes for yourself than to leave only one, or that it is better to cross-reference a paper under two headings in a file cabinet: You are twice as likely to be able to retrieve the messages.

Of course, the two explanations above for why visual images may help memory are not mutually exclusive. It may be that pictures are inherently more memorable than words *and* that pictures are coded both visually and verbally. However we try to explain it, we will see in chapter 4 that visual imagery can indeed improve recall dramatically. We will also see in later chapters that visual imagery (as well as the use of actual pictures) plays a central role in mnemonic systems.

HOW DO EXCEPTIONAL MEMORIES WORK?

Some people seem to have truly exceptional memory abilities, and do not seem to forget nearly as fast or as much as most of us do. Do their memories work differently from ours? In chapter 1 it was suggested that memory is a learned skill more than an innate ability, and that most of what people attribute to a photographic memory is merely the powerful application of learned memory techniques. However, it was also noted that there is a valid phenomenon that is somewhat similar to the popular notion of photographic memory, which psychologists call "eidetic imagery."[15] The word *eidetic* means "identical" or "duplicative." Eidetic imagery is a very strong visual afterimage that enables a person to duplicate a picture mentally and describe it in detail shortly after looking at it. No more than 5 to 10 percent of children possess eidetic imagery, and it is even rarer after adolescence. Eidetic imagery has been very hard to study objectively, but most research indicates that it differs from normal imagery in degree more than in kind: It is merely a more powerful version of the capacity for visual imagery that we all possess (see chapter 4).

Eidetic imagery is probably the source of the notion of photographic memory, but it differs from the popular notion of photographic memory in several ways:

1. The eidetic image fades away soon after viewing the scene. It does not stay with a person over a prolonged period of time, but lasts for a few seconds to a few minutes.
2. The eidetic image is affected by the subjective state of the viewer. The image may contain additions, omissions, or distortions, and the aspects of the scene that are of most interest to the person tend to be reproduced in the most detail. The image is not an objective reproduction like a camera photograph.
3. The person does not take a split-second snapshot but requires a viewing time of several seconds to scan the scene.
4. Images can not be brought back once they have faded away; thus, people with eidetic imagery do not seem to be able to use their eidetic images to improve long-term memory.

Psychologists have studied some people who seem to have exceptional memories that are not subject to all the limitations of eidetic imagery. For example, one twenty-three-year-old woman reportedly could look at a page of poetry in a foreign language and years later repeat it verbatim, reading either forward or backward. She could retain a pattern of 10,000 black-and-white squares in her mind for as long as three months. However, she did not just take a snapshot like a camera would but required some time to scan the pattern.[16]

Probably the best known example of a person who seemed to have a truly photographic memory is given in the account by Alexandr Luria of a Russian newspaper reporter named Shereshevskii, whom Luria referred to simply as "S". S was able to recall perfectly as many as 70 words or numbers presented once, and could later produce them in reverse order (you can get an idea how difficult this is by trying to repeat the alphabet backward). He invariably performed successfully in experiments to test his retention (without being given any warning) 15 to 16 years after the session in which he had originally recalled the words! Luria's description of these test sessions is interesting:

During the test sessions S would sit with his eyes closed, pause, then comment: "Yes, yes. . . . This was a series you gave me once when we were in your apartment. . . . You were wearing a gray suit and you looked at me like this. Now, then, I can see you saying . . ." And with that he would reel off the series precisely as I had given it to him at the earlier session. If one takes into account that S had by then become a well-known mnemonist, who had to remember hundreds and thousands of series, the feat seems even more remarkable. [17]

Like the twenty-three-year-old woman described above, S did not merely take a snapshot of the information but required time to study it. For example, memorizing a table of 20 digits required about 40 seconds of study, and memorizing a table of 50 digits required 2 to 3 minutes of study. One of the methods S used to perform such feats is similar to the Loci system discussed in chapter 10.

A "photographic memory" is not necessary to perform amazing feats of memory. For example, a man who could not pass a standard test for eidetic imagery and who reported that he does not "see" the numbers, could memorize a 16 × 16 matrix of 256 random digits. Another man (V. P.), who apparently relied on verbal memory rather than visual memory, could look at a 6 × 8 matrix of 48 digits for about 4 minutes and recall all 48 digits in any order two weeks later. A nineteenth-century memory prodigy could memorize a 100-digit number in 12 minutes if the digits were read to him, but he became confused if the digits were shown to him in writing; another person could recite two and one-half pages of material after reading it only once, although he had poor visual imagery. [18]

Other exceptional memories studied by psychologists include the following performances: a college student who could repeat a number up to 73 digits long after hearing it once; another college student who could do 79 digits; a waiter who could remember 19 complete dinner orders at once; a college student who could perform such feats as squaring 6-digit numbers in his head (for example, $716,723^2$); and one man (T. E.) who showed an exceptional memory for such varied material as numbers, prose, and people's names and faces (most exceptional memories focus on only one kind of material). [19] All of these performances have been attributed by the researchers, and by the performers themselves, to the use of learned mnemonics, interest, and practice more than to innate abilities. Another example of the role of learned mnemonics is a study I did with six students who had learned the Phonetic system (chapter 12).

They tried to duplicate S's feat of memorizing a 4 × 5 matrix of 20 digits in 40 seconds, so they could recall it by rows or columns, forward and backwards. Four of the six students did it in 1 minute or less, including one student who did it in 41 seconds and one who did it in 36 seconds.[20]

Although there are probably a few individuals with exceptional memories, such as Luria's S, who do possess some inborn abilities that make them innately different from other people (one psychologist called them "memorists" to distinguish them from the more common "mnemonists"),[21] the best conclusion regarding how most exceptional memories work seems to be consistent with the earlier conclusions regarding photographic and eidetic memories. Exceptional memories seem to differ from ordinary memories more in *degree* than in *kind*, and to depend more on learned than innate abilities. This means that when we see someone perform an amazing memory feat, we should probably admire her motivation more than her ability.

The following excerpt from a memory textbook represents the view of most psychologists regarding most exceptional memories:

Many of the devices the experts use are abilities we have studied in the preceding chapters, carried to unusual heights. . . . experts may not be so different from nonexperts as we once imagined. They seem to have finely honed talents, but they are talents that also exist in the "average" information processor we have been studying, even if they appear in lesser form.[22]

There is another interesting memory phenomenon that fits under the heading of exceptional memories. Some people possess one outstanding mental ability, such as a so-called photographic memory, a chess-playing ability, or the ability to do complex mathematical calculations in their heads, but lack general intelligence. Such a person is called an *idiot savant*, a term meaning "wise idiot."[23]

Having a so-called photographic memory, or any other outstanding mental skill, is not necessarily a blessing. Idiot savants are generally incompetent at anything other than their one feat, being unable to reason or to comprehend meaning. In some cases, they may even be retarded in areas other than that of their feat. Similarly, the photographic memory of Luria's S was in many ways more of a burden than a blessing. When he tried to read, every word brought forth an image; these images cluttered his mind and prevented him from understanding what he was reading. He also found it hard to erase images that were no longer useful. (Recall the discussion in chapter 2 of how difficult it would be to select relevant information if all the information were constantly at the fore of our awareness.) In addition, S could only understand what was concrete enough to visualize. Abstract ideas presented problems and torments to him, as did metaphors and synonyms (for example, when a person was called a "baby" on one page and a "child" on another, it was hard for S to understand that the words were referring to the same person). Thus, it was very difficult for S to understand the overall meaning of material he read.

HOW WELL DOES SLEEP LEARNING WORK?

Think about how much time and effort you would save in learning if you could just play a tape recording of the material while you were asleep and learn it. Isn't it a shame to waste all that time sleeping when you could be learning something useful at the same time? This is the kind of argument offered in advertisements for sleep-learning machines. Some radio stations have even broadcast messages during the night to help sleeping people lose weight, quit smoking, and reduce tension. Can you really learn in your sleep? Dozens of studies have been conducted on sleep learning in the United States and in the U.S.S.R. [24]

A central issue in determining whether you can learn in your sleep is what we mean by the term *sleep*. There are several stages of sleep, ranging from very light to very deep sleep. Early studies that showed positive effects of sleep learning did not determine whether people were really asleep or take into account how deeply asleep they were. In later controlled studies, the level of sleep was measured by observing the people's brain-wave patterns on an electroencephalograph. The people showed no evidence of remembering questions and answers or word lists that had been read to them while they were soundly asleep. In 1970 the New York attorney general banned the advertising of a language-learning machine that claimed to teach a person in his sleep, on the grounds that there was no evidence that a language could be learned while a person slept. [25]

What about light sleep? Is it possible to remember material that is read to you when you are just barely asleep? There is some evidence that people can learn while they are in states of drowsiness or of very light sleep. Most research of this kind has been conducted in the U.S.S.R. In one study that was conducted in the United States, people were read statements such as "*A* is for apple" during the different stages of sleep. After they awoke, they were asked to check any familiar word appearing on a list of 10 words beginning with *A*. Correct words were recognized from 28 percent of the statements presented in the lightest stage of sleep, 10 percent in the next lightest stage, and none in deep sleep. [26]

The suggestion that it may be possible to learn in very light sleep is subject to several conditions.

1. The material must be presented at just the right level of drowsiness or light sleep. If the person is not asleep enough the material will wake him up. If he is too deeply asleep, he will not remember any of it.
2. No complex material or material involving reasoning or understanding can be learned. Only material such as nonsense syllables, Morse code, technical expressions, facts, dates, foreign language vocabulary, and simple formulas constitute potential materials for sleep learning.
3. Even when conditions one and two are met, sleep learning is not sufficient by itself, but only as an aid to daytime studies.

Thus, although it may be possible to learn some kinds of material in some stages of sleep, it is an inefficient way to learn. You are better off staying awake while you are studying or listening to a lecture.

Some research evidence indicates that people can remember more if they go to sleep immediately after learning than if they stay awake during the same period of time, but that they remember less if they sleep immediately before learning. In both of these situations the learning itself took place when the people were awake.[27]

Subliminal Learning

An area of research that is related to sleep learning is subliminal learning and advertising. The term *subliminal* means below the level of conscious awareness and refers to messages that are too fast or too weak for us to be aware of them. During the 1950s "subliminal advertising" became publicized and people became concerned about its implications for mind control. A famous case indicated that messages saying "eat popcorn" and "drink Coca-Cola" were flashed on a theater movie screen during movies over a six-week period. They were flashed so fast that no one was consciously aware of them. Popcorn sales reportedly shot up 50 percent and Coke sales went up 18 percent. Many people were justifiably concerned at the implications of this report. In the 1980s this concern has arisen again, and now includes rock music with "Satanic messages" that are said to be consciously discernible when the recording is played backward and unconsciously persuasive when the recording is played normally.

During the 1980s there has been increasing research interest in unconscious processing, and there is some research evidence that people can process limited sensory information without conscious awareness in the artificial distraction-free setting of a research laboratory, where their attention is finely focused on the task.[28] However, no one has been able to duplicate the reported "subliminal advertising" effect of the 1950s, and well-controlled research studies have found no evidence that subliminal messages in ads or music have significant effects on either learning or behavior.[29]

Thus, you are not likely to learn and remember material, whether you are asleep or awake, if you are not consciously aware that it is being presented to you.

4

How to Remember Almost Anything: Basic Principles

Certain basic principles of learning and memory underlie almost all memory tasks. These principles are general enough so that one or more of them can be applied to help remember almost anything. Some of the basic principles on which virtually all learning and memory are based are meaningfulness, organization, association, visualization, and attention. Each of these principles is discussed in this chapter, and additional basic principles are discussed in chapter 5. The mnemonic systems discussed in later chapters use these principles.

MEANINGFULNESS: "THAT DOESN'T MAKE SENSE"

One of the main determinants of how easy something is to learn is how meaningful it is to the learner. If it doesn't make sense, it will be hard to learn; the more meaningful it is, the easier it will be to learn. The alternative to meaningful learning is learning by "rote." Rote memory refers to trying to remember something by repeating it over and over without doing anything to make it meaningful.

Words are easier to remember than nonsense syllables. Concrete words are easier to remember than abstract words. Words grouped into meaningful categories are easier to remember than words given in meaningless order. Sentences are easier to remember than words in ungrammatical order. And well-organized paragraphs and stories are easier to remember than disorganized ones. At all levels, meaningfulness affects memory. In one study that shows the effect of meaning on learning, people memorized a list of 200 nonsense syllables, a 200-word prose passage, and 200 words of poetry. The nonsense syllables took about 1½ hours to memorize; the prose took less than ½ hour, and the poetry took about 10 minutes.[1]

People who participate in experiments on learning sometimes try various personal strategies to give meaning to a list of words, foreign words, nonsense syllables, or nonsense drawings, so that they can learn them more easily. They may try converting a nonsense syllable into a meaningful word by using a substitute word (HAWK for HOK), adding a letter (TACK for TAC), or substituting a letter (CUT for KUT). Others try organizing material into meaningful units or try looking for a pattern. These people realize that you should try to make something meaningful in order to remember it.[2]

Some of the other basic principles discussed in this chapter can help make material meaningful; in fact, it is hard to define meaningful learning without referring to such principles as organization and association.[3] In addition to these other principles, familiarity, rhymes, and patterns also can help make material meaningful.

Familiarity

Generally, the more you know about a particular subject the easier it is to learn new information about it, not only in terms of remembering the information but also in terms of understanding it.[4] Learning builds on learning. If you already know something about a topic, if you are already familiar with it, then not only will the new information be more meaningful but you will also have something with which to associate it (association is discussed later). For example, if a list of cooking terms and sports terms is given to a group of men and women, more women may memorize the cooking terms faster and more men the sports terms; these terms are more familiar and thus more meaningful to them. We saw in chapter 2 that experienced chess players can remember chess positions better than inexperienced players. Familiarity plays an important role in this effect. In addition to being familiar with more patterns of these pieces, experienced players are better at integrating familiar configurations into a meaningful whole.[5]

The study described in chapter 2 in which a three-year-old child who was read passages of Greek showed some memory of the Greek at age eight suggests another advantage of familiarity. Exposure to something may result in partial learning of it even without the intent to learn. Thus, a child whose parents read to him may later learn to read more easily, or a child with music in his house may later learn music more easily.

Several recent research findings also illustrate the importance of familiarity in remembering. College students who heard a list of 12 sayings or proverbs (such as, "An apple a day keeps the doctor away") remembered more familiar sayings than unfamiliar sayings. Familiarity with the words on a word list reduced differences between young and elderly adults in recall (in fact, when the words used were more familiar to older adults, they actually outperformed young adults). In a series of studies on recall and organization of information by black and white adolescents, the researcher reported that the most noteworthy finding was the positive relationship between their performance and their familiarity with the information. [6]

Rhymes

Do you remember when Columbus discovered America? What happened in fourteen hundred and ninety-two? Most likely you learned this rhyme at one time: "In fourteen hundred and ninety-two, Columbus sailed the ocean blue." Similarly the rhyme, "*i* before *e* except after *c*; or when sounded like *a*, as in neighbor and weigh," helps you to remember how to spell words with *ie* in them. Many people rely on a rhyme to help them remember how many days are in each month: "Thirty days has September, April, June, and November . . ." Rhythm and rhyme are used by children in learning the alphabet with the following song (which also uses chunking):

AB-CD-EFG
HI-JK-LMNOP
QRS-TUV
WX-Y and Z.
Now I've said my ABCs,
Tell me what you think of me.

These are just a few examples of how rhyme can be used to impose meaning on material that is not inherently meaningful. If you can make up a rhyme involving the material to be learned, it will make the material more meaningful and thus easier to remember. Also, research has shown that when you are trying to recall a word, other words that rhyme with it may be effective cues to help recall it, and that when a list of words is recalled, words that rhyme tend to be recalled together, even when they were not together in the original list. [7]

Patterns

If you can find a pattern, rule, or underlying principle in the material, you will likely be able to learn it easier. It was noted in chapter 2 that the number 376-315-374-264 is easier to remember if you arrange it in four groups of three. The task is even easier if you can see some pattern or relationships among the four groups. For example, the first three groups all start with 3, and the first and third groups both have a 7 next; the second digits in the last two groups are only one digit apart (7 and 6), and the last digit is the same (4). Noticing such patterns helps make the number more meaningful. Similarly, looking for patterns in phone numbers, addresses, dates, or any other numbers will help you remember them. For example, the phone number 375-2553 might be analyzed as follows: 3 into 75 gives 25, followed by another 5 (2 fives), and ending with the same number it starts with (3).

Some people tried to memorize the following 24-digit number: 581215192226293336404347. Try it yourself before you read any further. Do you see any pattern in the number? Some of the people were asked to learn the number by rote repetition. Others learned a pattern. Three weeks later none of the people in the first group could recall the number, but 23 percent of the people who learned the pattern could recall the number. You may have figured out by now that the pattern is to start with 5, add 3 to get 8, then add 4 to get 12, then add 3, then add 4, and so on. Once you find the pattern, all you have to do is remember the pattern and use it to generate the sequence.[8]

This last example illustrates chunking as well as meaning. If you can find a pattern, you only have to remember one piece of information (5 plus 3 then 4, alternately) rather than 24 pieces of information. Finding a pattern is one way to code a number to put it in long-term memory; you no longer have to keep rehearsing it to remember it. Thus, in addition to making material more meaningful, patterns serve to chunk the material so there is less to remember. If you can see a pattern, then all you have to remember is the pattern, and you can generate the original material.

The use of patterns is not limited to memory for numbers. One study found that when a paired-associate word list had a pattern underlying the associations, the associations were remembered better a week later than when the list was tested without an underlying pattern. We have seen that a chess master can memorize the positions of pieces in a game at a glance because they form a pattern, but if the pieces are arranged randomly then he does not do much better than the beginner; similar findings have been reported in memory for bridge hands, for the game of Go, for maps, and even for music. Leon Fleischer is an internationally famous pianist who has to learn whole piano concerts of

00,000 distinct notes; he tries to notice underlying patterns in the music so that he comes away from studying a piece not only with a mere sequence of notes but with what he calls "profound understanding of the structure of the material."[9]

ORGANIZATION: "GET IT ALL TOGETHER"

How useful would a dictionary be if the words were listed in random order rather than alphabetically? One of the reasons you can find a particular word in a dictionary is because the words are organized in alphabetical order. Similarly, one of the reasons you can find a book in a library, or a particular document in a file cabinet, is because the information is organized. You do not have to search through all the words in the dictionary, all the books in the library, or all the documents in the file cabinet; you merely go to the section where the desired item is stored. Of course, not only must the information be organized but it must be cataloged if there is a large amount of information. You could not find much in a library without the card or computer catalog. The catalog's usefulness is extended even further if the materials in the catalog are cross-referenced.

Material is also organized in long-term memory so that you don't need to search through everything in your memory to find specific information.[10] A simple demonstration of this fact is to try recalling the names of all the states in the United States. Before you read any further, take 1 minute to recall as many state names as you can. You probably do not randomly start naming states, but make a systematic search of memory. Most likely you will name them geographically, starting with the states in a certain part of the country and working across the country; or you might start with the ones you have visited. Another possibility is that you may name them alphabetically, starting with the states that begin with the letter A. The important point is that your recall will be organized, not haphazard.

Similarly, if you try to make a list of men's names that begin with the letter R, you do not just start recalling words randomly (names and nonnames, men's names and women's names, R names and A names, etc.) but immediately go right to the section of your memory where "men's R names" are stored. Even within this section, your recall does not occur randomly. You may try to think of all your friends whose names begin with R, or you may proceed alphabetically (Ra, Re, etc.), or you may try to think of famous people whose names begin with R.

These examples of state names and R names show that information is organized in memory. The more you consciously organize material at the time you are first learning it, the easier it is to retrieve. It will be easier to find this material when you want it if you put it into memory in some organized way. Note, however, that a particular way of organizing material may not be equally effective for every recall task. For example, the organization of a dictionary is convenient for looking up the meaning of a given word or for finding out how many words start with the letters *cy* but it is not convenient for finding a word that rhymes with a given word or finding out how many words end in the letters *cy*. Similarly, if you originally learned the state names organized in alphabetical order sometime in the past, then using the letters of the alphabet to retrieve the names would be more effective than if you had not previously learned the names alphabetically. The power of sequential organization in recall can also be illustrated by trying to recite all the letters in the alphabet. This is an easy task for most people. But now try to recite all the letters in random order (*W, C, A, M,* etc.). You will soon find that you have a hard time keeping track of how many letters you have named and which ones.

In addition to arranging the order of material in a meaningful sequence, another way to organize material is to group it into similar categories. Research shows that presenting information organized into categories helps in learning the information. Learning and memory are helped even when items are not grouped into categories, but the people are told the categories into which the terms *could* be organized, or are told to pay attention to the categories.[11]

People may impose their own organization to help learn a list of items that is not presented in categories, and they still tend to recall the material by categories later even if they do not learn it organized by categories. For example, if you gave people the following list of words to learn—man, rose, dog, pansy, woman, horse, child, cat, carnation— they would likely recall the words grouped in similar categories: man, woman, child; dog, cat, horse; rose, pansy, carnation. Children as young as six years old were taught to use this organizing strategy well enough to significantly improve their memories for 18-item lists. If the items to be remembered could not be grouped by categories, they would likely be grouped by other criteria, such as the same first letter.[12]

It has been found that people who are instructed to just organize material remember it as well as people who are instructed to learn the material. The value of organization is not limited to word lists. Organized paragraphs are also recalled better than unorganized ones, and stories that are organized logically (with one event leading to another) are remembered better than stories that jump around from one point to another and do not make as much sense. Nor is the value of organization in memory limited to verbal material. Objects that are organized in a meaningful, coherent picture are remembered better than objects in a jumbled picture. [13]

One value of organization is that it can be used to make material meaningful. Consider the number 581215192226293336404347 discussed earlier in this chapter. If the number were regrouped as follows— 5 8 12 15 19 22 26 29 33 36 40 43 47—then you would be much more likely to see the pattern and thus learn the number faster. Similarly, the following set of letters may not be too easy to memorize: BUS HAW OR THIS T WOBIR DH AND INT HE INT HE. But if we reorganize the letters (not the order, but just the grouping) we get a more meaningful set of letters: BUSH A WORTH IS TWO BIRD HAND IN THE IN THE. Reorganizing the order of the words gives A BIRD IN THE HAND IS WORTH TWO IN THE BUSH. What makes this last set of letters so much easier to remember? It consists of the same elements, but they are reorganized to give them more meaning.

Another value of organization is that it can involve chunking. The previous example of the 12-digit number divided into 3-digit chunks (376-315-374-264) involved organizing the numbers by grouping them. People who are learning to type on a typewriter or computer keyboard may begin by coding each letter as a separate chunk. Soon they are able to group the letters into words; even phrases may be perceived as chunks. Thus, more efficient organization reduces the amount of material to be learned, which increases the length of the message that can be remembered. A somewhat similar situation exists for a child who knows the letters of the alphabet but does not know, for example, the word *automobile*. To remember this word he has to remember 10 things; the adult has to remember only one. Adults can chunk even further and remember phrases ("I beg your pardon") and even longer sentences ("A bird in the hand is worth two in the bush") as one chunk.

As a practical example of the use of organization, suppose you had the following items to remember for a shopping list: cookies, grapes, cheese, can opener, chicken, pie, butter, bananas, bread, pork, gum. It may help you to reorganize the items by categories: dairy—butter, cheese; bakery goods—cookies, pie, bread; meat—chicken, pork; fruit—grapes, bananas; and other—can opener, gum. You now have five chunks of 2 or 3 items each rather than 11 separate items to remember. Another possibility is to group the items by the same first letters: C— cheese, cookies, chicken, can opener; B—butter, bread, bananas; G— grapes, gum; and P—pie, pork. Then you could cue your memory by remembering ""four C's, three B's, two G's, and two P's."

The Serial Position Effect

The order in which items in a serial learning task are organized can affect how easy they are to learn and remember; this finding is called the "serial position effect." Items in the middle part of a list will take longer to learn and will be harder to remember than will items at the beginning and end of the list. For example, most people who tried to remember the names of the presidents of the United States could recall the first half-dozen and the last half-dozen but could not remember very many in between.[14]

The serial position effect is affected by the amount of time between learning and recall. When recall occurs immediately after learning, the last few items in the list tend to be remembered better than the first few; however, when there is some delay between learning and recall, the first few items tend to be remembered better than the last few. Regardless of the time between learning and recall, the first few items and the last few items are easier to remember than those in between.

The serial position effect is well supported by research evidence. It occurs in all serial learning tasks and for all modes of presentation and types of material (including spelling words and memory for lectures). Recent research has been aimed more at theoretical explanations of the effect than at demonstrating its existence.[15]

There are at least two ways you can use the serial position effect to help you remember better. First, if the items you are learning do not have to be in a certain order, arrange them so that the more complex, less meaningful items are at the ends of the list and the simpler, more meaningful items are in the middle. Second, when you have a learning task where you cannot change the order of the items, spend more time and effort studying the middle part of the list than the first and last parts.

ASSOCIATION: "THAT REMINDS ME"

Can you draw a rough outline of Italy? How about Denmark? Most likely you can do better with Italy. Why? One reason is that at some time it was probably pointed out to you that Italy looks like a boot. This illustrates the use of association. Association refers to relating what you want to learn to something you already know. This can be done with analogies (which is why several analogies have been used throughout this book), metaphors, and examples, and by comparing, contrasting, or rewording.[16]

One way to remember the difference in spelling between the kind of "principle" you learn in school and the "principal" of the school is that a principle is a rule, and a principal is a pal (whether or not that last statement is true, at least it is meaningful); to remember how to spell "believe," never believe a lie; to remember the difference between port and starboard, remember that "port" and "left" both have four letters; to remember the difference between stalactites and stalagmites, remember that stalactites grow from the ceiling and stalagmites grow from the ground. All of these simple examples illustrate the principle of associating something you want to remember with something you already know. You already know how to spell "pal" and "lie," how many letters are in "left," and what letters "ceiling" and "ground" start with.

A simple association helped my three-year-old son remember the difference between hotels and motels. We were on a lecture circuit in which we stayed only two or three days in any one city. He learned that we sometimes stayed in hotels and sometimes in motels, but it was hard for him to keep straight which was which. The way I defined the terms for him was that in motels you enter your room directly from the outside, but in hotels you enter your room from the hallway. He could remember the statement that "hotels have halls," and using this association of the two *h* words he was pleased that he could correctly identify the places where we stayed for the rest of the trip.

In memorizing a number, you might try to associate it with familiar numbers, dates, or events. For example, the phone number 375-2553 might associate for one person as follows: 3 is the number of digits in the prefix, 75 was the middle of the 1970s decade, 25 is my age, and 53 represents my parents' anniversary (May 3). Merely expressing a number in terms of familiar units can give it some meaning. For example, the number 1206 could be thought of as a price ($12.06), a time (12:06), or a distance (1,206 meters).

Association can even occur at the unconscious level. Have you ever seen or heard something and said, "Oh, that reminds me . . . ?" The reason for such an experience is that somehow in the past those two things became associated with each other, so that bringing one of them from memory drew the other with it. I had an interesting experience in college that illustrates unconscious association. A fellow student in one of my classes came up to me about halfway through the semester and said, "I just figured out why I don't like you." Naturally that caught my attention, so I asked him why. He said, "Every time I looked at you I felt that I didn't like you, but I could never really figure out why. Today it suddenly dawned on me. A few years ago in a health class I saw a movie on venereal disease, and you remind me of the bad guy in the movie." This example shows that we can form associations and have them affect us even without being consciously aware of them (incidentally, I was not in the movie).

Associating information with yourself and with events in your life can help you remember it. For example, you can remember when certain events happened by associating them with other more significant events that you know you will never forget, like the avid golfer who never got in trouble with his wife for forgetting their anniversary: He just remembered that they were married exactly one week after he got a hole in one. Although this example is fiction, research evidence shows that people do remember information (including personal and public events) better when they try to relate it to themselves and to events in their own lives.[17]

One way association helps memory is to make material meaningful. In fact, in research on learning, the meaningfulness of a word frequently has been defined in terms of the number of associations it has.[18] In discussing familiarity it was noted that learning builds on learning. Association plays an important role in this process. The more you know about a topic, the more you have to associate new facts with, and the more facts a fact is associated with the better you remember it. This leads us to the next point.

Besides giving meaning, association can help memory by giving us cross-referencing in our memories. You will have a greater likelihood of finding a letter from a bookstore concerning your account if copies of the letter are filed under "correspondence," "books," and "charge accounts" than if you file only one copy under a single category. Similarly, the more other information you can associate a particular fact with in your memory, the more pathways you can use to find it. In fact, there is evidence that information is represented in memory as a network of associations among concepts, even if we do not purposely make such multiple associations.[19]

This section on association is primarily oriented toward the use of association by the person doing the learning. Association can also be used by a teacher to help other people learn. Research has found that both remembering and understanding new information are improved when teachers help students relate the information to what they already know.[20] So you can use association (as well as the other principles) not only to improve your own memory but also to improve your ability to teach others.

Think Around It

By a technique that might be called "thinking around it," association can help you retrieve information that you know is stored in your memory but that you cannot quite get out. This technique consists of thinking of everything you can that might be associated in any way with the specific item you are trying to retrieve, including the context in which you learned it (see chapter 5). Thinking around it is one of very few memory techniques that can be applied at the retrieval stage of memory rather than at the recording stage.

Suppose, for example, you are trying to think of the name of that favorite teacher you had in school many years ago. You might try thinking of the classroom itself, where you sat, what he or she looked like, the names of other students in the class, or the names of other teachers you had that year. One of these other items might have become associated with your favorite teacher's name enough to bring it out. This approach was found to be an effective technique for people trying to remember the names of high school classmates. They would think of a variety of settings (such as who was on the football team or who dated whom) to help them recall names, and typically an image of a person or some fact about that person would be retrieved before the name itself. [21]

Thinking around it has been used to help crime and accident witnesses recall details such as license plate numbers. The witnesses were asked to mentally put themselves back at the scene and report everything they could think of, even partial information or things that seemed only remotely related. Sometimes seemingly irrelevant or incomplete information would help them remember something else more relevant or complete. People viewing a filmed simulation of a crime were able to remember up to 35 percent more using this approach than were those given a standard police interview. [22]

This technique of searching your memory for something that is lost is similar to what you do in searching for a lost object in your house. You do not know the exact spot to look in (or the object would not be lost) so you search in the general area where you think it might be, such as in the room where you saw it last. As with many memory techniques, thinking around it is not a new idea. This approach was described more than 150 years ago by James Mill, an English philosopher. After quoting Mill's description, William James explained the philosophy underlying the technique:

In short, we make a search in our memory for a forgotten idea, just as we rummage our house for a lost object. In both cases we visit what seems to us the probable neighborhood of that which we miss. We turn over the things under which, or within which, or alongside of which, it may possibly be; and if it lies near them, it soon comes to view." [23]

VISUALIZATION: "I CAN SEE IT ALL NOW"

How many windows are in your house? Your memory search is more likely visual than verbal in answering such a question. You conjure up a visual image of each room and count the windows, and then move on to the next room. This task, which is not too hard for most people, illustrates the use of visual images in memory.

There is research evidence from as long ago as the 1800s indicating that visual imagery can improve memory for verbal material. However, imagery was not considered an appropriate field of study for most psychologists from the early 1900s until the 1960s; it was viewed as being something going on inside the person that could not be objectively studied. In fact, in an extensive survey of the field of human learning published in 1952, mental imagery and visualization were not even mentioned. Research on conscious processes, including imagery, has become more acceptable the past two decades.[24]

The number of article references appearing under the heading of "Imagery" in *Psychological Abstracts* (a journal that publishes summaries of all of the research articles published in psychology) reflects the increased research interest since the 1960s: From 1960 to 1964, there was an average of 5 articles published per year; from 1965 to 1969, 22 articles per year; from 1970 to 1974, about 99 articles; from 1975 to 1979, about 165 articles; from 1980 to 1984, about 145 articles. (The total number of references has also increased since 1960, but not as fast as the "imagery" references.) The increased interest in imagery is also reflected in the establishment of an international association for imagery researchers (International Imagery Association) and a journal for imagery research (*Journal of Mental Imagery*) in the late 1970s. Much of the research done since the mid-1960s on imagery and its effectiveness in memory has been summarized in several books published in the 1980s.[25]

In chapter 2 we saw that memory for pictures is very powerful and that imagery is also effective for verbal material. Two possible reasons were suggested: First, images are inherently more memorable than words; second, words that evoke images are coded dually (in both verbal and visual memory) so that there is twice as great a likelihood of remembering them. There are other theories about why imagery is such a powerful memory aid, but regardless of what the reason is, the important point for our purpose is that visual imagery does help memory. We can take advantage of this fact by visualizing material we want to remember.

Visualization of verbal material does not mean picturing the words themselves in your mind but picturing the objects, events, or ideas the words stand for. There are several lines of evidence to indicate that such imagery helps in learning verbal material:[26]

1. Concrete (high imagery) words and sentences are almost always learned faster and remembered better than abstract words.

2. People report spontaneous use of mental pictures in learning particular paired-associate word pairs, and tend to learn these pairs most quickly.
3. Instructing people to use mental pictures relating two words of a pair greatly helps paired-associate learning of nouns.
4. People who report vivid visual imagery perform better in tests of recall than people who report poor visual imagery.

Many of the numerous studies showing the effectiveness of visual imagery in remembering have used a paired-associate learning task (see chapter 2). The general approach of studies on imagery in paired-associate learning is to instruct some people to use verbal techniques to associate the words, and to instruct others to form images representing the words and associate the images for each pair of words. For example, for "dog–broom" you might picture a dog sweeping the house with a broom, and for a "door–baby" you might picture a baby hanging onto a doorknob. The general finding of these studies is that the imagers learn and remember much more effectively than the verbalizers. In fact, in many of these studies, the effect of using imagery can be underestimated because people who are instructed to verbalize sometimes report using imagery spontaneously.

Many real-life learning situations involve paired-associate learning, such as capitals of states, names and faces, first names and last names, foreign languages, vocabulary words, and names and sounds of letters. Some mnemonic systems in later chapters also involve paired-associate learning, so that paired-associate research is relevant to their use also. The role of imagery in many of these areas is discussed in later chapters.

Most of this section has discussed the use of imagery to learn words, because most of the research has been done with pairs of nouns. However, research shows that the value of imagery is not limited to nouns; imagery has also been found to aid memory for verbs and adverbs. Nor is the value of imagery limited to memory for word lists or pairs of words. Visual imagery has been found to help in learning sentences, stories and other prose material, and even concepts.[27] Ways to use imagery effectively and some of its strengths and limitations are discussed further in chapters 7 and 8.

Of course, the main advantage of imagery is that it can make learning more effective. Another advantage is that it can make learning more fun. Most people find it more interesting to picture images and associate them than to merely repeat words over and over by rote methods to memorize them. One of the comments of my memory students that was included in the introduction to this book referred to the mnemonic systems based on visual imagery that are discussed in later chapters: "The systems make learning seem more like a game than work. I almost feel guilty, it's so fun."

ATTENTION: "I DON'T GET IT"

An important principle of memory is suggested by a statement that has been attributed to Oliver Wendell Holmes: "A man must *get* a thing before he can *forget* it."[28] Frequently when we say we forgot something, what we really should say is that we never actually got it in the first place: we were never consciously paying attention to it. The following quiz may help you recognize this distinction between forgetting and not getting.

1. Which color is on top on a stoplight?
2. Whose image is on a penny? Is he wearing a tie?
3. What four words besides "In God We Trust" appear on most U.S. coins?
4. When water goes down the drain, does it swirl clockwise or counter-clockwise?
5. What letters, if any, are missing on a telephone dial?

Can you answer all of these questions? If not, don't feel too bad. One study of 20 adult U.S. citizens found that only 1 person was able to draw the head side of a penny accurately from memory (that person was an active penny collector), and only 15 out of 36 could recognize the correct drawing from a set of drawings of pennies.[29] If you were not able to answer some of the questions on the quiz, the reason is probably not that you forgot. Although you have seen pennies and used the phone many times, you probably have never consciously paid attention to these things; thus, you cannot accurately say that you do not remember what letters are missing on the phone dial. A more accurate answer is that you never really knew in the first place. The correct answers to the questions are: (1) red; (2) Lincoln, yes (a bow tie); (3) United States of America; (4) counterclockwise (in the Northern Hemisphere); (5) Q, Z.

Some of the difficulty people report with "bad memories" is not a matter of forgetting, but simply of not learning in the first place. People blame their memories for something that is not their memories' fault. If you want to remember something, you must pay attention to it, concentrate on it, and make sure you get it in the first place. We can talk about forgetting only if there is some evidence of learning.

A person can really only pay attention to one thing at a time. You might be able to read a newspaper while you are also watching TV, or listen to two different party conversations at the same time (the one at your table and the more interesting one you are eavesdropping on at the next table), but that is by switching your attention back and forth rather than by simultaneously attending to both things. One psychologist compared this characteristic of attention to a TV remote channel selector.[30] You can only watch one channel at a time, so you miss what is on another channel at the same time, but by switching back and forth between channels you can sit back and "watch" two shows simultaneously. This works satisfactorily for simple shows, but if we try it with complex shows, we get lost. Similarly, if we try to learn material that is complex or difficult, we will not get it very well if our attention is divided or distracted.

Sometimes when students complain about forgetting things they studied, it may be true that they do not know what they studied; however, it may also be true that they did not really study the material enough for it to be considered learned in the first place. They might not have remembered much more immediately after study than they did later. Just because people sat through a lecture or ran their eyes over a textbook does not necessarily mean that they learned. If they were not paying attention, then the later recall failure (such as a flunked test) is due to the fact that they never learned the material in the first place. This is one problem with cramming as a study method (see chapter 6), and is also one reason why students might not be able to "remember" what they studied when they were watching television, listening to their stereo headset, or in the midst of other distractions. Research has found that attention to learning tasks correlates more highly with school achievement than does amount of time spent on the task.[31]

The failure to pay attention may be the most common reason for "forgetting" the names of people we meet. Frequently when we are introduced to someone we are not really paying attention; we never really get the name in the first place. We are waiting for our own name to be said or trying to think of something to say to the person. Thus, one way to reduce the problem of forgetting names is to make a special effort to concentrate on the name.

The failure to pay attention is also a common reason for absentmindedness. Usually when you forget where you parked your car or left your umbrella it is because you were not consciously paying attention to what you were doing when you parked the car or put your umbrella down. Your mind was on something else. Thus, one way to reduce absentmindedness is to pay attention to what you are doing. You might even tell yourself as you put the umbrella on the store counter, "I am putting the umbrella on the store counter." This will focus your attention on what you are doing and reduce the likelihood that you will walk off and forget it. Names and absentmindedness are discussed further in chapters 13 and 14.

Attention is the last of the basic principles discussed in this chapter, but it is certainly not the least. In fact, none of the other principles can be applied if attention is not. You cannot make material meaningful, organize it, associate it, or visualize it if you do not get it in the first place.

5

How to Remember Almost Anything Else: More Basic Principles

Chapter 4 discussed some of the principles of learning and memory that serve as a foundation for learning almost any kind of material. This chapter continues with some more basic principles that can also be used to help remember almost anything: repetition, relaxation, context, interest, and feedback.

REPETITION: "WHAT WAS THAT AGAIN?"

Almost everyone knows the importance of repetition. We might be able to learn a few things the first time through (if they are short and simple), but most learning requires repeating the material over and over. Of course, repetition does help learning, but some people do not realize that although repetition is *necessary* for learning it is not *sufficient* for most learning. That is, you must repeat most material to learn it, but just repeating it does not guarantee that you will learn it; repetition should be combined with other principles of learning to be effective.[1]

The examples illustrating the importance of attention in chapter 4 show that repeated exposure to something is not sufficient to learn it. The insufficiency of repetition alone is also illustrated by the story of the young boy who used the phrase "I have went" in a paper he wrote in school. The teacher made him stay after school and write on the board

100 times, "I have gone." She told him that when he finished he could go home, and then she went to a faculty meeting. When she returned to the classroom later she found "I have gone" written 100 times on the board, and scrawled at the end of it was "I have finished, so I have went." Another example of the inadequacy of repetition is the experience of Professor Edmund Sanford, who had read a morning prayer at least 5,000 times over a period of 25 years and could read it almost automatically with a minimum of attention, but still could not recite it from memory.[2]

What about continued repetition *after* you have learned something? Suppose you reach the point in your study where you can say your poem or your speech once without any mistakes. You may think that you have learned it now so you might as well stop studying; further study would be inefficient. This is not true. *Overlearning,* which is continued learning beyond the point of bare mastery or of mere recall, has been shown to be effective in strengthening learning and improving retrieval speed.[3]

Three groups of people memorized a list of nouns. One group quit studying as soon as they could recall the list perfectly once (0-percent overlearning). The second group continued to study the list for half as many trials as they had needed to reach one perfect recall of the list (50-percent overlearning). The third group continued to study the list for as many trials as they had needed to reach one perfect recall (100-percent overlearning). For example, if it took 10 repetitions to reach the criterion, the second group studied the list for 5 more repetitions, and the third group studied the list for 10 more repetitions. Memory for the lists was measured by recall and relearning at various intervals from 1 to 28 days later. The greater the degree of overlearning, the better the memory at all time intervals, although the improvement from 0-percent to 50-percent overlearning was greater than the improvement from 50-percent to 100-percent overlearning.[4]

Overlearning shows one reason why cramming for an exam does not result in retention of the material for very long after the exam: You have barely learned the material so it is forgotten quickly. You have probably had the experience of going in to take an exam that you have crammed for with the feeling that lots of facts are floating around in your head but none of them is really tied down or fully learned. You just hope the teacher asks the questions in the right way. Then the teacher comes in and has some business to conduct before handing out the exams, and you are wishing he would hurry so that you can start writing down answers immediately before you forget too much. You can almost "feel" your knowledge running out your ears and piling up on the floor around you where it will not do you any good. This feeling of underlearning accompanies most cramming.

In a study of people's memory for names and faces of high school colleagues, the relatively high level of recall (40 percent even after 48 years) was attributed by the researchers in part to overlearning: People learned most of their colleagues' names very thoroughly.[5] Overlearning also accounts for the fact that you can still remember some things you learned as a child (the multiplication tables, the alphabet, how to ride a bicycle), even though you may not have used them for a long time.

Not only does overlearning help you remember material better but it can give you more confidence that you really do know the material. People learned a list in which various items were acquired to a criterion of either one correct recall, two correct recalls, or four correct recalls. Four weeks later they had a recall test, and then rank-ordered the nonrecalled items in terms of how well they felt they knew them. They then had a recognition test on the nonrecalled items. Both their recall and their confidence in how well they knew the nonrecalled items increased with how much they had overlearned them.[6]

Repetition can result not only in *more* learning (and more confidence) but can result in *different kinds* of learning when studying technical and unfamiliar information. In one study learners appeared to notice the main conceptual framework as they repeated unfamiliar technical material, so that repetitions helped transform the material into more meaningful ideas. Verbatim learning actually decreased over repetitions, while problem-solving skills and the ability to transfer learning increased.[7]

RELAXATION: "TAKE IT EASY"

Have you ever taken a test where you just could not remember the answers to some questions, but right after you turned the test in and relaxed the answers came flowing into your mind? Have you ever forgotten what you had prepared to say when you stood up in front of a group of people to give a speech or report? (As one speaker said, "Friends, just before I stood up to speak to you, only God and I knew what I was going to say; now only God knows.") Have you ever lived through or witnessed a disaster, such as a fire or accident, and found later that you remembered very little about it or did not remember it accurately?

These are examples of the kinds of situations that can cause stress—situations where you are under time pressure or pressure to perform well, where lots of people are watching you, or where physical danger or pain is involved. Any kind of stressful situation that gives rise to strong emotional arousal (especially negative emotions such as anxiety, fear, embarrassment, nervousness, and worry) can interfere with your ability to learn and remember. The negative emotion that has been studied most often in connection with memory is anxiety.[8]

Even stressful situations that are not directly related to the memory task itself (for example, divorce, death of a close friend, loss of a job) can hinder learning and memory. Young adults (in their twenties) reported that most memory problems occurred when they were under stress.[9] In fact, anxiety can interfere with memory even without a specific stressful situation being involved; people with a high general anxiety level (who are generally anxious about life) tend to do worse in memory tests than people with a low general anxiety level. One kind of general anxiety level involves anxiety associated with any situation where performance is being evaluated, such as taking tests in school. This is called "test anxiety." Several scales have been developed to measure test anxiety, and a lot of research has been done on it.

The relationship between memory and anxiety, whether situation-specific anxiety or more general anxiety, is not a simple one. A little anxiety can help memory, but beyond a certain level, continued increasing anxiety hinders memory. For example, the person who does not care at all about his next exam or an upcoming speech is not likely to do too well on it; the person who is moderately anxious about his performance will probably do better; but the person who feels excessive amounts of anxiety will probably not be as able to prepare effectively or to recall during the exam or speech.

Although it is well documented that high anxiety often interferes with performance, exactly why or how it does so is not yet clear. Some problems may be caused by narrowing the focus of attention; high stress and anxiety may cause a person to not pay adequate attention to things outside of himself, and thus miss information necessary for accurate memory. There is also some evidence that anxiety can cause problems in encoding (reading) material, in organizing it (when studying or reviewing), and in retrieving it during an exam. Some research on test anxiety has suggested that it causes three sources of interference in recall: (1) worry—cognitive concern about one's performance (such as performance consequences and comparison to others); (2) emotionality—self-perceived arousal of negative feelings (physiological arousal); and (3) task interference—tendency to be distracted by task irrelevancies (for example, inability to leave unsolved problems and preoccupation with time limits). The source of interference that appears to be the most important in influencing memory is worry.[10]

Whatever the reasons are for why or how anxiety affects memory, an important practical question is, what can we do about it? There are two approaches you can take to help you deal with anxiety—cure it or prevent it. A cure for anxiety is to learn and use relaxation techniques like meditation to calm your mind, and muscle relaxation techniques to calm your body. Elderly people who were taught a mnemonic technique for remembering names and faces were able to use the mnemonic more effectively after they had relaxation training. In athletic performance, relaxation enhances ability to focus attention on critical aspects of a situation—to discriminate the important features of the performance and generate useful images to mentally practice them.[11]

There are steps you can take to prevent anxiety from arising in addition to attacking the anxiety directly with relaxation techniques. Generally, the better prepared you are for the exam or the performance, the less anxious you will feel. This means extensive practice for a skill performance, and overlearning for a recall peformance. We have seen that overlearning increases your confidence in your ability to remember, and increased confidence helps reduce anxiety.[12] Anxiety is more likely to interfere with your memory for material that you have just barely learned than with material that is well learned.

In addition to overlearning, improving your learning and recall skills can also increase your confidence and reduce anxiety. Of course, improved skills in learning and recall are not relevant just to formal school settings, but that is the area in which most research has been done, in the form of study skills and test-taking skills. For example, research has found that learning effective study skills can reduce test anxiety, and that students who experience high test anxiety benefit most from a course on learning strategies.[13] In another study students were taught test-taking strategies, such as concentrating on only one test item at a time, marking harder items to return to later, and giving themselves instructions that are used by effective test takers (for example, "I have plenty of time—read the questions carefully"). These students performed better on a later test than did other students who had practiced taking similar tests or who were taught relaxation techniques. The students who learned test-taking skills also reported that they thought less often during the test about their level of ability, about how hard each item was, and about how poorly they were doing. They also had better cumulative grades the next term. The researchers suggested that so-called test anxiety may not even be an anxiety-based problem as much as a problem in ineffective test taking as a result of deficient test-taking skills.[14]

Sometimes you cannot remember something right at the time you need it, even though you know that you know it. Something else keeps intruding. This is a "mental block." You may temporarily block on the name of a good friend when you start to introduce her, or on the answer to a test question that you studied thoroughly. Stress is a frequent cause of mental blocks; you are more likely to block when you are under pressure. In addition to the above techniques for overcoming anxiety, abandoning the search for a while has been found to help overcome mental blocks; quit trying to recall that item. Often one of two things will happen. First, when you come back to the item later it may come right to your memory immediately, because you are more relaxed and not trying so hard. Second, the item may just pop into your mind when you are thinking about something else.[15]

CONTEXT: "WHERE AM I?"

Although most of the basic principles deal with *what* you learn or *how* you learn, context deals with *where* you learn. Context refers to the situation, surroundings, environment, or setting in which learning and recall occur. The essence of the context effect is that if you learn something in a particular context, you can recall it better in the same context than in a different context. Presumably, contextual features become associated with material being learned, and can serve as cues later for recall. Studies have found the context effect in diverse examples ranging from the finding that material learned under water in a diver's suit is later recalled better in the diver's suit under water than on the beach, to the finding that material learned standing up or lying down is remembered better in the same posture in which it was learned than in the other posture.[16]

The interest of most people in context effects is in less exotic, more everyday settings than learning under water in a diver's suit. For students, being tested in the same room as the study room has been found to aid recall, as compared with being tested in a different room. Even imagining the study room when being tested in a different room restored some of the contextual cues and helped recall. The effects of context are enhanced by purposely associating the learned material to a feature of the room; in fact, one study found that the same context resulted in better recall only when such an association was made. It has been hypothesized that the context serves as a memory landmark when it becomes associated with the learned material, and that such landmarks can later be generated from memory and used to guide retrieval of the material.[17]

Research has also found that learning different word lists in several different rooms produced better recall on a comprehensive test of all the lists than did learning them all in the same room, when the test was in a new room. It was hypothesized that studying in different rooms gives variability in contextual cues and allows for more flexibility in retrieval, so that the learners are not so context bound.[18]

How can you use the research on context effects? There are at least four possibilities:

1. Practice in the same place where you will perform, so that all the contextual cues that were present in practice will be there during performance. For students this means studying each subject in the classroom where the exam will be given. For other learning tasks, such as a speech, delivering lines for a play, or a musical performance, it means practicing in the hall or on the stage where you will be performing.

2. When the first strategy is not possible, practice in settings that are as similar as possible to the setting where you will perform. For example, studying in a similar classroom, or even in the library, would be better than studying out on the lawn. Similarly, practicing your speech standing behind the kitchen table would probably simulate the final setting better than practicing while lying in bed.

3. Use the context effect while you are taking the exam. When you cannot remember an answer, try to recall the conditions in which you studied that material. For example, if you were in a library study room when you read a chapter, imagine yourself there and some mental context cues might help. We saw in chapter 4 that people who try to remember the names of school classmates after many years often find this imagining approach helpful as they try to mentally reconstruct scenes from school days and then name the people present. Besides imagining the learning context during recall, you can also benefit by imagining the recall context during learning. Mental rehearsal of speeches, reports, or musical performances can involve imagining the context in which you will be performing as you are practicing. Much research on performance in sports has found that such mental practice helps.[19]

4. "Immunize" against contextual changes beforehand. This approach applies when you know that you will be tested in a different context or when you do not know what the context will be for the test. Study the material or practice the performance in several different contexts to avoid being dependent on one context for recall. This should give you more flexibility in any retrieval that is affected by contextual cues. One study found that varying the learning contexts helped memory for information students learned in a minicourse in statistics. This strategy also helps brain-damaged patients relearn activities so that they can transfer to home and everyday life outside the hospitals. The patients practice the new skills in as many different environments as possible. Ideally, the environments should resemble the eventual environment in which they will be living, but if that is not possible then practice in a wide range of hospital contexts is better than in a single situation.[20]

These four ways to use the context effect all deal with improving memory for what you studied. If your problem lies more in making yourself study than in remembering what you study, you might use context in another way. Have at least one place where you do nothing but study (no food, radios, games, television, friends, etc.). Studying will become associated with that place, and when you go to that study area it will be easier to get something done.

This section on context has focused so far on effects of the physical environment. In addition to physical context, learning and memory can also be affected by "psychological" context and "material" context. Psychological context is an internal rather than external context; research has found that people can remember information better when they are in the same drug state or same mood as when they learned it. (This applies even to the effects of alchohol, caffeine, and nicotine.) Material context refers to the kind of material that surrounds the material to be learned. Words or pictures learned in the context of other words (as in a sentence or list) or other pictures are recalled better if the other context words or pictures are present during recall. [21]

Learners can become too context bound in terms of material context just as they can for physical context. Students often complain that they knew their notes and the book by heart, but did not do well on the test because they were unable to relate the questions to their notes. If allowed to reproduce their notes instead, they could do so, even telling where on the page the answer to a question is located. Perhaps they know the material *too* well: It is overly tied to a particular context. This may be one reason why word problems in math are difficult for many people. [22] For example, many children who can easily handle a problem like "9 − 3 = 6" may have trouble when the problem is embedded in a context like "If John has nine marbles, and gives three to his friend Joe, how many marbles will he have left?"

It should be noted that context effects can vary with the way memory is measured, and that none of the context effects (physical, psychological, or material) is as strong as the effects of using good study skills or mnemonic techniques. [23] Thus, any attempt to use context effects to aid recall should not be done *instead of* using such skills and techniques, but should be used *in addition to* them.

INTEREST: "WHAT'S IT TO YA?"

We saw how important attention is in chapter 4. Attention is influenced by interest. You pay attention to the things you are most interested in; thus, you are most likely to remember those things. If something is not important to you, you are not very likely to remember it. Any two people who walk through a department store, read a restaurant menu, or read a book are likely to remember different things because of their different interests. The influence of interest on attention and memory is illustrated by the story of the returning serviceman who was greeted at the airport by his girlfriend. He casually mentioned as the attractive stewardess walked by, "That's Laura Nelson." His girlfriend asked him how he happened to know her name. "Oh," he said, "the names of all the crew members were posted at the front of the plane." She stumped him with the next question: "What was the pilot's name?"[24]

The value of interest in memory may be illustrated by comparing two people who are studying French. Suppose that one of them is planning to take a trip to France in a few months. Other things being equal, which one would be more likely to learn and remember the French? Similarly, suppose you are introduced to two people, and one of them borrows $5 from you. Which person's name are you more likely to remember? Or suppose you have been told that pericholecystitis is an inflammation of tissue around the gall bladder. You may not remember this fact. But suppose that you were told by your doctor that *you* have pericholecystitis. Now wouldn't you be much more likely to remember it? These simple examples show that you tend to remember the things that interest you.

Some people complain that they are "just no good" at such subjects as math or mechanics. Frequently the reason for this is that they have no interest in those subjects; they see no value in them and thus have not, and do not want to, put forth effort to learn them.[25] Women who claim to have bad memories may be able to remember the birthdays and anniversaries that their husbands have a hard time keeping track of, or may be able to describe in detail what other women at a party were wearing. Boys who cannot seem to learn in school may be able to tell you everything you want to know (and more) about sports or cars. The reason is simply interest.

Interest is one possible reason why some adults, especially the elderly, may find it hard to learn and remember new information. Many elderly people are more interested in the past than they are in the present or future, and spend more time thinking about the past. When you go to visit your parents or grandparents, anyone in their seventies or older, what do they talk about? Do they talk about current events or future plans? Not usually. Most of the time they talk more about past experiences and family history. That is what they are more interested in, so they may have a hard time remembering new things they learn.

It was suggested in chapter 4 that one reason some people fail to remember names is that they do not pay attention to them. We may take this one step further and suggest that one reason they pay little attention to names is that most people are not as interested in other people as they are in themselves. (When you look at a picture of a group of people that includes you, who do you look at first?) Most people are more interested in what they are going to say, or in what the other person will think of them, than they are in the other person.

Two ways in which interest helps in memory have been suggested so far: It helps us pay attention and it motivates us to try to remember. Another way interest helps memory is that people spend more time thinking about things that interest them than they do thinking about things that do not interest them, and we have seen that repetition aids learning.

The importance of interest can be illustrated by referring again to the 12-digit number that has been used to illustrate several points: 376-315-374-264. You may not have learned this number by now. It is not especially easy to learn, but more important you see no reason for doing so. Therefore, you are not motivated to learn it. But I did not make up that number from nowhere; I have been using that particular number on purpose. If you memorize that number you will in effect have the calendar for all of 1988 memorized (you can do the same for any other year with the appropriate 12-digit number). You will be able to answer questions like "What day of the week is June 18?" "How many Mondays are in November?" or "What date is the second Sunday in April?" Now are you interested? Do you think you could learn the number? Having a reason for learning it may have increased interest, which will make it easier to learn. Chapter 7 describes how the number can be used.

The principle of interest suggests that you should increase your interest in certain things if you having trouble learning and remembering them. A natural question is, how? If you are not interested in something it probably will not work just to say to yourself, "From now on I am going to be interested in that." One way to develop an interest in something you need to learn is to try to find ways to relate it to your present motives and interests. Try to find some use for the material. Homemakers who have a difficult time in math may be able to learn it better if they can see some ways to use the information to make measurements in cooking and sewing. Carpenters who have a hard time learning math may improve if they can see how it will help them be faster and more accurate in their carpentry work. Salespeople who have a hard time remembering names may be able to improve if they can realize how important people's names are to them, and how remembering customers' names can help sales.

It might help to realize that virtually every subject is interesting to someone. Try to figure out what it is that someone may find interesting about the material you are learning. Do not depend on authors, speakers, or teachers to make books, lectures, or courses interesting. If you actively seek for something of interest and bring an inquiring mind to your learning, you will find most learning more interesting than if you just passively depend on the provider of the material to entertain you.

In addition to developing interest internally, you might also be able to stimulate interest externally or artificially. External motivations, such as rewards or punishments, may help create interest. For example, you might put off a pleasant task until a certain learning goal is achieved.

FEEDBACK: "HOW ARE YOU DOING?"

Suppose you are shooting with a rifle at a target that is too far away for you to see where you hit. You take a total of 50 shots without ever looking at the target to see where they are hitting, so that you have no idea how you are doing. How interesting would this kind of target practice be? How much do you think you would improve? On the other hand, looking through a spotting scope after every few shots would not only help maintain your interest in what you are doing but would also give you information about how you are doing so that you could make adjustments to improve.

Feedback in learning serves the same two functions. First, knowing how you are progressing in learning something helps sustain your interest in the task. You will soon grow bored and lose interest if you constantly study and never know whether you are remembering any of the material. First-grade children were taught to rehearse material to help them remember it. Some of them were given feedback on how well it worked and others were not. When later given the option of rehearsing, only those who had received feedback on its value persisted in using it. Second, you will be able to make adjustments to improve if you get feedback on how much you can remember. You can correct your recall errors and put more effort into the parts you cannot remember.[26]

Feedback can help you learn and remember material better. Some people were tested on written material right after they finished reading it. Half of them received feedback as to how they did on the test, and the other half received no feedback. The people who received feedback remembered the material better a week later than did the people who did not receive feedback.[27] Research shows that students in school learn more efficiently when teachers provide corrective feedback during practice and application, and a whole program of instruction has been based on feedback from teachers to students.[28]

In addition to helping you learn material better, feedback can increase your accuracy in assessing how well you know the material. Some people studied a list of paired associates for several trials, alternating study trials with test trials (which gave them feedback on how well they were learning the materials). Others had the study trials only, without the practice tests. The first group was more accurate in predicting how well they would do on a final recall test.[29]

You can apply the principle of feedback by using any technique that gives you information about how you are doing. One method is to study with a friend and quiz each other. Another method is recitation (see chapter 6). Recitation in effect involves testing yourself. If you are memorizing a poem or learning a speech, then try saying it to yourself after a few readings and look at it only when you get stuck. If you are studying a chapter, then glance at the headings and words in italics and try to explain to yourself what they mean. You might even make up test questions. This gives you feedback on how you are doing. It will help you to sustain your interest and make adjustments to improve your learning.

6

Strategies for Effective Learning: Study Skills

A number of strategies can help you learn and remember more effectively: Take steps to reduce interference; space your learning sessions out over time; use whole learning and part learning in appropriate circumstances; recite the material; and use a study system. Each of these learning strategies is discussed in this chapter. These strategies are the kinds of skills that are typically covered in books or courses on study skills in school. Most such books and courses also cover some of the principles in chapters 4 and 5, as well as school skills that are not covered in this book (for example, goal setting, managing time, taking exams, writing papers).[1]

The strategies in this chapter are discussed from the viewpoint of students in school, and can help students develop better study skills. (The *quality* of a student's study is more important than the *quantity* of study, good students do not necessarily study more than poor students, but they use their study time more effectively.) Poor students are not the only ones who can benefit from improved study skills. Research has found that most students in high school and college use a narrow range of learning strategies over a wide range of learning materials and objectives, and that good students know very little about effective strategies to better learn and remember even though they use more strategies than poor students.[2]

Although this chapter focuses on students in school, the scope of the chapter is broader than just the school setting. In research on learning strategies, a "learner" includes any person who is trying to acquire new knowledge or skills in formal school settings, on-the-job training, or informal learning.[3] Learning strategies will help not only in remembering material for exams but also in many other tasks, such as remembering names of people you meet, learning a foreign language, learning a speech or report, or memorizing scriptures, poems, songs, or lines for a play. Thus, even if you are not currently in school you will still find that you can use these learning strategies. One of the students' comments included in the introduction to this book was written by a middle-aged woman in my memory course: "I honestly did not think any of this memory business would be of help to me now that I am out of school, but it really has."

REDUCE INTERFERENCE

In chapter 3 we saw that interference from other learning is one of the main causes of forgetting. What factors affect interference and what can you do about them?

How Well the Material Is Learned

The more thoroughly something is learned, the less it will be affected by interference.[4] Material that is just barely learned is more subject to interference than is material that is learned very well; thus, if you want to remember something, overlearn it (see chapter 5).

Meaningfulness of the Material

The more meaningful the material is, the less subject it is to interference. This does not mean that interference occurs only with meaningless material like nonsense syllables (which have been used in much of the research on interference). Interference can also occur with meaningful prose,[5] but the effects of interference are generally not as great for meaningful material as for less meaningful material. Any of the principles you can use from chapter 4 to make the material meaningful will help reduce interference.

Amount of Intervening Activity

How much you do, especially in terms of mental activity, during the period between the time of learning and the time of recall can affect interference. Generally, the more you do, the more opportunity there is for interference to occur. Suppose one student studied for an exam, and then went to a movie, read the newspaper, read a magazine, and studied another subject before the exam. Suppose a second student studied for the exam, and then slept or rested until the exam. Other things being equal, there would be more interference for the first student than for the second. Minimum interference should occur if you sleep between studying and testing (assuming you studied well and are not sleeping *instead* of studying). As we saw in chapter 3, there is research evidence that a person who goes to sleep right after learning will remember more than a person who stays awake. One study found that even three-month-old infants showed a positive correlation between how well they remembered a simple motor task (moving an overhead crib mobile by kicking) and how much they slept during the 8 hours after learning; the researchers attributed the correlation to the amount of intervening activity.[6]

Similarity of Intervening Activity

The previous item referred to *how much* you do between learning and recall. *What* you do can also affect interference. Two kinds of information that are similar will interfere with each other more than two that are dissimilar.[7] Therefore, if you cannot sleep all the time after study (to reduce the amount of intervening activity), then you should do something that is different from what you have studied (to reduce the similarity of intervening activity). It is best not to study two similar subjects close together when you can help it. For example, if you had to study French, Spanish, and biology in the next few days, it would be better to study biology in between French and Spanish. French and Spanish are more similar, and thus more likely to interfere with each other. (Of course, a student who has tests in French and Spanish on Friday and has not studied either one by Thursday night may not have much choice.)

Similarity of Learning Contexts

The context in which you learn something affects your ability to remember it. For example, you are more likely to recognize a person you have met only once, and to remember her name, if you see her in the office where you first met her rather than if you see her walking down the street. Similarly, other recall will be helped if it occurs in the same context in which the material was learned (see chapter 5). The contexts in which you study different subjects can also make a difference in how much they interfere with each other. For example, studying two different subjects in two different rooms instead of in the same room can reduce the interference between the subjects by as much as half. It has even been found that it is easier to keep straight which of two speakers said what if the speakers are observed in different places.[8]

The practical implication of the context effect is that if you need to study subjects that are likely to interfere with each other, you should study them in different places. For example, having one place to study your French and another place to study your Spanish will help you keep the two subjects separate when you recall them. When teachers teach two different sections of the same class covering the same subject matter during one semester, a common problem is that they cannot remember what they talked about in one section and what they talked about in the other section. I find that it helps me to teach the sections in different rooms rather than in the same room.

In addition to different places of study, you can also create different contexts for the materials to be learned. For example, you could write your French notes in blue ink and your Spanish notes in black ink, or write your French vocabulary words on the top half of each page and your Spanish words on the bottom half. When you try to recall them later, the color of the ink or the location on the page will help you keep straight which language is which.

Time Between Learning Sessions

If you have more than one subject to study, you may have less interference if you study each one in a separate study session rather than studying all subjects in one session. Some people learned two paired-associate lists on Thursday and were tested on the second one on Friday. Others learned the first list on Monday and the second one on Thursday, and were also tested on the second one on Friday. The first group recalled 38 percent; the second group recalled 65 percent. In a similar study, people learned four different sets of words paired to the same cue words and then recalled the fourth set later. This situation is also very susceptible to interference. Some of the people studied all four sets in one session; others studied them on a spaced-out basis over a period of three days. Those who did all their studying in one session could recall only 31 percent of the fourth set of words after one day, and 7 percent after a week. Those who had learned the four lists separately in the spaced schedule recalled 89 percent after one day, 72 percent after a week, and 34 percent after a month.[9]

What if you do not have several days? Suppose you have to know the material tomorrow. It will still help to take a break. The time between study sessions does not have to be very long. Merely going to get a drink of water between two learning sessions has been found to reduce interference. (In fact, taking such a break and coming back to the same room reduced interference as much as going to a different room for the second session.)[10] Suppose, for example, that you need to study two similar subjects, such as French and Spanish, for 2 hours in one night. You could study French and Spanish intermittently for 20 to 30 minutes at a time during the 2 hours; or you could study French for 1 hour, take a short break, and then study Spanish for 1 hour. The second strategy is preferable.

SPACE IT OUT

Suppose you have allotted a certain amount of time to studying some material. Should you do all of your studying in one session, or should you distribute your study time across shorter time periods? For example, if you can allot 3 hours to study the material, you could either spend one 3-hour session studying it or you could space it out over three 1-hour sessions.

The first strategy will be easily identified as "cramming" by almost anyone who has been a student. Cramming consists of trying to learn a large amount of material in a relatively short period of intense study, usually just before the exam. Psychologists call it "massed learning." They call the second strategy "distributed learning." Distributed learning is what most teachers tell students to do but what few students actually do—probably because they do not start studying for a test far enough ahead to be able to space their study. They study by the "brush-fire" method, stamping the fire out wherever it flames up, with little planning ahead. This is one reason why most books on how to study in school include a chapter on budgeting your time.

In the previous section on time between learning sessions, we saw that spacing of study sessions helps reduce interference among different sets of material. How effective is spacing in terms of efficiency in learning one set of material? Quotations from three sources that summarize the relevant research can answer this question. The first quote is from a review of research on memory. "Spaced repetitions almost always benefit memory more than massed repetitions. . . . [There is] a beneficial effect of greater spacing between learning trials under many circumstances." The second quote is from a textbook on memory: "One of the most potent variables influencing forgetting is spaced practice."[11]

The third quote is from a booklet titled *What Works: Research About Teaching and Learning,* which was published by the U.S. Department of Education in 1986. It summarizes 41 "findings" of educational research for parents and teachers. Each of the 41 findings is a strategy or activity that has substantial research support and that could be followed by a home or school educator to enhance student learning. The booklet has been well received by most educators, and several of its findings are noted in this book. One of the "examples of sound study practices" listed in *What Works* is, "Good students space learning sessions on a topic over time and do not cram or study the same topic continuously."[12]

As the above quotes suggest, research evidence indicates that spaced learning is generally more effective than massed learning for a number of different kinds of learning tasks, and for intervals between study and recall from a few seconds to much longer. Three studies illustrate the variety of the research. In the first study, high school students studied French vocabulary words 10 minutes each day for three days. Other students studied the words during one 30-minute period. Their performance on a test immediately after studying was the same, but the distributed study group did better four days later. In the second study, postmen in Britain were taught to type on a new postal-code keyboard. Some practiced two 2-hour sessions per day; some practiced one 2-hour session or two 1-hour sessions per day, and some practiced one 1-hour session per day. The more spaced their training was, the less practice time it took to learn the keyboard and the greater the subsequent rate of improvement. In the third study, people who had studied Spanish for three years by both spaced and massed study when they were in school retained about 72 percent of the vocabulary up to 50 years later; those who relied only on cramming typically retained less than 10 percent.[13]

In addition to benefiting study, research evidence shows that spacing may also benefit reviewing, improve teaching, and aid memory for names. When reviewing material that was previously learned, it has been found that spaced reviews are more effective than continuous reviews in helping retention. Along with spaced study, spaced tests and spaced presentations of material by the teacher seem to make the most efficient use of classroom time. We saw in chapter 5 that in a study of people's memory for names and faces of former high school colleagues, the relatively high level of recall was attributed in part to the effects of overlearning. The other contributing factor suggested by the researcher was distributed learning: We learn the other students' names over a period of four years. You might have a hard time remembering the names of 10 people you met in one evening, but you would do better if you met one of those people each day for 10 days. Similarly, people who saw faces for three 5-second viewings separated by several minutes to 2 hours remembered the faces better than did people who saw the faces for one 15-second viewing.[14]

There are at least three possible reasons why spaced learning is generally better than massed learning. [15]

1. You can concentrate only so long before your attention wanders; thus, if you try to do all your studying in one session, you may not be able to pay attention for the whole time.

2. There is evidence that what you have learned during a study session may consolidate in your mind during a break. You can help the process along by consciously reviewing the material in your mind between study sessions. Students remembered more from a 21-minute lecture when the lecture was broken up by three 2-minute pauses to allow consolidation.

3. You are more likely to study the material in different contexts and moods in several study sessions. Chances are better that the mood and setting of the exam will be similar to at least one of the study sessions. Even if it is not, you still have the advantage of being less bound by context than if you had done all your studying in only one context (see chapter 5).

Spaced learning reduces the amount of actual study time it takes to learn the material. Of course, the total amount of time between the beginning of study and final mastery increases with spaced learning, because the total time consists both of actual study time and time between study sessions. Thus, the student who starts studying for Friday's exam on Wednesday will find it easier to space his study than will the student who starts on Thursday night.

There is a limit to the improvements in performance with spacing. As the length of the study session is decreased and the interval between them is increased, performance improves to a point, and then declines. For example, distributing your 3 hours of study into eighteen 10-minute periods may be worse than cramming for one 3-hour period. A practical problem is deciding what length is best for the study periods and for the intervals between periods. It has been recommended that the study period should be shorter for difficult tasks, young, inexperienced learners, and early stages of learning, than for easier tasks, more mature learners, and tasks that are in an advanced stage of learning. [16]

Massed learning may be better for tasks that require a lot of preparation or for certain problem-solving tasks. For example, if it takes you 15 minutes of each study session to settle down, get your supplies together, and get "warmed up" before you can actually start studying, then it may not make much sense to divide your study time into 30-minute sessions. Massed learning may also be more efficient if recall is going to be required right after learning; distributed learning is usually more efficient when there is a delay between learning and recall.[17] (This suggests one reason why many students are not able to recall material for very long after an exam: They have learned it by cramming the night before the exam.)

BREAK IT UP?

Another choice that you are faced with in learning material is whether you should study it by the part method or by the whole method. In the part method you break up the material into smaller parts, and study each part (section, verse, paragraph, stanza, etc.) separately: Study the first part until you have learned it, and then study the second part until you have learned it, and then the third part, and so on. In the whole method you study the whole thing from beginning to end, all the parts together, over and over until you have learned it.

The following seven conditions can determine whether whole learning or part learning is more efficient.[18]

1. One of the main advantages of the whole method is that it gives a context of meaning to each part and prompts recall of the next part. This holds especially for material in which there is a developing theme (for example, a poem or speech). Whole learning gives you an overall picture of how the parts fit together, and this overview of the context helps you to remember the material. Learning the parts without having an overall picture of how they go together is somewhat like putting a jigsaw puzzle together without looking at the picture on the box to see what the completed puzzle is supposed to look like. In the part method, putting the parts together will take up as much as half of the total learning time and will be the source of most errors. Thus, the difficulty in the part method is not learning the parts but putting them together.[19]

2. One of the main advantages of the part method is that people get feedback on how much they are learning sooner than they do using the whole method. You may not realize that you are learning anything if you keep studying the whole thing over and over. However, the person who is studying the separate parts may be able to recite each part as he finishes it. He gets immediate feedback. If the whole learner keeps studying, he will soon find that he can recite most of the material, but he may give up before he reaches this point without feedback on progress along the way. As we saw in chapter 5, feedback helps sustain interest.

For example, suppose that it takes a person an hour to memorize a passage of 500 words, and that a 100-word portion of this passage requires only 9 minutes to memorize. After 9 minutes of study, part learners have something to show for their efforts, whereas whole learners may not be able to recall even a single sentence correctly. This may discourage the whole learners and they may give up. For this reason, the part method may be better for adults who are not used to the whole method, and for children who need feedback to keep them going.

3. Continued practice using the whole method will improve its efficiency, whereas continued practice with the part method will not. Let us consider further the above example of memorizing a 500-word passage. The first 9 minutes spent by the whole learner is not wasted, but it is leading toward mastery. The part learner still has four parts left to memorize and may forget some of each part while memorizing the others. In addition, he still has to work on putting the parts together (see number 1 above). People who have had practice using the whole method realize these things, and that they are learning even though it does not show yet. Because of past experience they know that even though they may not be getting feedback for some time, the final results will probably justify their patience and endurance.

4. The more material there is to be learned, the more efficient the part method will be. Incidentally, it may be helpful to note that regardless of whether you use the whole or part method, a passage that is twice as long as another requires more than twice as long to learn. For example, in one study, a passage of 100 words required a total learning time of 9 minutes; 200 words required 24 minutes; 500 words required 65 minutes; and 1,000 words required 165 minutes.[20] Thus, if it takes you 1 hour to master a 20-page chapter, it will probably take you more than 2 hours to master a 40-page chapter.

5. The more distinctive the parts are, the more efficient the part method will be. For example, the part method may be more appropriate for learning the constitutional amendments than for learning the Gettysburg Address.

6. The advantages of the whole method are greater for distributed learning than for massed learning.

7. The more mature and intelligent the learner is, the more efficient the whole method will be for him.

For much of your learning you would probably want to use a combination of whole and part learning. For example, you might study by the whole method, but select certain parts for extra study. Or you might try using a compromise between the whole and part methods that has been called the "whole-part-whole" method: You first go through the whole thing once or twice, then break it up into logical parts and learn them, and finally review the material as a whole. This method can be very effective for long, difficult material. [21]

Another combination method is the "progressive part" method: You learn the first part and then the second part, and then study the first two parts together. After you know the first two parts, you learn the third part and then study all three parts together, and so on. The progressive part method has an advantage over the part method in that you connect the parts together as you learn them, rather than learning them as disconnected parts. It has an advantage over the whole method in that you get feedback to realize that you are really learning something. The progressive part method may be particularly helpful for older adults; forgetting takes place during learning, and because many elderly people need more trials than young adults do to learn something, they are likely to forget more while they are learning large amounts of material. The progressive part method may reduce this effect. [22]

RECITE IT

Reciting means repeating to yourself what you have studied without looking at it. In recitation you recall as much of what you are trying to memorize as you can, looking at the material only when necessary, after you have read it once or twice. For example, if you are studying a book chapter, you might look at the headings and try to tell yourself what they are about; if you are studying a poem, you might look at the first few words of each line or stanza and try to recall the rest; if you are studying a foreign language, you might look at each English word and try to recall the foreign word. Talking to yourself out loud is not necessary, but it may be better than just repeating material in your mind because it forces you to pay more attention.

Suppose you have 2 hours to study a textbook chapter that takes a half-hour to read. Would it be more effective to read it 4 times or to read it once or twice and spend the rest of the time reciting, testing yourself, and rereading to clear up the points you could not recall? The findings of several studies suggest that it would be more effective to spend as much of the time as possible reciting.

For example, in one study students read an 800-word passage containing 10 paragraphs. Students who recited after each paragraph performed better on a recall test than students who reread the whole passage again (however, the reciting took about twice as long as rereading). In a second study people listened to eight lists of 5 words each. Some of them then listened to each list 3 more times and others recalled (recited) each list 3 times, for the same total amount of study time. They were then tested by recognizing the words from a larger list of 160 words. There was no significant difference between the two groups after 10 minutes, but after 48 hours the recitation group performed better. Recitation can also give you feedback on how well you know the material so that you can focus your study time on what you do not know as well. [23]

One reason recitation is so effective is that it forces you to use many of the other principles and strategies discussed in chapters 4, 5, and 6. For example, recitation forces active learning, it gives you feedback on how you are doing, it involves repetition, and it forces you to pay attention to what you are doing.

Also, in reciting you are practicing the very thing that will be required of you later—recall. You are actually rehearsing retrieval or testing yourself. In several studies, people who were given a test on material right after reading it remembered it better a week or two later than did people who were not given the test, and better even than people who spent the same amount of time reviewing the material. These results are due in part to the fact that the test groups had practiced retrieving the material. Even young children can benefit by an immediate test as a review. [24]

The effectiveness of some of the strategies in this chapter is affected by various conditions, such as the kind of material learned or who is doing the learning. The effectiveness of recitation does not depend on whether the learners are dull or bright, whether the material is long or short, or whether the material is meaningful or not; in virtually every case it is more efficient to read and to recite than to just read. One recent book on study skills said, "No principle is more important than recitation for transferring material from the short-term memory to the long-term memory," and a memory textbook said, "The importance of practicing retrieval activities cannot be overemphasized." [25]

If recitation is so helpful, why don't more people do it? Why do some people spend all of their study time reading the material over and over? There are at least two possible reasons. First, some people probably do not realize the value of recitation. Second, recitation takes more work than reading. It is easier to let your eyes wander down the page (while your mind may be wandering somewhere else) than to concentrate on trying to recall what you have read.

Of course, recitation can be done by yourself, but you can also use recitation by studying with another person. You ask the other person questions about the material to give her a chance to rehearse retrieval, and then she does the same for you. Not only do you benefit by answering questions but your recall will also benefit from making up questions to ask the other person. [26]

USE A STUDY SYSTEM

An effective study method should:

1. Be based on the strategies for effective learning
2. Help you identify and understand the important parts of the material
3. Help you remember the important parts of the material
4. Be more efficient than merely reading the material over and over
5. Be easy to learn

Many study systems have been developed to meet these criteria. The names of the systems are acronyms in which the first letters represent the steps in each system. The following is a representative, but not exhaustive, list of systems: SQ3R, OK4R, PQRST, OARWET, PANORAMA, PQ4R, REAP, SQ5R, MURDER. I have selected SQ3R to discuss as a typical study system for two reasons. First, it is the granddaddy of study systems, dating from 1946. [27] All of the others have been developed since the 1960s (the next oldest being OK4R, which dates from 1962). Second, most of the other systems are modifications of SQ3R, containing essentially the same steps but dividing them up differently and/or using different names for them.

SQ3R consists of five steps: Survey, Question, Read, Recite, Review. It is a general-purpose system that combines several specific learning strategies. It is used with large bodies of material (for example, textbook chapters), and can be used in a wide range of tasks and content areas. One textbook for teaching reading to high school students illustrates how SQ3R can be applied to content areas such as English, social studies (history), science, and math. The following is a brief description of the SQ3R system based on more extensive discussions in books on study skills. [28]

Survey

To survey a book, read the preface, table of contents, and chapter summaries. To survey a chapter, study the outline and skim the chapter, especially the headings, pictures, and graphs. Surveying consists of getting an overview of what the book or chapter is about, and should not take more than a few minutes. Many books have a summary at the end of each chapter; reading this summary before you read the chapter may help you get an overview. (In fact, reading a summary has even been found to yield better memory for the main points of a chapter than reading the chapter itself and similar results have been found in memory for lectures.)[29] The overview is somewhat like looking at a map before taking a trip, or at a picture of the finished product before starting to put together a jigsaw puzzle. Surveying gives a framework within which to place the parts as you learn them, which not only can make the parts easier to remember but also can speed up your reading time by allowing you to comprehend the parts more rapidly.

Memory for reading material can be increased significantly merely by giving the reader a short title reflecting the main idea of the material. To illustrate the effect of knowing what a passage is about, read the following passage once, then try to recall as much you can:

The procedure is actually quite simple. First you arrange things into different groups. Of course, one pile may be sufficient depending on how much there is to do. If you have to go somewhere else due to lack of facilities, that is the next step; otherwise you are pretty well set. It is important not to overdo things. That is, it is better to do too few things at once than too many. . . . After the procedure is completed, arrange the materials into different groups again. They can then be put in their appropriate places. Eventually they will be used once more and the whole cycle will then have to be repeated.

Your recall of this passage was probably not too good because the passage did not make much sense to you. Now I'll tell you that this paragraph is about washing clothes. Try reading it again and see how much better you understand it and remember it now that you have the general idea of what it is about.[30]

"Advance organizers" are methods that give an introduction to, or overview of, the material to be studied (for example, a summary or outline to look over before studying). Research shows that they help in learning and remembering reading material, for elderly adults as well as younger adults. The reason authors of textbooks organize their material under different chapters and headings is to tell the readers the main idea of each chapter and section, how the material is put together, and how the topics relate to each other. If you do not use the headings, you are failing to take advantage of an important source for learning the material. Using text headings can aid both in understanding and remembering textbooks.[31]

The same holds true for pictures and graphs as for headings. The reason pictures are included in a textbook is not just to take up space, make the book thicker, or give the reader something to look at to break up the monotony of reading. Rather, including pictures that illustrate material in the text has been found in a number of studies to increase learning of the text material.[32]

Question

Skim again, asking yourself questions based on the headings so that you will know some things to look for when reading. For example, the heading to this section—"Use a Study System"—may raise some questions: What constitutes this system? A system for what? How can I use this system? Several studies have found that inserting written questions before, within, or after text material helps in learning and remembering the material, as do questions made up by the learner.[33] Since most material you read does not have questions inserted, you can benefit by asking your own questions as your read. Questions can maintain interest, focus attention, foster active involvement in learning, and give a purpose to your reading, all of which help you to learn the material. Also, some textbooks provide review questions at the end of the chapter; you might try reading them before reading the chapter so that you will know what to look for as you read the chapter.

Read

Read the chapter without taking notes. Answer the questions you have asked. Read everything. Sometimes tables, charts, and graphs convey more information than the text does. Note that this is the *third* step in SQ3R; for most students it is the *first* step in studying. In fact, for some students it is the only step: Some students think that when they have run their eyes over the textbook they have studied it (after reading this section on SQ3R one of my memory students commented that he used the 3R method—read, read, and reread).

A student in one of my psychology courses came to talk with me about her low quiz scores. She said she studied for the chapter quizzes, but she just could not remember what she had studied. I asked her to describe how she studied. She said, "Well, I read the chapter the night before the quiz or the morning of the quiz." That was it—one reading, no survey, no review. Reading was the only one of the SQ3R steps she was using. I suggested to her that her problem was not in remembering the material, but in learning it well enough in the first place. She probably could not have told me much more about the chapter right after reading it than she could later on the quiz.

Underlining while reading is a very popular learning tactic among high school and college students. Research on the effectiveness of underlining shows that it can help people get more from their reading if it is done right, but there are several ways that students can misuse underlining.[34] One misuse is to read a chapter and underline, and then only review the underlined parts in studying for a test. One problem with this approach is that you usually do not know what is important, or what relates to what, the first time you read a chapter. Thus, when you review the underlined parts you may miss much of what is important. Underlining while you are reading for the first time also has other problems. It is easy to do, so most students underline too much; this results in reviewing pages that have marked not only the important points but also repeated and conflicting points.

Another problem with underlining the first time through is that some students develop the habit of reading to *mark* important points rather than reading to understand and remember the points; thus, a student may underline an italicized sentence and continue reading without having even read the italicized sentence! To use underlining properly, you should wait until reaching the end of a section before underlining, think about what the important points were, and then go back and underline only the key phrases. Underlining the wrong things may actually interfere with learning.[35]

Recite

Recitation is discussed as a separate strategy earlier in this chapter. Reread, asking yourself questions about the headings and italicized words and answering the questions as much as you can. This can be done after each section or after each chapter, depending on their length. How much of your study time should you spend reciting? For most textbooks about half of your time should be spent reciting. You may want to spend more time reciting for disconnected, meaningless material, such as lists of rules and formulas, but somewhat less for storylike, connected material.

Review

Review is a very basic learning strategy that is often overlooked in popular memory books. Some authors give the impression that if you just use the right technique (theirs) to learn something, you will never forget it. The fact is that no matter how you learn something, if you do not use it occasionally you are likely to forget it unless you review it. Three studies illustrate the variety of learning tasks in which review has been found to help. One psychologist studied her memory for events that she had recorded in a diary during a period of four and one-half years. She recalled only 36 percent of events that she never reviewed, but her recall went up to 88 percent for events that she had reviewed at least 4 times during four years. In another study students remembered more from a lecture when a short pause for review was provided at the end. In a third study Pakistani college students remembered nonsense syllables better after 6 hours when they reviewed than did other students not given a chance to review. [36]

To use review as a part of SQ3R, survey again, reviewing what you could recite and noting what you could not. Question yourself again. Like the Survey, the Review should take only a few minutes. In chapter 2 we saw that it takes fewer trials to relearn old material (even when it has apparently been forgotten when measured by recall) than to learn new material; thus, it pays to review the material occasionally to refresh your memory so that you will not have to spend as much time going over the material for the exam.

It was noted earlier that spaced reviews are better than continuous (massed) reviews. The best times to review are: during study, by reciting after each major section; immediately after studying; and just before the exam. A review immediately after studying helps you consolidate the material in your memory, and a later review helps you relearn forgotten material. One study found that having one review immediately after learning and one a week later was more effective than only one review, or two reviews immediately after learning, or two reviews a week later. For eight-year-old children, an immediate review-test was more effective than a review-test a week later. [37]

Many students have reported a saving in study effort by the following rule: Never finish a reading session without reviewing in outline the main points of what has just been read. This rule has been found by many students to be the most important single step to reduce forgetting. Not only does it help you see what you have learned, but it also helps you learn the material further before forgetting it (in chapter 3 it was noted that most forgetting occurs soon after learning). In addition, such review saves time and effort; because you remember more, you do not have to spend so much time rereading and reviewing the material for the exam later. [38]

One study found that the best review schedule for remembering people's names was a series of gradually increasing intervals between reviews. [39] For example, you might review the name of a person immediately after meeting her, then again 15 seconds later, then maybe a minute later, and then several minutes later. I used an increasing-interval review schedule during a 16-month period when I was memorizing scriptures. I learned one new scripture each day, and carried with me seven scriptures on cards—the new one I was learning that day plus the six I had learned the previous six days. After seven days a card would go in a file to be reviewed once a week for a month, then once a month for several months, and then once every three months. This schedule of gradually increasing review intervals helped me memorize about 500 scriptures (averaging about two verses each) in 16 months.

Note that reviewing just before an exam is different from cramming for the exam. The key word in the difference is "new." If the material you are studying is new to you (that is, you are learning it for the first time) then you are cramming. If it is not new (that is, you are going over what you have studied before) then you are reviewing. Although a final review just before the exam is recommended, cramming is not.

This section on reviewing applies to lecture or reading notes as well as to textbooks. Researchers have studied two possible benefits that can come from taking notes. The "encoding" function of notes is the benefit that comes from putting the material in your own words in order to write it down. The "external-storage" function is the benefit that comes from having something in writing to review later. Although research has provided some support for the encoding function, the external storage function is more consistently supported by research evidence. Notes give you something to review later, and reviewing notes usually produces higher achievement than not reviewing notes.[40]

When my students come to my office to talk about an exam they have taken, I ask them to bring their class notes with them; I often find that their notes have the answers to several of the questions they missed. They took good notes but did not study them well enough. Similarly, research found that the lecture notes of most college students contained the answers to many of the test questions they had missed. A common mistake was to wait until just before the exam to review their notes, which by then usually had lost much of their meaning. You can demonstrate the importance of reviewing your lecture notes soon after the lecture by comparing your ability to read and interpret your own notes taken during a recent lecture with those you took several weeks ago and have not looked at since.[41]

HOW WELL DO THE PRINCIPLES AND STRATEGIES WORK?

The distinction between "principles" in chapters 4 and 5 and "strategies" in this chapter is somewhat arbitrary; some principles could be viewed as strategies (for example, "associate it" or "overlearn it"), and some strategies could be viewed as principles (for example, "review"). The strategies themselves also are highly overlapping and interrelated. For example, spaced study allows for review and use of part learning, and the study systems include some strategies, such as recitation, discussed in other sections. You have probably used some of the principles and strategies, but you may have used them without knowing for sure what you were doing or why you were doing it. You may have used others without knowing whether they were really doing any good, and you may even have used others in such a way that they did not do much good.

Do the principles and strategies discussed in chapters 4, 5, and 6 really help? One classic study indicates that they do. People were taught seven rules for memorizing. One group was instructed in the seven rules, and then given 3 hours of practice using the rules. A second group also practiced memorizing for 3 hours, but they were given no instruction. Both groups were then given a memorization test involving many different kinds of material, such as poetry, prose, facts, foreign languages, and historical dates. The instructed group improved about 8 times as much in their memorizing ability as did the uninstructed group—an average of 36 percent compared with about 4.5 percent for the uninstructed group.[42]

The seven rules that the students were taught are listed below as they were given in the original study. After each rule, in parentheses, are the principles and strategies that are related to the rule.

1. Learn by wholes. (Whole Learning, "Survey" of SQ3R)
2. Use active self-testing. (Recitation)
3. Use rhythm and grouping. (Meaningfulness, Organization)
4. Attention to meaning and advantages of picturing. (Meaningfulness, Visualization)
5. Mental alertness and concentration. (Attention)
6. Use of secondary associations. (Association)
7. Confidence in ability to memorize. (Relaxation, Overlearning)

A lot of research done on various learning strategies, including those in this chapter, has produced a lot of evidence that people can become more effective learners when they are taught these strategies. A recent review of research on study skills courses in which students learned how to use most of the basic principles and learning strategies concluded that such courses have been found to increase reading comprehension, reduce anxiety, improve course grades, and improve academic performance. Training in learning strategies seems to be effective from elementary school through college.[43]

One of the conclusions listed in *What Works* regards study skills: The ways in which children study influence strongly how much they learn. Examples of sound study practices are listed, most of which are covered in this chapter, and it is stated that low-ability and inexperienced students can learn more information and study more efficiently when they use these skills. [44]

SQ3R and similar study systems have been found to increase the rate of reading, level of comprehension, and performance on examinations. A modified version of SQ3R (PQRST) has even helped brain-damaged patients accomplish memory tasks that they could not accomplish without the system. An analysis of SQ3R in the framework of a learning theory called "information processing" explains why each step of SQ3R can facilitate the processing of information, and the author suggested that students should be shown *why* SQ3R works so that they will use it. [45]

However, evaluation of the study systems has not been all positive. Reviews of research on the study systems have suggested that although SQ3R appears to have a good deal of intuitive appeal, there is not a great deal of empirical support for it, and that much of the perceived potency of the study systems is based on opinion more than fact. One of the main problems with SQ3R and other systems is simply that most students do not use them, probably because they are too much work (as I suggested earlier for recitation). Also, the systems may be too complex to be used effectively by children and other less-mature students. [46]

7

Working Miracles with Your Memory: An Introduction to Mnemonics

Can you remember a list of 20 or more words, in any order, after hearing it just once? Can you repeat a 30-digit number after hearing it once? Can you look through a shuffled deck of cards once and remember all 52 cards in order, or tell where any particular cards are in the deck? Can you memorize a 50-page magazine so that you can tell what is on any page?

These are examples of the kinds of memory feats performed by stage mnemonists in their acts. These feats are among those I have duplicated for public demonstrations, using the techniques and systems in this book. Other memory feats I have also done include memorizing the calendar for the second half of this century, so that I can give the day of the week for any date from 1950 to 1999; memorizing more than 100 telephone numbers of all the members of an organization to which I belong; memorizing the page numbers of nearly 200 hymns in a hymnal; memorizing the major contents of each of the 239 numbered sections of a book.

Feats such as these seem like miracles to people who are unfamiliar with the mnemonic systems involved, and they really *are* miracles when compared with the unaided memory. However, most people can do such feats if they want to badly enough to learn and practice the appropriate mnemonic systems. For example, my daughter did the 30-digit number and magazine demonstrations when she was thirteen years old and my son did the 20-word demonstration when he was eight. You may not *want* to perform these particular feats, but the important point is that you *can* do them; they are not beyond the reach of a normal memory. If you can do these feats, you can also do other things with your memory that you *do* want to do, but may have thought were beyond your ability. The purpose of this chapter, and the rest of the book, is to teach you how to use mnemonics to help you work your own memory miracles.

WHAT ARE MNEMONICS?

The word *mnemonic* (pronounced "ne MON ik") was briefly defined in the introduction to this book as "aiding the memory." It is derived from *Mnemosyne,* the name of the ancient Greek goddess of memory. The use of mnemonics is not new; the Loci system described in chapter 10 dates back to about 500 B.C., and was used by Greek orators to remember long speeches. An interesting book has traced the history of mnemonics from ancient times through the Renaissance, and several articles have reviewed the history of mnemonics since then.[1]

"Mnemonics" refers in general to methods for improving memory; a mnemonic technique is any technique that aids the memory. Most researchers, however, define mnemonics more narrowly as being what most people consider to be rather unusual, artificial memory aids. For example, the learning strategies discussed in chapter 6 aid the memory, but they are not usually referred to as mnemonic strategies. One characteristic of most mnemonic techniques is that they do not have an inherent connection with the material to be learned; rather, they impose meaning or structure on material that is otherwise not very meaningful or organized. Another characteristic is that they usually involve adding something to the material being learned to make it more memorable, and thus are referred to by many researchers as visual or verbal "elaboration." The elaborations create meaningful associations between what is to be learned and what is already known.[2]

Mnemonics can be either visual or verbal. Visual mnemonics use visual imagery to associate the items to be remembered; verbal mnemonics make the associations with words. For example, to associate the words *cats* and *rats,* you could either form a visual image of cats eating rats (visual mediator), or you could form a sentence such as "Cats like to eat rats" (verbal mediator). The first part of this chapter gives some examples of verbal mnemonics.[3] Most of the rest of the book, and most research on mnemonics, focuses more on visual mnemonics.

Most of the examples of mnemonics given in this chapter are single-purpose mnemonics used for remembering specific facts. Mnemonics discussed in later chapters include more general-purpose systems that can be used over and over to remember different sets of material. I will refer to the kinds of specific-purpose mnemonics discussed in this chapter as mnemonic "techniques," and will refer to the more general mnemonics discussed in chapters 9 through 12 as mnemonic "systems."

Some Sample Mnemonics

Some of the examples of association discussed in chapter 4 could be called mnemonic techniques (such as remembering *port* versus *starboard* and *stalactite* versus *stalagmite,* and spelling). Additional examples can also illustrate mnemonic associations. You can remember that a Bactrian camel has two humps and a Dromedary camel has one hump by noticing the two humps in the letter *B* and the one hump in *D.* You can remember that there are 52 white keys and 36 black keys on a piano by associating the white keys with a deck of cards (52 cards) or a calendar (52 weeks in a year), and the black keys with a yardstick (36 inches). Mnemonic associations are frequently used in spelling (for example, bad grammar will mar a report; stationERy is for a lettER; she screamed "EEE" as she passed by a cEmEtEry). A book has been published containing such mnemonic associations for 800 problem spelling words, and such spelling mnemonics have been found to be helpful for sixth graders.[4]

Rhymes such as those discussed in chapter 4 may also properly be referred to as mnemonic techniques. The following are some additional examples. A rhyme for remembering the books of the Old Testament in order begins: "That great Jehovah speaks to us, in Genesis and Exodus; Leviticus and Numbers see, followed by Deuteronomy," and continues for the remaining 34 books. A rhyme I once read on a cereal box (when I was hard-pressed for reading material at breakfast one morning) is aimed at helping children remember what each vitamin does for us. Part of the rhyme went as follows:

The vitamin called A has important connections
It aids in our vision and helps stop infections.
To vitamin C this ditty now comes,
Important for healing and strong healthy gums.
Done with both of these?
Here come the B's:

B_1 for the nerves.
B_2 helps cells energize.
Digesting the protein's
B_6's prize.

A rhyme helps us remember how to treat a shock victim: "If his face is red, raise his head; if his face is pale, raise his tail." Rhymes have also helped people in their cooking chores: "A pint's a pound, the world around" helps us remember a useful equivalence; "Cooking rice? Water's twice" helps us remember to cook one cup of raw rice in two cups of water; and "One big T equals teaspoons three" helps us remember that there are three teaspoons in a tablespoon.

A well-known mnemonic is used to remember which way to set the clock for daylight savings time: "Spring forward, fall back" (set the clock forward an hour in the spring, and back an hour in the fall). To remember long numbers, sentences can be constructed so that the number of letters in each word corresponds with each digit of the number in order (if the first digit is 3, the first word would have three letters, etc.). For example, to remember pi (π) to four decimal places (3.1416) remember "Yes, I know a number." For the ambitious memorizer, this technique can be combined with the use of rhyme to remember π to 30 decimal places, as the following example from the *Mensa Journal* shows:

> Sir, I send a rhyme excelling
> In sacred truth and rigid spelling,
> Numerical sprites elucidate
> All my own striving can't relate,
> It nature gain
> Not you complain
> Though doctor Johnson fulminate.

We saw earlier that a rhyme ("Thirty days has September . . .") can help us remember how many days are in each month, but some people have a hard time remembering the rhyme. (Someone once said that a more appropriate rhyme might be "Thirty days has September, all the rest I can't remember.") If you have a hard time remembering the rhyme, you can use another mnemonic technique to remember the number of days in the months (see the following diagram). Hold your hands out in front of you in fists, with the palms down and the hands together. The knuckle of the left little finger represents January, the valley between it and the ring finger represents February, the knuckle of the ring finger represents March, and so on until you reach the knuckle of the right ring finger, which represents December. All the knuckle months have 31 days, and the valley months are the short months. You can do the same with only one fist by starting over on the knuckle of the little finger for August after you reach July on the knuckle of the index finger.

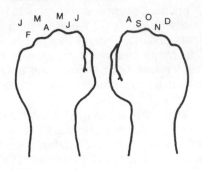

Memorizing the Calendar

While we are on the topic of calendars, let us consider again the 12-digit number that we have encountered several times: 376-315-374-264. In chapter 5, I told you that if you memorize this 12-digit number you will, in effect, have the calendar for the whole year of 1988 memorized. Here is how it works. Each digit represents the date of the first Sunday in each month; the first Sunday in January is the 3rd, the first Sunday in June is the 5th, and the first Sunday in December is the 4th.

Knowing that, all you have to know in addition are the months and the days of the week. If you can also add and subtract up to 7, then you can give the day of the week for any date. What day of the week is July 4, 1988? July is the seventh month. The seventh digit is 3, so the first Sunday in July is the 3rd. Add one day to determine that July 4, 1988 is a Monday. Try another one. What day is June 18, 1988? The sixth digit is 5, so the first Sunday in June is the 5th. Add 7 to get the second Sunday, the 12th, and add six more days to get the 18th, which is a Saturday. (In this example it may be simpler to add 7 more to the second Sunday to get the third Sunday, the 19th, and then subtract one day.)

Try a question like the following: How many Mondays are in May 1988? The digit for May is 1, so the first Monday is May 2. Add sevens to get the other Mondays—May 9, 16, 23, 30; there are five Mondays in May. Try the following: What date is the fourth Thursday in November (Thanksgiving)? The digit for November is 6. This means that the first Thursday (counting backward) is November 3, making the second Thursday November 10, the third Thursday November 17, and the fourth Thursday November 24.

Can you see how the principle of chunking is involved in this mnemonic? For all practical purposes you have 365 things memorized, when in fact you really have only 12 things memorized, but each of the 12 chunks represents about 30 bits of information (dates). Of course, you can use the technique for any year merely by memorizing the appropriate number for that year; memorizing a new 12-digit number once a year should not be too difficult a memory task (especially after reading this book).

One of my students memorized the calendar using this number and then amazed his colleagues at work the next day. He reported that one of them got a puzzled look on his face and then said, "Oh, I know you stayed up for 5 hours last night and memorized the whole thing." The student had actually spent less than 3 minutes memorizing and practicing the number, and reported that "it was truly a miracle of effectiveness." When he was age eleven my son did an impressive demonstration using the calendar number; several members of the audience called out their birthdays (month and date) and in less than 10 seconds he told them what day of the week their birthday was that year.

FIRST LETTERS AND KEYWORDS

The varied examples of mnemonics in the previous section help give a feeling for what mnemonics are. Many of the specific examples were discussed under the general categories of "associations" and "rhymes." This section discusses additional examples of verbal mnemonics that psychologists have studied under the headings of "first-letter" mnemonics and "keyword" mnemonics.

First-letter Mnemonics

Can you name the Great Lakes in the midwestern United States? Try it now before you read any further. What you have just attempted was a recall task. Let us now change it to an aided-recall task. The following word is composed of the first letter of the name of each lake: HOMES. Using the word as a cue, if you were not able to name all five lakes, can you do so now? Many people who cannot recall the names of the lakes can do so when given this cue. The cue is what is known as an *acronym*— a word that is made out of the first letters of the items to be remembered. In this example the acronym HOMES stands for Huron, Ontario, Michigan, Erie, and Superior. A mnemonic technique that is similar to the acronym is the *acrostic*—a series of words, lines, or verses in which the first letters form a word or phrase; for example, an acrostic for remembering the names of the Great Lakes might be, Healthy Old Men Exercise Some. Acronyms and acrostics are referred to by most mnemonics researchers as "first-letter mnemonics" (for reasons that should be obvious).

A well-known acronym that is used as an aid to remember the colors of the visible spectrum is the name ROY G. BIV. This name represents red, orange, yellow, green, blue, indigo, and violet. Similarly, suppose you have a shopping list of bananas, oranges, milk, and bread. The word BOMB could be used to help remember the list. An acronym does not even have to be a real word. What are the only four states in the United States that come together at a single point? The coined word CANU will help you remember Colorado, Arizona, New Mexico, and Utah. An acronym for remembering the excretory organs of the body is SKILL (Skin, Kidneys, Intestines, Liver, Lungs). An acronym that may help a French student remember most of the verbs that are conjugated with the helping verb "to be" is the name of a lady, MRS. VANDERTAMP (*Monter, Rester, Sortir, Venir, Aller, Naître, Descendre, Entrer, Rentrer, Tomber, Arriver, Mourir, Partir*).

Acronyms are widely used to represent associations (CORE for Congress of Racial Equality), organizations (NOW for National Organization for Women), government agencies (CAB for Civil Aeronautics Board), military titles and terms (WAVES for Women Accepted for Voluntary Emergency Service, SNAFU for "Situation normal, all fouled up"). Collections have been compiled of at least 10,000 such acronyms used on a national level.[5] One reason that so many groups identify themselves with an acronym is that it serves as an aid to help people remember them.

Many examples of acrostics can also be given. The colors of the visible spectrum have been remembered by the acrostic, "Richard Of York Gave Battle In Vain." Psalm 119 is divided into 22 eight-verse sections corresponding to the 22 letters of the Hebrew alphabet; the first word of every verse in each section begins with the same one of the 22 letters, in order. Many anatomy students have used acrostics like "On Old Olympus' Towering Top, A Finn And German Viewed Some Hops" to remember the cranial nerves (Olfactory, Optic, Oculomotor, Trochlear, Trigeminal, Abducens, Facial, Auditory, Glossopharyngeal, Vagus, Spinal Accessory, and Hypoglossal),[6] and many music students have used "Every Good Boy Does Fine" to remember the notes on the lines in the treble clef (EGBDF).

An acrostic for remembering the order of planets from the sun is "Men Very Easily Make Jugs Serve Useful Nocturnal Purposes" (Mercury, Venus, Earth, Mars, Jupiter, Saturn, Uranus, Neptune, Pluto). An acrostic that helped one woman line up her baking ingredients in their proper order is "Shirley Shouldn't Eat Fresh Mushrooms" (Sugar, Shortening, Eggs, Flour, Milk), and an acrostic that has helped mathematics students perform operations in their proper order of priority is "Bless My Dear Aunt Sally" (Brackets, Multiplication, Division, Addition, Subtraction).

Several research studies done on first-letter mnemonics have found that they are among the most frequent mnemonic techniques that people use on their own and that they can significantly improve memory for lists of items, even in people with brain damage.[7]

There are at least four ways in which acronyms and acrostics can help memory.

1. Acronyms and acrostics make the material meaningful; they give you something meaningful to remember, such as HOMES, ROY G. BIV, and Every Good Boy Does Fine.

2. Acronyms chunk the information so you do not have to remember a lot. Instead of five lakes or seven colors, for example, you only have to remember one word or one name. Of course, an acronym or acrostic itself is not the original information; it merely gives you some cues to help you retrieve the original information. After you remember the acronym or acrostic, you still must be able to generate the original information from it. (A physics professor may not be particularly impressed if a student wrote on an exam that the colors of the visible spectrum were ROY G. BIV.) Thus, acronyms and acrostics may be more useful for terms that are familiar to you than for terms that are not familiar, because a first letter might not be a sufficient cue for terms you do not know very well.[8]

3. First-letter mnemonics provide cues to help you retrieve the items; therefore, they change a recall task to an aided recall task. This makes your memory task easier by narrowing your memory search. Research has shown that the first letters of words help people recall the words (even patients with dementia and brain damage). Also, when people are trying to recall something they know, such as the name of a relative or the capital of a country, they frequently try to cue themselves by generating letters of the alphabet to trigger retrieval.[9]

4. First-letter mnemonics can tell you how many items are to be remembered, so that you know when you have recalled all of them. For example, if you have recalled the names of four Great Lakes, you know you have one more to go because there are five letters in the acronym HOMES or five words in the acrostic, Healthy Old Men Exercise Some.

These four advantages of first-letter mnemonics apply as long as you can remember which acronym or acrostic goes with which information, but what if you forget the mnemonic itself? It will not do you much good, for example, to remember that there is some acronym to help remember the names of the Great Lakes if you cannot remember what the acronym is. Here is a suggestion that may help prevent this problem: Associate the acronym with the information it represents. You might use a verbal association such as, "The Great Lakes make good HOMES for big fish," or a visual association such as an image of HOMES (houses) floating on the Great Lakes. Now when you try to think of the acronym for the Great Lakes, you think of what it was that was floating on the lakes and that leads you to HOMES.

The Keyword Mnemonic

A great amount of research has been done on a mnemonic that is usually called the "Keyword mnemonic." This term was used by Richard Atkinson in a 1975 article describing the use of this mnemonic in learning foreign language vocabulary.[10] Subsequent researchers usually attribute the Keyword mnemonic to him, probably because he was the first respected psychologist who brought it to their attention and initiated systematic research on it. However, the technique was developed and used by other people before 1975, particularly for foreign languages.

The Keyword mnemonic consists of two steps, one verbal and one visual. The first step is to construct a concrete keyword to represent the foreign word to be learned. For example, the Spanish word for duck is *pato,* which could be represented by the sound-alike keyword *pot.* The second step is to form a visual image connecting the keyword with the English meaning. For example, you could picture a duck cooking in a pot or wearing a pot on its head. To recall the meaning of the Spanish word *pato* you first retrieve the keyword *pot,* and then the stored image that links it to duck.

The Keyword mnemonic is really just the combined use of two mnemonic techniques discussed later in this chapter—substitute words and visual associations. It also shares several properties and principles in common with other mnemonics discussed in later chapters (such as the Loci system and face-name mnemonics). Research shows that the Keyword mnemonic is very effective in learning a foreign vocabulary, and it has also been used effectively to aid students in several other kinds of paired-associate learning tasks in school (see chapter 14).[11]

In my travels to other countries to speak on my memory research,

I have had occasion to learn some vocabulary and pronunciation in six languages—Spanish, French, Italian, German, Hebrew, and Japanese. I did not learn any of these languages well enough to give my research report in that language or even to carry on an intelligent conversation, but I learned just enough to be polite and to communicate some necessary ideas. This included three or four dozen basic words and phrases in each language, such as "please" and "thank you," "yes" and "no," "hello" and "goodbye," "Where is . . .?" "I don't understand . . . " "Do you speak English?" and "That costs too much." I used the Keyword mnemonic to help in learning many of the words, and found that it could even be used for some phrases. For example, the pronunciation of "You're welcome" in Hebrew is like "al lō da VAHR" (a load of air), and in Japanese the pronunciation is like "dō eTASHeMASHta" (don't touch the mustache).

BASIC PRINCIPLES OF MNEMONICS

A recent memory textbook suggested that the objections some people have (see pseudo-limitations in chapter 8) to the use of some memory methods might decrease if the reasons for the mnemonics' effectiveness were better understood. It helps to better understand mnemonics and to remove some of the mystical aura that can surround mnemonics if we realize that they are based upon well-established principles of learning and memory. More than 20 years ago, one psychologist observed that mnemonic techniques are oddities only in the sense that they enable their users to deal with memory tasks that most people do not even attempt in everyday life, "but they are not oddities in the sense that they employ any basic procedures which are absent from everyday activities. They are merely specialized elaborations of normal memory activities." During the 1970s other memory researchers made similar observations: [12]

The secrets of those who practice the art of memory ought to shed light on the organization and operation of the mechanisms involved in memory.

A study of mnemonics and mnemonists can provide cues as to the functioning of normal memory and a way of testing the generality of theories of memory.

No general theory of memory can be adequate without being able to account in principle for the efficiency of mnemonic systems.

The point is the same one that was made earlier, that mnemonic techniques and systems do not *replace* the basic principles of learning but *use* them. Mnemonics make use of all the basic principles of learning and memory that were discussed in chapter 4, as well as others.[13]

Meaningfulness. Mnemonic techniques and systems help make material meaningful by using rhymes, patterns, and associations. In fact, probably the main function of most mnemonics is to impose meaning on material that is not inherently meaningful; that is the kind of material for which mnemonics have best shown their value. Mnemonics are not needed for material that already has meaning. One of the most powerful examples of the use of this principle is the Phonetic system (chapter 12), which gives meaning to one of the most abstract, meaningless kinds of material—numbers—so that they will be easier to learn.

Organization. Most of the mnemonic techniques just described, and all of the mnemonic systems described in subsequent chapters, impose a meaningful organization on the material. As mental filing systems, they give a systematic way to record and retrieve the material. Again, mnemonics are not needed for material that already has an inherent logic and structure.

Association. We have seen some examples of mnemonic associations. The principle of association is basic to all the mnemonic systems discussed in subsequent chapters. In the Link system the items are associated with each other. In the Loci, Peg, and Phonetic systems, easily remembered material that is memorized previously serves as your filing system; you associate the new material that you want to learn with the material that has been memorized previously.

Visualization. Visual imagery also plays a central role in the mnemonic systems because the associations are usually made visually. Visualization is probably the most unusual aspect of mnemonic systems, and may also be the most misunderstood. For these reasons, it is discussed more thoroughly in this book than any other principle. Chapter 3 discussed the differences between remembering pictures and words; chapter 4 discussed the effectiveness of visual imagery in remembering verbal material; and this chapter offers some suggestions for the effective use of visual associations to remember verbal material.

Attention. Mnemonic systems force you to concentrate on the material in order to form pictures and associate them. Mnemonics can foster attention because they tend to be more interesting and fun than rote learning.

Other Principles and Strategies

In addition to making inherent use of all the basic principles of memory from chapter 4, mnemonic systems can also be used in connection with other principles and strategies discussed in chapters 5 and 6. For example, although learning with a mnemonic system frequently takes fewer repetitions than learning with the unaided memory, your retention of the material will still be increased if you overlearn it.

Although mnemonic systems do not completely eliminate interference, a considerable amount of evidence shows that they do reduce it as compared with using only the unaided memory. For example, mnemonic systems have been used to learn several successive lists, or several different orders of the same list, with very little interference among the different lists.[14] You will probably still get some interference among different lists if they are learned consecutively by the same mnemonic system, but the interference will be a lot less than if you did not use a system. Of course, you can reduce the interference even further by combining the use of mnemonics with the other methods for reducing interference that were discussed in chapter 6.

The effectiveness of mnemonic techniques can be increased if you combine them with other learning strategies. Space out your study sessions. Use whole and part learning where appropriate. Use recitation. Finally, use the relevant steps from the SQ3R study system where appropriate. For example, just because you use a mnemonic to learn something does not mean that you do not need to review the material occasionally. Mnemonic systems aid the memory by supplementing study strategies, not by replacing them, just as with the basic principles of learning.[15]

HOW TO MAKE EFFECTIVE VISUAL ASSOCIATIONS

Because visual association plays a central role in most mnemonic techniques and systems, it is useful to have some guides for making effective use of visual imagery in associations. Research has been done on three factors that can help to make your visual associations effective—interaction, vividness, and bizarreness.[16]

Interaction

Visual imagery by itself is not maximally effective. To make visual association effective, your imagery must both be "visual" *and* involve "association." The two items you are associating should be pictured as interacting in some way with each other (one of them doing something to or with the other), rather than as merely sitting next to each other or one on top of the other. For example, if you were associating the words *dog* and *broom* it would be better to picture a dog sweeping with a broom than to picture a dog standing by a broom.

Considerable research evidence supports the interaction effect: Visual imagery involving interaction among the items is more effective than separate images of the items. Several research studies in which pictures were shown to people have found that when the items in the picture were interacting they were remembered better than when they were not interacting—for kindergarten children through elderly adults.[17]

In other studies people made up their own mental pictures to remember words rather than having pictures shown to them. Again, interacting imagery was more effective than separate images in serial learning as well as in paired-associate learning. In fact, even when people were not instructed to remember the words, just telling them to compare the words in each pair with one another yielded better memory for the words than making judgments about each word individually. However, children as young as first graders may not benefit as much from interacting imagery when they are instructed to make up their own mental pictures as they do when pictures are shown to them.[18]

One possible reason for the effectiveness of interacting imagery is that images of separate items can be combined into a single image that is remembered as a unit; therefore, each part of the image serves as a cue for remembering the rest of the unit. This suggests that chunking plays a role in the effectiveness of interacting imagery: One image represents the relationship among two or more items. Interactive imagery is not much better than separate images for word pairs that are already meaningfully related, possibly because they are already remembered as a single unit better than are the arbitrary word pairs used in most research.[19]

Vividness

A vivid visual image is one that is clear, distinct, and strong—one that is as similar as possible to actually seeing a picture. Pictures have an even stronger effect on memory than instructions to visualize, so that the more you can see the image like you were actually looking at a picture, the better.[20] You should try to see your mental pictures as clearly as possible. For example, if you are associating the words *dog* and *broom* you should not just think about the two words together or think about the idea of a dog sweeping with a broom, but you should try to actually *see* the dog sweeping with the broom in your mind's eye. People who are not accustomed to visualizing (and many adults are not) may find that it helps at first if they close their eyes when trying to see the mental picture. It also seems to help if you make the mental picture detailed.[21] What kind of dog is it? What kind of broom? Where is he sweeping? What is he sweeping? Picture a dachshund sweeping mud off your porch with a pushbroom; or a bulldog sweeping food off the kitchen floor with a straw broom.

In addition to detail, three suggestions that are frequently recommended to help make visual associations effective are aimed at making them more vivid (and maybe even more bizarre—see the next section):

1. *Motion.* See the picture in action (the dog is sweeping with the broom, not just holding it).
2. *Substitition.* See one item in place of the other (you are sweeping with a dog instead of a broom, or a broom is coming out of a doghouse).
3. *Exaggeration.* See one or both of the items exaggerated in size or number (a Chihuahua is sweeping with a giant broom, or a large St. Bernard is using a small whisk broom).

Another factor that may help enhance vividness is *familiarity;* images that are familiar in terms of prior experiences have been found to be more vivid.[22]

Researchers have had a hard time defining and measuring vividness, which can affect whether or not they conclude that vividness helps memory. Even so, several different kinds of studies suggest that visual associations should be vivid to be remembered better. In one study of imagery in paired-associate learning, people rated the vividness of their images as they constructed them. For every person, the more vivid the images were rated, the better they were recalled. In another study, people who were instructed to make vivid visual images tended to remember a list of words better than people who were told only to make visual images; people instructed to make vivid, active visual images tended to perform even better.[23]

Effects of mental practice on motor skills were greater for people who were able to form vivid and/or controlled memory images of the process. People who tended to form vivid visual images of other people not only remembered their appearance better than those who did not but also remembered other information (attitudes, values, history) about them better. Finally, people whose images were generally high in vividness could use imagery mnemonics more effectively than those whose images were low in vividness (although their general, overall memory performance was not significantly different).[24]

Bizarreness

Popular memory-training books typically recommend that visual associations should be bizarre (unusual, weird, implausible, incongruous, ludicrous). The opposite of bizarre would be plausible—imagining a picture that makes sense and could really occur. For example, a picture of a dog being chased out of a house by a person with a broom is plausible; a dog sweeping with a broom would be somewhat bizarre; and a dog riding a broom like a witch, or a person sweeping the floor with a dog tied to the end of a broomstick, would be bizarre.

At least 30 research studies have been done on the effectiveness of bizarre versus plausible imagery.[25] Most of the studies have found no difference between bizarre and plausible images in their effectiveness, but a few studies have found that bizarre images were more effective than plausible images under some conditions, and a few have found that bizarre images were less effective. Some of the differences in findings are probably due to methodological differences among studies (such as different definitions of bizarreness, immediate versus delayed recall, pictures versus mental images, and paired-associates versus free recall).

When bizarreness does help, it may be because bizarre images also incorporate other factors that help memory, such as interaction, vividness, uniqueness, and time. Some studies have found that bizarreness can be confounded with interaction; some interacting images may almost *have* to be bizarre in order to involve interaction (for example, it is hard to think of a plausible picture showing an elephant and a piano interacting). Bizarre images may be more striking and attention-getting, and thus more vivid than plausible images. We saw in the previous section that vivid images tend to be remembered better than nonvivid images.

Bizarre images tend more to be unique (distinctive or novel) than plausible images, and the uniqueness of an image helps memory. Novel visual associations between objects have been found to help memory for the objects more than common associations, as long as the novel associations were plausible; implausible novel associations were no more effective than common plausible associations.[26] (An example of a common plausible association is a man playing a harp; a plausible novel association is a man sitting on a harp; an implausible novel association is a harp playing a man.) Bizarre images generally take more time to form than do plausible images, and extra time and effort spent thinking of an image may help you remember it better.

However, it is not necessary that an image be bizarre in order to benefit from these factors (interaction, vividness, uniqueness, extra time). You can use all of these factors in images that are not bizarre. One popular memory-training book illustrated the advantages of ridiculous, impossible, or illogical associations by the following examples for associating airplane and tree: A logical picture would be an airplane parked near a tree. Since that is possible, the book said, it probably will not work; better pictures would be airplanes growing on trees, or trees boarding an airplane.[27] It is true that the latter examples would be more memorable than a plane parked near a tree. However, it is also true that more plausible pictures involving interaction, vividness, and uniqueness would also be more memorable; for example, a low-flying airplane shearing the tops off the trees, or an airplane crashing into a tree.

One reason why bizarreness may be ineffective for some people is that some people have a hard time making up bizarre images. Similarly, elderly adults tend to not want to use bizarre imagery, and natural interacting imagery works just as well for them.[28] If you find it difficult to make up bizarre images or you feel uncomfortable doing so, then I recommend that you concentrate on making the images interacting and vivid—do not worry about making them bizarre. On the other hand, if you do not have any trouble imagining bizarre associations and you feel comfortable with them, then I recommend that you go ahead and use them.

MORE ON EFFECTIVE MNEMONICS

In addition to making effective visual associations, there are some other considerations that can help you use mnemonics effectively. How can you use visual associations on abstract verbal material? Is it more effective to use your own images and associations or to use ones provided by someone more experienced? How do the guidelines apply to using effective verbal associations? The answers to these questions suggest further guidelines for using mnemonics effectively.

How Can You Use Images for Abstract Material?

In chapter 3 we saw that concrete words are easier to visualize than abstract words. It is not hard to picture concrete words like *apple, car, book,* and *horse,* but it is harder to picture more abstract words like *nourishment, liberty, justice,* and *happiness.* Since most mnemonic systems use visual imagery, how can the systems be used to remember abstract material?

The procedure for using imagery to help remember abstract terms is the same as for concrete terms except that you add a step using "substitute words." You substitute a concrete word to represent the abstract word. One way of doing this is to use objects that typify the abstract term: for *liberty,* you might picture the Liberty Bell; for *justice,* a judge; for *happiness,* a smiling face; for *education,* a schoolhouse; for *fashion,* a model; for *depth,* a hole; for *agree,* a nodding head; for *salary,* a paycheck. A second way of substituting a concrete word for an abstract one is to use objects whose names sound like the abstract term: celery for *salary;* fried ham for *freedom;* happy nest for *happiness.* You can even use this technique to remember nonsense syllables: Cage for KAJ; rocks for ROX; seal for ZYL; sack for XAC.

The techniques of substitute words is frequently recommended in memory-training books, and we will see in chapter 13 that it plays an important role in remembering names and faces. We saw that the substitute-word technique is part of the Keyword mnemonic described earlier in this chapter. Research on the Keyword mnemonic has found that people are quite adept at using the above two approaches to "concretize" abstract materials for effective visual images. However, one study found that for college students who had no experience with substitute words, the first approach (based on meaning) was more effective than the second approach (based on sound-alikes) but was also more difficult to use.[29]

Do substitute words really help in learning abstract material? Pictures of concrete substitute objects have been found to help in learning abstract paired associates. For example, a picture of a hammer hitting a vacuum cleaner helped people to remember the pair, "impact-vacuum," and a picture of a big flower in an open doorway helped people to remember "blooming-portal." By using concrete substitute words, people can use visual imagery to learn abstract words almost as well as concrete words, and to remember verbal material that is more complex than words (for example, sayings like "history repeats itself"). People can even use visual imagery to help in concept learning.[30]

Should You Make up Your Own Mnemonics?

Someone once said that ideas are like children: Your own are very wonderful. Some research evidence supports this saying. People tend to remember information that they generate themselves better than information that is given to them. In addition to memory for words and sentences, this "generation effect" has also been found for such varied items as physical movements, product names in advertisements, and computer commands.[31]

Does the generation effect apply to mnemonics? Is it more effective to make up your own mnemonics (substitute words, images, and associations) or to get them from someone else (expert, teacher, researcher, etc.)? Popular memory treatises since ancient times have suggested that it is better to form your own mnemonics. Several studies have found that associations do tend to be more effective and easier to use if the people think them up themselves than if the associations are provided by the researcher; however, more of this research has been done with verbal associations than with visual associations and a few studies have yielded mixed results.[32]

There are several possible reasons why you are likely to remember your own mnemonics better. You may put more thought and effort into them than into mnemonics that someone else gives you. Your own mnemonics are likely to be the first associations to come to you at recall time. Another possible reason is that because other people suggest mnemonics different from the ones you would think of yourself, they are not as meaningful to you. Sometimes in my memory class after we have done an activity that involves using verbal or visual mnemonics, I will ask some of the students to explain some of their mnemonics to the rest of the class. Many mnemonics that are very meaningful to a particular person, and came easily and naturally to him in a split second, may take several minutes to explain to other people and may sound very cumbersome. You do not have to explain mnemonics that you devise to yourself.

When teaching young children (or anyone else who does not know how to make effective visual associations) how to use visual associations, it would probably be best to help them with the associations at first until they have some practice and experience. Research has found that people such as young children or the mentally retarded, who may not be able to construct good associations on their own, benefit by having associations suggested to them. The problem with very young (preschool) children is not so much that they cannot generate visual images; rather, the problem is that most of them cannot generate *effective* visual images.[33]

But even people who cannot form effective associations on their own can still make effective use of mnemonic pictures provided for them. For example, in a study on learning foreign language vocabulary, when preschoolers were provided with mnemonic pictures, their learning increased as much as 1,000 percent! Most children from eleven years old appear to be able to use self-generated imagery as effectively as adults can, but teacher-supplied pictures still worked better than self-generated images even for gifted students in the fourth, fifth, and sixth grades. In addition, people with severe brain damage were not able to benefit from using their own images, but they still benefited from pictures drawn for them. (People with only slight brain damage benefited from both.)[34]

How Can You Make Effective Verbal Associations?

Much of this chapter has focused on visual mnemonics. However, we have also seen that not all mnemonic techniques involve visual imagery. Examples of nonvisual (verbal) mnemonics were given earlier (verbal associations, rhymes, acronyms, acrostics), and there are nonvisual equivalents of most visual associations (see the previous example of associating the words *cats* and *rats* in the section, "What Are Mnemonics?").[35]

Verbal mnemonics may come more naturally to some people than visual mnemonics. The mnemonics used by college students to remember classroom notes tend to be nonvisual, and surveys of techniques they use in learning word lists did not find visual imagery among the many different techniques used. A survey of college students and housewives in England found that rhymes and acrostics were among the most frequently used memory aids. It has been suggested that elderly adults might benefit more from verbal mnemonics than visual mnemonics, because many of the elderly who have difficulty with memory problems seem to have more difficulty with visual skills than with verbal skills.[36]

Although some studies have not found a significant difference between visual and verbal associations in their effectiveness, visual associations are more often found to be more effective than verbal ones for remembering concrete material, whereas verbal associations may be more effective for abstract material.[37] Are there ways to maximize the effectiveness of verbal associations?

Much of the previous discussion of factors determining the effectiveness of visual associations is also relevant to verbal associations. There is some evidence that vividness can affect memory for verbal material as well as for images. The positive relationship between recall and rated vividness of images has also been found for sentences. In other studies, people learned concrete sentences or paragraphs that described events with either high or low vividness. (The vivid descriptions were emotional, colorful, and forceful, and yielded more graphic imagery.) The vivid sentences and paragraphs were recalled better than the nonvivid ones. Similarly, including vivid adjectives in paragraphs can result in better recall of the paragraphs than using "dull" adjectives. We saw that familiarity can add to the vividness of an image; similarly, sentences that were personalized by including familiar names or places were rated as higher in imagery value and were remembered better.[38]

Some of the research on bizarreness in associations has been done on bizarre sentences as well as pictures, so the conclusions regarding bizarreness can reasonably be taken as applying to verbal associations as well as visual associations. The discussion on constructing your own mnemonics versus having them supplied by others can also be applied to verbal mnemonics.

The use of substitute words to make abstract verbal material more concrete is not as directly relevant to verbal associations as it is to visual associations, but the basic idea of trying to make verbal material more concrete is relevant. One possible way to make abstract verbal material more concrete is suggested by a study on memory for abstract sentences such as, "The regulations annoyed the salesman," or "The set fell off the table." Such sentences were remembered better when concrete modifiers were added to yield sentences such as, "The strict parking regulations annoyed the salesman," and "The ivory chess set fell off the table."[39]

8

The Legitimacy of Mnemonics: Limitations and Pseudo-Limitations

Although the practical use of mnemonics dates back more than 20 centuries, the research interest dates back only about 20 years. During the first half of this century mnemonics were widely taught in popular memory books and commercial courses, used by mnemonists and some laymen, and ignored by most psychologists. Until the 1960s, American psychologists concentrated on outwardly observable behavior in order to be "scientific," and did not consider mental processes to be a very legitimate area for research. In addition, many psychologists associated mnemonics with sensationalism, showmanship, and commercialism. (In 1960 some researchers observed that the attitude of many experimental psychologists was that "mnemonic devices are immoral tricks suitable only for . . . stage magicians.")[1] Thus, until about 20 years ago, many researchers thought that research on mnemonics would not yield useful knowledge about memory, or that such gimmicks were not worthy of serious scientific study.

Incidentally, it is interesting to note that the skepticism of some psychologists regarding the value of mnemonics is not limited to the twentieth century. In 1888 a psychologist quoted the following from a seventeenth-century document referring to teachers of mnemonics: "Many there be that at this day profess the same, though they get more infamy and disrepute than gain thereby; being a sort of rascally fellows that do many times impose upon silly youth, only to draw some small piece of money from them for present subsistence." The psychologist then went on to say, "There is at least this difference between the mnemonic teachers of Agrippa's time and those of the present. The latter generally get, not a small piece of money but a larger piece, and they sometimes impose upon others as well as silly youth."[2]

Research interest in mnemonics began in the mid-1960s, aided by the return of mental processes as a legitimate area of scientific investigation (see chapter 4). Virtually all of the experimental research on mnemonics has been published since then. By the early 1970s, several respected psychologists and reputable researchers had suggested that mnemonics should be taken seriously, and had encouraged research on mnemonics. In 1973 mnemonics research finally earned its own heading—"Mnemonic Learning"—in *Psychological Abstracts,* and since then about 20 references per year have been cited under the heading. By the mid-1980s, there had been enough research on mnemonics to fill a book consisting of 20 chapters, each reviewing an area of mnemonics research. (I have written a more detailed account of the legitimacy and rise to respectability of mnemonics research elsewhere.)[3]

However, there are psychologists, researchers, educators, and others who still doubt the legitimacy of studying and using mnemonics. Some of the reasons for their skepticism are valid limitations of mnemonics and some are not. This chapter discusses both kinds of limitations. (Other psychologists have also analyzed the limitations and problems in mnemonics research and applications.)[4]

SOME LIMITATIONS OF MNEMONICS

You learned in chapter 7 that you can work miracles with your memory using mnemonics. However, you also learned in chapter 1 that there are no memory techniques that are magical, all-powerful answers to all learning and memory tasks. In addition to their power and strengths, mnemonics also have weaknesses and limitations. Some of the limitations of mnemonics are primarily a result of using visual imagery, and thus apply primarily to visual mnemonics; other limitations apply also to verbal mnemonics. The limitations include time constraints, abstract material, learning versus retention, imagery ability, verbatim memory, decoding interference, and transfer and maintenance.

Time

We saw in chapter 2 that visual memory processes may be somewhat slower than verbal processes. It may take a little longer to think up an image of the object that is represented by a word than to think of the word itself. Many studies have shown that you may not have time to form images and associate them if material is presented too fast.[5] Thus, visual associations may not be an effective strategy when material is presented too fast.

What is "too fast"? The Peg system (chapter 11) has been found to be effective at a presentation rate of 4 or 8 seconds per item, but not at 2 seconds per item. Two seconds is apparently not long enough for the unpracticed person to form effective visual associations. In using visual or verbal associations, 5 seconds is typically sufficient study time to produce retention for hours or days; for pictures (versus generated images) 1 or 2 seconds may be sufficient. A difference of only 1 or 2 seconds per item (5 versus 6 seconds in one study, 3 versus 5 seconds in another) has been found to make a significant difference in how well visual associations help in remembering the items. Studies using visual imagery in paired-associate learning typically give people at least 5 seconds per pair; when allowed to set their own rate, people average about 7 seconds per pair. If verbal material is presented to you at the rate of 1 or 2 seconds per item, you will probably not be able to use visual imagery to remember it.[6]

It may be noted that you can improve your speed of making visual associations with practice; the more people practice forming visual associations, the less time it takes for them to do it. The average time of 7 seconds per association is for people who are using visualization for the first time. College students who were given more training than usual were eventually able to use a mnemonic involving visual imagery (Keyword mnemonic) to learn German vocabulary at a 2.5-second rate as well as they had first done with the mnemonic at a 10-second rate. In addition, the time limitation does not matter in many practical learning tasks because you can determine your own rate; the material does not come one item at a time at a set rate. Finally, it should be noted that even though it may take longer to go through some materials once using visual associations than not using them, the overall learning time may be less because you may not have to go back through the material as many times to learn it.[7]

We have seen previously that any kind of coding to transfer material from short-term memory to long-term memory takes time—whether it be visualizing, chunking, associating, organizing, or seeking meaning. Thus, the time limitation is not unique to mnemonic systems using visual imagery (although time is a more serious problem for visual imagery with abstract words than with concrete words, as discussed in the next section). For example, people instructed to make up eight acrostics to help them learn eight lists of six words took longer to learn the lists than did people not using acrostics (although they remembered more words on a later memory test for all eight lists).[8]

Retrieval time is another way in which time may limit the use of mnemonics. It may take longer to decode a mnemonic association than to just think of the information directly. There is some research evidence that visual associations do require longer retrieval than rote remembering, but also that they will reach the same retrieval speed as rote remembering with repeated practice.[9]

In addition to presentation time and retrieval time, mnemonics also often require extra study time to learn the mnemonic itself. For example, a system such as the Peg system (chapter 11) may not be worth the extra time it takes to learn the system if it were to be used only once. However, if it were used many times, the time saved in the subsequent uses may outweigh the extra learning time accompanying the first use (see "Mnemonics Give You More to Remember" later in this chapter). The cost-effectiveness of mnemonics, in terms of time and effort to learn relative to payoff, is still an open research question.[10]

Abstract Material

We saw in chapter 7 that you can use visual imagery to aid memory for abstract terms by using concrete substitute words. However, the use of concrete substitute words for abstract terms has at least three possible limitations:

1. To form an image for abstract words takes somewhat longer than for concrete words because of the extra step of thinking of a concrete word to represent the abstract term.[11]

2. The substitute word is only a cue to remind you of the abstract idea, and there is always the chance that you will remember the word without remembering the idea it represents. It is possible that you might recall the picture of the Liberty Bell or a judge or a smiling face and not be able to recall that they represent liberty or justice or happiness. This may be one reason why it has been found to be more difficult to decode abstract mediators than concrete mediators.[12]

3. It may be very hard to form good concrete words for some abstract terms and ideas (for example, *assertion, theory, analysis, inference*). Even if you can come up with some concrete words for such terms, they may take inordinately long to construct and may not be very good representations of the abstract terms they represent.

Although visual imagery can help you remember abstract material, the above limitations suggest that verbal mediators may be more effective than visual mediators for some abstract material. Verbal mediators are not as dependent on the concreteness of the material for their use. For example, to associate *theory* and *analysis* you could say, "That theory is worthy of analysis," but it would be hard to think of a good image for this association. In addition, research has shown that verbal mediators do not take more time for abstract terms than for concrete terms, as visual mediators do.[13]

Learning Versus Retention

There is some debate among researchers as to whether mnemonics help only learning or also help retention. In chapter 3 we saw that the rate of forgetting depends on how well you learn something more than it does on how fast you learn it; thus, it is possible to learn material faster without necessarily retaining it longer. Some researchers have said that although mnemonic techniques and systems help in learning material faster they do not help in remembering it longer. In fact, it has been claimed that we cannot really improve memory, but that memory systems work by improving learning. On the other hand, there are those who say that mnemonics help a person remember material longer as well as learn it faster. Reviews of the relevant research indicate that although a few studies do show that imagery does not help long-term retention, most studies show that imagery does help retention at least as much as it helps learning.[14]

There are two considerations that we should keep in mind concerning this issue of learning versus retention. First, whether mnemonics help retention depends on how retention is measured, and retention has been measured different ways in different studies. A simple example illustrates the differences. Suppose one group of people learned a list of 20 items using a mnemonic, and a second group learned the list without using a mnemonic. After going through the list once, the first group remembered an average of 18 items, and the second group remembered an average of 12 items. This finding would indicate that the mnemonic helped in learning the list better with one exposure. A week later, the mnemonic group may remember 12 items and the other group, 8 items. Did the mnemonic help retention a week later? Using the *amount remembered* it did: The mnemonic group remembered 4 more items than the other group (12 versus 8). Using the *amount forgotten* it did not: The mnemonic group forgot 2 more items than the other group (6 versus 4). Using the *percentage remembered or forgotten* there was no difference between the two groups: They each forgot one-third of what they had learned (6/18 versus 4/12).

The second consideration to keep in mind is that the issue of learning versus retention may be an important theoretical distinction to the researcher, but it may not make much practical difference to the person doing the learning. Suppose that mnemonics did help learning only, and that one group used a mnemonic system to learn material and another group did not. Each group learned the material until they could recite it perfectly once. Now, if mnemonics helped learning but not retention, then we would expect that the two groups would remember the same amount of material a week later. But the mnemonic group may have taken only 15 minutes to learn the material and the other group may have taken 30 minutes. (In one study with learning-disabled students, the mnemonic group learned twice as many science facts as a direct-instruction group did in the same amount of time.)[15] This means that the mnemonics helped the people to make more efficient use of their study time: They remembered as much as the other group with only half as much study. Now suppose that both groups studied for 30 minutes. This would mean that the mnemonic group could then spend 15 minutes overlearning the material, so that they would have it learned better and thus would retain it longer.

Imagery Ability

At the end of chapter 7 we saw that some adults are not accustomed to thinking in images, so verbal mnemonics may come more naturally than visual mnemonics. Perhaps this is because visualizing is harder work than verbalizing, or perhaps as children acquire language skills they rely more on verbal ability and less on imagery, or perhaps our culture and educational system with its emphasis on facts and its verbal orientation destroys the childhood reliance on imagery. Whatever the reason, there is evidence that young children tend to rely on visual imagery for memory more than older children and adults do.[16]

Even among adults, people differ in their habits of visual or verbal thinking and in their imagery ability. We have seen that elderly people in particular tend not to use visual imagery. Because many adults are not used to picturing things, visualization may seem unnatural to them. Those adults and children who do have the ability to use imagery have been found to benefit more by instructions to make visual associations than those who lack this ability. Thus, mnemonic systems using visual imagery may have limited usefulness for some adults.[17]

However, even though some people may not be in the habit of visual thinking or have the current ability to use imagery effectively, most people do have the *capacity* to do so and can be trained to use imagery. Use of visual imagery is a learned skill that requires instruction, training, and practice just like other memory skills.[18] Adults, elderly adults, and young children, as well as learning-disabled children, mentally retarded and brain-damaged patients, and other inefficient learners, have all been trained to use visual mnemonics effectively.[19]

People who can visualize well can benefit from the start by the mnemonic systems; those who have difficulty visualizing may require some time to develop the ability, but if they practice they can acquire the skill. Some people do not do too well when they first try to use visual associations to remember because they may not try as hard, or may resort to other methods because they do not trust the procedure; the reason is not that they are incapable of imagery. The few people who cannot use visual imagery at all, and cannot learn to do so, may be able to use mnemonic techniques involving verbal mediation; but the visual imagery part of mnemonic systems may be less powerful for them.

Verbatim Memory

Some memory tasks may require word-for-word memorizing (for example, learning scriptures, poems, scripts, etc.). Mnemonic systems are not especially appropriate for such verbatim memory tasks. When people ask me how to memorize these kinds of materials verbatim, I refer them to the memorizing strategies discussed in chapter 6. We will see in subsequent chapters that mnemonic systems can help in remembering the main points or ideas covered in such materials and in getting these points in the right order, thus providing a framework within which the exact words can then be learned. But the systems do not help much directly in the word-for-word memory part of the task.

Interference

We have seen that mnemonic systems can reduce interference among different sets of material. Now I will suggest that visual images may actually increase interference. There is really no inconsistency, because I am now talking about a different kind of interference.

An image may be easy to remember, but when used to remember verbal material, the image must be decoded back into the appropriate verbal response. The interference problem arises in recalling a concrete noun that has synonyms that could be represented by the same picture; thus, one picture could represent more than one word. For example, the picture of a small *child* could also represent the words *infant* or *baby;* the picture of a *dog* could also represent *canine* or *wolf;* and the picture of a *car* could also represent *automobile* or *vehicle.*

This interference problem is most likely to arise when we are using imagery to learn abstract material. For example, if we use an image of a smiling face to represent the word *happiness,* then later when we recall the smiling face we might think of *smile, face,* or *head.* A number of studies indicate that although high imagery is superior to low imagery, this kind of decoding error is more likely with visual images than with verbal material alone.[20]

Maintenance and Transfer

Do people who are taught how to use mnemonics continue to use them later on their own? Do they transfer their mnemonic skills to tasks other than the one they were trained on? These two questions refer to the problems of maintenance and transfer (or generalization), respectively. Most research on such autonomous use of mnemonics has been done with children, and has not been entirely encouraging. Even though children who are very young or mentally retarded can be taught to use mnemonics effectively for a particular task, they often fail to use the mnemonics on their own on subsequent tasks and fail to generalize to other tasks.[21]

Probably the most important factor influencing children's autonomous use of mnemonics is how much training and practice they receive before they are left on their own. In most studies the children are given brief instruction and little or no practice. Their transfer of a mnemonic to new tasks increases when they are given comprehensive instructions on how, when, why, and where to use the mnemonic and additional practice with the mnemonic during instruction. With sufficient training even kindergarten prereaders have been able to transfer a visual imagery mnemonic to other similar tasks.[22]

Children's use of mnemonics on later tasks can be increased by prompting, or being reminded to use the mnemonic on a task. The fact that they often fail to think of using the mnemonic on their own indicates that even though they have learned it well enough to use it, they may not have learned it well enough for it to become ingrained in their habitual way of remembering. Older children may not need as much prompting or training as younger children; for example, eighth-grade children taught to use a mnemonic were able to use the technique several weeks later without being prompted.[23]

Some researchers have suggested that children's failure to use mnemonics autonomously may not be a very serious problem. If the goal is to increase the child's learning, then autonomous use is important only if there is nobody or nothing around to prompt the child to use the mnemonic. The effectiveness of the mnemonic is the same whether children use it on their own or only under instruction. When children are learning in most natural settings, there is often someone around who could provide such prompting (for example, parents or teachers).[24]

The problems of maintenance and transfer are not limited to children. I have found that adults may not continue to use mnemonics on their own. For example, many students from my college memory courses have reported a significant decline in use of their skills a few months after completing the course (although their reported use was still higher than it was before taking the course). Also, in one study in which we taught elderly adults to use visual associations and the Peg system (chapter 11) effectively, we found several months later that virtually none of them had used it for anything since the study. This finding is consistent with other research that shows that most elderly adults who have been taught imagery mnemonics do not use them when they are not reminded to do so.[25] In addition to how well they learned the mnemonic skills, level of motivation and opportunity for use probably also play a significant role in whether adults continue to use mnemonics.

It may be noted that this failure to continue to use new skills after training is not limited just to mnemonics. Maintenance and transfer of *any* kind of mental skill (learning strategies, creative thinking, problem solving, etc.) is hard for children, and even for college students and adults. Likewise, a constant problem for any kind of therapy, including memory therapy, is the extent to which improvements observed in the clinic actually generalize to the patient's everyday life.[26] Research on learning strategies has found that autonomous use of other learning and memory skills can be increased in the same two ways as for mnemonics— increased training and practice with strategies, and thorough explanation of how and why they work and when to use them.[27]

SOME PSEUDO-LIMITATIONS OF MNEMONICS

This chapter so far has discussed some of the valid limitations and problems of mnemonics. There are also "pseudo-limitations"—problems and limitations that are not as valid as the ones just discussed, or that are not as serious as some critics would have us believe. For example, a recent book on how to study listed three main limitations of mnemonics: material memorized by rote lacks understanding; mnemonic devices just add to the memory's overall load; material learned through mnemonics is soon forgotten.[28] The first two of these limitations are discussed in the following sections; the third one does not need to be addressed.

One psychologist has observed that "like many things, mnemonic techniques are easy to parody and poke fun at." But, he noted, that makes them no less effective, "and there is nothing like success to reinforce someone in a new method of learning." He also observed that critics rarely make it explicit that the alternatives to mnemonics in memorizing are either "dumb, blind repetition or simply outright failure, and no one seems to want to champion these alternatives."[29] Critics of mnemonics have suggested five limitations that I classify as pseudo-limitations:[30]

1. They are not practical.
2. They do not aid understanding.
3. They give you more to remember.
4. They are crutches.
5. They are tricks.

Mnemonics Are Not Practical

Both the kinds of memory tasks studied in the research laboratory and the kinds of memory demonstrations done by performers can contribute to the impression that visual imagery mnemonics are not practical. In the research laboratory, much research on visual imagery in verbal learning and memory has concentrated on paired-associate and serial learning of unrelated nouns. Although these paradigms are convenient for psychological researchers, many people's practical memory problems do not fit well within either paradigm.

People sometimes come up to me after a lecture and demonstration in which I have performed one or more of the feats described at the beginning of chapter 7, and say that they do not have much use for remembering a long list of unrelated nouns or for memorizing a magazine. After all, they are not planning to go on tour giving memory shows. Many of them act as if they were watching a magic show rather than an exhibition of applied psychology. Similarly, one memory textbook said of mnemonics: "A major difficulty with many of these memory tricks is that they are largely useful for recalling simple lists such as lists of grocery items. This may help in a pinch, but in general they don't help a great deal when it comes to the kinds of memories that play a major part in everyday life."[31]

If, in fact, the memory tasks contained in research studies and in demonstrations were all that mnemonics were good for, people might have a good case for claiming that mnemonics have little practical value in everyday life. After all, how often do you need to memorize a list of pairs of nouns, or a list of unrelated words, or a magazine? I anticipate these objections in my teaching, and emphasize that mnemonic systems are not just for research or for show. I point out to the audience what I pointed out at the beginning of chapter 7—whether or not people *want* to do such feats, the important point is that they *can* do them; and that means they can also do other things with their memories that they *do* want to do, but may have thought were beyond their abilities.

What are some of these "other things" that people can do with their memories? Research has shown effective uses of mnemonic techniques and systems for many areas of schoolwork (see chapter 14) as well as for such other practical memory tasks as learning foreign languages, overcoming absentmindedness, and remembering errands, people's names, numbers (phone numbers, dates, etc.), scriptures, and advertisements. Researchers have suggested that the vocational domain is also a fruitful domain for the application of mnemonics, and that in industrial and military settings there is widespread need to memorize lists and learn operational models. In fact, mnemonics have been developed for areas of military training such as Morse code, signal flags, and orders to sentries. In addition, mnemonics help not only for material in paired-associate or list form, but also have been found to help in learning prose material.[32] Many of these applications, and others, are discussed in other chapters.

The potential applicability of mnemonics beyond the research lab and mnemonists' demonstrations is also suggested by the wide range of people that have been able to use mnemonics effectively (see the section on "Imagery Ability" earlier in this chapter). Many mnemonic techniques and systems have been incorporated into memory rehabilitation therapy for patients with acquired brain damage.[33]

As a final comment on practical uses of mnemonics, it may be noted that what is "practical" depends on individual interests and needs. For example, one person may see no practical need for memorizing lots of people's names, while that ability may be very useful to someone who deals with a lot of people (for example, a teacher or salesperson); one person may see the ability to memorize numbers as impractical, while another who works with measurements, prices, or schedules may find it very useful; one person may not be interested in learning a foreign language, while another one preparing to visit another country may find it very useful; and memorizing a list of items may not be practical to some people, but very useful to a waitress or short-order cook. Even the educational uses of mnemonics may not seem as practical to someone who is not in school. Thus, what is practical to one person may not be practical to another.

Mnemonics Do Not Aid Understanding

Some people (and some psychology textbooks) have dismissed mnemonics with the comment that they are effective for certain kinds of rote memory tasks, but that many learning tasks involve understanding (comprehension) more than straight memory for facts. The implication is that mnemonics are not worth learning because they do not help with understanding.

There are two ways of responding to this criticism. First, the statement that mnemonics cannot help with understanding may not be entirely accurate. One psychologist has recently suggested that even though imagery techniques are not often used to facilitate comprehension, they may have potential value for doing so, and some research supports this suggestion. Research on mental elaboration in instruction indicates that the images learners generate often increase both their understanding and their memory, and that mnemonic pictures and diagrams given to learners can also facilitate both understanding and memory.[34] Visual imagery may be involved in the internal representation of such abstract verbal concepts as clock time, monetary value, and months of the year, and there is evidence that pictures and visual imagery can help in understanding concepts and sentences and prose reading material. Imagery mediation has been used in the development of broad-based programs for teaching cognitive strategies and in the training of generalized cognitive strategies for learning. Mental imagery has even been found to help in problem solving.[35]

But suppose that mnemonics do not help with understanding. In fact, it is probably true that mnemonics are not as useful for comprehension tasks as they are for straight memory tasks. A second way of responding to the criticism then is, So what? Mnemonics are not *intended* for such tasks as reasoning, understanding, and problem solving; they were not developed for that purpose. They are intended to aid learning and memory. Should we discard something if it does not do what it is *not* intended to do as effectively as it does what it *is* intended to do?

In chapter 1, an analogy was drawn between memory tools and carpentry tools. It was pointed out that what a hammer does, it does very powerfully, but it is not intended to do everything. We would not discard it because it does not saw boards or turn screws. Similarly, mnemonics enable people to do amazing feats that cannot be done with the unaided memory; and what they are supposed to do, they do very powerfully. It is not valid to criticize mnemonics because they are not as powerful in doing what they are not supposed to do.

To say that mnemonic systems are not worth using because many learning tasks do not involve straight memory is somewhat like saying that the multiplication tables are not worth learning because many math problems do not involve multiplication, or that Spanish is not worth learning because many people do not speak Spanish. There are also many math problems that do involve multiplication and many people who do speak Spanish. Likewise, it is true that many tasks do *not* involve straight memory, but it is also true that many tasks *do* involve straight memory. Whether we like it or not, most of us have many things to remember—names, phone numbers, things to do, things to buy, addresses, dates, errands, speeches, reports, and schoolwork. Thus, even if mnemonics did help only remembering and not understanding, many people may still have enough to remember to make the use of memory aids worthwhile. (See chapter 14 for a discussion of remembering and understanding in school.)

The experiences of the Russian mnemonist S, described in chapter 3, have been used as an example of how mnemonics not only may not help understanding but may actually interfere with it. S used visual imagery to remember everything: Given a list of numbers that had an inherent pattern, he did not see the pattern; rather, he remembered the list by visualizing the numbers. This finding has led some people to a conclusion such as that made by one psychologist: "Apparently, the mnemonist exhibited little talent for abstract thinking, which is not unexpected considering that mnemonic techniques use concrete methods of organization and hence interfere with organizing information according to abstract principles."[36] The implication is that our use of mnemonics will also interfere with our ability to see and understand abstract patterns and principles.

However, S was *compelled* by his cognitive style to form visual images; he could not help it. Just because we choose to use mnemonics to impose meaning on some material does not mean that we will not be able to learn other material that is meaningful without mnemonics; nor does using mnemonics on unorganized material mean that we must also use them on organized material.

Mnemonics Give You More to Remember

Most mnemonic techniques and systems actually increase the amount of material you must remember. Mnemonic systems require you to memorize material constituting a mental filing system in addition to the information to be remembered. In fact, that is the meaning of the word *elaboration* when psychologists talk of visual and verbal elaboration. For example, to use the Loci system (chapter 10) to memorize a series of

10 items, you must remember 10 locations in addition to the 10 items to be remembered. This fact has led some critics to suggest that the systems are actually more work than it would be just to learn the information by itself (something like determining the number of horses in a herd by counting the number of legs and dividing by four).

It is true that most mnemonic systems do add to the amount of material to be remembered, and as a result they may require extra effort when they are first being learned. But this extra effort may be illusory for three reasons:

1. Once the locations (or other mnemonic elaborations) are learned, they are used over and over to learn new material. One does not memorize a new set of locations for each list to be remembered. Thus, the extra effort of learning the locations occurs only once.

2. No matter how it is done, remembering is work, and memory aids are not necessarily supposed to make it easy, just more effective (as noted in chapter 1). Learning to use mnemonics is a skill that requires practice just like acquiring any other skill. For example, when a person is first learning to use a typewriter, typing may be slower than writing and may seem that it is more trouble that it is worth; but typing is more efficient than writing once the person masters the skill. Or a golfer may find that learning a new grip or a new swing may hinder her game at first, but if she keeps practicing it she will find that her game improves. Similarly, mnemonic systems may seem at first to be more trouble than they are worth, but people who have made the effort to learn them and get used to using them usually report that they are worth the effort. The extra effort of learning a system can be partially offset by the fact that it may now take less time and effort to learn other material than it does without a system. People who used visual mnemonics to remember a list of sayings or a list of errands reported that the task was easier than did people who did not use the mnemonics.[37]

3. Memory capacity is not a function of the amount of material to be learned as much as it is a function of other factors, such as how organized or meaningful the material is. For example, we saw in chapter 2 that the number of chunks is more important than the number of items: You can remember a sentence containing 40 letters better than a series of 10 unrelated letters. We also saw in chapter 7 that a sentence such as "The set fell off the table" is actually easier to remember when concrete details are added ("The ivory chess set fell off the table").

Other studies have also found that adding relevant details to a sentence improves memory for the sentence. For example, sentences such as the following were found to be easier to remember when the parts in parentheses were added: The fat one bought the padlock (to place on the fridge door); The bald one cut out the coupon (for the hair tonic); The funny one admired the ring (that squirted water). In another study people were given facts about famous people: "At a critical point in his life, Mozart made a journey from Munich to Paris." Some facts had relevant details added: "Mozart wanted to leave Munich to avoid a romatic entanglement." The people recalled more facts when given added details than when facts were presented alone.[38]

Thus, the amount of material to be remembered is not the primary concern in assessing memory capacity. Once a person learns the additional material involved in acquiring a mnemonic system, he usually finds that the advantages in terms of organization and meaningfulness outweigh the disadvantage of having additional material to remember.

Mnemonics Are Crutches

Some people criticize mnemonics on the basis that a person may become dependent on a mnemonic and use it as a memory crutch. (In fact, one psychologist referred to a mnemonic as an "artificial memory-crutch.") Then he will not be able to remember the material without the crutch. That is, a person who memorizes a given set of material with a mnemonic will become dependent on that mnemonic to remember that material. For example, how many people can remember the number of days in November without going through the rhyme, "Thirty days has September, April, June, and November. . . ."? The critic says, "What happens if you forget the crutch?"

There are at least three responses to this question:

1. The "crutch" itself is frequently not forgotten as easily as the items would be without the crutch. People may remember some mnemonics long after they have forgotten the material. One psychologist learned a rhyme from a friend for memorizing π to 20 decimal places; later he still remembered the rhyme but had to telephone his friend to remember how to decode it into the appropriate digits. Similarly, some people can remember the sentence they used to memorize the names of the cranial nerves ("On Old Olympus' Towering Tops . . .," chapter 7) long after they have forgotten the names of the nerves. However, remembering the mnemonic is not responsible for their having forgotten the material.

2. Such dependency frequently does not happen. It is possible that it can happen with some material that a person does not learn very thoroughly and/or use very often. However, especially if the material is something that a person will be using regularly, he will eventually find that he no longer needs to recall the original mnemonic association in order to recall the material.[39] The material may come automatically. I can recall material that I learned years ago using mnemonics, but I cannot remember some of the associations I originally used to learn the material.

3. Even if a person did become dependent on a mnemonic to remember certain material, is that bad? Is it undesirable for a person with poor eyesight to become dependent on eyeglasses to help him see better? Even a person with good eyesight may need a telescope to see distant objects clearly. Is that worse than not being able to see the distant objects? Is it worse for a person to depend on mnemonic associations to remember the names of everyone he meets than to forget their names? I used the Phonetic system (chapter 12) to memorize the telephone numbers of more than 100 people in a group to which I belong. I must refer to my mnemonic associations to remember all of the numbers, but is this worse than not remembering the numbers? I do not think so. Even if the crutch criticism of dependency were true, it may be better to remember material using a mnemonic than to not remember the material.

An irony of the crutch criticism is that it actually serves as the basis for two conflicting criticisms. On one hand, the critic says that you cannot remember the material without the crutch (meaning that you are lost if you forget the crutch). On the other hand, the critic says that you become too dependent on the crutch for remembering the material (meaning that you cannot forget the crutch).

Another aspect of the crutch criticism involves a general dependency on mnemonics. It is the argument that a person who gets in the habit of using mnemonics may not be able to learn material without mnemonics. As one psychologist explained it: "Some success with mnemonics may set up a vicious circle: The more we use them, the more we need them, and the more we are inclined, or even forced, to be perfunctory in our attempts to understand new information."[40] Luria's S is often used as an example of how a dependency on mnemonics can lead to a failure to be able to learn without mnemonics (but see the discussion of S in the section on mnemonics and understanding).

Actually, the appropriate use of mnemonics can lead to greater self-confidence in other remembering, rather than making a person a helpless memory cripple. The following comments of two of my memory students are representative of many:

I have found that mnemonic devices have not only helped me in the obvious ways, but have also improved my sensitivity to my normal memory. Now when I go to use the rote system, I find it easier because of the self-confidence that mnemonics gave to me.

I find myself going about my daily activities applying mnemonics to every situation that I possibly can. I find myself in return to be more effective and more organized, and to have a considerable amount of self-confidence that I had not experienced before.

Mnemonics Are Tricks

Isaac Asimov described an experience which illustrates a view of intelligence that is similar to some people's view of memory. When Asimov buys several objects at a store, he watches the clerk write the numbers on a slip of paper (for example, $1.55, $1.45, $2.39, and $2.49) and automatically mutters the total—$7.88. When the clerk finishes his addition and gets $7.88, he looks up in awe and says, "That's amazing. You must be very smart to be able to do a thing like that." Then Asimov explains how to do it. "You don't add $1.45 and $1.55. You take 5 cents from one and add it to the other so you have $1.50 and $1.50 which comes to $3.00 at once. Then instead of adding $2.39 and $2.49 you add a penny to each and add $2.40 and $2.50, which comes to $4.90, remembering that you will have to remove the pennies you added. The $3.00 and the $4.90 are $7.90, and when you take off the two pennies, you have $7.88 and that's your answer. If you practice that sort of thing, you can . . ."

At about this point, Asimov has to stop because he cannot ignore the clerk's cold stare as the clerk says, "Oh, it's just a trick." Asimov observed, "Not only am I no longer intelligent, I am nothing but a faker. To the average person, in other words, understanding the properties of numbers and using those properties is *not* intelligent. Performing mechanical operations *is* intelligent."[41]

In doing memory demonstrations, I have observed some people react like the clerk in Asimov's story. They are impressed by my amazing memory until I explain a little about the mnemonic system used, at which time I no longer have an amazing memory but am just a faker. (Perhaps this is why some memory "experts" do not divulge their secrets.) To some people understanding the principles of memory and applying them via mnemonic techniques is not memorizing. Rote repetition and drill *is* memorizing. I have several memory and psychology textbooks published in the 1980s that refer to mnemonics as "tricks," and some psychologists refer to mnemonics as "artificial memory."

The distinction between "natural" memory and "artificial" memory aids may be an artificial distinction; the distinction between what is natural memory and what is artificial memory is often not clear, and there may be more similarities than there are differences (see "Basic Principles of Mnemonics" in chapter 7).[42] It seems to me that the natural–artificial distinction stems in part from equating "unaided" with "natural"; but unaided rote rehearsal feels no more natural to many people than do their attempts to impose meaning on material.

The view that rote repetition and drill is real remembering and the use of mnemonics is artificial can lead to the claim that the use of mnemonics is unfair. Since a mnemonic is a trick or gimmick, it is not fair to use a mnemonic system because you are not really remembering. The 12-digit number for memorizing the calendar is a good example: You have not really memorized all 365 dates; therefore, you have not really memorized the calendar for a year. This argument seems to be saying that you are cheating if you do not do things the hard way. You are cheating to use an aid. Actually, the "unfairness" to the critics may lie in the fact that you can remember so much more than they can. It is no less fair to use aids to train the memory than it is to use special training techniques to train long-distance runners, keyboard-learning aids to teach piano lessons, or a mathematical formula to find the circumference of a circular field given the diameter. (Is it somehow more "fair" to walk around the field and measure it with a tape measure than to just use the formula $c = \pi d$?)

It was noted at the beginning of the chapter that viewing mnemonics as tricks and gimmicks probably contributed to the hesitancy of many psychologists to accept mnemonics as a legitimate area of investigation. It is probably also one reason people applaud a memory demonstration as if it were a magic show (after all, magicians do tricks) rather than a demonstration of applied psychology. Unfortunately, some commercial memory trainers contribute to, and even encourage, this image. One memory course that uses parts of an automobile as the basis for a Loci system (see chapter 10) is titled "Auto-magic," and another commercial course is titled "Memory Magic."

9

Mental Filing Systems: Link and Story Mnemonics

In chapter 7 mnemonic "techniques" and mnemonic "systems" were distinguished. The examples of mnemonics discussed so far in this book illustrate specific-purpose techniques. For example, the "1492 . . ." verse helps us remember when Columbus discovered America, but it does not help remember other dates. "*I* before *e* . . ." helps us remember how to spell words with *ie* in them, but it does not help spell other words. HOMES helps us remember the names of the Great Lakes, but it does not help remember other names. Of course, other rhymes and acronyms can be constructed to remember other dates, spelling words, and names, but these particular mnemonics lack generality; they can be applied only for one purpose.

Mnemonic systems are more general-purpose methods that can be applied to different kinds of memory tasks; they are not limited to only one set of material, but can be used over and over to learn different material. Chapters 9 through 12 discuss five mnemonic systems—Link, Story, Loci, Peg, and Phonetic. Each of these four chapters has three major sections. The first section describes and explains the mnemonic system. The second section describes some recent research evidence concerning how well the system works, to give you confidence in its effectiveness. The third section suggests some ways you might be able to use the system in practical memory tasks.

All of the principles, characteristics, applications, strengths, and limitations of mnemonics in chapters 7 and 8 apply to mnemonic systems as well as to mnemonic techniques. After you have read chapters 9 through 12, read chapters 7 and 8 again; many of the points regarding mnemonics will be even more meaningful when you are familiar with the mnemonic systems.

YOUR MENTAL FILING SYSTEM

In chapter 1 the efficiency of an organized 3″ × 5″ file box was compared with a larger unorganized box as filing systems in discussing the capacity of memory. Then in chapter 2 the analogy of a mental filing system was used in discussing short-term and long-term memory. Mnemonic systems may be viewed quite literally as mental filing systems. They allow you to store information in your memory in a way that you will be able to find it and get it back out when you want it.

Suppose you were asked to go to your local library and get a certain book. Even though the library may have thousands of books, the task would not be too hard because the books are filed systematically. You would go to the card or computer catalog, look up the call number of the book, and then go to the part of the library where that number was located and get the book (unless your luck is like mine, in which case the book would probably be checked out).

Now suppose all the books in that library were dumped into one big pile in the parking lot or on the street, and you were asked to get a certain book. Your task would be much more difficult. Why? The pile contains the same number of books as the library, but the difference is that you now have no systematic way to locate a particular book. You have to search through all the books to find a particular one.

Similarly, suppose you are given a list of 10 items to remember. Later, when the time comes for recall, you begin looking through your memory for the 10 items. For most people the task is like finding a book in a pile of thousands of books. You know the 10 items were put in your memory somewhere. But you know thousands of words; how can you systematically search through all these words and identify the 10 you are looking for? Unless the items were originally stored in some systematic, orderly manner, you have no good way to systematically search for them. For people who use a mnemonic system to learn the 10 items, the task is more like finding a book in a library. They have stored the items in such a way that they can identify them and cue themselves as to where the items are.

When you are trying to find items in your memory, a mnemonic system can help in at least three ways as a mental filing system:

1. It will give you a place to start your search, a way to locate the first item.
2. It will give you a way of proceeding systematically from one item to the next.
3. It will let you know when your recall is finished, when you have reached the last item.

Even for material that you know very well, you may have a hard time without steps 2 and 3. For example, we saw in chapter 4 that if you try to recite the alphabet in random order you are likely to find that you are lost by the time you are halfway finished. You are not sure which letters you have named or how many you have named—problems that do not occur when you recite the letters in alphabetical order.

WHAT IS THE LINK SYSTEM?

The Link system, which could also be called the "Chain system," consists of two steps. First, form a visual image for each item in the list to be learned. Second, associate the image for each item with the image for the next item. Thus, you form a visual association between the first two items, then between the second and third items, then between the third and fourth items, and so on. You do not try to associate every item with every other item in one big picture; rather, you associate the items two at a time. The reason for the name of this system should be obvious: You are linking the items together to form a chain of associations.

The Link system is the most elementary of the mnemonic systems. In fact, it may really be too simple to be called a "system." I sometimes describe the Link system when I give a short lecture on mnemonics, because, although it is simple, it is adequate to illustrate the principles on which mnemonic systems are based and how powerful they can be for appropriate kinds of material. The Link system is appropriate for serial learning tasks, where you have a series of items to remember: The Link system helps you remember all the items in order.

Much of the discussion on mnemonics in chapters 7 and 8 was illustrated with paired-associate learning, but serial learning is really not very different. Serial learning can be viewed as a series of paired-associate tasks where each item in the list serves first as the response to the previous item and then as the cue for the next item. For example, suppose we have four items identified by the letters *A, B, C,* and *D*. A paired-associate task would consist of two pairs, *A-B* and *C-D*. You would be cued with *A* and *C* and would respond by recalling *B* and *D*. A serial learning task would consist of the series *A-B-C-D*, which could be viewed as consisting of three pairs—*A-B, B-C,* and *C-D*. Thus, serial learning is similar to paired-associate learning, so that everything discussed previously on remembering pairs of items is also relevant to the Link and Story systems.

As an example of the Link system, suppose you were given a list that begins with the following five items: paper, tire, doctor, rose, ball. To use the Link system in remembering these five items, you first form a visual association relating *paper* and *tire*. You might picture a car driving on paper tires, or using a tire to erase writing from a paper. Next associate *tire* and *doctor*. You might picture a tire running over a doctor, or a tire performing an operation. To associate *doctor* and *rose*, you might picture a doctor operating on a rose, or a doctor giving roses to a patient. To associate *rose* and *ball*, you might picture two people playing catch with a rose, or balls growing on a rose bush. Of course, it may be just as easy for some people to remember only five items without using a system; however, the procedure is the same whether you have 5 items or 50 items.

The visual associations I have suggested for these five items are some possibilities that come to my mind; they may not be the most memorable ones for you. We have seen that both visual and verbal mediators tend to be more effective if you think them up yourself than if they are given to you by someone else. Some of the associations I suggested above are bizarre and some are plausible. If you like bizarreness, you can use bizarre images; if not, you can use plausible ones as long as they are vivid and interacting. Generally, you should use the first association that comes to your mind, because it will likely also be the first one to come to your mind when you want to recall the items. Whatever your association is, use the guides and principles discussed in chapter 7 to form good images and effective visual associations.

Whenever I read a list of items to an audience so that they can try using the Link system, or any other mnemonic system, I emphasize two additional points. I first tell them, "Make sure you actually *see* each of your associations, even if it is only a brief second. If it helps at first to cut out distractions, close your eyes." Then I tell them, "After I have given you several items you are going to start worrying about forgetting the first few items, and you will want to go back and review them. Don't go back and review, or you will miss the new associations. Just concentrate on making a good association for each item as it comes, and trust your memory that you will be able to get the items back when you want them."

To recall a list that you have learned with the Link system, you begin with the first item and proceed in order as each item leads to the next one. For our example, think of paper; see the image that involves paper; and it reminds you of tire; tire leads to doctor; doctor leads to rose; and rose leads to ball.

In the Link system each item is cued by the previous item except for the first one. You need some way to cue yourself to remember the first item. One way to do this is to associate the first item with something that is related to the list and that is easy to remember. For example, you might associate the first word with the source of the list: If a person is giving you the list, associate the first item on the list with that person (that is what I tell my students to do when I read a list to them); if the list comes from a textbook, associate the first item with the book. If the list is a shopping list, associate the first item with the door to the store.

WHAT IS THE STORY SYSTEM?

The Story system is a variant of the Link system in which you weave the items into a connecting story. It is an extension of the use of sentences as mediators in paired-associate tasks; you just continue with additional sentences to form a story based on the items you want to remember. For example, you might use something like the following for the previous five-item list: The *paper*boy rolled a *tire* down the sidewalk, and it hit the *doctor* coming to make a house call (now that's a bizarre idea!); it knocked him into a *rose*bush, where he picked up a *ball* and threw it at the boy. The procedure for recalling items learned with the Story system is essentially the same as with the Link system. Begin with the first item and proceed through the story, picking the key words out as you come to them.

Although the Story system is very similar to the Link system, there are at least four differences:[1]

1. In the Link system you link each pair of items independently of the previous links; in the Story system you link the items in a continuous, integrated sequence. This logical sequence may be an advantage of the Story system over the Link system for some people who find it easier to recall a story than a series of unrelated associations.
2. The Story system may require a little more time to make each association than the Link system does, because you must think of an association that fits the narrative of the story rather than using the first association that comes to your mind.
3. The longer the list, the harder it is to work each succeeding item into an integrated story. Most people find it hard to put together a story to remember a list of 20 items. However, it is not much harder to use the Link system on a list of 20 items than on a list of 10 items.

4. Items learned by the Link system can be recalled in backward order almost as well as forward, but items woven into a story may be harder and take longer to recall backward.

The Story system can be used effectively in verbal form without accompanying visual imagery, but it is probably more powerful if you actually picture the events happening as you think of them. In fact, the Link system also can be used with verbal mediators by a person who cannot use visual imagery. (Verbal associations may also be effectively used in the mnemonic systems discussed in subsequent chapters).[2] If you use verbal mediators for the Link or Story systems, then you may be able to apply them more directly to abstract material without having to use concrete substitute words.

HOW WELL DO THE LINK AND STORY SYSTEMS WORK?

Several research studies up to the mid-1970s found that the Link and Story systems can be effective in learning and remembering word lists. People using the Link system typically remembered 2 to 3 times as many words from a 20-word list as did people who were not taught the system. Similarly, people using the Story system to learn a dozen or more lists of 10 words remembered 2 to 7 times as many words as did people not using the system. The research also found that the Story system could be used effectively on abstract words (although not quite as effectively as on concrete words), and even that sentences strung together as stories were remembered better than when they were presented as unrelated sentences.[3]

Recent research has supported some of the older findings and produced a few new insights into the Link and Story systems. Some of the recent findings on the Link system include:[4]

1. The same list of 20 words was learned and recalled in a new order every few minutes for 5 times with surprisingly few errors, as compared with people learning five different lists.
2. Instructing people in the Link system reduced the range of differences among people but did not eliminate the differences. (Recall of people using the Link system ranged from 55 to 97 percent versus 29 to 95 percent for those not using the Link system.)
3. The Link was effective for 12 words in immediate recall but not one week later.
4. The Link system was more effective than just imagery or rehearsal in a free recall task, but its effectiveness was even greater when the order of recall of the words was considered.

5. People who were given some practice using the Link system (which they are usually not given in research studies) were able to improve their performance to where they could soon remember lists of 30 to 40 words.

Most of these recent studies, like the earlier ones, used word lists. One of the mnemonists (T. E.) described in chapter 3 who had an exceptional memory for stories used the Link system and substitute words. In a study to see if the Link system could be used to remember errands, or things to do, college students were given a list of 22 errands to remember (get a haircut, get gas in the car, etc.). They heard the list once with a 10-second pause after each errand. The students who had been taught the Link system remembered significantly more errands than those not taught the system. Students from the second group who used their own visual imagery mnemonic also recalled significantly more errands than did the other students (about the same as the students who were taught the Link system).[5]

Several studies on the Story system have also found it to be effective for elementary school children and college students, for immediate and delayed memory, and for free recall, serial recall, and recognition. Experimenter-provided stories were found to be effective for remembering five lists of six words each. However, although studies have found that the Story system helps in learning several short lists (up to 16 words), the findings for learning a longer list (up to 30 words) have been mixed; some research found that self-generated stories were effective for a long list, but one study did not.[6]

The Link and Story systems have also been found to be effective in a nonwestern culture and for special populations. The Link system was used effectively by college students in India. A story helped chronic organic amnesiac patients remember word lists; they improved as much as the normal comparison group, although their recall was lower. Other research compared acronyms and the Story, Link, and Loci systems (chapter 10) for word lists with normal people and with brain-damaged patients. The Link and Story systems were both found to be more effective than no method, and the Story system was the most effective mnemonic for both groups for recall 24 hours later.[7]

Demonstrations

In addition to the research studies, demonstrations by my audiences and memory students show the effectiveness of the Link and Story systems. I frequently use the Link system to help people demonstrate to themselves the power of visual association, because I can explain the system to them in about 5 minutes and let them try it. I read to them a list of 20 words to remember, and have them write as many as they can recall in order. Then I teach them the Link system. Finally, I read to them a second list of 20 words to remember using the Link system, and have them recall as many as they can in order. Very few people recall all 20 words from the first list (those who do generally use some kind of mnemonic technique). However, after learning the Link system, about half the audience generally recalls all 20 words from the second list. Many of them are astounded at their own performance.

In my memory course I give my students several memory tests during the first couple of class periods, and then give them the same tests later in the course. One of the tests is the same one I described for my lecture audiences—to remember a list of 20 words after hearing them once at a rate of one word every 10 seconds. The following summarizes the performance of about 100 students in several recent classes: Before learning the Link and Story systems, 18 percent of the students recalled all 20 words. (Most of the 18 percent used the Link or Story system or a similar mnemonic that they had learned before the class.) Several weeks later, using the systems, the percentage of students recalling all 20 words increased threefold to 54 percent. At the other end of the performance scale, the percentage of students recalling fewer than 14 words was 40 percent before learning the systems and 15 percent after learning the systems.

These results from my memory classes are more striking than those found in some research studies because of several procedural differences. For example, I give my students about 10 seconds per word; this presentation rate is slower than that used in most research studies. Also, the same people learn both lists of words (one list before learning the systems and one using the systems), rather than comparing some people who used the system with others who did not use it, as is done in most research studies.

Thus, there is considerable evidence that the Link and Story systems really can make a difference in memory. It is important to note also that people in the research studies and some of the demonstrations were using the systems for the first time. With practice, you could expect to become even more effective in using the systems. (This consideration also applies to the research on the Loci, Peg, and Phonetic systems discussed in the next three chapters.)

HOW CAN YOU USE THE LINK AND STORY SYSTEMS?

After hearing these systems described to this point some people wonder about their use, because most people do not need to memorize a list of 20 unrelated words. Of course, if this were the only application, then the systems would probably not be worth the effort of learning them (except perhaps to amaze your friends). What are some practical situations in which the systems could be used?

Lists

The Link and Story systems can be used in almost any situations where you want to remember lists of things. This may seem to be rather restrictive, but actually there are many kinds of everyday memory tasks that involve serial learning, or even free recall where the order of the items is not important (the systems just order the items to help recall them). One category would include shopping lists and lists of things to do. The use for shopping lists is fairly straightforward—just link the items on the list. One woman who attended one of my lectures reported later that since she had started using the Link system, she hardly ever wrote down her shopping lists anymore. Not only did the Link system enable her to remember the items but she had more fun doing it that way.

The use of the Link or Story system for lists of things to do may not be quite as straightforward as for shopping lists, but the procedure is the same. Suppose that you need to do the following tasks tomorrow: Call the newspaper office about your subscription, get the flat tire on your car fixed, go to the doctor's office, have some roses sent to a friend, and pick up the tickets for the upcoming ball game. To help you remember these items, you might pick a key word to represent each of these tasks: *paper, tire, doctor, rose, and ball.* (Do these words look familiar?) Then link the words together or weave them into a story, as described at the beginning of this chapter.

The systems can also be used for learning material that consists of separate, ordered parts, such as the amendments to the Constitution, the Ten Commandments, or the names of the presidents. The procedure for such a task is to pick a key word representing each item and then link the words together or form a story with them. For example, to remember the Ten Commandments you might link the following: One god, graven image, swearing, Sabbath, parents, kill, adultery, steal, lie, covet. You could use concrete substitute words and their pictures to represent the terms that are abstract; thus, you might picture a church meeting to represent *Sabbath* and a person whose face is green with envy and who has dollar signs in his eyes to represent *covet*.

The procedure for remembering a series of people's names would be similar, and can be illustrated by the experience of a woman who attended one of my lectures. She reported that she had used the Link system to learn the 12 apostles named in the New Testament for a Sunday School lesson she was giving. She made up a substitute word to represent each of the names (mat for Matthew, beater for Peter, etc.) and linked them together. Then she surprised her class (and herself) by being able to name all 12 men in order. Other students of mine have done the same thing with the names of the books in the Old and New Testaments.

Remember that items to be remembered by the Link or Story systems do not necessarily have to have a natural order to them. A wife may think of things that she wants her husband to do when he comes home, link the first task to him, and link each succeeding task in the order they come to her mind (take out the garbage, mow the lawn, replace the hall light bulb, etc.). Similarly, she may use the same procedure to remember things that happened during the day to tell him (a letter came from his folks, their son got an "A" on his homework, the dog had puppies, etc.).

The Story system using substitute words has been used to remember the names of the cranial nerves (an alternative to the acrostic we learned in chapter 7—"On Old Olympus'. . ."):

At the *oil factory* (olfactory nerve) the *optician* (optic) looked for the *occupant* (oculomotor) of the *truck* (trochlear). He was searching because *three gems* (trigeminal) had been *abducted* (abducens) by a man who was hiding his *face* (facial) and *ears* (auditory). A *glossy photograph* (glossopharyngeal) had been taken of him, but it was too *vague* (vagus) to use. He appeared to be *spineless* (spinal accessory) and *hypocritical* (hypoglossal).[8]

A similar example of a use of the Story system is the following story used to remember the names of the 13 original states in the order they entered the Union:

A lady from *Delaware* bought a ticket on the *Pennsylvania* railroad. She packed a *new jersey* sweater in her suitcase, and went to visit her friend *Georgia* in *Connecticut*. The next morning she and her friend attended *mass* in a church on *Mary's land*. Then they took the *South car line* home, and dined on a *new ham*, which had been roasted by *Virginia* (the cook from *New York*). After dinner they took the *North car line* and *rode to the island*.[9]

A student in one of my memory classes, who was a second-grade teacher, tried this story with her students and was so impressed with how fast they learned the states that she called the principal in to see what the children had accomplished in such a short time. Two weeks later, with some intermittent review, 26 of the 33 children could still recall at least 12 of the 13 states.

A kind of Story method can even be used to learn equations, such as the equation for changing Fahrenheit (F) temperature to Centigrade (C): $F = 9/5C + 32$. The sentence is "Friday (F) is the same (=) 9 to 5 (9/5) drag in College (C); but I've only got 32 minutes (32) to go!"[10]

Speeches or Reports

Another possible use of the Link or Story system is for remembering speeches. (Bishop Fulton J. Sheen said that the reason he spoke without notes was because an old Irish lady watching a bishop read his sermon remarked, "If he can't remember it, how does he expect us to?")[11] Suppose you want to make the following points in a speech to your local PTA group: A traffic light should be installed at the intersection by the school; a fence should be constructed along the side of the playground by the street; funds need to be raised to buy more musical instruments for the school; classrooms are too crowded; some changes should be made in the route of the school bus; and the media section of the library needs expanding.

The first step in using the Link or Story system to remember your points is to pick a concrete key word to represent each point: traffic light, fence, musical instruments, crowded classroom, bus, audiovisual supplies. (You may want to be more specific and use trombones for musical instruments and videotapes for audiovisual supplies.) Once you pick your key words, you just link them in the order you want to talk about them.

Mark Twain reportedly tried several systems for remembering his speeches. Finally, he hit on the idea of creating visual images. He would actually draw the pictures representing his ideas. Here is an example.

First a haystack with a wiggly line under it to represent a rattlesnake—to remind him to begin talking about ranch life in the West. Then there were slanting lines with what must be an umbrella under them and the Roman numeral II. That referred to a great wind that would strike Carson City every afternoon at 2 o'clock.

Next came a couple of jagged lines, lightning, obviously telling him it was time to move on to the subject of weather in San Francisco, where the point was that there wasn't any lightning, or thunder either, he noted.

From that day, Twain spoke without notes, and the system never failed him. He drew a picture of each section of his speech, all strung out in a row, then he'd look at them and destroy them. When he spoke, there was the row of images fresh and sharp in his mind. He'd make notes based on the remarks of a previous speaker—just insert another picture in the set of images. [12]

Twain's system was so good, he said, that 25 years after he had given a speech he could remember the whole thing by a single act of recall. Of course, you will be able to recognize Twain's system as an application of the Link and Story systems.

The same system for learning your speech could be applied also to remembering speeches other people give, or to remembering lectures in school. You can link the points together in order as the speaker covers them. Of course, this requires skill at forming associations rapidly, and also requires that you concentrate on the speech to be able to select the key points. With practice, you may even be able to apply the same procedure to remembering what you read. [13]

Other Uses

Experiences reported by several students in my memory class suggest that the Link and Story systems can be used profitably in school. One student used the Link system to help him complete a self-paced physics course. The course employed a 24-chapter textbook, a 6-unit study guide, a series of films on the major units, and optional filmed lectures. The student linked the information under each unit to acquire a chain of information relating to each unit, and then associated each chain to the appropriate film. Thus, he could use the films to cue himself as to which chain of information he needed, and the chain to get the information. Using this filing system, he completed the one-semester course in two weeks—and obtained A's on all four exams! He wrote, "The class was a first of its kind for me, so I was a little leery of how I would perform," and he reported (rather surprised) that "the results were quite amazing."

Another student reported that one test containing five fill-in-the-blank questions from four chapters of reading had her thinking that she had to spend at least 4 hours just acquainting herself with the material. She reported that, "When time was eaten away to 1 hour I had to make a last-ditch effort and felt that the only help I had was mnemonics. Using the Link system, after 1 hour of study I was able to answer five of five questions correctly, with less recall time than usual."

One student described how she used the Link system to prepare for an essay test on a text chapter on Roosevelt's New Deal programs. After learning the Acts and Administrations he created, she grouped them into three categories of about a half-dozen each and used the Link system to remember the lists. She reported that there were 10 essay questions, and using these lists, "I was able to recall the whole chapter and could effectively answer each question. Results of the test? A!" Another student used the Link and story systems to remember 20 FCC rules and regulations regarding radio stations. She took about 45 minutes to make up substitute words and link them, and remembered all the rules three days later with no review in between.

The Link system can help in learning foreign languages. Jacques Romano, who died in 1962 at the age of 98, was noted for his remarkable memory. He was especially noted for his ability to speak many foreign languages. Romano found that he needed only about 125 basic words to communicate in a new language. He could acquire this basic vocabulary in about two weeks by learning 10 words a day. (This time could probably be shortened by using the Keyword mnemonic described in chapter 7.) He then built interlocking chains of new words by linking them to the 125 basic words and increased his vocabulary until he became fluent in the language.[14]

Some learning tasks may involve both serial learning and paired-associate learning, and thus could combine the Link system and the Keyword mnemonic. For example, being able to give the capital city of each state when someone tells you the state name, or the vice-president when someone tells you each president's name, is a paired-associate task. But how about being able to recall each state name *and* its capital? You could use the Link system to link the state names together, and the Keyword mnemonic to associate the capital to each state.

Of course, these examples of possible uses of the Link and Story systems do not exhaust all the possibilities. They are given to show that mnemonic systems really do have practical value, and to suggest ideas that may stir up your imagination for applications that might better fill your own needs. In addition, popular memory-training books contain numerous examples of how to put the mnemonic systems to practical use; some of the examples in this chapter, as well as in following chapters, are adapted from these books.[15]

10

Mental Filing Systems:
Loci Mnemonic

One limitation of the Link and Story systems discussed in the previous chapter stems from the fact that each item is associated with the previous item so that forgetting one item affects memory for subsequent items. The Loci system does not have that limitation. In the Loci system you build up a mental file of previously memorized images with which you can associate new information to be learned. These images exist independently of the information to be learned. Thus, the Loci system fits the analogy of a mental filing system better than does the Link system.

WHAT IS THE LOCI SYSTEM?

The Loci system is the most ancient mnemonic system, dating back to about 500 B.C. It was *the* mnemonic system until about the middle of the seventeenth century, when other systems, such as the Peg and Phonetic systems (discussed in the next two chapters), began to evolve. The history of the Loci system has been traced in detail from 500 B.C. through the seventeenth century.[1] This chapter notes just a few interesting facts about the origin and ancient uses of the Loci system.

Origin

The origin of the Loci system is generally attributed to the following story told by Cicero. A poet named Simonides was speaking at a banquet when a message was brought to him that someone was outside waiting to see him. While Simonides was outside, the roof of the banquet hall collapsed, crushing the occupants beyond recognition. Simonides was able to identify the bodies by remembering the places at which the guests had been sitting. This experience suggested to Simonides a system for memorizing. Noting that it was his memory of the places where the guests were sitting that had enabled him to identify them, he inferred that a person could improve memory by associating mental images of the items to be remembered with mental images of locations for the items. This observation reportedly gave rise to the Loci system.

The word *loci* (pronounced LŌ si) is the plural of *locus*, which means "place or location"; this is also the meaning of the Greek *topo*. Thus, the Loci system, which has also been called the "Topical" system, is the system that uses places or locations. The Loci system was used by Greek and Roman orators to remember long speeches without notes. Orators visualized objects that represented the topics to be covered in their speeches, and then mentally placed the objects in different locations—usually parts of a building. They then moved through this building mentally while delivering the speech, retrieving the object images from the locations as they came to them. This use of places to remember speeches may be the origin of the expression, "in the first place," and of the reference to "topics" in speeches.

How to Use It

The Loci system consists basically of two steps. First, memorize (overlearn) a series of mental images of familiar locations in some natural or logical order. This series of locations is your mental filing system, which you can use over again for different lists of items. This is an important feature, because the system would hardly be worth the effort if you had to memorize a new set of locations every time you wanted to memorize a new list of items; you would have twice as much to learn each time. Second, associate a visual image of each item to be remembered with a location in the series; do this by visually placing the items, in the order they are to be remembered, in the locations as you take an imaginary walk past the locations. Locations have the advantages of being concrete (thus easy to visualize) and of being learned in a natural serial order.

Let us consider an example. Picture in your mind each of the following locations in a house with which you are very familiar. The first location is the front walk that leads up to the house. The second location is the front porch. The third location is the front door. The fourth location is the coat closet where you hang your coat after entering the house (or the corner where you throw it). The fifth location is the next logical place to go—the refrigerator. Picture yourself taking a walk up the front walk, onto the porch, through the door, to the closet, and then to the refrigerator. Make sure you see each of these locations in your mind as clearly as possible while taking your mental walk.

Now suppose you want to use these locations to remember the same five items we discussed in chapter 9: paper, tire, doctor, rose, and ball. (As I noted in chapter 9, it may not be worth the effort to learn a system for only 5 items, but the procedure is the same for 50 items.) You might proceed as follows: Associate *paper* with your front walk; you might see it made of paper (which you can hear crinkling under your feet as you walk on it), or see your newspaper coming down the walk to meet you. Associate *tire* with porch; you might see tires rolling off your porch, or see your porch made of tires. Associate *doctor* with door; you might see a doctor hanging on the doorknob, or stuck in the doorway. Associate *rose* with front closet; you might see the closet completely empty except for a rose bush growing from the shelf, or see a large red rose hanging from a coat hanger. Finally, associate *ball* with refrigerator; you might see your refrigerator in the shape of a giant ball, or hundreds of balls rolling out of the refrigerator when you open the door.

Now take a mental walk through these five locations and try retrieving the five items. You will probably find this task to be rather easy. The Loci system enables you to change a free-recall task in three ways to help recall:

1. The task is changed to an aided-recall task because you can use the locations as aids to cue yourself.
2. The task incorporates paired-associate learning, with the location serving as the first word in each pair and the item serving as the second word.
3. The task incorporates serial learning because the locations are organized in a natural serial order.

It is not difficult to construct several extensive mental files of locations. In the house you could continue to the living room, to the bedroom, and then on to each room in your house; then you could go downstairs, out into the yard, etc. You could increase the number of loci in your series by visualizing two or three distinctive locations in each room (for example, the refrigerator, table, and sink in the kitchen; the couch, window, and television in the living room; and the bed, dresser, and clothes closet in the bedroom). Other buildings could also be used, such as a familiar school building, office building, or store. Nor are you limited to buildings. You could take a walk through your neighborhood, or downtown, and construct a file of mental locations. A familiar golf course has at least 36 ready-made locations (18 tees and 18 greens). You could also use different parts of your own body, or of your automobile, for loci.

Other Features

The characteristics of the Loci system have been analyzed in some detail to explain *how* and *why* it works. (Research on *how well* it works is discussed later.) In addition to some of the characteristics we have seen so far, five more features are worth noting:[2]

1. The Loci system is similar in underlying structure and operations to most mnemonic techniques. For example, it is based on the same principles, and shares essentially the same steps, as other mnemonics like the Keyword mnemonic in chapter 7 and the name-face mnemonic techniques in chapter 13.

2. In ancient times it was recommended that the locations be widely spaced. However, it appears to be more important for the loci to be *distinct* than it is for them to be *distant,* at least with respect to how fast items can be retrieved. College students learned a list of 12 concrete words using 12 campus buildings as loci. They were then told different locations, one at a time, and were timed on how long it took to find a location that was either one, two, or three positions away from the named location. The search time was not related to the actual physical distances between the loci, but *was* related to the number of loci covered. It took twice as long to find a location two positions away as a location one position away and three times as long for a location three positions away. This finding indicates that people do not skip over loci to get directly to the desired one, but process the intervening loci one at a time, step by step (the same way you go through your chain of associations using the Link system).

3. The time it takes to retrieve an item of information when given the location is about the same for abstract items as for concrete items, but the time to retrieve a location when given the item is slightly longer for abstract items than for concrete items (in practice, of course, you will be more concerned with retrieving items when given the locations).

4. It is important to form a good, strong association between each item and its corresponding location (remember the same emphasis when associating pairs of items in the Link system). If people learn a series of locations but are not told how and when to use them, they show no memory improvement whatsoever. The locations are effective retrieval cues only if you consciously associate them with the list items when the items are presented. (Similarly, in remembering paired-associate items, imagining a context for each pair has been found to help remember them only if they are pictured as interacting with the context.)[3]

5. It is not necessary that only one item be associated with each location. You could associate more than one item with each location if you picture a grand scene showing interactions among all the items and the location. The important point is that the several items must be *simultaneously* in mind. Thus, for example, you could learn a list of 40 items using only 10 loci by associating 4 items with each location. However, you may lose the order of the items that are associated with each location. (A way to overcome this limitation is discussed later in the chapter.)

I noted at the beginning of this chapter that a disadvantage of the Link system is that forgetting one item affects memory for the following items; when a person does not recall a word, it is common that the next word in the sequence is also missing.[4] The Loci system has an advantage over the Link system in this respect: Forgetting one item does not affect recall of subsequent items in the Loci system, because the items to be remembered are associated with an independent series of locations rather than with each other.

Like the Link system, the Loci system enables you to remember all the items and to remember them in order. Of course, both systems can also be used to remember items where the order is not important. One limitation of both the Link and Loci systems is that they do not enable you to directly retrieve an item at a particular position on the list. For example, to find the twelfth item in the Link system you must proceed through your links until you reach the twelfth item. Likewise, as we saw earlier in this section, a mental walk through a series of loci is also a step-by-step process in which the loci are identified one at a time. Thus, for the Loci system you must walk through your mental locations until you reach the twelfth location, and then retrieve the item from that location. (Of course, the same limitation applies to any serially ordered information, even information that we have learned very thoroughly. For example, can you name the twelfth letter of the alphabet without having to count through the letters? Most people cannot retrieve a letter directly in this manner.) An ancient technique to help remember the order of the locations will also help alleviate this limitation of the Loci system: Give some distinguishing mark to, say, every fifth location. For example, you might always picture a hand (with five fingers) in the fifth location and a 10-dollar bill in the tenth location. Then, when you want to recall the twelfth item, you can find the tenth location quickly and have to count only two more locations from there.

HOW WELL DOES THE LOCI SYSTEM WORK?

In chapter 3 some of the amazing memory feats performed by S, the Russian newspaper reporter, were described. The following passage describes one of the methods S used to perform such feats:

When S read through a long series of words, each word would elicit a graphic image. And since the series was fairly long, he had to find some way of distributing these images in a mental row or sequence. Most often (and this habit persisted throughout his life), he would "distribute" them along some roadway or street he visualized in his mind. . . . Frequently he would take a mental walk along that street . . . and slowly make his way down, "distributing" his images at houses, gates, and in store windows. . . . This technique of converting a series of words into a series of graphic images explains why S could so readily reproduce a series from start to finish or in reverse order; how he could rapidly name the word that preceded or followed one I'd selected from the series. To do this he would simply begin his walk, either from the beginning or end of the street, find the image of the object I had named and "take a look at" whatever happened to be situated on either side of it. [5]

Does that procedure sound familiar? Of course, it is essentially the Loci system. The Loci system is based on the assumption that memory for imagined locations will aid memory for items associated with those locations. Three lines of research relevant to this assumption have been conducted:

1. Research has found that people can remember the locations of things they have seen or heard at least as easily as they can remember the things themselves.
2. Research indicates that memory for locations helps memory for material and events associated with the locations. For example, remembering where we have seen a person helps us recall the person's name. Even children can use physical locations to aid memory.
3. Several studies on the Loci system itself have found that it can significantly improve memory for lists of items.

Considerable research up to the mid-1970s along all three lines above has been summarized elsewhere.[6] Let us look at some recent research in each of these three areas.

Memory for Locations

Have you ever had the experience of not being able to remember specific information but being able to remember where you saw it? You might remember that it was on the left page, in the upper right corner of the page. You may even remember what part of the book it was in (for example, toward the end of the book). A similar experience may occur when we see a person we have met before; we may be able to remember where we met her without remembering her name. Sometimes when I see former students of mine on campus, I can place which classroom they were in and even where they sat in class before I can recall their names. These experiences illustrate what is meant by memory for locations.

There have been several recent research studies on memory for locations and on using locations to aid memory. Such research is relevant to the Loci system because the basis of the Loci system lies in associating events with distinctive imagined locations. Also, good memory for location of pictures on the pages of a book was found to be positively related to the ability to use the Loci system effectively.[7]

Research has indicated that locations of objects and of printed material on a page are remembered automatically. That is, when you are studying the details of an object you see or the content of material you read, its location seems to be recorded without conscious effort. Thus, for example, when people are trying to remember what a speaker said or something they read, they can remember where the speaker was or where the reading material was on the page even though they did not try consciously to record that location during the original learning.[8]

Research on memory for locations has found some differences between elderly and young adults. For example, both elderly and young adults remembered the positions of pictures on a page better than the corresponding words, but the young adults did better on both kinds of remembering. Another study also found that elderly people had less accurate recall of location than younger adults; the young adults remembered urban landmarks and their locations better than the elderly did. When they were trying to remember the landmarks, young adults seemed to use a mental walk more to recall buildings, suggesting it may be more natural for them. This may be a possible weakness in using the Loci system as opposed to the Link system for the elderly, although it has been suggested that they might use the Link system to help them remember the routes in their mental loci.[9]

Using Locations to Aid Memory

We have noted the story of how Simonides used the locations of people to recall the people themselves. Similarly, locations may provide us with a systematic way of searching memory for people. For example, when trying to recall the names of my colleagues it helps me to take a mental walk past their offices and picture each person as I come to his office. I have used a similar approach to recall the names of all the students in a particular class; I proceed mentally down each row, picturing and naming the occupant of each seat. These are examples of using locations to aid memory.

We saw in chapter 5 that recall can be affected by whether it occurs in the same context as the original learning; the section on "thinking around it" in chapter 3 is also relevant to this section. This finding that physical location can help recall also applies to memory for verbal material on a page. One study found a positive correlation between how well people remembered key words from prose and how well they remembered where the words were on the page. In addition, cuing the people with a word helped them remember its page location, and cuing them with the page location helped them remember the word.[10]

Placing words on a pattern on different parts of a page helps you learn the words better than if they are just listed in a vertical column, because you can use the locations on the pattern as cues to retrieve the words. One study found that lists of words (including abstract terms from a psychology textbook) that were placed on different visual patterns were recalled better than words placed on the same pattern. Many learning and note-taking strategies (webbing, networking, mapping, flow-charts, diagrams, etc.) have been developed to make use of this visual organization or patterning of words and notes on the page. Such spatially arranged note-taking has been found to work better than regular note-taking for students as young as fourth graders.[11]

A survey of students at the University of London found that about half of them had often used such a place-on-a-page method.[12] One of my memory students reported that in her Spanish class she wrote regular verbs on the left side of the page and irregular verbs on the right. When taking the test, she was able to remember whether a verb was regular or irregular by thinking of which side of the page it was on. I used the same approach to help my son learn a fifth-grade spelling list containing several words ending in *-able* or *-ible* (for example, *indomitable* and *reversible*); we wrote the *-able* words on the left side of the page and the *-ible* words on the right side.

Research using maps also shows the power of location for helping memory. People learned the names of fictitious provinces and capitals better when the names were arranged on a map than when they were just listed. Other information arranged on maps is also recalled better. People heard a passage describing events on an imaginary island. As they listened, some studied a map of the island with features located on it; some studied a map outline with the features listed next to it; and some studied an outline without any feature information. People who saw the map recalled more information from the passage as well as more feature-related information. In another study, people who created their own maplike representation while learning a passage remembered more than those who did not. Such findings show that a knowledge in visual form of locations can help us remember a related message.[13]

Effectiveness of the Loci System

The research discussed so far shows that we can remember the locations of things we see and hear, and that we can use these locations to help us remember the things themselves. Can these two factors be combined to make the Loci system effective? The research on location and memory is interesting and useful in itself, but it provides only indirect support for the Loci system. The Loci system involves using imagined locations rather than locations that are physically present, and imagining the to-be-remembered items in those locations where the items may never have been in reality. Recent studies on the Loci system itself provide more direct support for it.

Several studies have found the Loci system to be effective for remembering word lists under various conditions, including memory for abstract nouns as well as concrete nouns. One study found that recall performance with well-learned loci is equivalent to having the loci physically present. In fact, recall was actually hindered if the loci were visible during learning but not during recall, which suggests that memorized loci have an advantage over visible loci that might not be there during recall. The use of the Loci system is not limited to word lists or lists of separate items. Freshmen in a college "Study Skills" course were taught to use the Loci system to remember the main ideas in a prose passage. They recalled 50 percent more ideas from a 2,200-word passage than did students who were taught traditional study skills.[14]

Most research studies on the Loci system—like those on most other mnemonics—do not give the participants much training, and also measure their performance on their first attempt to use the system. In one study people who were provided with more instruction and more practice than usual performed substantially better than people who were merely given the usual instruction.[15]

Research has also demonstrated that the Loci system can be used effectively by special populations, such as the elderly (including using the system to remember a grocery list while purchasing groceries), blind adults (both elderly and young), and brain-damaged patients.[16]

HOW CAN YOU USE THE LOCI SYSTEM?

All of the uses of the Link system discussed in chapter 9 are also possible uses of the Loci system—remembering shopping lists, lists of things to do, naturally ordered material like the Ten Commandments, lists of names, speeches, and so on. The only difference is that you associate each item with a location rather than with the previous item. In addition to all of the above uses, there are some further uses for the Loci system.

A Mental Filing System

The Loci system can be used literally as a mental filing system. For example, do you ever think of an idea at a time when it is inconvenient to write it down? Maybe you think of something you need to do tomorrow, or of an idea for a speech you are preparing, just as you are falling asleep at night; but you do not want to get up and turn on the light to hunt for paper and pencil to write the idea down. Or an idea might come to you when you are in a movie theater where it is too dark to write, or while you are driving down the street (your passengers might get a little nervous if you let go of the steering wheel to write), or in the middle of doing dishes or mowing the lawn, or in any other situation in which you cannot immediately write an idea down when it comes to you. The next morning, or after the movie, or at the next stoplight, or when the dishes or lawn are done, you have lost the idea. You might remember that you had an idea, but you cannot remember what it was. One solution to this problem is to associate the idea to one of your locations as soon as the idea comes to you. You can retrieve it later and write it down for more permanent storage if you wish.

Suppose, for example, that you use a series of loci around your house. You recall as you are drifting off to sleep that you must give your children lunch money for school tomorrow morning. You might picture nickels, dimes, and quarters rolling down your front sidewalk. When you wake up in the morning and remember that there was something you needed to remember, you can search your loci for it. Or suppose that while you are sitting in a dark movie theatre you remember that you need to put a letter out for the mailman when you get home. You might picture letters cluttering up your front sidewalk. When you get home and think, "Now what was it I needed to do before I go to bed?" you can search your loci and recall the task.

If you write things down in a notebook or put things in a file cabinet for more permanent storage, you must still remember to look at your notebook or file cabinet occasionally if they are going to do you any good. Likewise, using the Loci system as a filing system in which you can record items for future reference requires that you remember to search the loci. Often this is not a problem; you can remember that you wanted to remember something—you just cannot remember what it is. However, if you cannot even remember that you wanted to remember something, or if you use the Loci system regularly, then you may want to get into the habit of having a set time (or times) each day to search your loci. For example, if you take a few minutes to review your loci before breakfast, during lunch, and/or just before going to bed, then you will not need to make a special effort to remember to search your loci.

Using the Same Loci Over and Over

It was noted that the same loci can be used more than once for new lists. This presents a potential problem in practical uses of the Loci system: Learning several lists attached to the same loci might lead to unwanted interference. For example, suppose you have a series of 20 loci and you want to learn three different lists of 20 items each. If all the items are associated with the same set of loci, you might have interference as to which items are on which list.

Such interference is the basis of one of the most frequent questions people ask when I am teaching the Loci system: "If I use the same loci over to learn new material, won't there be some confusion between the new and old material?" I answer: "Yes, of course . . . but there won't be nearly as much interference as you would get if you tried to memorize several different sets of material *without* any system." I also point out that this problem is not as serious in situations where you only want to remember a list for a short time or where there is enough time (for example, a day or two) between learning the two lists to allow some forgetting of the first list, because when you put the new list in the locations it will weaken the old list.

In addition, there are two ways to reduce such interference. First, you can construct multiple sets of locations so you do not have to use the same set many times in close succession. A student could select a set of loci in one part of campus to use in memorizing material for one class and loci in a different part of campus for material for another class. People could similarly have one set of loci around the house, another around the office, and another on a familiar neighborhood street. This way, if you have three lists to learn close together, you could use your home loci for the first list, your office loci for the second list, and your neighborhood loci for the third list. You might even use each set of loci for specific kinds of memory storage; for example, your home loci could be used to remember things that concern your home and family, your office loci to remember things connected with work, and your school loci to remember things connected with school. If you use the Loci system every day, it might be worth your time to construct seven sets of loci so that you can use a different set every day.

A second way to reduce interference among several lists learned with the same loci is "progressive elaboration"—adding each subsequent word at a particular location to a progressive picture. Reimagine each earlier item in its location when you associate the new item by elaborating a grand scene of interacting objects. For example, if your front porch were the second location in your set of loci, and the second word in each of three lists were *swing, hat,* and *fish,* then the scenes might be: list one—a swing hanging from your porch; list two—a hat swinging on the swing on your porch; list three—a fish wearing a hat while swinging on your porch. Several research studies have found that such progressive elaboration does help reduce interference among different lists.[17]

Which of these two methods of reducing interlist interference— multiple sets of loci and progressive elaboration—is preferable? The answer depends on the person who is using them, but I recommend that the person who may make frequent use of the Loci system learn several different sets of loci and use the multiple-sets method. The benefits of having several sets of loci are probably worth the effort it takes to learn them.

Other Uses

You may recognize that the method of progressive elaboration is sort of a combination of the Loci system and the Story or Link system. The loci are used to start each story or link, and a story or link serves to retrieve the items in order at each location. Notice that the item order would be lost if the items at each location were just pictured in a single photo-graphic image rather than ordered sequentially using the Link or Story system.

There is another way in which the Loci system can be combined with the Link or Story system. A set of 10 loci could be used to remember 100 items. Place the first item in the first location; then use the Link or Story system to associate the next nine items in order; then place the eleventh item in the second location and link the next nine items onto it; and so on, until you place the ninety-first item in the tenth location and link items 92 to 100 onto it. In recall, you then use your loci to cue you for the first item in each group of 10, and your inter-item associations (links) to recall the next 9. You can thus recall 100 items with no single chain of associations longer than 10 items.

The students in my memory course have tried this combining of the Link and Loci systems to remember a list of 40 words. The words were read to the students once, with a 5- to 10-second pause after each word. Students used 10 loci with four words linked at each one. The following are the results for a little more than 100 students: About one-third of the students (34 percent) got a perfect recall score of 40, and about one-half of the students (52 percent) recalled at least 39 of the 40 words; at the other end of the performance scale, only 2 percent of the students recalled fewer than 26 words.

The experience of one person who used 40 loci to memorize a 40-digit number may suggest additional ways in which you could use the Loci sysem (although a more efficient way to learn numbers is described in chapter 12). He associated something representing each number with each location. For example, to associate the digit "1" with the location "ice cream store," he used, "I am rather a fat little boy so I can have only 1 ice cream cone"; to associate "6" with "fire station," he used, "They tell me there is a 6-alarm fire. It must be very unusually exciting, for I had never heard of as many as 6 alarms for a fire before"; to associate "2" with "the market," he used, "I have been sent to the market to get 2 bags of potatoes."[18]

I often give my memory students a homework assignment to apply the mnemonic systems to something they want to learn. The variety of possible uses of the Loci system is illustrated by the following examples of a few of the things students have learned with the system in response to this assignment: errands, 11 wedding preparation items, 11 old-car models and years, 10 company names in a stock portfolio, the Bill of Rights, 8 major Jewish holidays, 30 psychoactive drugs, 16 main components of cerebrospinal fluid, and the countries of Westen Europe.

As with the Link system, these uses of the Loci system do not exhaust all the possibilities. They are intended to suggest the different kinds of possible applications of the system. You might adapt some of these suggestions to your own needs, or even be stimulated to think up some additional uses for the Loci system.

11

Mental Filing Systems: Peg Mnemonic

As was noted in chapter 10, direct retrieval of an item at a certain position in a memorized list (for example, the twelfth item) is difficult for both the Link and Loci systems. They are both dependent on sequential retrieval. The Loci system associates items to be learned with prememorized information. To use the same approach in such a way that you can retrieve an item directly, you might associate items to other information that you already have memorized and know very well: the number sequence. If you could associate the first item with number 1, the second item with number 2, and so on, then for recall you could just recall what item was associated with each number. If you wanted to retrieve the twelfth item directly, you would just think of number 12 and see what item was associated with it. The main problem with this strategy is that numbers are abstract and thus are hard to associate with items. But the strategy would be feasible if a way could be found to make the numbers concrete, or to substitute something concrete for the numbers. This is what the Peg system does.

WHAT IS THE PEG SYSTEM?

The Peg system is a mental filing system consisting of a series of prememorized concrete nouns. The concrete nouns are not arbitrarily selected; rather, they are selected in such a way as to correspond meaningfully with numbers.

Origin

The Peg system can be traced to the mid-1600s, when Henry Herdson developed an extension of the Loci system. Herdson dispensed with the spatial locations of the objects and merely used the objects themselves. Each digit was represented by any one of several objects that resemble the numbers (for example, 1 = candle, 3 = trident, 8 = spectacles, 0 = orange).

A system that used rhyming syllables and words to represent the numbers was introduced in England around 1879 by John Sambrook.[1] The nouns rhyme with the numbers they represent so that it is easy to remember what noun represents each number. The following is a widely used version of the Peg system based on rhymes, indicating the word that represents each number:

one-bun	six-sticks
two-shoe	seven-heaven
three-tree	eight-gate
four-door	nine-wine
five-hive	ten-hen

How to Use It

Most people can learn these rhyming pegwords with little effort. In fact, many people already know half of them from the nursery rhyme, "One–two buckle my shoe, three–four shut the door . . ." Each of the pegword objects should be pictured as vividly as possible. The bun should be a specific kind of bun, such as a breakfast bun, a dinner roll, or a hamburger bun. The shoe could be a man's dress shoe, a woman's high-heeled shoe, a gym shoe, or a boot. The tree could be a pine tree in the forest, a Christmas tree, or a palm tree.

The Peg system gets its name from the fact that the pegwords serve as mental pegs or hooks on which the person "hangs" the items to be remembered. To use the Peg system to learn new material, you associate the new material with each of the pegwords in order. For example, the first five pegwords could be used to learn the list we have used in the last two chaters—paper, tire, doctor, rose, ball—as follows: Associate *paper* with *bun;* see yourself eating a bun made of paper, or reading the evening news-bun. Associate *tire* with *shoe;* see yourself wearing tires on your feet, or see a car that has four shoes in the place of tires. Associate *doctor* with *tree;* see a doctor operating on a tree, or a doctor climbing a tree. Associate *rose* with *door;* see a rose in the place of the doorknob, or a rosebush growing from the middle of the door. Associate *ball* with *hive;* see a round beehive in the shape of a ball, or balls rather than bees flying out of the hive. Of course, all the considerations involving effective visual associations that were discussed in chapter 7 are relevant in making these associations.

To recall the items in order, you recall the pegwords and retrieve the items associated with them. Recall of items out of order proceeds in the same manner. For example, what was the fourth item? Think of "door" and retrieve the item associated with it. What was the third item? Retrieve the item associated with "tree."

Other Pegs

The rhyming Peg system that was just described is one that is commonly used and the one on which most research has been done; however, there are actually a number of Peg systems. They all have in common the characteristic of using a concrete object to represent each number, but there are various ways to choose the object that represents each number. The system discussed to this point uses pegwords that rhyme with the numbers. Other rhymes have also been used: one-gun, two-glue, three-bee, four-core, five-knives, six-picks, seven-oven, eight-plate, nine-line, ten-pen. Pegwords that represent objects that look like the numbers can also be selected: 1 = pencil, 2 = swan (the curve of the neck resembling the digit 2), 8 = hourglass, 10 = knife and plate. Pegwords can be selected on the basis of meaning also; one-me (there is only one me), three-pitchfork (three prongs), five-hand (five fingers), nine-baseball (nine players on a team). Peg systems often do not include a pegword for 0 (zero), but on the basis of rhyme you could use "Nero," on the basis of look-alikes you could use "donut," and on the basis of meaning you could use an empty "box."

One limitation of the Peg system is that it is difficult to find good pegwords to represent numbers beyond 10. It is hard to find words, for example, that rhyme with (or look like) the numbers 24 or 37. However, it is possible to find rhyming words for the numbers from 11 to 20. Most of them are verbs representing an action that can be visualized. The following are some examples: eleven-leaven, or a football eleven; twelve-shelve, or elf; thirteen-thirsting, or hurting; fourteen-fording, or courting; fifteen-fitting, or lifting; sixteen-Sistine, or licking; seventeen-leavening, or deafening; eighteen-aiding, or waiting; nineteen-knighting, or pining; twenty-plenty, or penny.

Another possible approach to generate pegwords for the numbers from 11 to 20 is to use rhyming pegwords for 1 to 10, and then to use pegwords based on look-alikes or meaning to represent the second digit of each number from 11 to 20 (for example, 11 = pencil, 12 = swan, 13 = pitchfork, etc.). Also, some people have tried using the rhyming pegword for each digit of a two-digit number (for example, 11 = bun-bun, 12 = bun-shoe, 13 = bun-tree), but this approach can cause some interference due to many similar visual images.

Alphabet Pegs

It was suggested at the beginning of this chapter that numbers would make a good series of pegs if they were not so abstract because they are naturally ordered and you know them very well. There is another possible source of pegs that also consists of information that is naturally ordered and that you know very well—the alphabet. The alphabet provides a ready-made series of 26 prememorized pegs. However, the letters have somewhat the same problem that numbers have: They are not very concrete and meaningful. If we could make them concrete, then we could use the alphabet as a Peg system. One way to do this is to associate a concrete word with each letter in such a way that the words are easy to learn.

Each of the following alphabet pegwords either rhymes with the letter of the alphabet it represents or has the letter as the initial sound of the word. The few words that are not concrete objects can be visualized by using substitute objects (for example, effort—a person working; age—an old person).

A-hay	N-hen
B-bee	O-hoe
C-sea	P-pea
D-deed	Q-cue
E-eve	R-oar
F-effort	S-ass
G-jeep	T-tea
H-age	U-ewe
I-eye	V-veal
J-jay	W-double you
K-key	X-ax
L-el	Y-wire
M-hem	Z-zebra

A second alphabet Peg system could be compiled from concrete words that begin with each letter of the alphabet but do not rhyme:

A-ape	N-nut
B-boy	O-owl
C-cat	P-pig
D-dog	Q-quilt
E-egg	R-rock
F-fig	S-sock
G-goat	T-toy
H-hat	U-umbrella
I-ice	V-vane
J-jack	W-wig
K-kite	X-X ray
L-log	Y-yak
M-man	Z-zoo

Alphabet pegwords can be used in exactly the same way as number pegwords. The only difference is that if you do not know the numerical positions of the letters (which most people do not), the alphabet pegwords are not amenable to direct retrieval of an item at a given numbered position. The alphabet pegwords could also be used in other ways. For example, if you want to learn the alphabet backward, you could link the words from *zebra* to *hay* or *zoo* to *ape*.

Peg and Loci Compared

There are a number of similarities between the Peg system and the Loci system, and performance of the two systems has been found to be equivalent.[2] The following are four similarities:

1. In both the Peg system and the Loci system items to be learned are associated with previously memorized concrete items. These previously memorized items make up the mental filing system to which new items are attached. The pegwords are used in exactly the same way as the locations are used in the Loci system. As with the locations in the Loci system, the pegwords can be used over again to learn new items. Recall is also similar for both systems; you proceed through your locations or pegwords and retrieve the items associated with them.

2. In the Peg system the mental filing system consists of a series of concrete objects rather than of locations, but locations are merely objects that are spatially ordered. For example, the five loci used in the example in the previous chapter are a sidewalk, a porch, a door, a closet, and a refrigerator.

3. As with the Loci system, the Peg system changes a free-recall task to aided recall via a paired-associate task, with the pegwords serving as the first word in each pair. Thus, the Peg system and the Loci system

are essentially the same as paired-associate learning, except that the learner generates his own cue words rather than having them given to him by someone else.

4. The Peg system and the Loci system have several advantages over free recall. First, you have a definite and consistent learning strategy; you know exactly what to do with each item as you study it (that is, associate it with a location or pegword). Second, you have definite pigeonholes (pegwords or locations) into which the items can be filed. Third, you have a systematic retrieval plan telling you where to begin recall, how to proceed systematically from one item to the next, and how to monitor the adequacy of recall. (You can tell how many items you have forgotten, and which ones.) Thus, both systems overcome one of the major problems in free recall—how to remind yourself of all the things you are supposed to recall.

Although the Peg and Loci systems are similar, they have at least three significant differences. First, as has been noted, the Peg system has the advantage of permitting direct retrieval. If you want to know what the eighth item is without going through the first seven, you merely think of "gate" and see what is associated with it. Second, the Loci system has the advantage of allowing a large number of mental images to make up the mental filing system: There is really no limit to the number of locations you can use, but it is difficult to find a large number of pegwords that rhyme with or look like the numbers greater than 10 and especially greater than 20. A third possible difference is suggested by comments of some of my memory students: The Loci system may be a little easier to learn and use. Some of my students who have used both systems report that the Loci system seems a little more natural (at least at first) because it uses knowledge that they already have, rather than requiring them to learn a new set of arbitrary associations between pegwords and numbers, and then make up images for the pegwords.

HOW WELL DOES THE PEG SYSTEM WORK?

Some psychologists described an interesting experience in teaching the Peg system to a skeptical friend. They told him the pegwords and told him how to use them. Then, despite his protestations that it would never work because he was too tired, they gave him a list of 10 words to learn.

The words were read one at a time, and after reading the word, we waited until he announced that he had the association. It took about five seconds on the average to form the connection. After the seventh word he said that he was sure the first six were already forgotten. But we persevered.

After one trial through the list we waited a minute or two so that he could collect himself and ask any questions that came to mind. Then we said, "What is number eight?"

He stared blankly, and then a smile crossed his face, "I'll be dammed," he said, "It's a lamp."

"And what number is a cigarette?"

He laughed outright now, and then gave the correct answer.

"And there is no strain," he said, "absolutely no sweat."

They then proceeded to demonstrate, to his amazement, that he could in fact name every word correctly.[3]

Research Evidence

It was noted in the previous section that the Peg system is similar to paired-associate learning, except that the learners provide their own pegwords rather than having them given to them by someone else. This means that the research that shows the effectiveness of visual imagery in paired-associate learning also suggests the effectiveness of the Peg system. As we learned in chapter 4, there are numerous studies showing that visual imagery aids learning and memory in paired-associate learning.

Several research studies were done on the Peg system from the mid-1960s to the 1970s. The findings from those studies, which mostly used word lists, include the following: College students typically recall about 7 of 10 words without the Peg system, and 9 or more with the Peg system; people have been able to use the Peg system effectively on lists of up to 40 words; the Peg system is effective at a presentation rate of 4 to 5 seconds per word or at a slower rate, but not at a rate as fast as 2 seconds per word; people can effectively learn up to six consecutive lists of 10 words with the same pegwords; alphabet pegwords as well as numerical pegwords are effective; concrete words are learned better than abstract words, but abstract words can also be learned using substitute words; results are mixed on how well abstract pegwords work, so it is probably best to use concrete pegwords.[4]

Since the mid-1970s, several additional studies have supported the earlier research in showing the Peg system to be effective in learning lists of words under various conditions. However, in one study people used the pegwords to memorize either random nouns or nouns from a categorized list. The pegwords worked better with the random nouns than with the categorized nouns because the categories seemed to interfere with the use of the pegwords. This finding suggests that you may not want to use the Peg system when there is some meaningful way to group the items to use organization.[5]

The above studies were done on college students. A recent study had junior high school students, half of whom were learning disabled, learn the Peg system and then use it to learn four 10-word lists. The students who used the Peg system recalled more than twice as many words as the students who were not taught the Peg system, immediately after learning as well as one week and even five months later.[6]

All of the research described so far shows that the Peg system can be effective in remembering word lists, but what about remembering more complex material such as concepts or ideas? One study found that the Peg system not only can help remembrance better but can even help in forming concepts in a task requiring high memory demands. Also, in several studies people used the Peg system to remember ideas in the form of sayings. Some of the sayings were concrete (for example, "Don't rock the boat") and others were abstract (for example, "History repeats itself"). College students using the Peg system remembered more sayings from lists of 10 to 15 sayings than did students not using the system. They also reported that it took less effort to remember the sayings than students not using the pegwords reported. Children in the fourth grade and middle-aged and elderly adults also remembered more sayings using the Peg system.[7]

In addition to these research studies on memory for sayings, I have also tested the students in my memory classes with the sayings. I have them try to remember a list of 10 numbered sayings in correct numerical order at the beginning of the semester, and again later using the Peg system. The following are the results for nearly 200 students in several classes: The percentage of students with perfect recall of all 10 sayings doubled when the Peg system was used (from 20 percent to 40 percent); the percentage recalling at least 9 of 10 sayings increased even more dramatically—from 28 percent to 62 percent. At the other end of the performance scale, the percentage of students recalling five or fewer sayings decreased from 22 percent to 2 percent.

I have also taught the Peg system as part of a short memory course for elderly adults. One class consisted of 28 students between the ages of sixty-two and seventy-nine. Before learning the Peg system, they recalled an average of 5.2 of 10 sayings; their average increased to 7.9 when they used the Peg system. The percentage of students recalling at least 9 of 10 sayings increased from 11 percent without using the Peg system to 50 percent when using the system. The students in their seventies performed just as well as the students in their sixties. Most students also rated the Peg system as the most interesting and worthwhile part of the course.[8]

Schoolwork

We have seen that the Peg system can be used effectively on word lists and even on more complex material. Can it help in learning the kinds of material students must learn in school? A recent book on study skills gave a negative answer to this question. It stated that the Peg system "has two important limitations with regard to schoolwork. First, it can be used with only one list of items for only one exam at a time. Second, no permanent knowledge is gained, for items so memorized are quickly forgotten."[9] Let us look at a few recent research studies that have investigated the effectiveness of pegwords in the classroom.

The Peg system was used to teach the hardness levels of minerals to learning-disabled high school students and to junior high school students. They first learned a substitute word for each mineral, and then saw an interacting picture associating the substitute word with the appropriate pegword (for example, pyrite is hardness level six so the picture showed a *pie* being supported by *sticks*). Students also learned the colors and uses of the minerals. They also learned the reasons for extinction of prehistoric reptiles in order of plausibility. For all these tasks, the Peg system was more effective than traditional instruction.[10]

Eighth-grade students used the Peg and Loci systems to learn the names of the U.S. presidents. They used the pegwords for the numbers from 1 to 10. Seasonal loci represented decades of numbers; 1–10 was a spring garden scene, 11–20 a summer beach scene, 21–30 a fall football scene, and 31–40 a winter snow scene. Presidents' names were represented by substitute words, and the associations were presented in pictures. Two sample associations are: Tyler (tie)–10 (hen)–garden, and Garfield (guard)–20 (hen)–beach. The students also learned biographical information on the presidents. This combined Keyword-Loci-Peg system has been expanded for extreme cases to learn up to 260 items, using alphabet scenes from an *airplane* scene to a *zoo* scene (10 pegwords × 26 alphabet loci = 260 items of ordered information).[11]

Sixth-grade students who were trained over several days in the use of the Peg system used it to learn a list of names and recipe ingredients. In another study, learning-disabled students in the sixth to eighth grades used the Keyword mnemonic (substitute words) and the Peg system to learn information on dinosaurs. In both studies, students who used the Peg system remembered the information better than those who did not use it.[12]

Other studies show that the Peg system can also be used to remember how to do something. College students and high school students were taught 10 steps to prepare a daisy wheel printer for operation. (For example, step 1—open clamps on side of printer; step 2—put end of paper over the sprockets; step 6—set dip switch to "feed"; and step 10—push self-test switch.) For both age groups, students who used the Peg system spent less time learning the steps, remembered more steps in order, and followed more steps correctly in actually preparing the printer (whether the steps were presented orally or in writing).[13]

We have seen that the Peg system can be used by special populations, such as young children, learning-disabled children, and elderly adults. In addition, the Peg system has been profitably used by an amnesiac patient to help remember things to do after getting up in the morning, and has been incorporated in a training program for rehabilitating memories of people with brain damage.[14]

HOW CAN YOU USE THE PEG SYSTEM?

The Peg system can be used for any of the uses suggested for the Link and Loci systems, including learning lists, naturally ordered material, names, and speeches, or as a mental filing system for temporary storage when it is inconvenient to write something down, or as a mental filing system for more permanent storage on a regular day-to-day basis.

Remembering Ideas

The Peg system can also be used for tasks for which direct access is desirable. For example, I used the Peg system to teach the Ten Commandments to my two daughters (who had just turned five and seven years old) so that they could recall them out of order as well as in order. The first step was to teach them the Peg system. Both girls were able to recall all the pegwords after two times through the list. The second step was to teach them how to use the pegwords. I gave them a list of 10 items to memorize and coached them in forming visual associations between the pegwords and the items. Both girls recalled all 10 items after the list was presented, and recalled 9 of the 10 items the following day. They were given additional practice with a second list of 10 items, and again recalled all 10 items on immediate recall. When tested the next day, they each needed prodding—"What is the pegword?" and "What is (pegword) doing?"—on two items.

The final step was to use the pegwords to learn the Ten Commandments. A concrete item representing each commandment was associated using visual imagery with the corresponding pegword. For example, an image of the girls' parents holding a beehive (five-hive) represented the

Fifth Commandment ("Honor thy father and thy mother") and a thief stealing a gate (eight-gate) represented the Eighth Commandment ("Thou shalt not steal".) Both girls learned all 10 of the commandments in order and out of order, and were even able to recall them in a surprise test two months later. Not only was the system effective but it was fun for the girls, and they were anxious to apply it to learning new things. [15]

A few years later I tried the same experiment with my son when he was still four years old, and recently I tried it with my youngest daughter when she was still three years old (about a month before her fourth birthday). Of course, it took a little more practice, but the four- and three-year-olds were also able to use the Peg system for this task. I did not ask the three-year-old to practice using the pegwords on word lists, and also did not require her to learn the exact words of some of the Ten Commandments, but only the ideas. (For example, instead of "Thou shalt not bear false witness" she learned, "Don't lie.")

Nine months later I quizzed my four-year-old daughter on her memory of the pegwords. There had been no review, or even mention, of either the pegwords or the Ten Commandments during that time. I started by asking her if she could remember that a long time ago she learned some rhyming words that sound like the numbers from 1 to 10. Her first response was, "Huh? I don't know what you're talking about." Then, after a few seconds, "Oh, yeah, now I remember—six-sticks." I said, "That's right! Now I want you to say as many of the rhyming words as you can remember. Say each number first, then the rhyming word that goes with it."

She recalled 7 of the 10 pegwords correctly, drawing a blank for numbers 3 and 9, and recalling "den" (rather than "hen") for 10. I then made the questions multiple-choice for those three numbers, telling her four words that rhymed with each number. She correctly recognized the pegwords for 3 and 9, but still chose "den" for 10.

About a week later I tested her memory for the Ten Commandments. She was not able to remember any of them without prompting, but remembered four of them when I described the associations we had used. After one review she was able to recall all 10 of the commandments without prompting, and did it again three days later with no further review.

The significance of this discussion on the Ten Commandments does not lie in knowing the commandments as much as it does in showing how the Peg system can be used to learn ideas, most of which are rather abstract. A student in my memory class related an experience which shows that the Peg system can help with this kind of task even when the user does not believe it will work. After teaching his wife the Ten

Commandments using the procedure described above, the student reported, "She was amazed that they could be learned so easily. Previous to this experiment she had told me that she couldn't do it. She also had mentioned that it seemed like more work [having to memorize pegwords], but she doesn't feel that way now."

Remembering Numbers

A use of the Peg system that goes beyond the Loci system is for learning numbers. (The Phonetic system in the next chapter is even more efficient for learning numbers). You can remember a long number by linking the pegwords together. For example, the 10-digit number 1639420574 could be remembered by using the Link system to remember bun-sticks-tree-wine, and so on. Your capacity for a string of numbers can be extended far beyond the short-term memory span of about seven digits, which was discussed in chapter 2 (as long as the digits are presented slowly enough for you to make associations).

The Peg system could be used to remember the 12-digit number representing a calendar year (see chapter 7); the number for 1988 (376-315-374-264) could be remembered by linking tree-heaven-sticks-tree, and so on. This method has a disadvantage of requiring sequential retrieval (to remember the digit for September, for example, you must remember that September is the ninth month, and then run through the number until you reach the ninth digit). A more efficient method would be to make up a substitute word for each month, based either on rhyme or meaning (for example, January = jam, February = valentine, April = ape, September = scepter). Then associate the pegword for each digit with the pegword for the corresponding month as paired associates (jam-tree, valentine-heaven, ape-tree, scepter-door). Now to find the key digit for September you do not have to run through the number sequentially until you reach the ninth digit; you can directly recall September-scepter-door-four.

The Peg system can be used to count things in any kind of a repetitious task in which you may lose count of how many times you have done it. For example, I use the pegwords to count laps around the track when I jog. One track where I run is an indoor track that is one-fifth of a mile around. This means that to run two miles, for example, I must circle the track 10 times. After running for a while, it is easy to lose track (pun intended) of how many laps I have completed. To help me overcome this problem, I picture myself jumping over a bun as I complete my first lap, jumping over a shoe as I complete lap two, running into a tree at the end of lap three, and so on. Another day I might picture the appropriate item sitting off to the side of the track as I complete each lap, or picture each item damaged in some way (squashed bun, broken shoe, sawed tree, etc.), or picture each item on fire. Varying the images from day to day helps reduce interference from the previous day so that I can tell that I am counting today's laps rather than yesterday's laps. Of course, the procedure could be adapted to count repetitions in any kind of a routine task; one of my memory students used this procedure to keep track of swimming laps and another one kept track of repetitions in practicing piano exercises.

Using the Same Pegwords Over and Over

A question was raised in chapter 10 regarding possible interference from using the same loci to learn several different lists. This issue is also relevant to using the same pegwords for several lists. Research evidence shows that there will be some interference, but not as much as when you do not use any system. For example, in one study some people used the Peg system to learn six consecutive lists of 10 items each, and other people learned the lists without the Peg system. The average recall of all six lists for the people using the Peg system was 63 percent; it was 22 percent for the other people. In addition, people using the Peg system recalled words equally well from all six lists, whereas the others recalled most of their words from the last two lists presented.[16]

Chapter 10 discussed two possible ways of reducing interference among different lists that are learned in close succession with the Loci system. First, you can construct several different sets of loci so you will not have to use the same ones as often. Second, you can use progressive elaboration. These two methods can also help reduce interference that may come from using the Peg system on several successive lists. You could either construct several sets of pegwords (perhaps one based on rhymes, one on look-alikes, one on meaning, and one on the alphabet), or you could attach more than one item to each pegword by using progressive elaboration. (One study on progressive elaboration that was cited in chapter 10 found equivalent results for the Loci and Peg systems.)[17]

Other Uses

As with the Link and Loci systems, the Peg system can also be used in school settings. We have seen some research on the use of the Peg system by students in school. Experiences reported by some of my memory students suggest additional ideas for possible applications of the

Peg system. One student took an exam on logarithms in a precalculus math class and reported that he "emerged dazed, confused, and with a score of 73 percent." The exam consisted of 11 types of problems, and each could be solved easily if the key manipulation could be remembered. The student used the pegwords to learn these key theorems and retook the exam. He reported, "There wasn't any problem or perplexity in retaking the exam, and I emerged this time with a 92 percent."

Another student used the Peg system to prepare for an open-book test on the content of about 50 Bible scriptures that had been marked in class. She linked all the scriptures in each chapter together, and then used pegwords for chapter numbers and associated them with the first scripture in each link of associations. She then linked the chapter pegwords together to remember which chapters had scriptures marked. She got 98 percent on the test and reported: "The test was timed and the majority of the class did not finish in the time limit. I had no difficulty finishing; in fact, I even had time to look over the test to make sure I did not want to change any of my answers."

One student used the Peg and Loci systems to help remember the numerical designations for the nine components in the radio compass system. She was attending a technical school in which students had to learn many different navigational systems. Each system has several components and each component has a number of designations. The Peg system helped her remember the numbers, and the Loci helped her remember which components go with which systems.

Another student was employed in training mentally and emotionally handicapped people to do custodial work, to prepare them for job placement. One custodial job they learned to do was cleaning lavatories, which involved 14 steps. My student first used the Peg system to learn the steps himself so that he could teach them more effectively; he then used the peg system to help his trainees learn the steps. He reported that developmentally disabled and emotionally handicapped trainees were successful in memorizing the steps, and that their quality rate according to competitive standards increased from approximately 20 percent to more than 80 percent of competitive norms.

Other examples of uses of the Peg system reported by my memory students include learning such varied materials as 6 trigonometry functions, 13 principles of motivation, campus building names, 18 kinds and symptoms of shock, 12 food groups for a diet, 10 short stories and authors, the numbers from 1 to 10 in Japanese, 10 points to remember for a dental-school interview, 11 periods of history in evolution, 20 most important events in U.S. history, and 8 aids in horseback riding. Another application for the Peg system had been developed in the military to teach new recruits the 11 "orders to sentries" comprising the duties that a sentry must be able to recall by number.[18]

Like the Loci system, the Peg system can be combined with the Link system to remember as many as 100 items. Associate the first item with "bun" and link the next nine items; associate the eleventh item with "shoe" and link the next nine items, and so on. Using this approach, you do not have any link longer than 10 words, and you use the pegwords to cue you for the first word in each link.

You could use the pegwords as a mental filing system for keeping track of daily appointments. For example, if you need to go to the dentist today at 10:00 and take your car in for an oil change at 3:00, you could associate "dentist-hen" and "oil-tree." If you made up a substitute word for each day of the week (for example, Monday = money, Wednesday = windy), you could construct a mental filing system for keeping track of weekly appointments. Thus, if you need to go to the dentist next Monday at 10:00 and take your car in for an oil change on Wednesday at 3:00, you could associate "dentist-money-hen" and "oil-windy-tree."

Additional practical applications of the Peg system can be found in popular memory-training books, such as those referenced at the end of chapter 9.

12

Mental Filing Systems: Phonetic Mnemonic

The Phonetic system is the most sophisticated and most versatile of the mnemonic systems discussed in this book. It is also the most complex and thus requires the most study and effort to master. However, for use as a mental filing system, the Phonetic system overcomes a limitation of the Peg system by allowing construction of more than 10 to 20 pegwords. At the same time it retains the Peg system's advantage of direct retrieval. In addition, the Phonetic system enables us to remember numbers better by making them meaningful.

WHAT IS THE PHONETIC SYSTEM?

The system discussed in this chapter has been referred to by such terms as *figure-alphabet, digit-letter, number-alphabet, hook, number-consonant,* and *number-to-sound.* Of these many terms, the most descriptive is the last one, the number-to-sound system. The other labels are more descriptive of older versions of the system. The reason why I have chosen to call the system the "Phonetic system" will become clear as it is described.

In the Phonetic system each of the digits from 0 to 9 is represented by a consonant sound; these consonant sounds are then combined with vowels to code numbers into words, which are more meaningful and thus easier to remember than numbers.

Origin

The origin of the Phonetic system has been traced back more than 300 years to 1648, when Winckelman (also spelled *Wenusheim* or *Wennsshein* in some sources) introduced a digit-letter system in which the digits were represented by letters of the alphabet. These letters were then used to form words to represent a given number sequence. Richard Grey published a refinement of Winckelman's digit-letter system in 1730.[1]

In these early systems the digits were represented by both consonants and vowels, and the letters representing each digit were selected arbitrarily. In 1813, Gregor von Feinaigle described a further refinement of the system. In his system the digits were represented by consonants only; vowels had no numerical value. In addition, the consonants representing each digit were not selected arbitrarily; rather, they were selected on the basis of their similarity to, or association with, the digits they represented (for example, "t" = 1 because it resembles the digit 1, "n" = 2 because it has two downstrokes; "d" = 6 because it resembles a reversed 6). Words were then formed to represent numbers by inserting vowels; thus 6 could be represented by *aid,* and 16 could be represented by *tide.*[2]

Further modifications of the digit-consonant system were made by mnemonists during the 1800s. In 1844, Francis Fauvel-Gouraud published an attempted classification of all the words in the English language that could represent numbers up to 10,000. By the end of the nineteenth century the digit-consonant system had evolved into its present form. During the 1890s it was briefly described in William James's classic psychology textbook, and more thoroughly described by Loisette as the system of "analytic substitutions." The digits were represented not by consonants themselves but by consonant *sounds.* This version of the system has remained essentially unchanged in memory books and commercial courses during the twentieth century.[3]

Description

The following display summarizes the digit-sound equivalents that are the basis of the Phonetic system:

Digit	Consonant Sound	Memory Aid
1	t, th, d	"t" has one downstroke
2	n	two downstrokes
3	m	three downstrokes
4	r	last sound for the word *four* in several languages
5	l	Roman numeral for 50 is "L"
6	j, sh, ch, soft g	reversed script "j" resembles 6 (*l*)
7	k, q, hard c, hard g	"k" made of two 7's ($\mathcal{K}$)
8	f, v	script "f" resembles 8 (*f*)
9	p, b	"p" is mirror image of 9
0	z, s, soft c	"z" for "zero"

There are several advantages to the way the consonant sounds have been selected to represent the digits in the display above:

1. The digit-sound equivalents are not too hard to learn (see the memory aids in the display).
2. The sounds are mutually exclusive: Each digit is represented by only one sound or family of similar sounds.
3. The sounds are exhaustive: All the consonant sounds in the English language are included, except for "w," "h," and "y," which you can easily remember by the word *why* (the letter *h* has value only as it changes the sounds of other consonants—th, ch, ph, sh).

All of the digits except 2, 3, 4, and 5 are actually represented by *families* of similar sounds rather than by a single sound. The memory aids in the display above can help in remembering the primary letter (the one listed first) for each digit. Here are some phrases and sentences (acrostics) that can help in remembering all of the sounds that go together in each family: for 1—train the dog; for 6—Jack should chase giants; for 7—kings and queens count gold; for 8—fun vacation; for 9—pretty baby; for 0—zero is a cipher.

It is important to realize that in the Phonetic system it is the consonant *sounds* that are important, not the letters themselves. This is why I have chosen to call it the Phonetic system. To understand why certain sounds are grouped together, say the following words aloud and pay close attention to how similarly the underlined sounds in each group are formed with your mouth and tongue: for 1—toe, though, doe; for 6—jaw, show, chow, gem; for 7—key, quo, cow, go; for 8—foe, vow; for 9—pay, bay; for 0—zero, sue, cell. Actually, there are only three sounds for 6 because "soft g" is the same as "j," two sounds for 7 because "hard c" and "q" are the same as "k," and two sounds for 0 because "soft c" is the same as "s."

The emphasis on sounds is important because different letters or letter combinations can take on the same sounds. For example, the "sh" sound can be made by the letters s (sugar), c (ocean), ci (gracious), and ti (ratio). Not only can different letters take on the same sound, but the same letter can take on different sounds. For example, sound the t in *ratio* versus *patio;* the c in *ace* versus *act;* the g in *age* versus *ago;* the gh in *ghost* versus *tough;* the ch in *church* versus *chronic;* the ng in *sing* versus *singe;* and the s in *sore* versus *sure.* The letter x takes on two consonant sounds ("k" and "s") as it is pronounced in most words (ax), but it can also be sounded as "z" (xylophone).

When a repeated consonant makes only one sound it counts as only one digit (button = 912 not 9112, and account = 721 not 7721), but when a repeated consonant makes two different sounds it counts as two digits (accent = 7021). A silent consonant is disregarded; it has no value if you don't hear it when pronouncing a word: limb = 53 not 539 (but limber = 5394); bought = 91 not 971; knife = 28 not 728; could = 71 not 751; scene = 02 not 072 (but scan = 072). Two different consonants together represent only one digit if they form only one sound (tack = 17 not 177; acquaint = 721 not 7721).

Two special combination sounds are not included in the display above. One is the "zh" sound (as in measure, vision, azure), which is very similar to the "sh" sound and is usually treated the same (representing 6). The other is the "ng" sound (as in sing and sang, which is usually treated the same as "hard g" (representing 7). However, some people treat "ng" as two different sounds, "n" and "g" (representing 27). The important consideration, as with the other examples, is that you go by what *you* hear and that you be consistent. Whichever method you prefer, remember that it is the sound that is important: angle = 75; angel = 265; engage = 276.

By now you can appreciate what I meant when I said that the Phonetic system is more complex than the other mnemonic systems, and thus takes more effort to learn. You will need to spend some time studying this section. However, I believe that the many potential uses of the Phonetic system justify the effort expended in learning it. The sounds representing each digit should be learned thoroughly.

Many of the examples already discussed, plus others that will help illustrate the differences between sound and letter, are contained in the following display. This display shows examples of different consonants and consonant combinations that can represent each digit. (It includes consonant combinations that make a unique sound, but does not include numerous consonant combinations in which one of the consonants is simply silent, such as debt, psalm, island, and mnemonic.

Digit	Sound	Examples
1	t	tot (11), letter (514)
	th	then (12), thin (12)
	d	did (11), ladder (514)
2	n	noon (22), winner (24)
3	m	mummy (33)
4	r	roar (44), barrel (945), colonel (7425)
5	1	lilly (55)
6	j	judge (66), gradual (7465)
	sh	she (6), ratio (46), ocean (62), anxious (angshus = 760), special (0965), tissue (16), emulsion (3562), fascism (8603), machine (362), sure (64)
	ch	choose (60), witch (6), conscious (7260), cello (65), Czech (67)
	soft g	gem (63), exaggerate (70641)
7	k	kite (71), back (97), chaos (70), xerox (zeroks = 0470)
	q	quit (71), acquit (71)
	hard c	cow (7), account (721)
	hard g	gagged (771), exam (egzam = 703)
8	f	food (81), off (8), phone (82), cough (78)
	v	oven (82), savvy (08), of (8), Stephen (0182)
9	p	popped (991)
	b	bobbed (991)
0	z	zoo (0), buzz (90), xerox (zeroks = 0470), scissors (0040),
	s	sue (0), tossed (101), scissors (0040), pretzel (94105), xerox (zeroks) = 0470
	c	circus (0470)

How to Use It

After the consonant sounds representing each digit have been thoroughly learned, the Phonetic system can then be used in two general areas: words can be constructed to serve as a mental filing system for use in the same way as the Loci and Peg systems, and any numerical information can be coded into words to make it easier to learn.

Mental filing system. The Phonetic system can be used to construct words to serve as a mental filing system just like the Loci and Peg systems. To keep it straight whether I am talking about the Peg system or the Phonetic system, I will refer to the Peg system words as "pegwords" and the Phonetic system words as "keywords" (not to be confused with the Keyword mnemonic in chapter 7). The keywords are constructed by combining vowels with the consonants. For example, there are many words that could represent the number 1: *doe, day, die, tie, toe, tea, eat, hat, head, wade,* and *the.* For reasons discussed in chapter 7, it would be best to use a concrete word; thus, *toe* would be better than *the.* Also, it will probably work better for most people to choose a keyword that begins with the consonant sound (such as *tea* or *doe*) than one that ends with the sound (such as *eat* or *head*).

We saw in the last chapter that one problem with the Peg system is that rhyming or look-alike pegwords are hard to find for numbers beyond 10 and even harder for numbers beyond 20. The Phonetic system does not have this limitation. Two-digit numbers are represented by a keyword that begins with a consonant sound representing the first digit and ends with a consonant sound representing the second digit. For example, the number 13 could be represented by *tomb, dome,* or *dime,* and the number 25 could be represented by *nail, Nile,* or *kneel.* The procedure for three-digit numbers is the same: for 145 you could use *trail, drill,* or *twirl.* Numbers of more than two digits are sometimes difficult to represent by a single word, and may require two words or a phrase. For example, 889 may be represented by "ivy fob," and 8890 by "five apes."

Keywords for numbers up to 100 can easily be constructed by combining consonants and vowels. Examples of possible keywords for the numbers from 1 to 20 are the following:

1 = tie	11 = tot
2 = Noah	12 = tin
3 = ma	13 = tomb
4 = ray	14 = tire
5 = law	15 = towel
6 = jay	16 = tissue
7 = key	17 = tack
8 = fee	18 = taffy
9 = pie	19 = tub
10 = toes	20 = nose

The sample keywords above all start with the primary digit from the previous display, but that is not essential (for example, *cow, dime,* and *dish* could be used for 7, 13, and 16, respectively). Several possible keywords for each number from 1 to 100 are listed in the appendix.

(Additional phonetic keywords for each number up to 1,000 have been listed elsewhere; and, as has been mentioned, several keywords for most numbers up to 10,000 were listed by Fauvel-Gouraud.)[4] You should choose one keyword that you can visualize easily for each number and use it consistently. The keywords serve as your mental filing system. They are used in the same way as the locations are used in the Loci system and the pegwords are used in the Peg system. Thus, the first item to be learned would be associated with *tie,* the second item with *Noah,* and the twentieth item with *nose* (or whatever keywords you select). Recall also proceeds the same as with the Loci and Peg systems. You think first of the number, then the keyword, and then the item that was associated with the keyword.

You can expand your basic 100-word list to 1,099 words by learning only 10 more words. The 10 words are adjectives that represent the numbers from 1 to 10; examples might be: wet = 1, new = 2, my = 3, hairy = 4, oily = 5, huge = 6, weak = 7, heavy = 8, happy = 9, dizzy = 10. For numbers from 101 to 1,099 you would use your regular keyword to represent the last two digits of each number, and the adjective to represent the first digit; for example, wet tie = 101, new tie = 201, hairy chin = 462, happy movie = 938, and dizzy baby = 1,099.

Remembering numbers. The second major area in which the Phonetic system is useful is in coding numerical information into words, so that the information will be more meaningful and easier to associate. Numerous examples of this use are presented later in this chapter.

The appendix lists several possible keywords for each number in order to provide additional keywords so that you can avoid using the same word too many times in coding a series of numbers. For example, you will have less interference if you code the number 6149234949 by linking "sheet-rope-gnome-rib-robe" than if you linked "sheet-rope-gnome-rope-rope." Also, if you were memorizing several phone numbers, for example, that had the number 72 in them, you would likely get less interference among them if you used several different words for 72 than if you used the same word in all of your associations.

HOW WELL DOES THE PHONETIC SYSTEM WORK?

Less research has been done on the Phonetic system than on the Link, Loci, and Peg systems for the obvious reason that it takes more time and effort to master the Phonetic system before it can be used. Thus, it is harder for a researcher to teach the system to a group of people and have them use it effectively in the same experimental session. Nevertheless, a few studies have investigated the effectiveness of the Phonetic system.

Research Evidence

The earliest experimental studies on the Phonetic system were three studies done in the 1960s, which indicated that the Phonetic system keywords helped in learning lists of 20 words. Additional research in the early and mid-1970s found that the keywords were effective in learning three consecutive 20-word lists and two 25-word lists, that the keywords were equivalent in effectiveness to the loci and pegwords, and that one person's similar system was effective in learning three-digit numbers.[5]

Whereas most earlier studies investigated the use of the Phonetic system as a mental filing system, a few studies in the 1980s have investigated its use for remembering numbers. One study found that the Phonetic system did not help in learning metric equivalences or in remembering them four weeks later. A second study corrected what the researchers felt were methodological weaknesses in the first study; people were given 5 minutes of instruction in the Phonetic system and 3 minutes to learn 20 two-digit numbers. They remembered more than twice as many digits as did people who were not taught the Phonetic system (15.7 versus 7.0). A third study found that with 10 minutes of instruction people could even remember four- and six-digit numbers more effectively. However, when people had to make up their own keywords to code the numbers while learning them (rather than use keywords provided by the researcher), the Phonetic system actually hindered their performance. This finding suggests the system cannot be used effectively unless it is learned well and practiced before it is used.[6]

Several of the mnemonists with exceptional memories featured in chapter 3 used the Phonetic system to achieve their feats. One person (T. E.) who was well practiced in using the Phonetic system was able to use it to duplicate the memory feats of Luria's S with number matrices as well as feats of other famous mnemonists. Six students who completed my memory course also tried to use the Phonetic system to duplicate S's feat of memorizing a 4×5 matrix of 20 digits in 40 seconds. As we saw in chapter 3, one student did it in less than 40 seconds (36 seconds), and three other students did it in less than 60 seconds. One mental calculator used the Phonetic system to store numbers in his memory while doing complex math problems, such as squaring six-digit numbers in his head.[7]

Using a system similar to the Phonetic system, another person was able to learn a number sequence of 1,152 digits in 34½ hours over several days, and after three months he could still recall two-thirds of the digits. In the same amount of study time without the system he learned only about one-third as many digits, and after three months he could not recall any of them.[8]

The Phonetic system has been studied in a unique application to learning French vocabulary words. The learners first learned a list of Phonetic keywords in French; for example, *thé* (tea) = 1, *roi* (king) = 4. They then associated these keywords with new French vocabulary words. The meanings of the vocabulary words were learned using the Keyword mnemonic described in chapter 7. By associating the words with the Phonetic keywords, learners could practice mentally recalling the new vocabulary words by using the keywords as cues. Several research studies found that this approach helped people learn lists of French vocabulary words (both concrete and abstract, familiar and unfamiliar), and even helped in learning a grammatical gender.[9]

Some researchers have analyzed the effectiveness of the Phonetic system in terms of trying to explain why it works, and have suggested that it makes effective use of principles such as meaningfulness and organization, illustrating the point made in chapter 7 that mnemonic systems use the basic principles of memory.[10]

Demonstrations

When I give lectures on memory I often begin with a demonstration for which I use the Phonetic system keywords. I write the numbers from 1 to 20 on the chalkboard, and the audience makes up a list of 20 words by calling out the numbers one at a time with a word to write after each number. A volunteer from the audience writes the words on the board as they are called out, while I stand facing the audience with my back to the board. After the list is completed I tell the audience that I am going to repeat all the words back to them without looking at the board, and I usually ask, "How do you want them—forward, backward, or odd and even?" This question generally produces looks of disbelief and a low roar of incredulous murmurs, and occasionally someone suggests something like "start in the middle and work both ways," or "every third one." (If there are no suggestions, I usually just recall them in reverse order from 20 to 1.) Of course, the order of recall does not matter with the Phonetic system.

I have done this demonstration about 60 to 70 times since 1970 and almost always recall all 20 words, although once I recalled only 18 words and about a half-dozen times I recalled only 19 words. I have also tried this feat 4 times with 100 words but have not yet recalled all 100 words; my recall has ranged from 93 to 97 words.

At age eleven, my son did this same demonstration with 20 words, and my daughter at age thirteen remembered 49 of 50 words the first time she tried the feat after learning keywords for numbers from 1 to 50. Further evidence that most people can achieve such feats is provided by students in my memory course. On the first night of class I read the students a list of 20 numbered nouns in random order, and have them recall as many as they can in correct numbered order. Later in the course, after they have learned the Phonetic system, I give them the same task with another 20-noun list. The following are the results for more than 100 students in several classes: The percentage of students achieving perfect recall of all 20 words was 7 percent before learning the Phonetic system and 51 percent after using it on the later test. The percentage recalling at least 18 of 20 words was 19 percent before learning the Phonetic system and 83 percent after learning it. At the other end of the performance scale, the percentage of students recalling 10 or fewer words was 28 percent before learning the Phonetic system and 2 percent after learning it.

HOW CAN YOU USE THE PHONETIC SYSTEM?

The Phonetic system can be used for all of the uses described previously for the Link, Loci, and Peg systems. Its main advantage over the Peg system is that you can use it for long lists. Its main advantage over the Loci system is that you can retrieve numbered items directly (of course, the items do not *have* to be numbered). It has an additional advantage over all previous systems in that you can use it to remember numbers.

A Mental Filing System

The Phonetic system keywords can be used as a literal mental filing system, in a way similar to that described for the Loci system in chapter 10. I have used my keywords from 50 to 99, in groups of 10, for this purpose: 50 to 59 for miscellaneous things to do; 60 to 69 for home and family; 70 to 79 for church and civic; 80 to 89 for school; and 90 to 99 for miscellaneous ideas. Suppose that just as I am drifting off to sleep one night I remember several things I have to do the next day. I remember that I need to leave some money home for my son (home and family), mail a letter on the way to work (miscellaneous things to do), pick up some income tax forms (miscellaneous things to do), grade the exams for a class (school), and order a book for another class (school). I may form associations between: *lot* (51) and *letter*, *lion* (52) and *tax*, *juice* (60) and *money*, *vase* (80) and *exam*, and *fit* (81) and *books*. Then in the morning before I leave for school, I can take a quick mental search in each category, do the things that need to be done in the morning, and write the others down in my notebook if I wish.

Another way you could use at least 70 keywords is similar to previous suggestions concerning use of the Loci and Peg systems every day. To reduce day-to-day interference, it was suggested that you might have a different set of loci or pegwords for each day. Similarly, you could use your Phonetic keywords from 1 to 10 on Sunday, 11 to 20 on Monday, 21 to 30 on Tuesday, and so on; this approach would eliminate the interference that could result from using the same 10 keywords day after day.

In chapter 1, a memory demonstration using a 50-page magazine was described. To memorize a magazine I use my keywords to represent the page numbers, and link what is on each page to the keyword. Suppose, for example, that page 36 contained a picture of three people in the upper right-hand corner, a report to the left of the picture on how they broke the world's record for trio-flagpole-sitting, a poem on love in the lower left-hand corner, and two ads in the lower right-hand corner (one for vitamin pills and one for an effortless exerciser). I could remember that information by using the Link system to form the following link: match (36), picture of people, flagpole, heart (for love), pill, and exerciser. This would give me the basic framework of what is on page 36. I could fill in the details by reading the material carefully. Remembering where each item was located on the page usually comes almost without conscious effort (as was discussed in chapter 10), but it may be aided by linking the items in order, say, from upper right to upper left to lower left to lower right. The same procedure can be adapted to studying other kinds of textual material.

If the material you want to remember is presented orally rather than in written form, such as in a lecture or speech, you can associate the first main point to *tie*, the second point to *Noah*, and so on. Of course, this procedure requires active concentration and participation in the listening process.

The Phonetic system can serve as the basis for some amazing memory feats with playing cards. One method involves representing each card by a keyword that begins with the first letter of the suit of the card and ends with the Phonetic sound representing the number of the card. For example, the four of clubs could be *car* or *core*, and the nine of spades could be *sub* or *soap*. Special procedures may be required for the face cards. The card keywords can then be associated to help remember them.

For people who play cards there are a number of card games in which there are obvious advantages to being able to remember what cards have been played. For those who do not play cards, a number of amazing memory feats can be performed. You can look through a shuffled deck of cards once and use the Link system to link the card keywords together, and then name all the cards in order. Or you can associate each card keyword with the Phonetic keywords from 1 to 52 and not only name all the cards in order but tell what card is in any location. (For example, "You'll find the four aces at positions 3, 17, 37, and 41.") A fast and easy, but impressive, demonstration is the missing-card stunt. Have someone remove one or more cards from the deck. You look through the deck once and tell which cards are missing. This is done by mutilating each card keyword as you come to it (see it broken, burned, etc.). Then after you have looked through the deck, run through the card keywords in your mind; the ones that are not mutilated are the ones that were missing. This is also a way to keep track of cards that have been played in some card games.

You could learn the numerical order of the letters of the alphabet by associating each alphabet pegword from chapter 11 with the corresponding Phonetic keyword for 1 to 26; for example, hay-tie (A = 1), eye-pie (I = 9), oar-taffy (R = 18). This would enable you to retrieve the letter at any given numbered position without having to count through all the letters until you reach that number. One of my memory class students taught this method to his daughter, who was having a hard time arranging words in alphabetical order. She then had no difficulty alphabetizing words by converting the initial letters to numbers and ordering the words numerically.

Phonetic keywords (or loci or pegwords) could be used for studying lists of spelling words in a way similar to the research studies on French vocabulary words. The keywords would not help you to remember the spelling of the words themselves, but they would allow you to mentally run over the word list and practice spelling the words at times when it is not convenient to study the list or to have someone else read the words to you.

Remembering Numbers

The unique advantage of the Phonetic system over the previous systems is its usefulness in learning numbers. Much of the information we need to remember consists of numbers: phone numbers, street addresses, historical dates, financial data, stock numbers, population figures, ages, identification numbers, social security numbers, license plates, time schedules, prices, style numbers, and so on. Unfortunately, numbers are about the most abstract kind of material to remember.

There are at least two ways to use the Phonetic system to remember numbers. Both of them involve turning the numbers into words, which are more meaningful. (When possible, of course, the words should represent something concrete that can be visualized, but even when this is not possible, most words will still be easier to remember than numbers.) The first way is to make up a word or phrase in which each of the digits in the number translates into one of the consonant sounds in order. The second way is to make up a phrase or sentence in which each digit in the number translates into the first consonant sound in each word. For example, to remember the number 60374 by the first approach, you might use "juicemaker;" by the second approach, you might use, "She sews many gowns readily."

The following are a few examples of how selected numbers might be coded: To remember my former automobile license plate number (KFK 207) I thought of the German psychologist Koffka as a "nice guy." A clothes locker in a gym I once visited was number C12-B (aisle C, booth 12, locker B), which I remembered by cotton ball. The deepest hole drilled by man is a gas well that went down 31,441 feet, which I can picture being measured by a meter rod. The Empire State Building is 1,250 feet tall, and I can see it filled with tunnels. The highest man-made structure in the world is a radio mast in Poland that rises 2,119 feet; I can see myself on the top. The Carlsbad Caverns reach a depth of 1,320 feet, at which depth I can imagine demons. The highest waterfall in the world is in Venezuela; it falls 3,212 feet, as high as a mountain. I can remember the 1980 population of the town where I was born and raised—Spokane, Washington—by imagining myself returning home "to get mazes" (171,300). I can see a square mile covered with chairs to remember that it equals 640 acres, or associate a mile with digit to remember that it equals 1.61 kilometers.

If the word or phrase bears some meaningful relationship to the item it represents (such as the Carlsbad Caverns example) then the association will be most memorable, but even if the relationship is arbitrary (such as the Spokane population example), the association will still be more memorable than an abstract number would have been.

You can make modifications for numbers with decimals by using words beginning with "s" only for decimals, and using the s as the initial letter to represent a decimal point. If no number precedes the decimal, "s" indicates the decimal point (.51 = salt, .94 = sparrow, .734 = skimmer, etc.). If a number precedes the decimal, use two separate words; the decimal word begins with "s" (945.51 = barley sold, 3.1416 = my store dish, etc.).[11]

People who must remember formulas, equations, and other mathematical expressions may be able to adapt a procedure that one of my memory students suggested to me. The procedure incorporates several mnemonics. Letters are represented by alphabet pegwords. Numbers are represented by Phonetic words. Symbols are represented by objects that remind you of the symbol; examples include a house for the square-root sign ($\sqrt{\ }$), a slide for the slash representing division (/), a pie for pi (π), and a cross for the plus sign (+). Thus, you might remember the formula for finding the volume of a sphere (4/3 πr^3) by linking "sphere-ray-slide-ma-pie-oar-cube."

I used the Phonetic system to memorize all the phone numbers of more than 100 members of a group to which I belong. The first two digits are the same for all phone numbers in our area, so I made up a word or phrase to represent the last five digits of each number. Then I made up substitute words to represent the names of the people (see chapter 13). The association of each name with its number was a paired-associate task. The following are a few examples: Evans, 59941 (ovens, wallpapered); Wille, 79812 (will, cup of tin); James, 77970 (Jesse James, cookbooks); Taylor, 41319 (tailor, ready-made bow).

Suppose you memorized a four-digit number like 1478 by associating your keywords (say, *tire* and *cave*) with the person. Later when you recall the number you think of *tire* and *cave*, but are not sure which comes first: Is the number 1478 or 7814? One way to avoid this problem is to use your regular keyword for the last two digits of a four-digit number, and any word other than your keyword for the first two digits. Thus, 1478 might be coded as "door cave" or "dry cave," and 7814 might be coded as "calf tire" or "goofy tire."

A useful application for remembering numbers is remembering the 12-digit number we learned earlier for memorizing a year's calendar. For example, the number for 1988 (376-315-374-264) could be represented by the following: my cash, motel, mugger, injury. These terms could be linked together in order by the Link or Story system. This procedure requires sequential retrieval. To allow direct retrieval of a given month's digit, associate each digit's keyword directly with the month's substitute word in a way similar to the procedure described previously for the Peg system (associate *ma* with *jam*, *key* with *valentine*, *jay* with *march*, *ma* with *ape*, etc.).

Methods have been devised using the Phonetic system to learn one 12-digit number for the months and a key digit for each year by which you could remember the day of the week for every date in the twentieth century.[12] I used one of these methods to memorize the calendar for half of the century (1950–1999). The mental arithmetic is a little more complex than that required for the use of a different 12-digit number each year, but this feat can be accomplished by a person with a normal memory using the appropriate system: It is not limited to mental wizards, lightning calculators, or idiot savants.

You could also use the Phonetic system to remember dates of birthdays and anniversaries. Suppose, for example, that a friend's birthday is on January 23 and that your parents' anniversary is on April 16. One method for remembering these dates is to form associations among the person, the month substitute word, and the date—"friend-jam-name" and "parents-ape-tissue." Another method is to use a number where the first digit represents the month and the last digit represents the date, then turn that number into a word to associate with the person—"friend-denim"(1–23), and "parents-radish" (4-16).

You could construct a mental filing system for keeping track of daily or weekly appointments in the same way as described for the Peg system. Thus, if you need to go to the *dentist* next *Monday* at *10:00* and take your car in for an *oil* change on *Wednesday* at *3:00*, you could associate "dentist-money-toes" and "oil-windy-ma." Another approach to remembering appointments involves numbering the days of the week rather than making up substitute words for them (Sunday = 1, Monday = 2, etc.). Then you could represent each appointment by a number indicating the day and time (Monday at 10:00 = 210, Wednesday at 3:00 = 43), and associate the appointment with a Phonetic keyword for that number (for example, "dentist-nuts" and "oil-room.").

The keywords could also be used in the same manner as the pegwords to count things and keep track of your count. Thus, in keeping count of my laps around the track (as I described for the Peg system) I can vary the monotony and reduce interference by using the pegwords one day and the keywords another day. In addition, with the Phonetic keywords I would not be limited to counting only 10 laps but could easily count up to 100 (not that I will ever run that many laps, but I do often run more than 10; also, there may be other things that a person would want to count that do go up to 100).

Other Uses

A program developed for learning scriptures is based on the Phonetic system. Phonetic phrases were constructed for 1,200 selected verses in the Bible. Each phrase is meaningfully related to the content of the verse and also identifies the book, chapter, and verse numbers by the Phonetic system. The books are represented by numbers giving their numerical order in the Bible, rather than by their names. Here are a few examples: A verse on the creation ("Let there be light," Genesis 1:2) is the phrase "the dawn," 1-1-2, representing the first book, first chapter, second verse; the Ten Commandments (Exodus 20) are "no-nos," 2-20, representing the second book, twentieth chapter; the names of the 12 apostles (Matthew 10:2) are "the dozen," 1-10-2, representing the first book in the New Testament, tenth chapter, second vese. A scripture-learning game has been developed based on this system, and the system and all 1,200 phonetic phrases have been put in book form. [13]

I used the Phonetic system to turn the multiplication tables into word associations (for example, new ma = witch [2 × 3 = 6] and wash key = rain [6 × 7 = 42]). Then I used these associations to help my son learn all the times tables through the twelves when he was age seven and in the second grade (the year before they started studying the times tables in his school). One of my students had a sixteen-year-old learning-disabled nephew who had started over learning the times tables every year in school but had never been able to learn them. She used these associations to teach him the times tables, and reported that he was finally able to learn them (and that this gave a positive boost to his self-image).

Reports from my memory students show additional ways they found to use the Phonetic system in response to a homework assignment to use it for something they wanted to learn. These included learning such items as phone numbers, postal ZIP codes, scripture verses and chapters, birthdays, highs and lows for selected Dow Jones stocks, page numbers of hymns in a hymnal, spectral frequencies in organic chemistry, 19 parts of a saddle, exercises in a routine, 62 terms in a psychology class, and the starting checklist for operation of a tram.

As was the case with the other mnemonic systems, there are many more possible uses for the Phonetic system besides those mentioned in this chapter. Memory-training books suggest additional uses, give more detail on some of the possible uses suggested in this chapter (for example, the mental filing system for remembering daily appointments, and the methods for remembering dates and playing cards), and give examples of how the system can be applied in various occupations. [14]

In chapter 9 I suggested that you might get more out of chapters 7 and 8 after you have read about the mnemonic systems. Now that you have read about the systems, you might find it interesting and beneficial to reread those two chapters; some of the points in those chapters might be more meaningful now.

13

Using Mnemonics: Remembering People's Names and Faces

Perhaps the most common memory complaint is the inability to remember people's names. This was demonstrated in one of my recent memory workshops consisting of a broad cross-section of people—more than 500 people ranging in age from thirteen to eighty-one, and representing more than 80 different occupations and two dozen states (and two other countries). At the beginning of the workshop I asked them for written questions they would like to have answered about memory. By far the largest number of questions (41 percent) were on the subject of remembering people's names. (The next most common subject was studying and schoolwork at 15 percent.) Memory for names is also among the most frequent memory concerns of special populations, such as the elderly and brain damaged. One large survey that included more than 500 elderly people found forgetting of names to be the most frequent of 18 potential memory complaints, and name memory has also been found to be one of the most frequent complaints of memory-impaired patients.[1]

Just because people learn how to remember lists, speeches, numbers, cards, or anything else discussed so far in this book does not necessarily mean they will be able to remember names and faces.

Memory for names must be trained just like any other kind of memory. You must learn the techniques and practice using them. The following two examples illustrate this fact, as well as the importance of interest.

In chapter 3, a man (V. P.) with an amazing verbal memory was discussed. Despite his impressive memory for verbal material, V. P. observed that his ability to remember faces was not unusually good. He failed to recognize the wife of one of the researchers on meeting her at the store where he works, although he had met her socially on two or three occasions. He commented, "It's really applications of memory that are of importance in the learning process. That politician . . . would certainly remember your wife by name and face, no matter what the circumstances in which he met her."

Similarly, Bob Barker, the host of a TV show, meets many people on each show and remembers their names. When he was asked what his secret was for remembering people's names, he replied, "It's all concentration. People on the show are my tools. I must know their names. It's my job. But introduce me to people at a cocktail party, and I can't remember who they are two minutes later."

When we forget a person's name we may be subject to embarrassing moments. For example, Clare Boothe Luce, former ambassador to Italy, was introduced at a gathering to David Burpee, flower- and vegetable-seed distributor. A short time later she could not remember his name, but did not say anything. Sensing her embarrassment, he said quietly, "I'm Burpee." Mrs. Luce replied, "That's quite all right. I'm sometimes troubled that way myself."[2]

In this chapter we will look at some research on how we remember names and faces, at a system for improving memory for names and faces, and at some evidence on how well the system works.

HOW DO WE REMEMBER NAMES AND FACES?

There has been a great deal of research on memory for people, including personality traits, behavior, physical features, faces, and names. More of this research has focused on memory for faces than on any other area (and it has been conducted in short-term tasks in the research lab more than in real-world settings). One reason for this interest in face memory is the real-world task of eyewitness identification in crimes; several books reporting research on eyewitness testimony have been published in the 1980s.[3]

Despite the widespread practical interest in remembering people's names, there was very little research on memory for names before the mid-1970s. Since then, research interest in name memory has grown, resulting in more than three dozen studies on memory for names from the mid-1970s to the mid-1980s. However, this is still much less research than has been done on memory for faces. [4]

Remembering names and faces is a paired-associate task: In most situations we see the face and recall the name; the face serves as the cue and the name serves as the response. Remembering faces is easier for most people than remembering names for at least three reasons:

1. We generally see the face but only hear the name, and most people remember things they see better than things they hear.
2. We saw in chapter 3 that pictures (faces) are easier to remember than words (names). Faces are treated differently from names in memory, and may even be treated differently from other pictures. [5]
3. As was noted in chapter 2, face memory is a recognition task whereas name memory is a recall task. If name memory were put in the form of a multiple-choice question (people had four names printed on their foreheads and we just had to recognize the right one), we would not have nearly as much trouble "remembering" people's names.

Recognizing Faces

A common form of paramnesia (mild amnesia involving distortion more than forgetting) is the everyday experience of encountering a relatively well-known person but not being able to identify him. This "I can't quite place him" phenomenon usually occurs when we meet the person outside the normal context, and often leads to a perplexed and preoccupying attempt to place the person. One interesting characteristic of the phenomenon is that it seems to represent recognition without complete recall. [6]

Almost all of the research on memory for faces uses recognition rather than recall as the memory measure. The procedure in most such research is to show pictures of faces to people, and then have them pick the faces they have just seen from a larger number of faces. Let us look at some of the revelant findings concerning such recognition memory for faces.

There is a considerable amount of difference among people in their ability to remember faces accurately. One study found no significant correlation for college students between memory for pictures of faces in the research lab and memory for faces of real people (their classmates). In fact, the students were not even very consistent in how well they remembered real people. A study of housewives found no relationship between how good they said their memory for faces was and how good it actually was. Several studies have found differences between male and female subjects in their memory for faces, but the results have not been consistent in terms of which sex remembers faces better.[7]

Young adults usually remember single-view pictures of faces better than the elderly do. For example, young women in their late teens or twenties remembered single-view pictures better than elderly women. However, the elderly women remembered multiview pictures (which more closely resemble how we see people in real life) just as well as the younger women did. Similarly, a study of college professors from ages 36 to 75 found no significant age differences in their memory for names and faces of former students. However, one study found that while there were only minimal age differences between young and elderly adults in recognizing faces and judging whether the faces had changed (in expressions or poses), the elderly did not perform as well in specifying exactly *how* the faces had changed.[8]

Although there are differences among people in their recognition memory for faces, such memory for most people is quite good. One study found a 96-percent recognition accuracy; another study found that people in their fifties and sixties still recognized 75 percent of their high school classmates' faces, and that memory for faces declined more slowly than memory for names.[9]

Recognition Versus Recall

Recall of faces is much harder than recognition because most people have an inadequate vocabulary to describe faces, and because face recall is less frequently needed than recognition; yet recall of faces has been called the most important and most difficult practical problem for research on memory of faces.[10]

One problem in studying recall of faces is the difficulty of checking the accuracy of recall. Methods have been developed to try to overcome this problem. The Photo-Fit Kit consists of a number of separate features that a person puts together to construct a face. It was designed to enable witnesses to reconstruct the faces of people who were wanted for police questioning. However, people using the kit have difficulty reconstructing a face even when the original face is present, and it is even harder when the face has to be recalled from memory.[11] This poor recall of faces contrasts with the typically high scores for recognition measures of face memory.

One study compared recall of names and faces. People were given the names of some famous people, and were asked to imagine the faces. They were shown the faces of other people, and were asked to recall the names. Reported recall of the face given the name was more frequent than recall of the name given the face (but accuracy of recall was not measured). Another study tried measuring both names and faces by both recognition and recall. For the recognition measure people were shown a series of names or faces, and then shown a larger set of names or faces and asked to pick the ones they had just seen. They were then tested for recall of names by being shown the faces and being asked to recall the names. They were tested for recall of faces by being shown the names and by reporting whether they could recall the faces. Recognition yielded higher accuracy scores than recall both for names (97 percent versus 36 percent) and for faces (91 percent versus 54 percent).[12]

In a study of college professors' memory for former students, name recognition was actually better than face recognition. The strength of recognition in measuring memory for names is also shown by the finding that 15 years after graduation from high school, people can recall only about 15 percent of their classmates' names but can recognize 90 percent of the names from a list of names. Recognition of names has also been found to be faster than recogniton of faces.[13]

All of this evidence points to the fact that one of the main reasons why name memory is more of a problem than face memory for most people is because name memory is usually a recall task and face memory is usually a recognition task.

Other Factors Affecting Name Memory

In a study on the tip-of-the-tongue phenomenon (see chapter 2), at least half of such experiences reported by both young and elderly adults involved memory for proper names.

Names tend to be harder to remember than other words. One reason might be that most names are not as common as most words. One study found that surnames were more difficult to recall than other verbal items because of a difference in objective frequency, and the researcher suggested that there also may be a different associative memory network for surnames than for other verbal material.[14]

We saw in earlier chapters that one strategy that may help in recalling a name is to try to recall anything else about the person you can, such as where you met her. For example, we saw that people who tried to recall the names of high school classmates 4 to 19 years after graduation were aided by thinking of settings in which they saw them; they reconstructed scenes and tried to think of who was there. Similarly, in trying to remember a famous person's name when shown his picture, people first try to locate the person's profession, then the place where they may have seen him, and then when they last saw the person. The more you know about a person the more paths you have to try to retrieve the name. Thinking of what a person looks like when trying to recall his or her name also may help bring the name to you. When people tried to recall the name of an object when given its definition, they frequently could recall a visual image of the object before—or even instead of—recalling the name. Even recognition memory for faces can be affected by the context, including the context of other information about the person as well as the physical context. [15]

One study investigated the effect of "priming" on recall of authors' names given the titles of their well-known literary works. Priming is a brief glance at a list of authors' names before testing of the names with the titles of their works. Recall of the names was better if the people were primed beforehand with a list of the names. [16] Suppose you were going to attend a high school reunion or an organization picnic. You might apply this idea of priming by looking over the names of your former classsmates or fellow employees before going. This review calls the names to the fore of your awareness and makes them more readily accessible.

One study found that introducing a person's name later in the course of a conversation produced better recall than early introductions. College students were introduced to another student via a 3- or 6-minute videotape. The other student talked about herself, her family, and school. On the short tape she gave her name in the first minute and talked for 2 more minutes; on the longer tape she gave her name in the fourth minute and talked for 2 more minutes. For the early introduction only 4 of 22 students remembered her name, but for the late introduction all 22 students remembered her name. The researcher suggested that if people were given a little time to familiarize themselves with a new person beore they were introduced to the new name, they might have better attention, experience less interference, and have more retrieval cues to which the name could be associated. [17] However, this finding may be difficult to apply; in introducing people it is hard not to say the name first because that is what people expect. Perhaps the introducer could repeat the person's name again later. If you are trying to remember someone's name, ask about it later in the conversation after you have learned a little about the person.

This section has focused on research that shows some of the factors influencing memory for names and faces. These factors include recognition versus recall, context, priming, and timing of name introduction. In the next section we will look at additional factors that are incorporated into a system for improving memory for names and faces.

A SYSTEM FOR REMEMBERING NAMES AND FACES

One of the most common reasons people enroll in memory-training courses is to improve memory for names and faces. Most popular memory-training books devote at least one chapter to memory for names and faces, and an entire book has even been devoted to the subject.[18] Virtually every memory author and expert proposes his "system" for remembering names. One system may consist of three steps, another of five or six steps. All the systems contain essentially the same basic strategies but differ in how they divide them. The first four of the five steps in this section capture the essence of virtually all memory systems for names.

Further details on each of the following steps for remembering names and faces may be found in many memory-training books, and you can read those books if you want more explanation and examples of these strategies. However, the main determinant of your memory for names is your awareness of these steps, and then your *practice* of them.[19] Nowhere are the myths from chapter 1 concerning the search for a simple, easy "secret" to memory more applicable than in remembering names. I have met many people who want to know the secret of remembering names, but when they are told the secret (as described in this system), they dismiss it as too much work or they do not think it will really help.

The following five steps are used by most people who have exceptional ability to remember people's names:

1. Make sure you get the name.
2. Make the name meaningful.
3. Focus on a distinctive feature of the person's appearance.
4. Associate the name with the distinctive feature.
5. Review the association.

Each step is discussed below, along with some relevant research findings. As you read, notice how many of the memory principles and strategies from earlier chapters are involved in these steps (for example, meaningfulness, association, attention, visual imagery, review, repetition, recitation, and substitute words).

Step 1: Get the Name

It was suggested in chapter 4 that failure to pay attention may be the single most common reason why we "forget" the names of people we are introduced to: We never really *got* the name in the first place. Often when we are introduced to someone our mind is on something else. Maybe we are waiting to hear our own name said, or are trying to think of something clever to say after the introduction.

An "I know the face but not the name" phenomenon is a milder version of the "I can't quite place him" phenomenon noted earlier. A person is recognized and appropriately identified, but his name cannot be recalled. One psychologist suggested that this phenomenon seems to involve partial forgetting due to lack of attention in the original situation; we typically pay less attention to names than to appearances. The importance of attention is also shown by the finding that people who are highly self-conscious recall names worse than people who are not particularly self-conscious. The researchers suggested that this may be because the attention of self-conscious people is focused more on themselves than on other people.[20]

Even when you are paying attention, you may not get a person's name if it is spoken too fast or too quietly. If this happens, stop the person or introducer and ask him to repeat the name. This seems obvious, so why don't people do it more often? One reason may be that they do not want to seem rude by interrupting the flow of the conversation. Or it may be that they are somewhat embarrassed that they did not get the name; but they are likely to be even more embarrassed later when they cannot remember the name.

Regardless of how many steps are in any "expert's" system for remembering names, the first step in virtually every system consists of some way of forcing you to get the name. Use the name in the conversation, repeat it, spell it aloud, work it over, ask about it. These activities help you make sure you get the name. They force you to concentrate your attention on it. Repeating the name and using it involves applying the principles of repetition and recitation discussed in chapters 5 and 6. Of course, this can be overdone, but you can use the name at least 3 times without appearing too obvious—once when you first meet the person, once during the conversation, and once when parting. (For example, "I'm happy to meet you Mr. Jones," then later, "What do you think about that, Mr. Jones?" and finally, "It was nice talking with you, Mr. Jones.")

Another technique that can help you get the name is to write it down when possible. This forces you to pay attention to it. In addition, people remember words better when they see and hear them than when they only see or only hear them.[21] Similarly, looking at a name in addition to hearing it should help fix it more firmly in your memory.

Research has found that memory for names can be improved significantly even without any additional steps or particular mnemonic technique if people merely concentrate on the name and pay attention to it.[22] Thus, you will notice an improvement in your ability to remember people's names even if all you do is form the habit of making sure you do something to *get* the name whenever you are introduced to someone. However, you can improve even more by going beyond this first step.

Step 2: Make the Name Meaningful

After you get the name, you should make the name meaningful and concrete. This is not hard for names that already have meaning. Many names have meaning in themselves or through association with something that is meaningful. Look through a phone book and you may be surprised at how many surnames already have meaning to you. There are names of cities or countries (London, Holland), colors (White, Green), occupations (Barber, Cook), adjectives (Strong, Short), famous people (Lincoln, Ford), metals (Silver, Steel), plants (Rose, Oaks), animals (Wolf, Lamb), things (Hammer, Ball), and commercial products (Dodge, Hershey).

For names that do not have any readily apparent meaning, you can use the principle of substitute words discussed in chapter 7 to give meaning to the name. For example, *hug bee* may represent "Higbee," *wood taker* may represent "Whittaker," *paw low ski* may represent "Paloski," *fresh neck* may represent "Frischknecht," *hunt singer* may represent "Huntzinger," *magnet mare* may represent "McNamara," *saw press key* may represent "Zabriski," *mule stein* may represent Muhlestein," *lamb or row* may represent "Lamoreaux," and *awl storm* may represent "Ahlstrom." I picked these examples from a telephone directory. A good way to acquire the skill of making substitute words is to practice with the names in a phone directory. One book on remembering people lists possible substitute words for hundreds of common given names and surnames.[23]

Even if you come across an occasional name that you cannot make meaningful in the time you have available, merely having *tried* to do so will help you remember the name better because you have had to focus your attention on the name in order to try to find a meaningful substitute word (step 1).

Step 3: Focus on the Face

The next step is to note a distinctive feature of the person's face or appearance, a feature that will be likely to first attract your attention the next time you meet him. The purpose of focusing on the face is to find something distinctive that will help you recognize it.

Carefully studying a face can increase your memory for it. Several studies have found that making a judgment about a person's traits (for example, honesty, friendliness, intelligence) improves face recognition even more than judgments about physical characteristics in children, young adults, and elderly adults. These findings suggest that to remember a person's face you should try to make a number of difficult personal judgments about his face when you are first meeting him. Of course, making personal judgments is just one way of producing a deeper level of processing by making you concentrate on the features of the person. In one study people who studied faces for the purpose of looking for their most distinctive feature remembered the faces as well as if they had made personal judgments. In fact, in another study people who were just told to remember the faces remembered them better than people who made superficial judgments.[24]

Many people who are not used to studying faces have a hard time at first finding something really distinctive about every face. All faces include the same basic features—two eyes, a nose, and a mouth, with a couple of ears sticking out from the sides. How can you make that distinctive? Actually, there are many distinguishing features in a face, but you must train yourself to look for them. Once you do, you will see much more in a face, just as a botanist on a walk through the forest sees many differences in plants that look the same to most people, or a geologist sees many differences in rocks that are indistinguishable to the untrained eye.

For example, studies teaching a computer to distinguish among faces used at least 21 different aspects of facial features.[25] These facial features included characteristics of the hair (coverage, length, texture, shade), mouth (upper-lip thickness, lower-lip thickness, lip overlap, width), eyes (width of opening, distance apart, shade), nose (length, tip, shape), ears (length, protrusion), eyebrows (bushiness, distance apart), chin (shape), forehead (slant), and cheeks (fullness). Each of the 21 features was further divided into two or three characteristics—for example, hair coverage (full, receding, bald), nose (tip upward, horizontal, downward), and cheeks (sunken, average, full)—for a total of more than 60 specific characteristics available to distinguish faces. In addition, you may note features that are unique to one person, such as dimples, a cleft in the chin, or lines in the forehead.

We tend to remember faces that are distinctive and distinguishable better than those that are not. For example, we remember very attractive and very unattractive faces better than moderately attractive faces; we remember faces of members of our own race better than those of another race. Even an expression on a face, such as a smile, can help make it distinctive enough to aid memory for it.[26] However, a feature as changeable as a smile would not be a good feature to base your recognition on, because the person may not smile the next time you see him; the same suggestion holds for other nonpermanent features, such as whether the person is wearing glasses.

Which features are the most helpful in distinguishing among faces? Research findings are not consistent. One review of the research concluded that the hair is the most important single feature for the purposes of the studies reviewed (recognition of faces from still photographs in a research setting). Unfortunately, hair is also the most easily altered feature, and the reviewers suggested that other features may be more important in real-life interactions. There is also evidence that the eyes may be the most helpful; however, other studies have not found a clear superiority of any one facial feature.[27] It may be that most people's eyes reveal more about them than any other facial feature, but it may not be wise to try to distinguish a person on the basis of his eyes if he has a bulbous nose, protruding ears, curly red hair, or some other definite distinguishing feature.

A recent analysis of 128 research studies on eyewitness identification and face recognition found that ability to identify faces is significantly affected by such variables as reinstating the context, depth of processing strategies, face distinctiveness, and elaboration of the face at encoding.[28] You may recognize these variables as some of the factors that have been discussed so far in this chapter.

Step 4: Associate the Face with the Name

After you have made something meaningful of the person's name and noted a distinctive feature of his appearance, you can form a conscious, visual association between the name and the distinctive feature. For example, if Mr. Ball has red hair, you could picture hundreds of red balls coming out of his hair; if Ms. Cook has long eyelashes, you could picture her eyelashes cooking; if Mr. Whittaker has large ears, you could picture him carrying wood (*wood taker*) with his ears; if Mrs. McNamara has a round mouth, you could picture a *magnet* riding a *mare* out of her mouth; if Miss Huntzinger has dimples, you could picture a *hunter* sitting in her dimple and *singing*.

The common criticism of this step (especially by people who have not tried it) is that the next time you see that person you might think of the substitute word but not the name. You might even call the person by the substitute word or some other related name. I have lost count of how many people have told me a story such as the one about the memory student who met Mrs. Hummock. She had a big stomach so he decided to use "stomach" as his association. Several weeks later when he saw Mrs. Hummock again he looked at her large stomach (belly) and said, "Hello, Mrs. Kelly!"

It is possible that you might remember a substitute word without remembering the name it represents. That is one of the hazards of using substitute words in visual associations (see chapter 8). Although this system improves your memory, it does not necessarily make memory perfect. But even if you did fail to recall a few names, you would probably still recall more than you do without using substitute words.

Actually, although it is possible that the above problem can occur, it is not very likely in practice. Usually only people who have not tried the system will ask how they can be sure that they will not call Mrs. Hummock "Mrs. Kelly" by mistake. People who have tried it know that it usually does not happen. [29] If a person remembers the facial features and substitute word, he has about a 90 percent chance of remembering the correct name. When errors do occur, they are usually a result of poor association of the substitute word to the name. Thus, one psychologist has suggested that the trick is to practice being able to convert a name to a memorable substitute word (step 2); after that, step 4 is easy. [30]

Step 4 is, of course, the main reason for steps 2 and 3. We make the name meaningful and find a distinctive feature so that we can associate the two together. However, it should be noted that even if you did not do step 4 or if it did not work perfectly for some names, having done steps 2 and 3 would still increase the likelihood that you would remember the person better than if you did nothing.

Step 5: Review the Association

We saw in chapter 6 that no matter how you learn something, you are likely to forget it if you do not use it occasionally unless you review. Yet this step is not even mentioned in most popular name-memory systems; they give the impression that if you follow steps 1 through 4 you will never forget people's names. If you really want to remember a name for a long time, you should review it as soon as possible after meeting the person, and then occasionally afterward. Gradually expanding intervals between reviews have been found to be very effective. Repeat the person's name immediately, and then say it again to yourself 10 to 15 seconds later (remember that most forgetting occurs soon after learning). Review it again after a minute or so, and then again several minutes later.[31] If you meet several people at one party or meeting, you might review in your mind the names and faces of everyone you met immediately after the party or meeting is over.

Proactive interference (see chapter 3) has been found for faces as well as for verbal material, suggesting that interference can affect memory for faces as well as for names.[32] To reduce the negative effects of such interference when you meet several people in succession, you might try to apply some of the principles for reducing interference from chapter 6 when possible—meet the people in different rooms or different parts of the room, space the introductions, and so on.

Since it takes some time to form associations, you may want to arrange to meet people with a little break between introductions when possible rather than having a lot of names thrown at you one after another. Spacing the introductions not only helps reduce interference and gives you time to make good associations but also gives you a chance to review the names of the people you have met so far.

Whenever you can do so, write the names of people you have met recently. In addition to the advantages already mentioned in step 1, writing the names also makes it easier to review the names later.

HOW WELL DOES THE SYSTEM WORK?

It should not be too surprising to find evidence that this system works, because the five steps incorporate the same principles and structure as other effective mnemonics like the Keyword mnemonic and the Loci system. In fact, one psychologist who felt that "memory tricks" are helpful only for simple tasks, such as remembering a grocery list, even conceded that an exception to the lack of practicality of mnemonics is their use for associating names and faces.[33]

One student in my memory class reported meeting with a new study group where the members all introduced themselves, and he tried to apply as many of the techniques as he could from this chapter (which he had just read that afternoon). After the introductions one group member suggested that they all say their names once more so that he could remember them. My student reported, "I asked if I could try to repeat everyone's names, as I was taking this class in mnemonics and I wanted to see if the techniques discussed in the book really worked. Well, it was really easy. The names came back so quick I couldn't believe it. It was really a good experience because now I realize that it can be done even by someone who has as hard a time at it as I do."

Another student, a man in his fifties, told the class how he had been a member of a club of about 150 men for 10 years, and he knew the names of only about 30 or 40 of the members. At their next dinner meeting, which was held after we had discussed names and faces in our class, he made it a point to sit at a table where he did not know any of the men. When they introduced themselves he made a special effort to make sure he got each of the eight names. He then made a visual or verbal association of each name with each person, used the names during the night, and reviewed the associations. He reported to the class that, somewhat to his surprise, he knew every man's name at the end of the evening, and that he was going to continue the same strategy until he knew the names of all 150 men in the club.

A man who attended one of my seminars for insurance agents in Maryland wrote me a note describing his experience in trying out the system. He reported that the morning after the seminar he practiced the steps at a laundromat: "The results were amazing to me; 10 of 14 names were properly recalled 15 to 30 minutes later. . . . It was fun. Most people cooperated with my request to ask me to recall their names if they left before I did."

One of the memory tests I give to the students in my memory classes during the first few days of class is to remember the names of 15 people. I show the slides of the people's faces on the screen and introduce each person to the class; I then give the students 10 to 15 seconds to look at the person before meeting the next person. Then I rearrange the order of the slides and show each face again for about 10 seconds while the students try to write down the name of each person. Near the end of the course, after they have studied this chapter and practiced some of the steps, I give the students the same test with 15 other people. The following summary highlights the performance of about 120 students in several classes: Before learning the system, 15 percent of the students remembered at least 12 of the 15 people's names, and another 28 percent remembered only 5 or fewer names. Using these steps on the second test, 3 times as many students (45 percent) remembered at least 12 names, and only 5 percent remembered 5 or fewer names.

Research studies also show the effectiveness of the system. In one study 40 college students learned the names of 13 people from their pictures; half of the students were then trained for 10 minutes on steps 2 through 4, and all of them were tested again. The trained group showed almost an 80-percent improvement, while the other group showed no improvement. (The trained group recalled an average of 10.2 names versus 5.4 for the other group.) In a second study college students were also taught steps 2 through 4 and were shown pictures of 20 people. Unlike the students in the first study, these students did not make up their own name-face associations; they were provided by the researcher. The students remembered 3 times as many names as did other students who were not taught the steps (an average of about 11 names versus about 4 names). The study also found that all three steps were necessary for maximum effectiveness, and that the weakest link was remembering the visual association given the prominent feature of the face.[34]

Elderly adults have also been able to increase their memory for names by using steps 2 through 4. They did even better when they were also taught relaxation training to reduce anxiety, or were given the additional task of rating their visual associations for pleasantness (which forced them to focus more attention on the associations). Attempts to help brain-damaged patients remember names by picturing the names (either with drawings or mental images) have also helped, but the whole system for name-face learning was too much for them to handle on their own.[35]

Even more striking proof that the system works is provided by people who are well trained in the system and who can remember the names of hundreds of people after meeting them once. For example, one memory performer has used these steps to meet several hundred people in one night and call them all by name.[36] Likewise, people have remembered thousands of names over periods of months or years by using these strategies. The mnemonist T. E. (see chapter 3) also used these steps in achieving his exceptional memory for names.

I use the system to help me learn the names of all the students in all my classes during the first week or two of each semester (sometimes as many as 200 students). To help me in using these steps with large classes, I take pictures of my classes so that I can study them outside of class. This overcomes the difficulty of trying to associate names and faces during class time when my mind must be on other things. I have been doing this since 1972, and I still have pictures of all the students who have taken classes from me since then. Not only do the pictures help me to learn students' names but they also give me a useful permanent file that I have occasionally referred to years later. Other teachers have also found similar approaches to be helpful, and one college instructor has his students apply these steps in small groups at the beginning of the semester so that they will also know one another's names.[37]

14

Using Mnemonics: Absentmindedness and Education

A college professor walking across campus was stopped by a student who asked him a question. When they finished talking, the professor asked the student, "Which way was I walking?" The student said, "You were going that way." "Good, then I've already had lunch," the professor said as he continued on his way.

This chapter discusses two areas in which memory aids can have practical value—absentmindedness and schoolwork. These two areas do not necessarily have any connection with each other except in "absent-minded professor" jokes like the one above. Absentmindedness and education are grouped together in this chapter merely because both areas represent practical uses of mnemonics that are of widespread interest and of relevance to many people.

ABSENTMINDEDNESS

Do you ever forget to mail a letter or to stop at the store for a loaf of bread on the way home? Do you ever forget to make a telephone call or to pass on a telephone message? Do you ever forget where you left your keys, your glasses, or your pen? Do you ever forget whether you locked the door, or turned off the lights or water at home? Have you ever forgotten where you parked the car, or found the lights still on when you returned to the car? Have you ever driven away from the gas pump with the gas cap on the roof of the car? Have you ever caught yourself squeezing shaving cream on your toothbrush or spraying deodorant on your hair? Have you ever found yourself pushing someone else's shopping cart in the store, or getting completely undressed and ready for bed when you just intended to change your shirt? Do you ever go into the other room to get or do something and then forget why you are there?

These are just a few examples of the wide range of experiences that fall under the heading of "absentmindedness." Is there something wrong with you if you can answer "yes" to some of these questions? No. Everyone has such experiences. One survey of 85 people yielded more than 600 specific examples of absentminded behavior like those listed above, falling into more than 30 different categories. There has been quite a lot of research interest in absentmindedness during the past decade, and much of the research has been summarized in two books from which some of the research and ideas in this chapter are drawn. [1]

Of all the principles of memory discussed earlier in this book, the one that is probably the most directly relevant to absentmindedness is attention. Failure to pay attention is a major contributing factor to most absentminded actions. In a very real sense, your attention is not focused where it should be because your mind is on something else; your mind is literally "absent." Two conditions have been found to promote absentminded actions, and attention plays an important role in both of them. You are likely to experience absentmindedness when either of the following conditions exists: Your actions are part of a habitual, well-established routine or occur in a familiar environment so that continued attention or vigilance is not required, or you are distracted by, or preoccupied with, something other than your actions so that your attention is diverted away from what you are doing.

One book describing research on absentmindedness concludes by noting that the authors have no prescriptions for how to avoid absentminded errors, because there are no simple remedies. Absentmindedness is the price we pay for being able to carry out so many complex activities with only a small investment of conscious attention, and we must accept the usually trivial consequences. The authors felt that the best they could do was to indicate the kind of circumstances where such slips are most likely to occur. [2] However, the situation might not be quite as hopeless as that. Although we might not be able to completely eliminate problems of absentmindedness, there are some things we can do that can help alleviate the problems.

When we talk about absentmindedness, we need to distinguish between two kinds of remembering—prospective and retrospective. *Prospective* memory concerns memory for future events in the form of actions that you intend to take in the future; it might be viewed as "remembering to remember." *Retrospective* memory concerns memory for past events, things we have learned in the past. For example, suppose you take a telephone message for a fellow office worker or family member. When that person returns, you need to remember to give him the message; that is prospective remembering. If he reminds you to give him the message by asking if there were any calls for him while he was out, then you need to remember what the message was; that is retrospective remembering.

PROSPECTIVE REMEMBERING

When people complain about being absentminded, or losing their memory, or having memory lapses, they are often more concerned with their failure to remember to do something they intended to do than with their failure to retrieve stored information from the past. When a person forgets something he has learned in the past, we say that his *memory* is unreliable, but when he forgets to do something he said he would do then we say that *he* is unreliable. Memory for intended actions is what makes an efficient, well-organized person.

A useful distinction may be drawn between two kinds of prospective memory. *Habitual* remembering involves things that we do on a regular basis, such as brushing our teeth or taking our daily vitamin pills. *Episodic* remembering involves things we do only occasionally or irregularly, such as picking up a loaf of bread, mailing a letter, or making a phone call.

One strategy for handling problems with habitual remembering is to incorporate the intended action in the regular stream of daily activities. For example, you could take your pill (which you might forget) each morning just before you eat breakfast (which you will not forget). Of course, the more routine you have in your life, the more effective this strategy will be. People who lead organized lives tend to notice fewer memory lapses in habitual remembering, because structure supplements—or even replaces—memory. One reason why some elderly people report fewer memory lapses than young adults is because many elderly are more reliant on a regular daily routine.[3] When the elderly do report more memory lapses, it is often because they were out of their normal routine or they had not used that information recently. Most reported problems for younger adults occur when they are under stress.[4]

Although habitual remembering can cause problems, most people have many more problems with episodic remembering than they do with habitual remembering. The wife may forget to tell her husband about an important phone call he needs to return or an appointment with the doctor; the husband may forget to mail a letter or may forget an anniversary; the student may forget to take a certain book to school or to take lunch money.

One way to remember intended actions is to make a list of what you need to do, either written in a notebook or filed mentally as described for the Loci and Phonetic systems. This method requires you to remember to look at the list frequently and regularly. Another way to help in remembering episodic intentions is to visualize some act or object that is related to the intended action, and associate it with the intended action. The wife may picture her husband coming home with a phone hanging around his neck; the husband may picture himself sitting on top of the mailbox that is next to his bus stop; the student may picture herself eating her breakfast out of her book. Then, when the wife sees the husband come in the door, the husband sees the mailbox by the bus stop, and the student sees her breakfast, they are more likely to remember the intended actions.

A simple example of my own use of this visual association technique occurred once while I was jogging around the track and remembered I needed to make a phone call concerning a piano. I could not make the call then or write a note to remind myself to do it so I pictured a piano sitting in my office. When I finished running and returned to my office, I thought of the piano as soon as I opened the door, and I made the phone call.

One woman reported that she often imagines a Dr. Suess type of household pet, a nine-foot Gleech, with bathmat ears and multicolored mink tail. When she must remember to do something, she pictures him doing it. For example, he may be at the telephone calling the rug cleaner. Later, when she calls him to mind, she sees him there and that reminds her of what she should be doing.[5]

External Reminders

Another technique that helps some people remember to perform intended actions is to make a physical change in their environment to cue them to remember the action. This is an external memory aid rather than an internal memory aid. Studies have found that in everyday life most people, from children through elderly adults, use external aids such as lists, memos to themselves, appointment books, timers and alarms, and physical changes in their environment, more than they use internal aids such as imagery, association, rhymes, acronyms, and mnemonic systems. For example, in one study elderly people reported using memory aids more often than did young adults, but the two groups were similar in the *kinds* of memory aids they used: External aids outnumbered internal aids by a ratio of about two to one.[6]

In research on the effectiveness of external aids in prospective remembering, people are typically given a set of addressed postcards or envelopes to mail on specified dates, or assignments to make phone calls at specified times. Most people use some kind of external memory aid, such as circling dates on the calendar to indicate when to mail the cards or putting the cards in a place that is frequently looked at like a bulletin board or dresser top. Several studies on remembering such "appointments" have found that the elderly remembered as well as young adults did. One study suggested that failure to do something on time (mail an envelope) is not always a failure in prospective memory—people previously identified as high procrastinators were late more than were low procrastinators.[7]

I suggested earlier that one reason why some elderly people report fewer memory lapses may be because their lives are more routine and organized; another reason the researchers suggested is that the elderly may make more use of external aids. External aids may be necessary if you are very busy, if you become engrossed in something else, or if you might be distracted by unexpected events. One of the problems in prospective remembering is that you might remember several times during the day that you need to mail a letter or make a phone call, but not at a time when you can do it.

Carrying out an intended action is not only a matter of remembering to do it but also of remembering to do it *at the right time*. Suppose that just before you left the house for work you thought of a phone call you needed to make or a book you needed to take; you could make the call or grab the book, and you would be glad you "remembered." But if you thought of them a few minutes later while driving down the street, you would complain about "forgetting." Thus, *when* and *where* we remember can be as important as *whether* we remember. We often need something to cue us, to call our attention to the intended action so that we are reminded to remember at the right time. Special cuing devices have even been developed for this purpose, such as special alarms and timers combined with visual or spoken messages.[8]

A straightforward example of a physical reminder is to put a book by the door so that you will remember to take it back to the library the next time you go out, or to hang your coat on the doorknob so that you will remember to take it to the cleaners. A similar method is to make a *symbolic* change in the environment to cue yourself, a change that is not directly related to the intended action. The well-known example of the string around the finger illustrates this strategy. The string is intended to remind you that there is something you need to remember, and the novelty of the string will usually serve that purpose (unless, of course, you normally wear a string around your finger). If you want to be less conspicuous than having a string around your finger, you might put a rubber band on your wrist, move your watch to the other wrist, move a ring to a different finger, turn your ring around so that the stone faces the palm, or put your keys in a different pocket. All of these changes serve to cue you that you need to remember something.

This strategy of symbolic reminders can also be used for the times when you remember at night (as you are trying to get to sleep) something that you need to do in the morning, and then in the morning you cannot remember what it was, or maybe do not even remember that you needed to remember something. A helpful technique is to reach over and turn your alarm clock on end, throw a book on the floor, or turn the radio around—something that you will notice in the morning. When you get up the next morning, you will see the thing that is out of place and be reminded that there is something you need to remember. I use this strategy sometimes when I turn my car lights on and do not want to forget to turn them off after parking. To remind me to turn them off before getting out of the car, I hang something (for example, a glove) on the door handle. When I park the car and reach for the handle to open the door, I am reminded to turn off the lights.

There is one limitation of these symbolic physical reminders. They do help you remember that you wanted to remember something, and thus start the search for retrieval, but they do not help you directly remember *what* it was you wanted to remember. Is the string around your finger to remind you to buy some string? Is the book lying in the middle of the floor to remind you to take it back to the library? Is the glove on the door handle to remind you to put on your gloves?

If you are concerned about remembering what it is you wanted to remember, an additional step that will make the symbolic external reminders more effective is to add an internal aid: Associate the physical change with the intended action. If the string on your finger is to remind you to mail a letter, you might picture yourself dropping string in the mailbox. If the book on the floor is to remind you to leave a note for the milkman, you might picture yourself stuffing the book into a milk bottle. If the watch on the wrong wrist is to remind you to make a phone call, you might picture yourself calling the person on your watch.

Actually, most of the time you will find that remembering what you wanted to remember is not a problem: As long as there is a cue to remind you that you need to remember something, your natural memory will usually tell you what it is you needed to remember. For example, in one study with six- and eight-year-old children the researcher sat a toy clown out where the children could see it, to remind them to have him open a "surprise box" for them at the end of the research session. About three-fourths of the children reminded him to open the box when the clown was out, as compared with only about half the children when the clown was not out.[9]

RETROSPECTIVE REMEMBERING

Almost all memory research (and almost all of this book) deals with retrospective memory: You do not need to remember to remember because the researcher tells you when it is time to recall the word list, or the teacher asks you a question or gives you the exam. Someone prompts you to recall. (This is different from "cued" or "aided" recall, where you are given a cue as to *what* you are to remember rather than *when* to remember.)

Some kinds of absentmindedness involve retrospective memory. Retrospective absentmindedness differs from the kinds of retrospective memory that have been the subject of most research in that it deals with memory for our own actions rather than memory for other information. It also differs from prospective memory in that research has been conducted on using imagery in retrospective memory more than in prospective memory (where, as we have seen, external aids are used more often than internal aids).[10]

One common kind of retrospective absentmindedness is forgetting whether you did something, such as turn off the lights when you left the house or lock all the doors before going to bed. Part of the problem in remembering such past actions is that you might have thought about doing it, and later cannot remember whether you actually did it or just thought about it. This is a normal experience. Some people are "checkers," having to continually check to confirm that a task has been completed. In its extreme form, continuous checking is a compulsive disorder, but in milder forms it also is very common among normal people.[11]

Another kind of retrospective absentmindedness is forgetting where we put something, such as our umbrella or car keys, or even the car itself. (Have you ever driven to a big concert or sports event, parked your car, and then after the event, as you looked over the thousands of cars, you could not remember where yours was?)

As I noted in chapter 4, a major cause of these kinds of retrospective

absentmindedness lies in the principle of attention. You were probably
not consciously paying attention to what you were doing at the time you
turned off the lights, locked the doors, set down your car keys, or
parked the car. Your mind was on something else. Thus, one way to
overcome these two kinds of absentmindedness (forgetting whether you
did something or where you put something) is to do something to focus
your attention on what you are doing. You might tell yourself as you
leave the house, "I am locking the door," or as you park the car, "I am
parking the car in the far northeast corner of the lot," or as you put
down the keys, "I am putting the keys on the refrigerator." It only takes
a fraction of a second to think this to yourself, and your attention is
focused on what you are doing; thus, there is a greater likelihood that
you will later be able to remember having done it. In addition, it may
help to actually form a mental picture of the car keys on the refrigerator.

One student in my memory class had a particular problem with
forgetting where she put her car keys. She was often rounding up her
roommates in search groups to help her hunt for her keys. She tried this
technique of telling herself whenever she put her keys down, only she
went one step further. She told herself *out loud* where she was putting
them. She reported that it almost drove her roommates crazy, but she
did not have any trouble remembering where her keys were (nor did her
roommates, and they did not even particularly want to know!).

If you did not pay attention to what you were doing at the time you
did it, there is a strategy that can help overcome retrospective absentmindedness at the retrieval stage (rather than at the recording stage).
Mentally retrace your steps. Go back in your mind and think about what
you were doing that led up to the act you are trying to remember; it
might help you remember whether you did the specific action or where
you put the item. This technique, which is similar to "thinking around it"
in chapter 4, was the most frequently used internal memory aid reported
in a survey of college students and housewives in England; nearly
everyone had used it at least once, and about 30 percent of them had
used it more than once a week. [12]

For most people retrospective absentmindedness is just an incon-
venience. But for urban elderly people such forgetfulness can endanger
not only their well-being but also their safety: It may be *annoying* to
misplace eyeglasses, but in a big city it is *dangerous* to leave front doors
unlocked. A memory course for people over age seventy in the Bronx in
New York City taught them the techniques in this chapter for overcoming
absentmindedness, and helped them reduce their problems of losing
things (eyeglasses, keys, canes, gloves, money) and of forgetting to lock
their doors. The imagery techniques were most successful with people

whose memories were more intact, whereas habit and repetition helped those people with serious memory deficits.[13]

Another kind of absentmindedness that is a source of irritation to many people is going into another room to get something or do something, and then forgetting why you are there. This is one memory lapse that can make people feel like they are really losing their minds, and thus we can take some comfort in knowing that it also is a common experience for many people. A national Roper survey found that 9 of 10 people admitted to having faulty memories, and that the most common lapse was going into a room and forgetting what they went in there for (reported by 59 percent of those surveyed).[14] Again, the most likely cause of this problem is failure to pay sufficient attention to what you are doing. Often you just have a passing thought enter your mind of something you need to do in the other room, and before you mentally grab the thought you start moving into the other room as your mind moves on to other things. If you stop and concentrate for just a second on the thought and actually tell yourself why you are going into the other room before you go, you are more likely to remember why you are there when you get there. Also, it may be of additional help to briefly picture yourself doing what you intend to do when you get there.

Association is another principle that can play an important role in the "other room" kind of absentmindedness. Sometimes when you find yourself in the other room wondering why you are there, you have probably looked around the room to see if there is something that will remind you of why you are there (because it may be associated with your errand). If that does not work, you might try going back to doing what you were doing at the time you first thought of going to the room. Suppose, for example, you were standing at the kitchen sink having a drink of water just before you went in the other room; go back to the sink and pick up your water again. Often this will remind you of what you needed to do, because the thought became associated with what you were doing when the thought came to you. Sometimes it can even help to mentally (rather than physically) go back and think of what you were doing when you first thought of going to the room. This strategy is similar to mentally retracing your steps to remember whether you did something or where you put something.

MNEMONICS IN EDUCATION

In addition to overcoming absentmindedness, memory aids can have practical value in schoolwork. We saw in chapter 8 that research on mnemonics began in the 1960s. By the early 1970s, several psychologists and researchers had suggested the potential value of mnemonics in education. Psychologists and researchers have continued to encourage educational applications of mnemonics in the 1980s. A book for high school teachers on how to teach study skills suggests that "mnemonic devices should not be scorned by study skills teachers. Too many of them have proved effective for students through the centuries and are still being used by successful students." One psychologist has listed 10 reasons why mnemonic techniques can and should be taught in the schools, and supported them with research evidence. A few of the reasons were: Mnemonics are versatile; mnemonics are time efficient; mnemonics are adaptable to student differences; and most children enjoy using mnemonics. [15]

A great amount of research published since the late 1970s has shown that mnemonics can help in the kinds of memory tasks required in school. Much of this research has been described in previous chapters and additional research is described in many recent review articles. [16] Examples of specific subjects that mnemonics have been found to help are spelling, foreign language vocabulary (concrete nouns, abstract nouns, verbs), English vocabulary words and definitions, states and capitals, people's names and their accomplishments, medical terms, reading, properties of minerals, the hardness scale of minerals, cities and their products, and U.S. presidents. Memory-training books give specific examples of how mnemonics could also be applied to many other school subjects. [17]

Much of this research on mnemonics in school has used the Keyword mnemonic, and has provided mnemonic pictures (rather than using self-generated mental images) to represent verbal material. The research has been done on material in textbook prose form as well as in list form, and has involved many different kinds of student of all ages.

Mnemonics have been found to benefit good students as well as poor students. Even gifted students in elementary school, as young as fourth graders, have improved their learning by using imagery mnemonics that they have been taught, although they already spontaneously use more elaborate and effective learning strategies than their peers. In fact, gifted students may benefit even more from mnemonics than other students do. [18]

One of the conclusions stated in the U.S. Department of Education book *What Works* is: "Mnemonics help students remember more information faster and retain it longer." Mnemonics that can be used in school have also been summarized from the teachers' perspective as well as that of the students. [19]

Extensive mnemonic programs based on stories, rhymes, and songs have been developed and used by a Japanese educator, Masachika Nakane, for learning mathematics (arithmetic, algebra, geometry, trigonometry, and calculus), science (chemistry, physics, and biology), spelling and grammar, and the English language. Japanese children as young as kindergarten have used these mnemonics to perform mathematical operations with fractions, to solve algebraic problems (including the use of the quadratic formula), to do elementary calculus, to generate formulas for chemical compounds and diagram their molecular structure, and to learn English.

Some of Nakane's mnemonics for adding, subtracting, multiplying, and dividing fractions have been adapted for use in the United States. One study found that third-grade children using these mnemonics learned all the mathematical operations with fractions in 3 hours as well as sixth-grade students had learned them in three years of traditional instruction. I also used these mnemonics to teach my son all the operations with fractions when he was still in the second grade (after he learned his times tables as described in chapter 12). Extensive mnemonic programs have also been developed in the United States for such areas as reading, spelling, grammar, and basic mathematics skills.[20]

We have seen many examples in previous chapters of ways my memory students have used mnemonics in their schoolwork. Several college students who have taken my memory course as juniors or seniors have commented that they wished they had taken the course when they were freshmen, because it would have done them more good in school. Also, many of my students, especially older students who have children of their own, have expressed their wish that these techniques were taught in school before college. One father who expressed such a wish wrote the following:

Today I sent an eight-year-old daughter to school feeling better about her chances of passing an exam on presidents of the United States. When I read such questions as which one liked fancy clothes or who formed the rough riders, I could see why Karen was upset. There were 50 such associations and she was ready to give up. It became a family project and everyone began to give ideas of associations. We could see the fancy clothes neatly packed in a chest of drawers (Chester Arthur). A teddy bear on a rough riding horse became Teddy Roosevelt. This could have been a situation that made Karen feel very inadequate but it turned into a fun session for the entire family.

I don't know how well she did on the test, but I do know that she will do better just because of her self-image improvement. . . . The rote learning that she had to do could have developed a thought pattern or a contorted self-image that could have been a negative experience that could stay with her for years.

. . . Karen just came home from school with an 88 percent on her presidents exam. She certainly is a happier, more confident little girl than she was last night.

In light of all the research support and other supportive evidence, you might think that there would be a trend toward teaching mnemonics in school, but this has not happened as much as the research might seem to justify. Mnemonics are not taught in most schools at any level. In fact, this is not only limited to mnemonics but is also true of other learning and memory strategies in this book. Explicit instruction in any strategies for effective thinking and learning rarely occur in the classroom. [21]

Two extensive programs on learning at the college level have been well researched and described at Texas Christian University and at the University of Texas at Austin. Both deal with learning how to learn, including mnemonics and other learning strategies in this book, and have been quite successful. There are also a few similar programs in other school districts below the college level, but generally little is taught at any school level about how to learn more effectively. [22]

It is strange that we expect students to learn, solve problems, and remember a lot of material, but we seldom teach them *how* to learn, solve problems, and remember. It is time to make up for this lack by developing applied courses in learning, problem solving, and memory, and by incorporating them in the academic curriculum. This was the justification that was given for including a chapter on learning strategies in a recent book on effective teaching.[23]

There are many obstacles to incorporating any kind of educational research into schools. [24] One reason why mnemonics are not taught more frequently in schools may be that many educators are not aware of the recent research showing how and why mnemonics could be used. A second reason probably lies in the pseudo-limitations discussed in chapter 8. Two psychologists who have done extensive research on memory have called these pseudo-limitations "the persisting nemesis" of mnemonic techniques in the classroom because, they said, as history has consistently shown with respect to most avenues of change, it takes far more than fact to combat the fiction of firmly entrenched personal philosophies. [25]

Although several of the pseudo-limitations have been espoused by many educators, the one that is probably most significant in preventing the teaching and using of mnemonics in schools is the one involving mnemonics and understanding. [26] Many educators feel mnemonics are not relevant to school subjects because most mnemonics help with learning and remembering more than they do with understanding and comprehending. To better understand this point, let us examine the role of memory in education (also see the section "Mnemonics Do Not Aid Understanding" in chapter 8).

MEMORY IN EDUCATION

Memorization is a low-level mental skill to many educators, so they usually state the purposes of education in terms of loftier goals than remembering, such as understanding and applying principles, critical and creative thinking, reasoning, and synthesizing. (You may often hear disparaging remarks about mere memorizing, but how often have you heard someone speak of "mere" understanding or "mere" creativity?) As one review of memory research observed, some educators "give the impression that they regard memory proficiency as antithetical to academic excellence, feeling that memorization interferes with the operation of more laudable, higher mental processes." The reviewers suggested that such misconceptions must be dispelled for research on memory to make a positive contribution to educational practice.[27]

Two points may be made regarding the role of memory relative to the loftier goals or "more laudable, higher mental processes" in school. First, whether we like it or not there is a lot of straight memory work in school. Education consists of "basic school tasks" involving list and paired-associate learning, as well as "complex school tasks" like meaningful prose learning. One history teacher argued that memory was unimportant in education today; then at an early class period he told his students that for a test they must list the U.S. presidents and their terms in office. ("You must all know the presidents in chronological order, and the dates, before the end of this term.") Psychologist Gordon Bower observed that the loftier educational goals are usually only extra requirements beyond the learning of basic facts that is demanded as a minimum standard.

Any geography student who thinks Istanbul is in France, or any art history student who thinks Salvador Dali painted the Sistine Chapel, is going to flunk his exams if he pulls such boners often enough. The point is that we do demand that students learn a lot of facts just as we are constantly required to do in our daily life. . . .[28]

The fact is that the loftier educational goals are *in addition to*, not *instead of*, memorization. One analysis of the goals of education divided general thinking and learning skills into three areas—knowledge acquisition (including memory aids and study techniques), problem solving, and reasoning. An analysis of the process of education viewed learning in terms of stages. In the early stages we acquire a number of relatively disparate pieces of information (the "basic facts" stressed in most classrooms). Mnemonics or other learning strategies may facilitate such learning by providing the "conceptual glue" necessary to hold these disparate pieces in memory. As a person begins to fit the pieces together, mnemonics may play a less important (or different) role, and other factors may be more important. Still later, when the performance is well established, mnemonics may have little or no effect on learning since the underlying knowledge structure now holds the information together in some meaningful, integrated whole. Both of these analyses include remembering facts as a significant part of the big picture, and both view mnemonics as playing a role in that part. [29]

Anyone who is a student in school, or can remember when he was, knows that success on exams depends heavily on remembering facts. I asked 33 college freshmen and 24 upperclassmen from many different majors to rate how important memorization was as compared with the "higher thinking skills (understanding, reasoning, critical and creative thinking, synthesizing, etc.)" in determining their exam scores in high school and in college. For their exams in high school, 76 percent of the freshman and 96 percent of the upperclassmen rated memorization as being of equal or greater importance than the higher thinking skills. Even for their college exams, half of the students (49 percent of the freshmen and 50 percent of the upperclassmen) still rated memorization as being of equal or greater importance. Whatever lofty goals teachers may espouse, or may think that they are testing, students still see memory as playing a significant role in their school success.

Memorizing the necessary routine things more efficiently may help to free our minds so that we can spend more time on the so-called loftier tasks. After his above observation that much of schoolwork is straight memory work, Bower went on to say:

But the solution to the problem is probably at hand. By systematically applying the knowledge that we now have about learning, we should be able to improve our skills so that we spend less time memorizing facts. By the strategic use of mnemonics, we might free ourselves for those tasks we consider more important than memorization.

The second point regarding the role of memory in education is that remembered facts serve as the basis for the loftier goals. One review of memory research began with this statement: "It is hard to think of any educational goal for which the ability to retain information is unimportant; human memory is crucial for acquiring the knowledge and skills we learn at school." In one study, students who took a comprehension test on a passage from memory did better than students who could refer to the passage while taking the test. The researchers suggested that memorizing individual facts may be a necessary precursor to a thorough understanding of the relations among the facts. Similarly, learning-disabled adolescents who learned attributes of minerals using mnemonic pictures were better able to make inferences about the attributes than were students taught the traditional way, even though such information was never explicitly presented in the lesson.[30]

Other researchers have also suggested that tasks involving reasoning and understanding still require that you remember the facts in order to be able to reason with them and understand them, and that one reason why mnemonics may help in acquiring concepts is that they reduce the memory load for the facts that are necessary for understanding the concept. In fact, one book on clear thinking even defined thinking as "the manipulation of memories."[31]

Memory also plays an important role in decision making and problem solving. Studies of problem solving in such areas as engineering, computer programming, social science, reading comprehension, physics, medical diagnosis, and mathematics have shown that effective problem solving depends strongly on the nature and organization of the knowledge available to the individuals. Mnemonics have even been conceptualized as problem-solving techniques for solving some memory problems.[32]

One of the conclusions contained in *What Works* is that ". . . memorizing can help students absorb and retain the factual information on which understanding and critical thought are based." The conclusion is explained further:

Memorizing simplifies the process of recalling information and allows its use to become automatic. Understanding and critical thought can then build on this base of knowledge and fact. Indeed, the more sophisticated mental operations of analysis, synthesis, and evaluation are impossible without rapid and accurate recall of bodies of specific knowledge.[33]

Thus, we have seen that even if we state the goals of education as going beyond "mere memorization" to understanding, reasoning, and problem solving, mnemonics can still help in school for at least two reasons: Many schoolwork tasks involve memorization, so memorizing these tasks more efficiently will free us to spend more time and effort on the advanced goals, and these memorized facts serve as the basis for achieving the more advanced goals.

Appendix: Keywords for the Phonetic System

The following list consists of several keywords for each number from 00 to 09 and from 0 to 100. These keywords are based on the Phonetic system (see chapter 12) and can be used in at least two ways. First, you can select a keyword for each number from 1 to 100 that will be meaningful and memorable to you, constructing a mental filing system for memorizing 100 items. Second, you can reduce forgetting caused by interference among different numbers that have the same pairs of digits in them by using a different keyword each time a pair of digits is repeated. For example, there will be less interference among the phone numbers 3905, 0542, and 4239 if they are remembered by *mop-sail, seal-rain,* and *horn-map* than if they are remembered by *mop-sail, sail-rain,* and *rain-mop.*

00   sauce zoos hoses seas seesaw oasis icehouse Zeus Seuss
01   suit seed sod seat soot waste waist city soda stew acid
02   sun scene zone sin snow swine swan
03   sum zoom Siam swim seam asthma
04   sore soar seer sewer sower hosiery czar
05   sail seal sale sly slow sleigh soil soul
06   sash sage switch siege
07   sack sock sick hassock ski sky whisky squaw
08   safe sieve sofa housewife
09   soap sub spy wasp asp soup subway

0 hose sew sow saw house zoo sea ace ice

1 tie tee tea hat head doe toe toy wheat dye hood auto weed

2 hen Noah hone inn honey gnu wine hyena

3 ma ham hem hymn aim home mow

4 rye ray hair hare row oar arrow ore wire

5 hole law hill hall heel owl eel ale whale awl halo hell wheel

6 shoe hash hedge ash witch show jaw jay wash

7 cow hog key hook cue echo hawk egg hockey oak wig

8 ivy hoof hive wave wife waif

9 bee pie hub hoop ape pea boy bay buoy oboe whip

10 toes dice heads woods toys daisy

11 tot date dot diet toad tide tattoo teeth

12 tin dune dean heathen dawn down twine

13 tomb dome team tummy dam atom autumn dime thumb

14 tire door tray tree deer tar tower dairy heater water waiter

15 towel doll tool dial hotel tail tile duel huddle Italy idol outlaw

16 dish dash tissue

17 tack dock deck duck dog toga twig dike attic

18 dove dive taffy TV thief

19 tub tape dope deb tube depot

20 nose news henhouse noose knees

21 net nut knot hunt window wand wind knight nude ant aunt

22 nun noon onion noun

23 gnome name enemy

24 Nero winner Henry wiener winery

25 nail kneel Nellie Nile

26 notch Nash winch hinge niche wench

27 hanky nag neck nick wink ink Inca

28 knave knife Navy nephew envoy

29 knob honeybee nap

30 mice mouse moose moss maze hams Messiah mass mess

31 mat mitt meat mate mud moth mouth maid meadow moat

32 moon man mane money mine woman human

33 Miami mom mummy mama mime

34 mayor mower moor hammer myrrh

35 mail mule male meal mole mill mall

36 match mooch mush mesh image

37 mug mike hammock

38 muff movie

39 mop map mob amoeba imp

40 rose rice horse rays ears race hearse warehouse iris

41 rot road heart wart rod reed yard radio rut art earth herd wreath

42 rain ruin heron horn Rhine iron urn
43 ram room harem worm rum arm army Rome
44 rower roar rear error harrier warrior aurora
45 roll rail reel role rule railway
46 roach rouge rash ridge rich raja Russia arch
47 rock rake rag rack rug arc ark
48 roof reef wharf
49 harp rope rib robe rabbi herb ruby
50 hails hills lace louse lice lassoe walls halls
51 lot lead loot hailed light wallet lady eyelid lid
52 line loon lion lane lawn
53 loom lime helm lamb llama limb elm
54 lyre lair lure leer lawyer
55 lily lolly Lulu
56 ledge leech latch lodge
57 log lake lock leak leg elk
58 loaf elf lava leaf wolf
59 lip lab lap loop lobby alp elbow
60 hedges cheese juice shoes chaise chess ashes
61 sheet chute jet washed jade shade shadow shed
62 chin gin jean gene chain ocean China
63 gem gym jam chum chime
64 shore jar cheer chair jury shower sherry usher washer
65 jewel jail Jell-O shale chili shawl jelly
66 hashish judge choo-choo
67 jack jug shock jock chalk check sheik jockey chick
68 chef chief shave shove java Chevy chaff
69 ship shop chop job jab sheep jeep chip
70 case gas hogs wigs wicks wax ox goose cows ax kiss gauze
71 cat coat goat cod kid gate cot kite caddie act
72 Cain cane can coin gown gun wagon coon queen canoe
73 comb game gum cam comma coma
74 car core gear cry choir crow
75 coal coil goal gill gale keel quail eagle ghoul glue
76 cage cash gauge couch coach
77 cake cook gag cog keg cock
78 calf gaff cuff cave coffee cove
79 cab hiccup cup cap cape cob gob coop cube cub
80 face fez fuse hoofs waves hives wives vase office
81 feed food feet foot vote photo
82 vein fin fan vane van oven heaven phone vine fawn
83 foam fame fume vim

84 fire weaver wafer fry heifer fur fairy fir ivory
85 veil fly filly veal foal fowl foil flue flea valley
86 fudge fish voyage effigy
87 fig fog fake havoc
88 fife five
89 fob fib fop VIP
90 pies bees bows boys peas base bus pizza abyss
91 beat pot pad bead pit boot boat path bat poet bed body
92 pin bean bun bone pan pine pane pony piano pen penny pawn
93 bomb boom beam bum poem puma opium
94 boar pear pray beer pier bar berry opera
95 bill bowl bell pile pill plow apple pail ball pillow bull eyeball
96 peach patch beach pitch bush page badge
97 bag bug peg pig back pack pick puck book beak bouquet
98 pave puff beef beehive buff
99 baby pipe pop Pope puppy papa
100 disease thesis doses diocese daisies

Chapter Notes

Each time a source is cited after the first time, it is identified by the last name of the author and the chapter and reference number where it was first cited. For example, "Hunter (1/5)" in chapter 1, reference 9, means that this is the same source originally cited in chapter 1, reference 5.

CHAPTER 1

1. F. I. M. Craik, "Paradigms in Human Memory Research," in *Perspectives on Learning and Memory*, ed. L. Nilsson and T. Archer (Hillsdale, N.J.: Erlbaum, 1985), 200.

2. M. K. Johnson and L. Hasher, "Human Learning and Memory," in *Annual Review of Psychology* vol. 38, ed. M. R. Rosenzweig and L. W. Porter (Palo Alto, Calif.: Annual Reviews, Inc., 1987), 631–68.

3. B. J. Underwood, *Attributes of Memory* (Glenview, Ill.: Scott, Foresman & Co., 1983).

4. Wechsler—N. Brooks and N. B. Lincoln, "Assessment for Rehabilitation," in *Clinical Management of Memory Problems*, ed. B. A. Wilson and N. Moffat (London: Croom Helm, 1984), 28–45. Nine scales—L. W. Poon, "Differences in Human Memory With Aging: Nature, Causes, and Clinical Applications," in *Handbook of the Psychology of Aging*, 2d ed., ed. J. E. Birren and K. W. Schaie (New York: Van Nostrand Reinhold, 1985), 427–62.

5. I. M. L. Hunter, *Memory*, rev. ed. (Middlesex, England: Penguin Books Ltd., 1964), 282–83.

6. R. F. Carlson, J. P. Kincaid, S. Lance, and T. Hodgson, "Spontaneous Use of Mnemonics and Grade Point Average," *The Journal of Psychology* 92 (1976): 117–22; B. J. Zimmerman and M. M. Pons, "Development of a Structured Interview for Assessing Student Use of Self-regulated Learning Strategies," *American Educational Research Journal* 23 (1986): 614–28.

7. P. R. Pintrich, D. R. Cross, R. B. Kozman, and W. J. McKeachie, "Instructional Psychology," in Rosenzweig and Porter (1/2, vol. 37, 1986), 611–51; M. Pressley, J. G. Borkowski, and W. Schneider, "Good Strategy Users Coordinate Metacognition, Strategy Use, and Knowledge," in *Annals of Child Development*, vol. 4, ed. R. Vasta and G. Whitehurst (Greenwich, Conn.: JAI Press, 1987), 89–129.

8. Schooling—M.T. Zivian and R. W. Darjes, "Free Recall By In-School and Out-of-School Adults: Performance and Metamemory," *Developmental Psychology* 19 (1983): 513–20. Habits—G. E. Rice and B. J. F. Meyer, "The Relation of Everyday Activities of Adults to Their Prose Recall Performance" (paper presented at the meeting of the American Educational Research Association, San Francisco, April 1986).

9. Hunter (1/5), 14.

10. Sources for this section include J. E. Birren and W. R. Cunningham, "Research on the Psychology of Aging: Principles, Concepts and Theory," in Birren and Schaie (1/4), 3–34; N. Datan, D. Rodeheaver, and F. Hughes, "Adult Development and Aging," in Rosenzweig and Porter (1/2), 153–80; Poon (1/4); P. Roberts, "Memory Strategy Instruction with the Elderly: What Should Memory Training Be the Training of?" in *Cognitive Strategy Research: Psychological Foundations*, ed. M. Pressley and J. R. Levin (New York: Springer-Verlag, 1983), 75–100.

11. S. L. Willis and K. W. Schaie, "Practical Intelligence in Later Adulthood," in *Practical Intelligence: Nature and Origins of Competence in the Everyday World*, ed. R. J. Sternberg and R. K. Wagner (Cambridge: Cambridge University Press, 1986), 236–68.

12. Poon (1/4); L. W. Poon, L. Walsh-Sweeney, and J. L. Fozard, "Memory Skill Training for the Elderly: Salient Issues on the Use of Imagery Mnemonics," in *New Directions in Memory and Aging*, ed. L. W. Poon, J. L. Fozard, L. S. Cermak, D. Arenberg, and L. W. Thompson (Hillsdale, N.J.: Erlbaum, 1980), 461–84; C. L. McEvoy and J. R. Moon, "Assessment and Treatment of Everyday Memory Problems in the Elderly," in *Practical Aspects of Memory: Current Research and Issues*, ed. M. M. Gruneberg, P. E. Morris, and R. N. Sykes (Chichester, England: Wiley, in press 1988).

13. M. Pressley and C. J. Brainerd, *Cognitive Learning and Memory in Children: Progress in Cognitive Development Research* (New York: Springer-Verlag, 1985); H. S. Waters and C. Andreassen, "Children's Use of Memory Strategies under Instruction," in Pressley and Levin (1/10).

14. First example—S. Witt, *How to Be Twice as Smart* (West Nyack, N. Y.: Parker Publishing Co., 1983), 7. Second example—L. Belliston and C. Mayfield, *Speed Learning, Super Recall* (Woodland Hills, Utah: SB Publishers, 1983), 10.

15. W. James, *Principles of Psychology*, vol. 1 (New York: Henry Holt & Co., 1890). Twelve-year-olds—S. A. Mednick, H. R. Pollio, and E. F. Loftus, *Learning*, 2d ed. (Englewood Cliffs, N.J.: Prentice-Hall, 1973), 131. College students—K. A.

Ericsson and W. G. Chase, "Exceptional Memory," *American Scientist* 70 (1982): 607–15.

16. For more discussion of mental discipline see M. L. Biggs, *Learning Theories for Teachers*, 4th ed. (New York: Harper & Row, 1982), 24–33, 256–59.

17. H. Lorayne, *How to Develop a Super-Power Memory* (New York: New American Library, 1974, originally published in 1957), 138.

18. The sources of the three quotes are, respectively, R. L. Montgomery, *Memory Made Easy* (New York: AMOCOM, 1981), 11; Belliston and Mayfield (1/14), 10; and Witt (1/14), 4.

19. 4 percent—C. Rose, *Accelerated Learning* (England: Topaz Publishing Ltd., 1985), 5. 1 percent—T. Buzan, *Making the Most of Your Mind* (New York: Simon and Schuster, 1984), 13.

20. Rose (1/19), 26.

21. Witt (1/14), 4.

CHAPTER 2

1. R. J. Baron, *The Cerebral Computer: An Introduction to the Computational Structure of the Human Brain* (Hillsdale, N. J.: Erlbaum, 1987).

2. Pintrich et al. (1/7).

3. A. Baddeley, *Your Memory: A User's Guide* (New York: MacMillan, 1982); V. H. Gregg, *Introduction to Human Memory* (London: Routledge and Kegan Paul, 1986); E. Loftus, *Memory* (Reading, Mass.: Addison-Wesley, 1980); L. Stern, *The Structures and Strategies of Human Memory* (Homewood, Ill.: Dorsey Press, 1985); A. Wingfield and D. L. Byrnes, *The Psychology of Human Memory* (New York: Academic Press, 1981); E. B. Zechmeister and S. E. Nyberg, *Human Memory: An Introduction to Research and Theory* (Monterey, Calif.: Brooks/Cole, 1982).

4. P. Muter, "Very Rapid Forgetting," *Memory & Cognition* 8 (1980): 174–79.

5. J. J. Watkins and T. M. Graefe, "Delayed Rehearsal of Pictures," *Journal of Verbal Learning and Verbal Behavior* 20 (1981): 276–88.

6. R. F. Schilling and G. E. Weaver, "Effects of Extraneous Verbal Information on Memory for Telephone Numbers," *Journal of Applied Psychology* 68 (1983): 559–64.

7. Elderly—Poon (1/4); Oriental cultures versus Western cultures—B. Yu, W. Chang, Q. Jing, R. Peng, G. Zhang, and H. A. Simon, "STM Capacity for Chinese and English Language Materials," *Memory & Cognition* 13 (1983): 202–07.

8. H. A. Simon, "How Big Is a Chunk?" *Science* 183 (1974): 482–88.

9. D. H. Holding, *The Psychology of Chess Skill* (Hillsdale, N. J.: Erlbaum, 1985). J. D. Milojkovic, "Chess Imagery in Novice and Master," *Journal of Mental Imagery* 6 (1982): 125–44.

10. K. A. Ericsson and H. A. Simon, *Protocol Analysis: Verbal Reports as Data* (Cambridge, Mass.: MIT Press, 1984).

11. R. R. Bootzin, G. H. Bower, R. B. Zajonc, and E. Hall, *Psychology Today: An Introduction*, 6th ed. (New York: Random House, 1986), 222.

12. W. F. Brewer and J. R. Pani, "The Structure of Human Memory," in *The Psychology of Learning and Motivation: Advances in Research and Theory*, vol. 17, ed.

G. H. Bower (New York: Academic Press, 1983), 1–38; E. Tulving, "How Many Memory Systems Are There?" *American Psychologist* 40 (1985): 385–98.

13. W. Penfield, *The Mystery of the Mind* (Princeton: Princeton University Press, 1975). Some psychologists have argued that such evidence does not necessarily prove that all memories are permanent. See E. Loftus and G. Loftus, "On the Permanence of Stored Information in the Human Brain," *American Psychologist* 35 (1980): 409–20; but compare M. B. Arnold, *Memory and the Brain* (Hillsdale, N. J.: Erlbaum, 1984), 50–52.

14. For more information about K. F. see T. Shallice and E. K. Warrington, "Independent Functioning of Verbal Memory Stores: A Neuropsychological Study," *Quarterly Journal of Experimental Psychology* 22 (1970): 261–73. For more information about H. M. see B. Milner, "Amnesia Following Operation on the Temporal Lobes," in *Amnesia*, ed. C. W. M. Whitty and O. L. Zangwill (London: Butterworth & Co., 1966), 109–33.

15. R. L. Klatzky, *Human Memory: Structures and Processes*, 2d ed. (San Francisco: W. H. Freeman & Co., 1980), 88.

16. These are the three most common direct measures of memory, although there are other direct and indirect measures—Johnson and Hasher (1/2).

17. 600 pairs—R. N. Shepard, "Recognition Memory for Words, Sentences and Pictures," *Journal of Verbal Learning and Verbal Behavior* 6 (1967): 156–63. Performance of the elderly—Poon (1/4).

18. H. P. Bahrick, D. O. Bahrick, and R. P. Wittlinger, "Fifty Years of Memory for Names and Faces: A Cross-sectional Approach," *Journal of Experimental Psychology* 104 (1975): 54–75.

19. L. K. Groninger and L. D. Groninger, "A Comparison of Recognition and Savings as Retrieval Measures: A Reexamination," *Bulletin of the Psychonomic Society* 15 (1980): 263–66.

20. H. P. Bahrick, "Memory for People," in *Everyday Memory, Actions, and Absent-mindedness*, ed. J. E. Harris and P. E. Morris (London: Academic Press, 1984), 19–34.

21. H. E. Burtt, "An Experimental Study of Early Childhood Memory: Final Report," *Journal of Genetic Psychology* 58 (1941): 435–39.

22. D. L. Horton and C. B. Mills, "Human Learning and Memory," in Rosenzweig and Porter (1/2, Vol. 35., 1984), 361–94.

23. G. Reed, "Everyday Anomalies of Recall and Recognition," in *Functional Disorders of Memory*, ed. J. F. Kihlstrom and F. J. Evans (Hillsdale, N.J.: Erlbaum, 1979), 1–28.

24. Most of the research in this section has been summarized by J. Reason, and K. Mycielska, *Absent-minded? The Psychology of Mental Lapses and Everyday Errors* (Englewood Cliffs, N.J.: Prentice-Hall, 1982); J. Reason and D. Lucas, "Using Cognitive Diaries to Investigate Naturally Occurring Memory Blocks," in Harris and Morris (2/20), 53–70.

25. A. D. Yarmey, "I Recognize Your Face but I Can't Remember Your Name: Further Evidence on the Tip-of-the-Tongue Phenomenon," *Memory & Cognition* 3 (1973): 287–90; L. T. Kozlowski, "Effects of Distorted Auditory and of Rhyming Cues on Retrieval of Tip-of-the-Tongue Words by Poets and Nonpoets," *Memory & Cogni-*

tion 5 (1977): 477–81; H. Lawless and T. Engen, "Associations to Odors: Interference, Mnemonics, and Verbal Labeling," *Journal of Experimental Psychology: Human Learning and Memory* 3 (1977): 52–59.
26. Research—Poon (1/4). Diary—D. Burke, "I'll Never Forget What's His Name: Aging and the Tip-of-the-Tongue Experience," in Gruneberg et al. (1/12).

CHAPTER 3

1. J. Deese, "On the Prediction of Occurrence of Particular Verbal Intrusions in Immediate Recall," *Journal of Experimental Psychology* 58 (1959): 17–22.
2. R. J. Harris, "Inferences in Information Processing," in Bower (2/12, vol. 15, 1981), 82–128.
3. A. Layerson, ed., *Psychology Today: An Introduction*, 3d ed. (New York: Random House, Inc., 1985), 111.
4. Syllables—H. Ebbinghaus, *Memory* (New York: Columbia University Press, 1913. Germany, 1885). Spanish—H. P. Bahrick, "Semantic Memory Context in Permastore: 50 Years of Memory for Spanish Learned in School," *Journal of Experimental Psychology: General* 113 (1984): 1–29. Drugs, amnesia—P. E. Gold, "Sweet Memories," *American Scientist* 75 (1987): 151–55.
5. Horton and Mills (2/22).
6. B. J. Underwood, "Forgetting," *Scientific American* 210 (1964): 91–99.
7. Poetry, Nigeria—J. R. Gentile, N. Monaco, I. E. Iheozor-Ejiofor, A. N. Ndu, and P. K. Ogbonaya, "Retention by 'Fast' and 'Slow' Learners," *Intelligence* 6 (1982): 125–28. Elderly—Poon (1/4).
8. R. G. Ley, "Cerebral Laterality and Imagery," in *Imagery: Current Theory, Research, and Application*, ed. A. A. Sheikh (New York: Wiley, 1983), 252–87; S. P. Springer and G. Deutsch, *Left Brain, Right Brain*, 2d ed. (New York: W. H. Freeman, 1985).
9. J. Levy, "Right Brain, Left Brain: Fact and Fiction," *Psychology Today*, May 1985, 38–44; K. McKean, "Of Two Minds: Selling the Right Brain," *Discover*, April 1985, 30, 34–36, 38, 40; S. P. Springer, "Educating the Left and Right Sides of the Brain," *National Forum: The Phi Kappa Phi Journal* 67, no. 2, (1987): 25–28.
10. Alphabet—R. J. Weber and J. Castleman, "The Time It Takes to Imagine," *Perception and Psychophysics* 8 (1970): 165–68. Object—J. M. Clark and A. Paivio, "A Dual Coding Perspective on Encoding Processes," in *Imagery and Related Mnemonic Processes: Theories, Individual Differences, and Applications*, ed. M. A. McDaniel and M. Pressley (New York: Springer-Verlag, 1987), 5–33.
11. 2,560 pictures—L. Standing, J. Conezio, and R. N. Haber, "Perception and Memory for Pictures: Single-trial Learning of 2,500 Visual Stimuli," *Psychonomic Science* 19 (1970): 73–74. 10,000 pictures, recall—L. Standing, "Learning 10,000 Pictures," *Quarterly Journal of Experimental Psychology* 25 (1973): 207–22. Memory after three months—D. Homa and C. Viera, "Long-term Memory for Pictures under Conditions of Difficult Foil Discriminability" (paper presented at the meeting of the Western Psychological Association, Long Beach, Calif., April 1987).
12. S. Madigan, "Picture Memory," in *Imagery, Memory and Cognition: Essays in Honor of Allan Paivio*, ed. J. C. Yuille (Hillsdale, N.J.: Erlbaum, 1983), 65–69; D.

C. Park, J. T. Puglisi, and M. Sovacool, "Memory for Pictures, Words, and Spatial Location in Older Adults: Evidence for Pictorial Superiority," *Journal of Gerontology* 38 (1983): 582–88; G. H. Ritchey, "Pictorial Detail and Recall in Adults and Children," *Journal of Experimental Psychology: Learning, Memory, and Cognition* 8 (1982): 139–41.

13. A. Paivio and K. Csapo, "Picture Superiority in Free Recall: Imagery or Dual Coding," *Cognitive Psychology* 5 (1973): 176–206; D. L. Nelson, "Remembering Pictures and Words: Appearance, Significance, and Name," in *Levels of Processing in Human Memory*, ed. L. S. Cermak and F. I. M. Craik (Hillsdale, N.J.: Erlbaum, 1979).

14. Clark and Paivio (3/10); A. Paivio, *Mental Representations: A Dual Coding Approach* (New York: Oxford University Press, 1986); A. Paivio, "The Empirical Case for Dual Coding," in Yuille (3/12), 307–32.

15. D. Marks and P. McKellar, "The Nature and Function of Eidetic Imagery," *Journal of Mental Imagery* 6 (1982): 1–28 (commentaries, 28–124); R. N. Haber, "Twenty Years of Haunting Eidetic Imagery: Where's the Ghost?" *The Behavioral and Brain Sciences* 2 (1979): 583–629.

16. C. F. Stromeyer III, "Eidetikers," *Psychology Today*, November 1970, 46–50.

17. A. R. Luria, *The Mind of a Mnemonist* (New York: Basic Books, 1968), 12.

18. 256 digits—J. C. Horn, "Ah Yes, He Remembers It Well . . . ," *Psychology Today*, February 1981, 21, 80–81. Study of V. P.—E. Hunt and T. Love, "How Good Can Memory Be?" in *Coding Processes in Human Memory*, ed. A. W. Melton and E. Martin (Washington, D.C.: V. H. Winston and Sons, 1972), 237–60. Nineteenth-century prodigy—A. Paivio, *Imagery and Verbal Processes* (Hillsdale, N.J.: Erlbaum, 1979), 45–76.

19. Students who could remember 73 and 100 digits—Ericsson and Chase (1/15); K. A. Ericsson, "Memory Skill," *Canadian Journal of Psychology* 39 (1985): 188–231; M. M. Waldrop, "The Workings of Working Memory," *Science*, 237 (1987), 1564–67. Waiter—S. Singular, "A Memory for All Seasonings," *Psychology Today*, October 1982, 54–63. Squaring feats—C. Wells, "Teaching the Brain New Tricks," *Esquire*, March 1983, 49–54, 59–61. Study of T. E.—J. Wilding and E. Valentine, "One Man's Memory for Prose, Faces, and Names," *British Journal of Psychology* 76 (1985): 215–19; J. Wilding and E. Valentine, "Searching for Superior Memories," in Gruneberg et al. (1/12).

20. K. J. Scoresby, T. Lowe, and K. L. Higbee, "Learning to Be a Born Mnemonist" (paper presented at the meeting of the Rocky Mountain Psychological Association, Tucson, Ariz., April 1985).

21. U. Neisser, "Memorists," in *Memory Observed*, ed. U. Neisser (San Francisco: Freeman, 1982).

22. Klatzky (2/15), 306, 317.

23. R. M. Restak, "Islands of Genius," *Science 82* 3 (1982): 62–67; M. Howe, "Memory in Mentally Retarded 'Idiot Savants'," in Gruneberg et al. (1/12).

24. Radio—J. Kasindorf, "Set Your Dial for Sleeplearning," *McCalls*, September 1974, 50. Studies—L. Aarons, "Sleep-assisted Instruction," *Psychological Bulletin* 83 (1976): 1–40; F. Rubin, *Learning and Sleep* (Bristol, England: John Wright & Sons, 1971).

25. Controlled studies—C. W. Simon and W. H. Emmons, "Responses to Material Presented During Various Levels of Sleep," *Journal of Experimental Psychology* 51 (1956): 89–97; W. H. Emmons and C. W. Simon, "The Non-recall of Material Presented During Sleep," *American Journal of Psychology* 69 (1956): 76–81; D. J. Bruce, C. R. Evans, P. B. C. Fenwick, and V. Spencer, "Effect of Presenting Novel Verbal Material During Slow-Wave Sleep," *Nature* 225 (1970): 873–74. Advertising—"Sleeping Students Don't Learn English," *Consumer Reports*, May 1970, 313.

26. F. J. Evans and W. Orchard, "Sleep Learning: The Successful Waking Recall of Material Presented During Sleep," *Psychophysiology* 6 (1969): 269.

27. A. Grosvenor and L. D. Lack, "The Effect of Sleep Before or After Learning on Memory," *Sleep* 7 (1984): 155–67; C. Idzikowski, "Sleep and Memory," *British Journal of Psychology* 75 (1984): 439–49.

28. Johnson and Hasher (1/2); A. Marcel, "Conscious and Unconscious Perception: Experiments on Visual Masking and Word Recognition," *Cognitive Psychology* 15 (1983): 197–37.

29. D. L. Moore, "Subliminal Advertising: What You See Is What You Get," *Journal of Marketing* 46 (1982): 38–47; J. R. Vokey and J. D. Read, "Subliminal Messages: Between the Devil and the Media," *American Psychologist* 40 (1985): 1231–39.

CHAPTER 4

1. D. O. Lyon, "The Relation of Length of Material to Time Taken for Learning and the Optimum Distribution of Time," *Journal of Educational Psychology* 5 (1914): 1–9, 85–91, 155–63.

2. Clark and Paivio (3/10).

3. T. J. Shuell, "Cognitive Conceptions of Learning," *Review of Educational Research* 56 (1986): 411–36.

4. I. L. Beck and P. A. Carpenter, "Cognitive Approaches to Understanding Reading: Implications for Instructional Practice." *American Psychologist* 41 (1986): 1098–1105; F. S. Bellezza, "Expert Knowledge as Mental Cues" (Paper presented at the meeting of the Psychonomic Society, New Orleans, November 1986).

5. Milojkovic (2/9).

6. Sayings—S. Markham, S. Crandall, and K. L. Higbee, "Factors Affecting Recall of Ideas Learned with a Visual Mnemonic" (paper presented at the meeting of the Western Psychological Association, San Jose, Calif., April 1985). Elderly—Poon (1/4). Adolescents—A. J. Franklin, "The Social Context and Socialization Variables as Factors in Thinking and Learning," in *Thinking and Learning Skills: Research and Open Questions*, vol. 2, ed. S. F. Chipman, J. W. Segal, and R. Glaser (Hillsdale, N.J.: Erlbaum, 1985), 81–106.

7. Cues—D. C. Rubin and W. T. Wallace, "Rhyme and Reason: Integral Properties of Words" (Paper presented at the meeting of the Psychonomic Society, New Orleans, November 1986). List—Kozlowski (2/25).

8. G. Katona, *Organizing and Memorizing: Studies in the Psychology of Learning and Teaching* (New York: Columbia University Press, 1940), 187–92.

9. Paired-associates—T. R. Barrett and B. R. Ekstrand, "Second-Order Associations and Single-List Retention," *Journal of Experimental Psychology: Human Learning and Memory* 104 (1974): 41–49. Bridge—N. Charness, "Components of Skill in Bridge," *Canadian Journal of Psychology* 33 (1979): 1–16. The Game of Go—Milojkovic (2/9). Maps—J. E. Ormrod, R. K. Ormrod, E. D. Wagner, and R. C. McCallin, "Cognitive Strategies in Learning Maps" (paper presented at the meeting of the American Educational Research Association, San Francisco, April 1986). Fleischer—R. Kanigel, "Storing Yesterday," *Johns Hopkins Magazine,* 32 (June 1981): 27–34. Quote is on p. 34.

10. M. McCloskey and K. Bigler, "Focused Memory Search in Fact Retrieval," *Memory & Cognition* 8 (1980): 253–64.

11. Presenting in categories—B. A. Folarin, "Is Grouping of Words in Memory a Fast or a Slow Process?" *Psychological Reports* 48 (1981): 355–58. Told categories—B. Z. Strand, "Effects of Instructions for Category Organization on Long-term Retention," *Journal of Experimental Psychology: Human Learning and Memory* 1 (1974): 780–86; M. E. J. Masson and M. A. McDaniel, "The Role of Organizational Processes in Long-term Retention," *Journal of Experimental Psychology: Human Learning and Memory* 7 (1981): 100–10.

12. Impose organization—Klatzky (2/15). Recall by categories—B. Ambler and W. Maples, "Role of Rehearsal in Encoding and Organization for Free Recall," *Journal of Experimental Psychology: Human Learning and Memory* 3 (1977): 295–304. Children—B. E. Moely and W. E. Jeffrey, "The Effect of Organization Training on Children's Free Recall of Category Items," *Child Development* 45 (1974): 135–43.

13. Instructed to organize—P. A. Ornstein, T. Trabasso, and P. N. Johnson-Laird, "To Organize Is to Remember: The Effects of Instructions to Organize and to Recall," *Journal of Experimental Psychology* 103 (1974), 1014–18. Organized Paragraphs—J. L. Myers, K. Pezdek, and D. Coulson, "Effect of Prose Organization upon Free Recall," *Journal of Educational Psychology* 65 (1973): 313–20. Organized Stories—J. B. Black and H. Bern, "Causal Inferences and Memory for Events in Narrative," *Journal of Verbal Learning and Verbal Behavior* 20 (1981): 267–75; Horton and Mills (2/22). Coherent Pictures—S. E. Palmer, "The Effects of Contextual Scenes on the Identification of Objects," *Memory & Cognition* 3 (1975): 519–26.

14. H. L. Roediger III and R. G. Crowder, "A Serial Position Effect in Recall of United States Presidents," *Bulletin of the Psychonomic Society* 8 (1976): 275–78.

15. Evidence—Wingfield and Byrnes (2/3), 26. Explanations—F. S. Bellezza, F. Andrasik, Jr., and R. D. Lewis, "The Primacy Effect and Automatic Processing in Free Recall," *The Journal of General Psychology* 106 (1982): 175–89; A. M. Glenberg, M. M. Bradley, J. A. Stevenson, T. A. Kraus, M. J. Tkachuk, A. L. Gretz, J. H. Fish, and B. M. Turpin, "A Two-Process Account of Long-term Serial Position Effects," *Journal of Experimental Psychology: Human Learning and Memory,* 6 (1980): 355–69; C. L. Lee and W. K. Estes, "Item and Order Information in Short-term Memory: Evidence for Multilevel Perturbation Processes," *Journal of Experimental Psychology: Human Learning and Memory* 7 (1981): 149–80.

16. C. M. Reigeluth, "Meaningfulness and Instruction: Relating What is Being Learned to What a Student Knows," *Instructional Science* 12 (1983): 197–218; C. M. Reigeluth, "The Analogy in Instructional Design" (paper presented at the meeting of the American Educational Research Association, San Francisco, April 1986); C. H. Hansen and D. F. Halpern, "Using Analogies to Improve Comprehension and Recall of

Scientific Passages" (paper presented at the meeting of the Psychonomic Society, Seattle, November 1987); S. Vosniadou and M. Schommer, "The Effect of Explanatory Analogies on Young Children's Comprehension of Expository Text" (paper presented at the meeting of the American Educational Research Association, San Francisco, April 1986).

17. A. D. Baddeley, V. Lewis, and I. Nimmo-Smith, "When Did You Last . . .?" in *Practical Aspects of Memory*, ed. M. M. Gruneberg, P. Morris, and R. N. Sykes (New York: Academic Press, 1978), 77–83; Johnson and Hasher (1/2); J. M. Keenan, P. Brown, and G. Potts, "The Self-Reference Memory Effect and Imagery" (paper presented at the meeting of the Psychonomic Society, New Orleans, November 1986).

18. Making material meaningful—Reigeluth (4/16, 1983) 197–218. Defining in terms of association—R. P. Stratton, K. A. Jacobus, and B. Brinley, "Age-of-Acquisition, Imagery, Familiarity, and Meaningfulness Norms for 533 Words," *Behavior Research Methods and Instrumentation* 7 (1975): 1–6.

19. J. R. Anderson, "Retrieval of Information from Long-term Memory," *Science* 220 (1983): 25–30; W. A. Wickelgren, "Human Learning and Memory," in Rosenzweig and Porter (1/2, Vol. 32, 1981), 21–57.

20. J. Brophy, "Teacher Influences on Student Achievement," *American Psychologist* 41 (1986): 1069–77; U.S. Department of Education, *What Works: Research About Teaching and Learning* (Washington, D.C., 1986), 37.

21. D. Williams and J. D. Hollan, "The Process of Retrieval From Very Long-term Memory," *Cognitive Science* 5 (1981): 87–119.

22. Witnesses—R. E. Geiselman, R. P. Fisher, D. P. MacKinnon, and H. L. Holland, "Eyewitness Memory Enhancement with the Cognitive Interview," *American Journal of Psychology* 99 (1986): 385–401; K. O'Reilly, D. P. MacKinnon, and R. E. Geiselman, "Enhancement of Witness Memory for License Plates: At Acquisiton and Retrieval" (paper presented at the meeting of the Western Psychological Association, Long Beach, Calif., April 1987). Simulation—R. P. Fisher and R. E. Geiselman, "Enhancing Eyewitness Memory with the Cognitive Interview," in Gruneberg et al. (1/12).

23. W. James, *Psychology* (New York: Henry Holt & Co., 1910), 290.

24. 1800s—E. A. Kirkpatrick, "An Experimental Study of Memory," *Psychological Review* 1 (1894): 602–09. 1960s—R. R. Holt, "Imagery: The Return of the Ostracized," *American Psychologist* 19 (1964): 254–64. Human learning—J. A. McGeoch and A. L. Irion, *The Psychology of Human Learning*, 2d ed. (New York: Longmans, Green and Co., 1952). Conscious processes—E. R. Hilgard, "Consciousness in Contemporary Psychology," in Rosenzweig and Porter (1/2, vol. 31, 1980), 1–26; T. J. Knapp, "The Emergence of Cognitive Psychology in the Latter Half of the Twentieth Century," in *Approaches to Cognition: Contrasts and Controversies*, ed. T. J. Knapp and L. C. Robertson (Hillsdale, N.J.: Erlbaum, 1986), 13–35.

25. For discussions of imagery see M. L. Fleming and D. W. Hutton, eds., *Mental Imagery and Learning* (Englewood Cliffs, N.J.: Educational Technology Publications, 1983); P. E. Morris and P. J. Hampson, *Imagery and Consciousness* (London: Academic Press, 1983); J. T. E. Richardson, *Mental Imagery and Human Memory* (New York: St. Martin's Press, 1980); Sheikh, Imagery (3/8); A. A. Sheikh and K. S. Sheikh, ed., *Imagery in Education* (Farmingdale, N.Y.: Baywood, 1985); Yuille (3/12).

26. See reference 25.

27. Prose—M. Denis, "Imagery and Prose: A Critical Review of Research on Adults and Children," *Text* 4 (1984): 381–401. Concepts—Markham et al. (4/6); K. L. Alesandrini, "Imagery Eliciting Strategies and Meaningful Learning," *Journal of Mental Imagery* 6 (1982): 125–40.

28. Lorayne (1/17), p. 22.

29. R. S. Nickerson and M. J. Adams, "Long-term Memory for a Common Object," *Cognitive Psychology* 11 (1979): 287–307.

30. L. S. Cermak, *Improving Your Memory* (New York: McGraw-Hill, 1976), 27.

31. M. C. Wittrock, "Students' Thought Processes," in *Handbook of Research on Teaching*, 3d ed., ed. M. C. Wittrock (New York: Macmillan, 1986), 297–314.

CHAPTER 5

1. D. A. Bekerian and A. D. Baddeley, "Saturation Advertising and the Repetition Effect," *Journal of Verbal Learning and Verbal Behavior* 19 (1980): 17–25; A. M. Glenberg and M. M. Bradley, "Mental Contiguity," *Journal of Experimental Psychology: Human Learning and Memory* 5 (1979): 88–97.

2. School boy—J. Brothers and E. P. F. Eagan, *Ten Days to a Successful Memory* (Englewood Cliffs, N.J.: Prentice-Hall, 1957), 61. Professor Sanford—E. C. Sanford, "Professor Sanford's Morning Prayer," in Neisser (3/21), 176–77.

3. Wickelgren (4/19).

4. W. C. F. Krueger, "The Effect of Overlearning on Retention," *Journal of Experimental Psychology* 12 (1929): 71–78. See also T. O. Nelson, R. J. Lonesio, A. P. Shimamura, R. F. Landwehr, and L. Narens, "Overlearning and the Feeling of Knowing," *Journal of Experimental Psychology: Learning, Memory, and Cognition* 8 (1982): 279–88.

5. Bahrick (2/20).

6. Nelson et al. (5/4).

7. R. F. Mayer, "Can You Repeat That? Qualitative Effects of Repetition and Advance Organizers on Learning from Science Prose," *Journal of Educational Psychology* 75 (1983); 40–49.

8. Many of the examples and research reported in this section are from Loftus (2/3); Pintrich et al. (1/7); I. G. Sarason, ed., *Test Anxiety: Theory, Research and Application* (Hillsdale, N.J.: Erlbaum, 1980); and H. M. Van Der Ploeg, R. Schwarzer, and C. D. Spielberger, ed., *Advances in Test Anxiety Research*, vol. 3 (Hillsdale, N.J.: Erlbaum , 1984).

9. J. C. Cavanaugh, J. G. Grady, and M. Perlmutter, "Forgetting and Use of Memory Aids in 20- to 70-Year-Olds' Everyday Life," *International Journal of Aging and Human Development* 17 (1983): 113–22.

10. Anxiety interference not clear—Pintrich et al. (1/7). Encoding, organizing, retrieving—W. J. McKeachie, "Does Anxiety Disrupt Information Processing or Does Poor Information Processing Lead to Anxiety?," *International Review of Applied Psychology* 33 (1984): 187–203. Three sources—J. L. Deffenbacher and S. L. Hazaleus, "Cognitive, Emotional, and Physiological Components of Test Anxiety," *Cognitive Therapy and Research* 9 (1985): 169–80.

11. Techniques—Sarason (5/8); D. C. Lapp, *Don't Forget: Easy Exercises for a Better Memory at Any Age* (New York: McGraw Hill, 1987). Elderly—J. A. Yesavage, "Relaxation and Memory Training in 39 Elderly Patients," *American Journal of Psychiatry* 141 (1984): 778–81; J. A. Yesavage and R. Jacob, "Effects of Relaxation and Mnemonics on Memory, Attention and Anxiety in the Elderly," *Experimental Aging Research* 10 (1984): 211–14. Athletics—J. E. Turnure and J. F. Lane, "Special Educational Applications of Mnemonics," in McDaniel and Pressley (3/10), 329–57.

12. Nelson et al. (5/4).

13. Study skills—C. E. Weinstein and V. L. Underwood, "Learning Strategies: The How of Learning," in *Thinking and Learning Skills: Relating Instruction to Research*, vol. 1, ed. J. W. Segal, S. F. Chipman, and R. Glaser (Hillsdale, N.J.: Erlbaum, 1985), 241–58. Learning Strategy Course—W. J. McKeachie, P. R. Pintrich, and Y. G. Lin, "Learning to Learn," in *Cognition, Information Processing, and Motivation*, ed. G. d'Ydwelle (Amsterdam: Elsevier, 1984), 601–18.

14. K. Kirkland and J. G. Hollandsworth, Jr., "Effective Test Taking: Skills-Acquisition Versus Anxiety-Reduction Techniques," *Journal of Consulting and Clinical Psychology* 48 (1980): 431–39.

15. Reason and Lucas (2/24).

16. These studies and others are described by Stern (2/3); Johnson and Hasher (1/2); and A. Memon and V. Bruce, "Context Effects in Episodic Studies of Verbal and Facial Memory: "A Review," *Current Psychological Research & Reviews* 4 (1985), 349–69.

17. Imagining—S. M. Smith, "Remembering In and Out of Context," *Journal of Experimental Psychology: Human Learning and Memory* 5 (1979): 460–71. Purposely associating—E. Eich, "Context, Memory, and Integrated Item/Context Imagery," *Journal of Experimental Psychology: Learning, Memory, and Cognition* 11 (1985): 764–70.

18. S. M. Smith, "Enhancement of Recall Using Multiple Environmental Contexts During Learning," *Memory & Cognition* 10 (1982): 405–12.

19. D. M. Landers, "Mental Practice and Imagery in Sports" (paper presented at the American Imagery Conference, New York, November 1987). R. M. Suinn, "Imagery and Sports," in Sheikh (3/8), 507–34.

20. Statistics course—S. M. Smith and E. Z. Rothkopf, "Varying Environmental Context of Lessons to Compensate for Massed Teaching" (paper presented at the meeting of the American Educational Research Association, New York, 1982.) Cited in Smith (5/18). Patients—A. D. Baddeley, "Memory Theory and Memory Therapy," in Wilson and Moffat (1/4), 5–27, see page 26.

21. Drugs, moods—P. H. Blaney, "Affect and Memory: A Review," *Psychological Bulletin* 99 (1986): 229–46; D. A. Overton, "Contextual Stimulus Effects of Drugs and Internal States," in *Context and Learning*, ed. P. D. Balsam and A. Tomie (Hillsdale, N.J.: Erlbaum, 1985); G. Lowe, "State-Dependent Retrieval Effects with Social Drugs," in Gruneberg et al. (1/12). Words, pictures—S. M. Smith, A. Glenberg, and R. A. Bjork, "Environmental Context and Human Memory," *Memory & Cognition* 6 (1978): 342–53; E. Winograd and S. D. Lynn, "Role of Contextual Imagery in Associative Recall," *Memory & Cognition* 7 (1979): 29–34.

22. L. Baker and J. L. Santa, "Context, Integration, and Retrieval," *Memory & Cognition* 5 (1977): 308–14.

23. Strong—S. M. Smith and E. Vela, "Outshining: The Relative Effectiveness of Cues" (paper presented at the meeting of the Psychonomic Society, New Orleans, November 1986); Johnson and Hasher (1/2). Measured—R. A. Bjork and A. Richardson-Klavehn, "Context Reinstatement and Human Memory: A Theoretical Taxonomy of Empirical Effects" (paper presented at the meeting of the Psychonomic Society, Seattle, November 1987).

24. Brothers and Egan (5/2), 24. On the importance of interest see S. Hidi and W. Baird, "Interestingness—A Neglected Variable in Discourse Processing," *Cognitive Science* 10 (1986): 179–94.

25. Hunter (1/5), 122.

26. Children—B. A. Kennedy and D. J. Miller, "Persistent Use of Verbal Rehearsal as a Function of Information About Its Value," *Child Development* 47 (1976): 566–69. Adjustments—J. M. Sassenrath, "Theory and Results on Feedback and Retention," *Journal of Educational Psychology* 67 (1975): 894–99.

27. R. E. LaPorte and J. F. Voss, "Retention of Prose Materials as a Function of Postacquisition Testing," *Journal of Educational Psychology* 67 (1975): 259–66. See also K. A. Kiewra and S. L. Benton, "The Effects of Higher-Order Review Questions with Feedback on Achievement Among Learners Who Take Notes or Receive the Instructor's Notes," *Human Learning* 4 (1985): 225–31; and A. W. Salmoni, R. A. Schmidt, and C. B. Walter, "Knowledge of Results and Motor Learning: A Review and Critical Appraisal," *Psychological Bulletin* 95 (1984): 355–86.

28. Corrective feedback—Brophy (4/20). Instructor Program—R. Van Houten, *Learning Through Feedback: A Systematic Approach for Improving Academic Performance* (New York: Human Sciences Press, 1980).

29. J. F. King, E. B. Zechmeister, and J. J. Shaughnessy, "Judgments of Knowing: The Influence of Retrieval Practice," *American Journal of Psychology* 93 (1980): 329–43.

CHAPTER 6

1. School skills are discussed in R. Carman and W. R. Adams, *Study Skills: A Student's Guide for Survival* (New York: Wiley, 1985); C. T. Morgan and J. Deese, *How to Study*, 2d ed. (New York: McGraw-Hill, 1979); W. Pauk, *How to Study in College*, 3d ed. (Boston: Houghton Mifflin, 1984).

2. Study time—Underwood (1/3). Narrow range of learning strategies—J. Snowman, "Learning Tactics and Strategies," in *Cognitive Classroom Learning: Understanding, Thinking, and Problem Solving*, ed. G. D. Phye and T. Andre (New York: Academic Press, 1986), 243–75. Good students—S. F. Chipman and J. W. Segal, "Higher Cognitive Goals for Education: An Introduction," in Segal et al. (5/13), 1–19.

3. Weinstein and Underwood (5/13).

4. B. Hayes-Roth, "Evolution of Cognitive Structure and Processes," *Psychological Review* 84 (1977): 260–78.

5. D. I. Anderson and J. L. Byers, "Effects of Test Items and Degree of Similarity upon Interference in Learning from Prose Materials," *Psychological Reports* 42 (1978): 591–600.

6. J. W. Fagen and C. Rovee-Collier, "Memory Retrieval: A Time-Locked Process in Infancy," *Science* 222 (1983): 1349–51.

7. Johnson and Hasher (1/2); W. N. Runquist, "The Generality of the Effects of Structure Similarity on Cue Discrimination and Recall," *Canadian Journal of Psychology* 37 (1983): 484–97; B. Gunter, C. Berry, and B. R. Clifford, "Proactive Interference Effects with Television News Items: Further Evidence," *Journal of Experimental Psychology: Human Learning and Memory* 7 (1981): 480–87.

8. Rooms—B. Z. Strand, "Change of Context and Retroactive Inhibition," *Journal of Verbal Learning and Verbal Behavior* 9 (1970): 202–06. Speakers—E. Z. Rothkopf, D. G. Fisher, and M. J. Billington, "Effects of Spatial Context During Acquisition on the Recall of Attribute Information," *Journal of Experimental Psychology: Learning, Memory, and Cognition* 8 (1982): 126–38.

9. First study—B. J. Underwood and J. S. Freund, "Effect of Temporal Separation of Two Tasks on Proactive Inhibition," *Journal of Educational Psychology* 78 (1968): 50–54. Second study—G. Keppel, "Facilitation in Short- and Long-term Retention of Paired Associates Following Distributed Practice in Learning," *Journal of Verbal Learning and Verbal Behavior* 3 (1964): 91–111.

10. Strand (6/8).

11. First quote—Wickelgren (4/19), 39–40. Second quote—Underwood (1/3), 218.

12. U.S. Dept. of Education, *What Works* (4/20), 39. Well-received—J. Bales, *"What Works:* Consensus Report Gets Good Marks from Researchers," *APA Monitor* 17 (May, 1986): 13; M. S. Smith, *"What Works,* Works!" *Educational Researcher* 15 (April 1986): 29–30; however, see G. V. Glass, *"What Works:* Politics and Research," *Educational Researcher* 16 (March, 1987): 5–10.

13. First study—K. C. Bloom and T. J. Shuell, "Effects of Massed and Distributed Practice on the Learning and Retention of Second-Language Vocabulary," *Journal of Educational Research* 74 (1981): 245–48. Second study—A. D. Baddeley and D. J. A. Longman, "The Influence of Length and Frequency of Training Sessions on Rate of Learning to Type," *Ergonomics* 21 (1978): 627–35. Third study—Bahrick (3/4); see also H. P. Bahrick and E. Phelps, "Retention of Spanish Vocabulary Over 8 Years," *Journal of Experimental Psychology: Learning, Memory, and Cognition* 13 (1987): 344–49.

14. Reviewing—J. H. Reynolds and R. Glaser, "Effects of Repetition and Spaced Review upon Retention of a Complex Learning Task," *Journal of Educational Psychology* 55 (1964): 297–308. Teaching—F. N. Dempster, "The Spacing Effect and Allied Phenomena: Educational Implications" (paper presented at the meeting of the Psychonomic Society, New Orleans, November 1986); C. P. Rea and V. Modigliani, "Educational Implications for the Spacing Effect," in Gruneberg et al. (1/12). Names— Bahrick (2/20). Faces—A. G. Goldstein and J. E. Chance, "Enhanced Face Recognition Memory After Distributed Viewing" (paper presented at the meeting of the Psychonomic Society, Seattle, November 1987).

15. Consolidate—H. Weingartner and E. S. Parker, ed., *Memory Consolidation: Psychobiology of Cognition* (Hillside, N.J.: Erlbaum, 1984). Lecture—F. J. Di Vesta and D. A. Smith, "The Pausing Principle: Increasing the Efficiency of Memory for Ongoing Events," *Contemporary Educational Psychology* 4 (1979): 288–96; Other possible reasons for the spacing effect have also been suggested; see, for example, R. L. Greene, "Spacing Effects in Memory: The Role of Rehearsal Strategies" (paper presented at the meeting of the Psychonomic Society, Seattle, November 1987).

16. R. M. Gorman, *Psychology of Classroom Learning* (Columbus, Ohio: Charles E. Merrill, 1974), 174; Hunter (1/5), 135.

17. A. M. Glenberg and T. S. Lehman, "Spacing Repetitions over 1 Week," *Memory & Cognition* 8 (1980): 528–38.

18. D. C. Candland, *Psychology: The Experimental Approach* (New York: Mc-Graw-Hill, 1968); J. M. Sawrey and C. M. Telford, eds., *Educational Psychology*, 4th ed. (Boston: Allyn & Bacon, 1973).

19. M. J. Breen and J. M. Jurek, "Serial Learning as a Function of Age and Part Versus Whole Learning Procedures," *Psychological Reports* 36 (1975): 767–73.

20. Hunter (1/5), 133.

21. Gorman (6/16), 173.

22. A. E. D. Schonfield, "Learning, Memory, and Aging," in *Handbook of Mental Health and Aging*, ed. J. E. Birren and R. B. Sloane (Englewood Cliffs, N.J.: Prentice-Hall, 1980), 214–44.

23. First study—V. P. Orlando and K . G. Hayward, "A Comparison of the Effectiveness of Three Study Techniques for College Students," in *Reading: Disciplined Inquiry in Process and Practice*, ed. P. D. Pearson and J. Hansen (Clemson, S.C.: National Reading Conference, 1978), 242–45. Second study—C. P. Thompson, S. J. Wenger, and C. A. Bartling, "How Recall Facilitates Subsequent Recall: A Reappraisal," *Journal of Experimental Psychology: Human Learning and Memory* 4 (1978): 210–21. Feedback—J. F. King, E. B. Zechmeister, and J. J. Shaughnessy, "Judgments of Knowing: The Influence of Retrieval Practice," *American Journal of Psychology* 93 (1980): 329–43.

24. Testing—R. J. Nungester and P. C. Duchastel, "Testing Versus Review: Effects on Retention," *Journal of Educational Psychology* 74 (1982): 18–22; W. B. Whitten and J. M. Leonard, "Learning from Tests: Facilitation of Delayed Recall by Initial Recognition Alternatives," *Journal of Experimental Psychology: Human Learning and Memory* 6 (1980): 127–34. Children—T. Petros and K. Hoving, "The Effects of Review on Young Children's Memory for Prose," *Journal of Experimental Child Psychology* 39 (1980): 33–43.

25. Pauk (6/1), 94; H. C. Ellis, *Fundamentals of Human Learning, Memory, and Cognition*, 2d ed. (Dubuque, Iowa; W. C. Brown, 1978), 125.

26. L. T. Frase and B. J. Schwartz, "Effect of Question Production and Answering on Prose Recall," *Journal of Educational Psychology* 67 (1975): 628–35.

27. F. Robinson, *Effective Study* (New York: Harper & Row, 1946).

28. General-purpose systems—D. F. Dansereau, "Learning Strategy Research," in Segal et al. (5/13), 209–39. Reading textbook—H. Singer and D. Donlan, *Reading and Learning from Text* (Boston: Little, Brown, & Co., 1980). For a more extensive discussion see F. P. Robinson, *Effective Study*, 4th ed. (New York: Harper & Row, 1970) and Morgan and Deese (6/1).

29. L. M. Reder, "Techniques Available to Author, Teacher, and Reader to Improve Retention of the Main Ideas of a Chapter," Segal, and Glaser in Chipman (4/6), 37–64; F. K. Aldrich, "Improving the Retention of Aurally Presented Information," in Gruneberg et al. (1/12).

30. J. D. Bransford and M. K. Johnson, "Contextual prerequisites for Understanding: Some Investigations of Comprehension and Recall," *Journal of Verbal Learning and Verbal Behavior* 11 (1972): 717–26.

31. Advance organizers—J. Luiten, W. Ames, and G. Ackerson, "A Meta-analysis of the Effects of Advance Organizers on Learning and Retention," *American Educational Research Journal* 17 (1980): 211–18; D. N. Thompson, K. Diefenderfer, and L. S. Doll, "The Use of Advance Organizers with Older Adults of Limited Verbal Ability" (paper presented at the meeting of the American Educational Research Association, San Francisco, April 1986). Headings—Dansereau (6/28); Snowman (6/2); S. C. Wilhite, "Headings as Memory Facilitators," in Gruneberg, et al. (1/12).

32. Alesandrini (4/27); J. L. Levin, "Pictures as Prose-learning Devices," in *Discourse Processing,* ed. A. Flammer & W. Kintsch (Amsterdam: North-Holland, 1982), 412–44; J. R. Levin, G. J. Anglin, and R. N. Carney, "On Empirically Validating Functions of Pictures in Prose," in *The Psychology of Illustration: Basic Reseach,* vol. 1; D. M. Willows and H. A. Houghton (New York: Springer-Verlag, 1987), 51–85.

33. J. R. Gavelek and T. E. Raphael, "Metacognition, Instruction, and the Role of Questioning Activities," in *Metacognition, Cognition, and Human Performance: Instructional Practices,* vol. 2, ed. D. L. Forrest-Pressley, G. E. MacKinnon, and T. G. Waller (Orlando, Fla.: Academic Press, 1985), 103–36; C. Hamaker, "The Effects of Adjunct Questions on Prose Learning," *Review of Educational Research* 56 (1986): 212–42.

34. Snowman (6/2); L. K. Cook and R. E. Mayer, "Reading Strategies Training for Meaningful Learning from Prose," in *Cognitive Strategy Research: Educational Applications,* ed. M. Pressley and J. R. Levin (New York: Springer-Verlag, 1983), 87–131; J. Hartley, S. Bartlett, and A. Branthwaite, "Underlining Can Make a Difference—Sometimes," *Journal of Educational Research* 73 (1980): 218–23.

35. J. P. Rickards and G. J. August, "Generative Underlining Strategies in Prose Recall," *Journal of Educational Psychology* 67 (1975): 860–65.

36. Psychologist—M. Linton, "Real World Memory After Six Years: An *In Vivo* Study of Very Long Term Memory," in Gruneberg et al. (4/17). Lecture—Di Vesta and Smith (6/15). Pakistani—M. Wasim, "Effect of Frequent Review upon Recall," *Journal of Social Sciences and the Humanities* 1–2 (1984), 69–73.

37. First study—L. R. Gay, "Temporal Position of Review and Its Effect on the Retention of Mathematical Rules," *Journal of Educational Psychology* 64 (1973): 171–82. Children—Petros and Hoving (6/24).

38. Hunter (1/5), 108–09.

39. T. K. Landauer and R. A. Bjork, "Optimum Rehearsal Patterns and Name Learning," in Gruneberg et al. (4/17), 625–32; R. A. Bjork, "Practical and Theoretical Implications of a Non-Semantic Mnemonic Technique," in Gruneberg et al. (1/12).

40. Snowman (6/2); K. A. Kiewra, "Investigating Notetaking and Review: A Depth of Processing Alternative," *Educational Psychologist* 29 (1985): 23–32; K. A. Kiewra and B. M. Frank, "The Encoding and External-Storage Effects of Personal Lecture Notes, Skeletal Notes, and Detailed Notes of Field-Independent and Field-Dependent Learners" (paper presented at the meeting of the American Educational Research Association, San Francisco, April 1986).

41. R. J. Palkovitz and R. K. Lore, "Note Taking and Note Review: Why Students Fail Questions Based on Lecture Material," *Teaching of Psychology* 7 (1980): 159–61.

42. H. Woodrow, "The Effect of Type of Training upon Transference," *Journal of Educational Psychology* 18 (1927): 159–72.

43. Learning strategies—Snowman (6/2); Dansereau (6/28); Weinstein and Underwood (5/13); J. Nisbet and J. Shucksmith, *Learning Strategies* (London: Routledge & Kegan Paul Ltd., 1986). Courses—Pintrich et al. (1/7).

44. U.S. Department of Education, *What Works* (4/20), 39.

45. Increase performance—J. L. Driskell and E. L. A. Kelly, "A Guided Notetaking and Study Skills System for Use with University Freshmen Predicted to Fail," *Journal of Reading* 1 (1980): 4–5. Brain-damaged people—Wilson and Moffat (1/4); B. A. Wilson, *Rehabilitation of Memory* (New York: Guilford Press, 1987). Analysis—D. F. Tadlock, "SQ3R—Why It Works Based on Information Processing Theory," *Journal of Reading* 22 (1978): 110–112.

46. Intuitive appeal, opinion—Cook and Mayer (6/34); J. L. Johns and L. P. McNamara, "The SQ3R Study Technique: A Forgotten Research Target," *Journal of Reading* 23 (1980): 705–08. Children—D. L. Forrest-Pressley and L. A. Gillies, "Children's Flexible Use of Strategies During Reading," in Pressley and Levin (6/34).

CHAPTER 7

1. F. Yates, *The Art of Memory* (London: Routledge & Kegan Paul Ltd., 1966); K. L. Higbee, "Recent Research on Visual Mnemonics: Historical Roots and Educational Fruits," *Review of Educational Research* 49 (1979): 611–29; R. A. Hrees, "An Edited Version of Mnemonics from Antiquity to 1985: Establishing a Foundation for Mnemonic-Based Pedagogy with Particular Emphasis on Mathematics," (Ph.D. diss., Indiana University, 1986).

2. These and other characteristics of mnemonics are discussed by F. S. Bellezza, "Mnemonic Devices: Classification, Characteristics, and Criteria," *Review of Educational Research* 51 (1981): 247–75.

3. Some of the examples not otherwise referenced are contained in *A Dictionary of Mnemonics* (London: Eyre Methuen, 1972); and P. Bracken, *The I Hate to Housekeep Book,* chap. 10 (New York: Harcourt Brace Jovanovich, 1962).

4. M. Suid, *Demonic Mnemonics: 800 Spelling Tricks for 800 Tricky Words* (Belmont, Calif.: Pitman Learning, Inc., 1981); G. A. Negin, "Mnemonics and Demonic Words," *Reading Improvement* 15 (1978): 180–82.

5. E. Pugh, *A Dictionary of Acronyms and Abbreviations* (London: Clive Bingley Ltd.; Hamden, Conn.; Archon Books, 1970); D. R. White, *A Glossary of Acronyms, Abbreviations, and Symbols* (Germantown, Md.: Don White Consultants, 1971).

6. A. G. Smith, *Irving's Anatomy Mnemonics,* 5th ed. (Edinburgh: Churchill Livingstone, 1972).

7. J. E. Harris, "Memory Aids People Use: Two Interview Studies," *Memory & Cognition* 8 (1980): 31–38; M. M. Gruneberg, J. Monks, and R. N. Sykes, "The First-Letter Mnemonic Aid," *IRCA Medical Science: Psychology and Psychiatry; Social and Occupational Medicine* 5 (1977): 304; B. Wilson and N. Moffat, "Running a Memory Group," in Wilson and Moffat (1/4), 171–98; Wilson (6/45). For a different viewpoint see L. Carson, J. W. Zimmer, and J. A. Glover, "First-Letter Mnemonics: DAM (Don't Aid Memory)," *The Journal of General Psychology* 104 (1981): 287–92.

8. P. E. Morris and N. Cook, "When Do First-Letter Mnemonics Aid Recall?" *British Journal of Educational Psychology* 48 (1978): 22–28.

9. Words—M. Ozier, "Access to the Memory Trace Through Orthographic and Categoric Information," *Journal of Experimental Psychology: Human Learning and Memory* 4 (1978): 469–85; D. C. Rubin, "Very Long-Term Memory For Prose and Verse," *Journal of Verbal Learning and Verbal Behavior* 16 (1977): 611–21. Alphabet— N. Moffat, "Strategies of Memory Therapy," in Wilson & Moffat (1/4), 63–88.

10. R. C. Atkinson, "Mnemotechnics in Second-Language Learning," *American Psychologist* 39 (1975): 821–28.

11. Properties, principles—Turnure and Lane (5/11). Vocabulary—M. Pressley, J. R. Levin, and H. D. Delaney, "The Mnemonic Keyword Method," *Review of Educational Research* 52 (1982): 61–91.

12. Recent textbook—Stern (2/3), 211. The four quotes are by, respectively, Ian Hunter (1964), Donald Norman, Alan Baddeley, and Lloyd Peterson and appear in K. L. Higbee, "Some Pseudo-Limitations of Mnemonics" (paper presented at the International Conference on Practical Aspects of Memory, Cardiff, Wales, September 1978). Available in *JSAS Catalog of Selected Documents in Psychology* 9 (1979): 19–20; condensed version in Gruneberg et al. (4/17), 147–54.

13. Bellezza (7/2); F. S. Bellezza, "Mnemonic Devices and Memory Schemas," in McDaniel and Pressley (3/10); R. De Beni, "La Ricerca Sperimentale Sulle Mnemotecniche: Una Rassegna" (Experimental Research on Mnemonics: A Review), *Girnale Italiano di Psicologia* 11 (1984): 421–56; M. J. Dickel, "Principles of Encoding Mnemonics," *Perceptual and Motor Skills* 57 (1983): 111–18; J. L. Oaks and K. L. Higbee, "Process Mnemonics and Principles of Memory" (paper presented at the meeting of the Western Psychological Association, San Jose, Calif., April 1985).

14. E. J. Forbes and H. W. Reese, "Pictorial Elaboration and Recall of Multilist Paired Associates," *Journal of Experimental Psychology* 102 (1974): 836–40; F. S. Bellezza, "Updating Memory Using Mnemonic Devices," *Cognitive Psychology* 14 (1982): 301–27.

15. W. D. Rohwer, Jr. and J. Thomas, "The Role of Mnemonic Strategies in Study Effectiveness," in McDaniel and Pressley (3/10), 428–44; Snowman (6/2); J. Snowman, "Explorations in Mnemonic Training," in McDaniel and Pressley (3/10).

16. For additional research references on interaction, vividness, and bizarreness see Higbee (7/1).

17. K. L. Alesandrini, "Cognitive Strategies in Advertising Design," in Pressley and Levin (1/10), 203–20; V. A. Bergfeld, L. S. Choate, and N. E. A. Kroll, "The Effect of Bizarre Imagery on Memory as a Function of Delay: A Reconfirmation of the Interaction Effect," *Journal of Mental Imagery* 6 (1982): 141–58; D. W. Kee and S. Y. Nakayama, "Automatic Elaborative Encoding in Children's Associative Memory," *Bulletin of the Psychonomic Society* 16 (1980): 287–90. E. Winograd and E. W. Simon, "Visual Memory and Imagery in the Aged," in Poon et al. (1/12), 485–506.

18. For more information on interacting imagery see reviews by I. Begg, "Imagery Instruction and the Organization of Memory," in Yuille (3/12), 91–115 and Richardson (4/25). Compare words—R. R. Hunt and M. Marschark, "Yet Another Picture of Imagery: The Roles of Shared and Distinctive Information in Memory," in McDaniel and Pressley (3/10), 129–50. Children—P. Cramer, "Imagery and Learning: Item Recognition and Associative Recall," *Journal of Educational Psychology* 73 (1981): 164–73.

19. Begg (7/18); I. Begg, "Images, Organization, and Discriminative Processes," *Canadian Journal of Psychology* 36 (1982): 273–90.

20. Alesandrini (4/27).

21. G. H. Ritchey and C. R. Beal, "Image Detail and Recall: Evidence for Within-Item Elaboration," *Journal of Experimental Psychology: Human Learning and Memory* 6 (1980): 66–76.

22. F. S. Bellezza, "Mnemonic-Device Instruction with Adults," in Pressley and Levin (1/10), 51–73.

23. Defining and measuring vividness—A. Ahsen, "Prologue to Vividness Paradox," *Journal of Mental Imagery* 10 (1986): 1–8; D. Reisberg, L. C. Culver, F. Heuer, and D. Fischman, "Visual Memory: When Imagery Vividness Makes a Difference," *Journal of Mental Imagery* 10 (1986): 51–74. Paired-associates—G. H. Bower, "Mental Imagery and Associative Learning," in *Cognition in Learning and Memory*, ed. L. W. Gregg (New York: John Wiley & Sons, 1972), 51–88. List of words—P. S. Delin, "Learning and Retention of English Words with Successive Approximations to a Complex Mnemonic Instruction," *Psychonomic Science* 17 (1969): 87–88.

24. Mental practice—A. Richardson, "The Voluntary Use of Memory Imagery as an Aid to Learning and Performance," in Fleming and Hutton (4/25), 21–32. Information about people—W. B. Swann, Jr., and L. C. Miller, "Why Never Forgetting a Face Matters: Visual Imagery and Social Memory," *Journal of Personality and Social Psychology* 43 (1982): 475–80. Imagery mnemonics—A. Katz, "Individual Differences in the Control of Imagery Processing: Knowing How, Knowing When, and Knowing Self," in McDaniel and Pressley (3/10), 177–203.

25. See reviews by G. Einstein and M. McDaniel, "Distinctiveness and the Mnemonic Benefits of Bizarre Imagery," in McDaniel and Pressley (3/10), 79–102. K. Wollen and M. G. Margres, "Bizarreness and the Imagery Multiprocess Model," in McDaniel and Pressley (3/10), 103–27.

26. H. S. Hock, L. Romanski, A. Galie, and C. S. Williams, "Real-World Schemata and Scene Recognition in Adults and Children," *Memory & Cognition* 6 (1978): 423–31.

27. H. Lorayne and J. Lucas, *The Memory Book* (New York: Ballantine Books, 1975), 25–26.

28. L. W. Poon and L. Walsh-Sweeney, "Effects of Bizarre and Interacting Imagery on Learning and Retrieval of the Aged," *Experimental Aging Research* 7 (1981): 65–70.

29. Adept—J. L. Levin and M. Pressley, "Understanding Mnemonic Imagery Effects: A Dozen 'Obvious' Outcomes," in Fleming and Hutton (4/25), 33–51. College students—F. S. Bellezza, J. C. Day, and K. R. Reddy, "A Comparison of Phonetic and Semantic Encoding Mnemonics," *Human Learning* 2 (1982): 49–60.

30. Paired associates—K. A. Wollen and D. H. Lowry, "Effects of Imagery on Paired-associate Learning," *Journal of Verbal Learning and Verbal Behavior* 10 (1971): 276–84. Abstract words—W. E. Montague, "Elaborative Strategies in Verbal Learning and Memory," in Bower (2/12, vol. 6, 1972), 225–302. Sayings—K. L. Higbee and R. J. Millard, "Effects of an Imagery Mnemonic and Imagery Value on Memory for Sayings," *Bulletin of the Psychonomic Society* 17 (1981): 215–16. Concepts—A. N. Katz and A. Paivio, "Imagery Variables in Concept Identification," *Journal of Verbal*

Learning and Verbal Behavior 14 (1975): 284–93; J. C. Dyer and P. A. Meyer, "Facilitation of Simple Concept Identification Through Mnemonic Instruction," *Journal of Experimental Psychology: Human Learning and Memory* 2 (1976): 767–73.

31. S. A. Soraci, Jr., J. J. Franks, J. P. Bransford and R. C. Chechile, "A Multiple-Cue Model of Generation Activity" (paper presented at the meeting of the Psychonomic Society, Seattle, November 1987); T. D. Lee and J. D. Gallagher, "A Parallel Between the Preselection Effect in Psychomotor Memory and the Generation Effect in Verbal Memory," *Journal of Experimental Psychology: Human Learning and Memory* 7 (1981): 77–78; C. P. Thompson and C. Barnett, "Memory for Product Names: The Generation Effect," *Bulletin of the Psychonomic Society* 18 (1981): 241–43; M. M. Sebrechts, C. T. Furstenberg, and R. M. Shelton, "Remembering Computer Command Names: Effects of Subject Generation Versus Experimenter Imposition," *Behavior Research Methods, Instruments, & Computers* 18 (1986): 129–34.

32. C. Clawson, L. Delano, S. Campbell, and K. L. Higbee, "Practical Applications of Visual Mnemonics: Errands" (Paper presented at the meeting of the Western Psychological Association, San Jose, Calif., April 1985); M. Dickel and S. Slak, "Imagery Vividness and Memory for Verbal Material," *Journal of Mental Imagery* 7 (1983): 121–26; Higbee (7/1); D. G. Jamieson and M. G. Schimpf, "Self-Generated Images Are More Effective Mnemonics," *Journal of Mental Imagery* 4 (1980): 25–33.

33. Associations suggested—Higbee (7/1); J. R. Levin, "The Mnemonic 80's: Keywords in the Classroom," *Educational Psychologist* 16 (1981): 65–82; C. Carrier, K. Karbo, H. Kindem, G. Legisa, and L. Newstrom "Use of Self-generated and Supplied Visuals as Mnemonics in Gifted Children's Learning," *Perceptual and Motor Skills* 57 (1983): 235–40. Effective images—Alesandrini (4/27).

34. Preschoolers—M. Pressley, J. Samuel, M. M. Hershey, S. L. Bishop, and D. Dickinson, "Use of a Mnemonic Technique to Teach Young Children Foreign Language Vocabulary," *Contemporary Educational Psychology* 6 (1981): 110–16. Most children from age eleven—Denis (4/27), 381–401. Gifted children—Carrier et al. (7/33), 235–40. Brain-damaged people—Wilson (6/45).

35. Levin (7/33), 65–82.

36. College students—R. Sommer, *The Mind's Eye: Imagery in Everyday Life* (New York: Dell, 1978), 127; K. A. Blick and C. J. Waite, "A Survey of Mnemonic Techniques Used by College Students in Free-recall Learning," *Psychological Reports* 29 (1971): 76–78. English college students and housewives—Harris (7/7), 31–38. Elderly—Winograd and Simon (7/17).

37. Snowman (6/2).

38. Positive relationship between recall and rated vividness—R. C. Anderson and J. L. Hidde, "Imagery and Sentence Learning," *Journal of Educational Psychology* 62 (1971): 526–30. Sentences and paragraphs—P. J. Holmes and D. J. Murray, "Free Recall of Sentences as a Function of Imagery and Predictability," *Journal of Experimental Psychology* 102 (1974): 748–50; W. E. Montague and J. F. Carter, "Vividness of Imagery in Recalling Connected Discourse," *Journal of Educational Psychology* 64 (1973): 72–75. Adjectives— E. P. Kirchner, "Vividness of Adjectives and the Recall of Meaningful Verbal Material," *Psychonomic Science* 15 (1969): 71–72. Familarity— B. A. Bracken, "Relative Image-Evoking Ability of Personalized and Nonpersonalized Sentences," *Journal of Mental Imagery* 5 (1981): 121–24. Some studies have not found vividness effects for verbal materials, due at least in part to differences in definitions and methods; see S. E. Taylor and S. C. Thompson, "Stalking the Elusive 'Vividness' Effect," *Psychological Review* 89 (1982): 155–81.

39. R. C. Anderson, "Concretization and Sentence Learning," *Journal of Educational Psychology* 66 (1974): 179–83; Alesandrini (4/27).

CHAPTER 8

1. G. A. Miller, E. Galanter, and K. H. Pribram, *Plans and the Structure of Behavior* (New York: Holt, 1960), 134.

2. W. H. Burnham, "Memory, Historically and Experimentally Considered: I. An Historical Sketch of the Older Conceptions of Memory," *American Journal of Psychology* 2 (1888): 39–90.

3. Book on mnemonics—McDaniel and Pressley (3/10). Detailed account of legitimacy—Higbee (7/12); Higbee (7/1); K. L. Higbee, "The Legitimacy of Mnemonics in Instruction," *The Journal of the International Learning Science Association* 1 (1982): 9–13.

4. C. Cornoldi, "Why Study Mnemonics?" in Gruneberg et al. (1/12); M. Pressley and M. A. McDaniel, "Doing Mnemonics Research Well: Some General Guidelines and a Study," in Gruneberg et al. (1/12); P. Morris, "Practical Strategies for Human Learning and Remembering," in *Adult Learning: Psychological Research and Applications,* ed. M. J. A. Howe (London: Wiley, 1977), 125–44; I. M. L. Hunter, "Imagery, Comprehension, and Mnemonics," *Journal of Mental Imagery* 1 (1977): 65–72.

5. Clark and Paivio (3/10).

6. Two seconds—B. R. Bugelski, E. Kidd, and J. Segmen, "Imagery as a Mediator in One-Trial Paired-Associate Learning," *Journal of Experimental Psychology* 76 (1968): 69–73. Associations, pictures—W. A. Wickelgren, *Learning and Memory* (Englewood Cliffs, N.J.: Prentice-Hall, 1977), 338. Significance of time difference— B. R. Bugelski, "The Image as Mediator in One-Trial Paired-Associate Learning: III. Sequential Functions in Serial Lists," *Journal of Experimental Psychology* 103 (1974): 298–303; R. R. Hoffman, A. Fenning, and T. Kaplan, "Image Memory and Bizarreness: There Is an Effect" (paper presented at the meeting of the Psychonomic Society, Philadelphia, November 1981). Paired associates—B. R. Bugelski, "Words and Things and Images," *American Psychologist* 25 (1970): 1002–12.

7. Practice improves speed—Katz (7/24). Learning German—J. W. Hall and K. C. Fuson, "Presentation Rates in Experiments on Mnemonics: A Methodological Note," *Journal of Educational Psychology* 78 (1986): 233–34.

8. Gruneberg et al. (7/7), 304.

9. A. Corbett, "Retrieval Dynamics for Rote and Visual Imagery Mnemonics," *Journal of Verbal Learning and Verbal Behavior* 16 (1977): 233–46.

10. Bellezza (7/22).

11. Clark and Paivio (3/10).

12. P. M. Wortman and P. B. Sparling, "Acquisition and Retention of Mnemonic Information in Long-term Memory," *Journal of Experimental Psychology* 102 (1974): 22–26.

13. Wortman and Sparling (8/12); F. J. Di Vesta and P. M. Sunshine, "The Retrieval of Abstract and Concrete Materials as Functions of Imagery, Mediation, and Mnemonic Aids," *Memory & Cognition* 2 (1974): 340–44.

14. Bellezza (7/2).

15. T. Scruggs, M. A. Mastropieri, J. R. Levin, and J. S. Gaffney, "Facilitating the Acquisition of Science Facts in Learning-disabled Students," *American Educational Research Journal* 22 (1984): 575–86.

16. D. W. Hutton and J. A. Lescohier, "Seeing to Learn: Using Mental Imagery in the Classroom," in Fleming and Hutton (4/25), 113–32; G. E. Speidel & M. E. Troy, "The Ebb and Flow of Imagery in Education," in Sheikh and Sheikh (4/25), 11–38.

17. People differ—Richardson (4/25), chap. 9.; M. E. Sutherland, J. P. Harrell, and C. Isaacs, "The Stability of Individual Differences in Imagery Ability," *Journal of Mental Imagery* 11 (1987): 97–104. Benefit more by making visual associations—J. A. Slee, "The Use of Visual Imagery in Visual Memory Tasks: A Cautionary Note," in Fleming and Hutton (4/25), 53–74; A. Katz, "What Does it Mean to be a High Imager?" in Yuille (3/12), 39–63; M. Denis, "Individual Imagery Differences and Prose Processing," in McDaniel and Pressley (3/10), 204–17.

18. Capacity to use imagery—Paivio (3/14), chap. 6; A. Richardson, "The Voluntary Use of Memory Imagery as an Aid to Learning and Performance," in Fleming and Hutton (4/25), 21–32; A. A. Sheikh, K. S. Sheikh, and L. M. Moleski, "The Enhancement of Imaging Ability," in Sheikh and Sheikh (4/25); 223–39. Learned skill—Bellezza (7/22); Katz (8/17). Practice activities to help develop imagery ability are given by K. Hanks and L. Belliston, *Rapid Viz: A New Method for the Rapid Vizualization of Ideas* (Los Altos, Calif.: William Kaufman, 1980).

19. M. Pressley and J. R. Levin, "Elaborative Learning Strategies for the Inefficient Learner," in *Handbook of Cognitive, Social, and Neuropsychological Aspects of Learning Disabilities,* ed. S. J. Ceci (Hillsdale, N.J.: Erlbaum, 1986); M. Pressley, C. J. Johnson, and S. Symons, "Elaborating to Learn and Learning to Elaborate," *Journal of Learning Disabilities* 29 (1987): 76–91; Poon (1/4); J. T. E. Richardson, L. S. Cermak, S. P. Blackford, and M. O'Connor, "The Efficacy of Imagery Mnemonics Following Brain Damage," in McDaniel and Pressley (3/10), 303–28; J. E. Turnure and J. F. Lane (5/11); M. Mastropieri, T. Scruggs, and J. R. Levin, "Mnemonic Instruction in Special Education," in McDaniel and Pressley (3/10), 358–76; Wilson (6/45).

20. Bugelski (8/6, 1974); A. Paivio, "Imagery and Long-term Memory," in *Studies in Long Term Memory,* ed. A. Kennedy and A. Wilkes (New York: John Wiley and Sons, 1975), 57–88.

21. Higbee (7/1); M. Pressley, "Elaboration and Memory Development," *Child Development* 53 (1982): 296–309; M. Pressley and J. Dennis-Rounds, "Transfer of a Mnemonic Keyword Strategy at Two Age Levels," *Journal of Educational Psychology* 72 (1980): 575–82.

22. Comprehensive instructions—J. T. O'Sullivan and M. Pressley, "Completeness of Instruction and Strategy Transfer," *Journal of Experimental Child Psychology* 38 (1984): 275–88; Snowman (7/15). Kindergarten—E. B. Ryan, G. W. Ledger, and K. A. Weed, "Acquisition and Transfer of an Integrated Imagery Strategy by Young Children," *Child Development* 58 (1987): 443–52.

23. Prompting—Pressley & Dennis-Rounds (8/21). Older children—B. F. Jones and J. W. Hall, "School Applications of the Mnemonic Keyword Method as a Study Strategy by Eighth Graders," *Journal of Educational Psychology* 72 (1982): 230–37; M. Pressley, J. R. Levin, and S. L. Bryant, "Memory Strategy Instruction During Adolescence: When Is Explicit Instruction Needed?" in Pressley and Levin (1/10), 25–49.

24. M. Pressley, D. L. Forrest-Pressley, E. Elliot-Faust, and G. Miller, "Children's Use of Cognitive Strategies, How to Teach Strategies, and What To Do If They Can't Be Taught," in Pressley and Brainerd (1/13), 1–47.

25. Students—K. L. Higbee, "What Do College Students Get From a Memory-Improvement Course" (paper presented at the meeting of the Eastern Psychological Association, New York City, April 1981). Elderly—J. D. Pratt and K. L. Higbee, "Use of an Imagery Mnemonic by the Elderly in Natural Settings," *Human Learning* 2 (1983): 227–35; L. E. Wood and J. D. Pratt, "Pegword Mnemonic as an Aid to Memory in the Elderly: A Comparison of Four Age Groups," *Educational Gerontology* 13 (1987): 325–37; Poon (1/4); Roberts (1/10).

26. Any mental skill—Turnure and Lane (5/11); P. L. Peterson and S. R. Swing, "Problems in Classroom Implementation of Cognitive Strategy Research," in Pressley and Levin (6/34), 267–87; E. C. Butterfield, "Toward Solving the Problem of Transfer," in Gruneberg et al. (1/12). J. R. Hayes, "Three Problems in Teaching General Skills," in Chipman et al. (4/6), 391–406. Therapy—Baddeley (5/20), 26.

27. S. J. Derry and D. A. Murphy, "Systems That Train Learning Ability: From Theory to Practice," *Review of Educational Research* 56 (1986): 1–39; Katz (7/24); M. Pressley, J. G Borkowski, and J. O'Sullivan, "Children's Metamemory and the Teaching of Memory Strategies," in *Metacognition, Cognition, and Human Performance: Theoretical Perspectives,* vol. 1, ed. D. L. Forrest-Pressley, G. E. MacKinnon, and T. G. Waller (Orlando, Fla.: Academic Press, 1985), 111–53; Pressley et al. (1/7).

28. Pauk (6/1), 111.

29. G. H. Bower, "Educational Applications of Mnemonic Devices," in *Interaction: Readings in Human Psychology,* ed. K. O. Doyle, Jr. (Lexington, Mass.: D. C. Heath & Co., 1973), 201–10. Quote is on page 209.

30. Numerous additional research references on these pseudo-limitations, including sources of research studies and quotations referred to but not cited in this chapter, can be found in Higbee (7/12).

31. Loftus (2/3), 187.

32. Vocational, military uses—Turnure and Lane (5/11). Military training—R. Braby, J. P. Kincaid, and F. A. Aagard, *Use of Mnemonics in Training Materials: A Guide for Technical Writers* (TAEG Report no. 60, Orlando, Fla.: U.S. Navy Training Analysis and Evaluation Group, July 1978); D. Griffith, *A Review of the Literature on Memory Enhancement: The Potential and Relevance of Mnemotechnics for Military Training* (Technical Report no. 436, Fort Hood, Tex.: U.S. Army Research Institute for the Behavioral and Social Sciences, December 1979). Prose—Denis (4/27); C. McCormick and J. R. Levin, "Mnemonic Prose-Learning Strategies," in McDaniel and Pressley (3/10); 392–406.

33. Wilson and Moffat (1/4); Wilson (6/45).

34. Potential value of imagery techniques—Wittrock (4/31). Research on mental elaboration in instruction—Levin (7/33); Levin and Pressley (7/29); J. R. Levin and M. Pressley, "Mnemonic Vocabulary Instruction: What's Fact, What's Fiction," in *Individual Differences in Cognition*, vol. 2, ed. R. F. Dillon (Orlando, Fla.: Academic Press, 1985), 145–72.

35. Problem solving—G. Kaufman and T. Helstrup, "Mental Imagery and Problem Solving: Implications for the Educational Process," in Sheikh and Sheikh (4/25), 113–44.

36. H. H. Kendler, *Basic Psychology: Brief Version*, 3d ed. (Menlo Park, Calif. W. A. Benjamin, 1977), 205.

37. Clawson et al. (7/32); T. Lowe, K. J. Scoresby, and K. L. Higbee, "The Role of Effort in Using a Visual Mnemonic" (paper presented at the meeting of the Western Psychological Association, San Jose, Calif., April 1985).

38. Sentences—J. D. Bransford and B. S. Stein, *The Ideal Problem Solver* (San Francisco: W. H. Freeman, 1984), 54–58. Facts—G. L. Bradshaw and J. R. Anderson, "Elaborative Encoding As an Explanation of Levels of Processing," *Journal of Verbal Learning and Verbal Behavior* 21 (1982): 165–74; see also Horton and Mills (2/22), 247–75.

39. Bellezza (7/2); Levin and Pressley (8/34).

40. Hunter (8/4), 70.

41. *Psychology Today: An Introduction*, 2d ed. (Del Mar, Calif.: CRM Books, 1972), 97.

42. Bellezza (7/2).

CHAPTER 9

1. Third difference—Bugelski (8/6, 1974). Fourth difference—L. W. Barsalou and D. R. Sewell, "Contrasting the Representation of Scripts and Categories," *Journal of Memory and Language* 24 (1985): 646–65.

2. D. L. Foth, "Mnemonic Technique Effectiveness as a Function of Word Abstractness and Mediation Instruction," *Journal of Verbal Learning and Verbal Behavior* 12 (1973): 239–45.

3. K. L. Higbee, "Mnemonic Systems in Memory: Are They Worth the Effort?" (paper presented at the meeting of the Rocky Mountain Psychological Association, Phoenix, Ariz., May 1976); Griffith (8/32).

4. First finding—Bellezza (7/14). Second finding—Bellezza (7/22). Third finding—F. S. Bellezza, "The Spatial-Arrangement Mnemonic," *Journal of Educational Psychology* 75 (1983): 830–37. Fourth finding—H. L. Roediger III, "The Effectiveness of Four Mnemonics in Ordering Recall," *Journal of Experimental Psychology: Human Learning and Memory* 6 (1980): 558–67. Fifth finding—B. R. Bugelski, "The Association of Images," in *Images, Perception, and Knowledge*, ed. J. M. Nichols (Boston: D. Reidel, 1977), 37–46.

5. Clawson et al. (7/32).

6. Studies of effectiveness—Snowman (6/2). Five lists—F. S. Bellezza, "A Mnemonic Based on Arranging Words on Visual Patterns," *Journal of Educational*

Psychology 78 (1986): 217–24. Long list—F. S. Bellezza, D. L. Richards, and R. Geiselman, "Semantic Processing and Organization in Free Recall," *Memory & Cognition* 4 (1976): 415–21; F. S. Bellezza, F. L. Chessman II, and B. G. Reddy, "Organization and Semantic Elaboration in Free Recall," *Journal of Experimental Psychology: Human Learning and Memory* 3 (1977): 539–50; G. Gamst and J. S. Freund, "Effects of Subject-generated Stories on Recall," *Bulletin of the Psychonomic Society* 12 (1978): 185–88.

7. India—S. K. Gupta, "Associative Memory: Role of Mnemonics in Information Processing and Ordering Recall," *Psycho-Lingua* 15 (1985), 89–94. Amnesiac patients—R. Kovner, S. Mattis, and R. Pass, "Some Patients Can Freely Recall Large Amounts of Information in New Contexts," *Journal of Clinical and Experimental Neuropsychology* 7 (1985): 395–411. Brain-damaged patients—Wilson (6/45).

8. G. H. Bower, "How to . . . uh . . . Remember!" *Psychology Today,* October 1973, 63–70. Quote is on page 63.

9. D. Carnegie, *Public Speaking and Influencing Men in Business* (New York: Association Press, 1926), 60.

10. D. W. Matheson, *Introductory Psychology: The Modern View* (Hinsdale, Ill.: The Dryden Press, 1975), 233.

11. T. B. Woodbury, "Be-attitudes in Business," in *Successful Leadership,* ed. M. L. Waters (Salt Lake City: Deseret Book, 1961), 236–50. Quote is on page 236.

12. Hanks and Belliston (8/18), 135.

13. Several examples of how to do this are provided in B. Furst, *Stop Forgetting,* chap. 10, rev. L. Furst and G. Storm (Garden City, N.Y.: Doubleday & Co., 1979).

14. C. V. Young, *The Magic of a Mighty Memory* (West Nyack, N.Y.: Parker Publishing Co., 1971), 67.

15. Some examples are T. Buzan, *Speed Memory* (London: Sphere Books Ltd., 1971); D. Hersey, *How to Cash in on Your Hidden Memory Power* (Englewood Cliffs, N.J.: Prentice-Hall, 1963); Lorayne and Lucas (7/27); T. G. Madsen, *How to Stop Forgetting and Start Remembering* (Provo, Utah: Brigham Young University Press, 1970); M. N. Young and W. B. Gibson, *How to Develop an Exceptional Memory* (North Hollywood, Calif.: Wilshire Book Co., 1974).

CHAPTER 10

1. Yates (7/1).

2. G. H. Bower, "Analysis of a Mnemonic Device," *American Scientist* 58 (1970): 496–510; C. Cornoldi and R. De Beni, "Imagery and the 'Loci' Mnemonic," *International Imagery Bulletin* 2 (1984): 10–13; C. Cornoldi and R. De Beni, "Retrieval Times in the Use of Concrete and Abstract Mnemonic Cues Associated to Loci," in *Imagery 2,* ed. D. F. Marks and D. G. Russell (Dunedin, New Zealand: Human Performance Associates, in press); G. Lea, "Chronometric Analysis of the Method of Loci," *Journal of Experimental Psychology: Human Perception and Performance* 104 (1975): 95–104; Turnure and Lane (5/11).

3. I. Begg and D. Sikich, "Imagery and Contextual Organization," *Memory & Cognition* 12 (1984): 52–59.

4. Bugelski (8/6, 1974).

5. Luria (3/17), 31–33.

6. Higbee (9/3).

7. Several studies on locations—Johnson and Hasher (1/2). Positively related—R. De Beni and C. Cornoldi, "Effects of the Mnemotechnique of Loci in the Memorization of Concrete Words," *Acta Psychologica* 59 (1985): 1–14.

8. R. N. Haber, "The Power of Visual Perceiving," *Journal of Mental Imagery* 5 (1981): 1–16; E. A. Lovelace and S. D. Southall, "Memory for Words in Prose and Their Locations on the Page," *Memory & Cognition* 11 (1983), 429–34; Rothkopf et al. (6/8), 50–54.

9. Remembering pictures versus words—Park et al. (3/12). Landmarks—G. W. Evans, P. L. Brennan, M. A. Skorpanich, and D. Held, "Cognitive Mapping and Elderly Adults: Verbal and Location Memory for Urban Landmarks," *Journal of Gerontology* 39 (1984): 452–57; Link system—Turnure and Lane (5/11).

10. Lovelace and Southall (10/8).

11. Effects of Different patterns on learning—Bellezza (7/14); Bellezza (9/6). Learning and note-taking strategies—C. D. Holley and D. F. Dansereau, eds., *Spatial Learning Strategies: Techniques, Applications, and Related Issues* (Orlando, Fla.: Academic Press, 1984). Fourth graders—R. D. Abbott and R. E. Hughes, "Effect of Verbal-Graphic Note-Taking Strategies on Writing" (paper presented at the meeting of the American Educational Research Association, San Francisco, April 1986).

12. R. E. Rawles, "The Past and Present of Mnemotechny," in Gruneberg (4/17), 164–71.

13. Provinces and capitals—A. I. Schulman, "Maps and Memorability," in *The Acquisition of Symbolic Skills*, ed. D. Rogers and J. A. Sloboda (New York: Plenum Press, 1982), 359–67. Imaginary island—N. H. Schwartz and R. W. Kulhavy, "Map Features and the Recall of Discourse," *Contemporary Educational Psychology* 6 (1981): 151–58. Creating maplike representation—R. S. Dean and R. W. Kulhavy, "Influence of Spatial Organization in Prose Learning," *Journal of Educational Psychology* 73 (1981): 57–64.

14. Word lists—De Beni and Cornoldi (10/7); R. De Beni and C. Cornoldi, "The Effects of Imaginal Mnemonics on Congenitally Total Blind and on Normal Subjects," in *Imagery 1*, ed. D. F. Marks and D. G. Russell (Dunedin, New Zealand: Human Performance Associates, 1983), 54–59; Roediger (9/4), 558–67; Snowman (6/2); Wilson (6/45). Visible loci—S. Kemp and C. D. van der Krogt, "Effect of Visibility of the Loci on Recall Using the Method of Loci," *Bulletin of the Psychonomic Society* 23 (1985): 202–04. Prose Remembering—J. Snowman, E. V. Krebs, and L. Lockhart, "Improving Recall of Information from Prose in High-risk Students through Learning Strategy Training," *Journal of Instructional Psychology* 7 (1980): 35–40; also see Snowman (7/15); and R. De Beni, "The Aid Given By the 'Loci' Memory Technique in the Memorization of Passages," in Gruneberg et al. (1/12).

15. C. E. Weinstein, W. E. Cubberly, F. W. Wicker, V. L. Underwood, L. K. Roney, and D. C. Duty, "Training Versus Instruction in the Acquisition of Cognitive Learning Strategies," *Contemporary Educational Psychology* 6 (1981): 159–66.

16. Elderly—J. A. Yesavage and T. L. Rose, "Semantic Elaboration and the

Method of Loci: A New Trip for Old Learners," *Experimental Aging Research* 10 (1984): 155–60; L. Anschutz, C. J. Camp, R. P. Markley, and J. J. Kramer, "Maintenance and Generalization of Mnemonics for Grocery Shopping by Older Adults," *Experimental Aging Research* 11 (1985): 157–60. Blind Adults—P. A. Raia, "Cognitive Skill Training of Adventitiously Blinded Elderly Women: The Effects of Training in the Method of Loci on Free Recall Performance" (Ph.D. diss., University of Maryland–College Park, 1979); De Beni and Cornoldi (10/14). Brain-damaged Patients—Wilson (6/45).

17. De Beni and Cornoldi (10/7); G. H. Bower and J. S. Reitman, "Mnemonic Elaboration in Multilist Learning," *Journal of Verbal Learning and Verbal Behavior* 11 (1972): 478–85; A. L. Brown, "Progressive Elaboration and Memory for Order in Children," *Journal of Experimental Child Psychology* 19 (1975): 383–400.

18. H. F. Crovitz, *Galton's Walk* (New York: Harper & Row, 1970), 44.

CHAPTER 11

1. Paivio (3/18), 173.

2. Bower and Reitman (10/17), 478–85; Bellezza (7/2).

3. Miller et al. (8/1), 135–36.

4. These findings have been summarized by Higbee (9/3) and by Griffith (8/32).

5. Additional studies on effectiveness—F. S. Bellezza and G. H. Bower, "Remembering Script-Based Text," *Poetics* 11 (1982): 1–23; Roediger (9/4); Wood and Pratt (8/25). Categories interfere with pegwords—B. G. Reddy and F. S. Bellezza, "Interference Between Mnemonic and Categorical Organization in Memory," *Bulletin of the Psychonomic Society* 24 (1986): 169–71.

6. J. L. Elliot and J. R. Gentile, "The Efficacy of a Mnemonic Technique for Learning Disabled and Nondisabled Adolescents," *Journal of Learning Disabilities* 19 (1986): 237–41.

7. Remembering concepts—Dyer and Meyer (7/30). College students—Higbee and Millard (7/30); Markham et al. (4/6); Wood and Pratt (8/25); Effort—Lowe, Scoresby, and Higbee (8/37). Children—T. P. Asay, K. L. Higbee, and R. K. Morgan, "Effects of a Visual Mnemonic on Children's Memory for Sayings" (paper presented at the meeting of the Rocky Mountain Psychological Association, Albuquerque, N.M., April 1982). Adults—Pratt and Higbee (8/25); Wood and Pratt (8/25).

8. Pratt and Higbee (8/25, study 1).

9. Pauk (6/1), 107.

10. Mastropieri et al. (8/19).

11. J. R. Levin, C. B. McCormick, and B. J. Dretzke, "A Combined Pictorial Mnemonic Strategy for Ordered Information," *Educational Communication and Technology Journal* 29 (1981): 219–25.

12. Snowman (7/15). D. T. Veit, T. E. Scruggs, and M. A. Mastropieri, "Extended Mnemonic Instruction With Learning Disabled Students," *Journal of Educational Psychology* 78 (1986): 300–08.

13. J. A. Glover and A. L. Harvey, "Remembering Written Instructions: Tab A Goes into Slot C, or Does It?" (paper presented at the meeting of the American Educational Research Association, San Francisco, April 1986); V. Timme, D. Deyloff,

M. Rogers, D. Dinnel, and J. A. Glover, "Oral Directions; Remembering What to Do When" (paper presented at the meeting of the American Educational Research Association, San Francisco, April 1986).

14. Amnesiac patients—C. D. Evans, *Rehabilitation of the Head Injured* (London: Churchill Livingstone, 1981), 72–73. Training Program—B. A. Wilson and N. Moffat (7/7).

15. K. L. Higbee, "Can Young Children Use Mnemonics?" *Psychological Reports* 38 (1976): 18.

16. B. R. Bugelski, "Images as Mediators in One-Trial Paired-Associate Learning. II: Self-timing in Successive Lists," *Journal of Experimental Psychology* 77 (1968): 328–34.

17. Bower and Reitman (10/17).

18. Braby et al. (8/32), 60–71.

CHAPTER 12

1. R. Grey, *Memoria Technica: or, a New Method of Artificial Memory*, 2d ed. (London: Charles King, 1732).

2. M. G. von Feinaigle, *The New Art of Memory*, 2d ed. (London: Sherwood, Neely, & Jones, 1813).

3. F. Fauvel-Gouraud, *Phreno-Mnemonotechnic Dictionary: A Philosophical Classification of all the Homophonic Words of the English Language*, part first (New York: Houel & Macay, 1844); James (1/15), 669; A. Loisette, *Assimilative Memory, or How to Attend and Never Forget* (New York: Funk & Wagnalls, Inc., 1899); 66–108.

4. Furst (9/13); Buzan (9/15); Hersey (9/15).

5. The research up to the mid-1970s is summarized by Higbee (9/3) and by Griffith (8/32).

6. Metric equivalences—D. Bruce and M. Cleamons, "A Test of the Effectiveness of the Phonetic (Number-Consonant) Mnemonic System," *Human Learning* 1 (1982): 83–93. Second study—P. E. Morris and P. J. Greer, "The Effectiveness of the Phonetic Mnemonic System," *Human Learning* 3 (1984): 137–42. Third study— G. W. R. Patton and P. D. Lantzy, "Testing the Limits of the Phonetic Mnemonic System," *Applied Cognitive Psychology* (in press). See also G. W. R. Patton, "The Effect of the Phonetic Mnemonic System on Memory for Numerical Material," *Human Learning* 5 (1986): 21–28.

7. T. E. Gordon, P. Gordon, E. Valentine, and J. Wilding, "One Man's Memory: A Study of a Mnemonist," *British Journal of Psychology* 72 (1984): 1–14. (3/19), 1–14. Scoresby et al. (3/20). Six students—mental calculation—Wells (3/19), 49–54/59–61.

8. S. Slak, "Long-Term Retention of Random Sequence Digital Information with the Aid of Phonemic Recoding: A Case Report," *Perceptual and Motor Skills* 33 (1971): 455–60.

9. Paivio, "Strategies in Language Learning" in Pressley and Levin (6/34), 189–210; Paivio (3/14), 254–55.

10. Dickel (7/13); S. Slak, "On Phonetic and Phonemic Systems: A Reply to M. J. Dickel," *Perceptual and Motor Skills* 61 (1985): 727–33.

11. Loisette (12/3), 73–74.

12. F. S. Hamilton, *Mastering Your Memory* (New York: Gramercy Publishing Co., 1947); see also the sources cited in note 15 of chapter 9.

13. The book is available from Ernest Weckbaugh, 1718 Rogers Place #1A, Burbank, Calif. 91504.

14. See the sources cited in note 15 of chapter 9.

CHAPTER 13

1. Elderly—E. M. Zelinski, M. J. Gilewski, and L. W. Thompson, "Do Laboratory Tests Relate to Self-assessment of Memory Ability in the Young and Old?" in Poon et al. (1/12), 519–44. Patients—B. Wilson, "Memory Therapy in Practice," in Wilson and Moffat (1/4), 89–111.

2. V. P.—Hunt and Love (3/18), 255. Barker—*Family Weekly*, September 1975. Luce—Brothers and Eagan (5/2), 104.

3. Memory for faces—Bahrick (2/20); G. Davies, H. Ellis, and J. Shepherd, *Perceiving and Remembering Faces* (London: Academic Press, 1981): Eyewitness testimony—S. J. Ceci, M. P. Toglia, and D. F. Ross, ed., *Children's Eyewitness Testimony* (New York: Springer-Verlag, 1987); J. W. Shepherd, H. D. Ellis, and G. M. Davies, *Identification Evidence: A Psychological Evaluation* (Aberdeen, Scotland: Aberdeen University Press, 1982); G. L. Wells and E. F. Loftus, eds., *Eyewitness Testimony: Psychological Perspectives* (New York: Cambridge University Press, 1984); S. Lloyd-Bostock and B. R. Clifford, ed., *Evaluating Witness Evidence* (Chicester, England: Wiley, 1982).

4. S. Parry and K. L. Higbee, "Remembering People: Research on Memory for Names and Faces" (paper presented at the meeting of The Rocky Mountain Psychological Association, Las Vegas, April 1984).

5. Horton and Mills (2/22).

6. Reed (2/23).

7. Difference among people—Bahrick et al. (2/18). College students—Bahrick (2/20). Housewives—Baddeley (2/3), 124. Sex differences—Behrick (2/20); K. A. Deffenbacher, E. L. Brown, and W. Sturgill, "Some Predictors of Eyewitness Accuracy," in Gruneberg et al. (4/17), 219–26; S. J. McKelvie, "Sex Differences in Facial Memory," in Gruneberg et al. (4/17), 263–69.

8. Women—J. C. Bartlett and J. E. Leslie, "Aging and Memory for Faces Versus Single Views of Faces," *Memory & Cognition* 14 (1986): 371–81. Professors—Bahrick (2/20). Changes—J. C. Bartlett, J. Leslie, and A. Tubbs, "Aging and Memory For Pictures of Faces" (Paper presented at the meeting of the Psychonomic Society, Seattle, November 1987).

9. 96 percent—K. Deffenbacher, E. Brown, and W. Sturgill, "Memory for Faces and the Circumstances of Their Encounter" (paper presented at the meeting of the Psychonomic Society, Denver, November 1975). 75 percent recognition of high school classmates—Bahrick et al. (2/18).

10. R. J. Phillips, "Recognition, Recall, and Imagery of Faces," in Gruneberg, Morris, and Sykes, (4/17), 270–77.

11. H. Ellis, J. Shepherd, and G. Davies, "An Investigation of the Use of Photo-Fit Technique for Recalling Faces," *British Journal of Psychology* 66 (1975): 29–37.

12. First study—J. D. Read and R. G. Wilbur II, "Availability of Faces and Names in Recall," *Perceptual and Motor Skills* 41 (1975): 263–70. Second study—H. M. Clarke, "Recall and Recognition for Faces and Names," *Journal of Applied Psychology* 18 (1934): 757–63.

13. Professors—Bahrick (2/20). Classmates—Bahrick et al. (2/18). Name recognition faster—A. Paivio and I. Begg, "Pictures and Words in Visual Search," *Memory & Cognition* 2 (1974): 515–21.

14. Tip of The Tongue—Burke (2/26). Objective frequency—J. F. Hall, "Memory for Surnames," *Bulletin of the Psychonomic Society* 19 (1982): 320–22.

15. Recalling names of classmates—Williams and Hollan (4/21). Recalling famous person's name—Yarmey (2/25). Object—J. E. May and K. N. Clayton, "Imaginal Processes During the Attempt to Recall Names," *Journal of Verbal Learning and Verbal Behavior* 12 (1973): 683–88. Recognition memory and context—A. Goldstein and J. Chance, "Laboratory Studies of Face Recognition," in Shepherd et al. (13.3), 81–104; Horton and Mills (2/22).

16. S. D. Cox and R. H. Hopkins, "Priming Treatments and Long-term Memory" (paper presented at the meeting of the Psychonomic Society, Phoenix, Ariz., November 1979).

17. S. J. Brant, "Name Recall as a Function of Introduction Time," *Psychological Reports* 50 (1982): 377–78.

18. H. Lorayne, *Remembering People: The Key to Success* (New York: Stein & Day, 1975).

19. A list of memory-training books is given in note 15 of chapter 9. Research with elderly people, for example, has found practice to be a very important factor in improving name-face memory, see Poon (1/4), 449.

20. "I know the face but not the name"—Reed (2/23). Self-conscious—C. E. Kimble and II. D. Zchr, "Self-Consciousness, Information Load, Self-Presentation, and Memory in a Social Situation," *Journal of Social Psychology* 118 (1982): 39–46.

21. B. M. Gadzella and D. A. Whitehead, "Effects of Auditory and Visual Modalities in Recall of Words," *Perceptual and Motor Skills* 40 (1975): 255–60.

22. D. L. McCarty, "Investigation of a Visual Imagery Mnemonic Device for Acquiring Face-Name Associations," *Journal of Experimental Psychology: Human Learning and Memory* 6 (1980): 145–55.

23. Lorayne (13/18).

24. Several studies—R. S. Malpass, "Training in Face Recognition," in Davies et al. (13/3), 271–84; Winograd and Simon (7/17). Distinctive feature—E. Winograd, "Encoding Operations Which Facilitate Memory for Faces Across the Life Span," in Gruneberg et al. (4/17), 255–62. Told to remember faces—P. G. Devine and R. S. Malpass, "Orienting Strategies in Differential Face Recognition," *Personality and Social Psychology Bulletin* 11 (1985): 33–40.

25. K. Laughery, B. Rhodes, and G. Batten, "Computer-Guided Recognition and Retrieval of Facial Images," in Shepherd et al. (13/3), 251–70.

26. Attractiveness—J. W. Shepherd and H. D. Ellis, "The Effect of Attractiveness on Recognition Memory for Faces," *American Journal of Psychology* 86 (1973): 627–33. Race—J. W. Shepherd, J. B. Deregowski, and H. D. Ellis, "A Cross-Cultural Study of Recognition Memory for Faces," *International Journal of Psychology* 9 (19747): 205–12. Smile—R. E. Galper and J. Hochberg, "Recognition Memory for Photographs of Faces," *American Journal of Psychology* 84 (1971): 351–54.

27. J. Shepherd, G. Davies, and H. Ellis, "Studies of Cue Saliency," in Shepherd, et al. (13/3), 105–32; K. Pezdek and J. K. Reynolds, "Facial Recognition Memory" (paper presented at the meeting of the Psychonomic Society, Seattle, November 1987).

28. P. N. Shapiro and S. Penrod, "Meta-Analysis of Facial Identification Studies," *Psychological Bulletin* 100 (1986): 139–56.

29. Lorayne (13/18), 201.

30. Loftus (2/3), 186.

31. Landauer and Bjork (6/39).

32. A. D. Yarmey, "Proactive Interference in Short-Term Retention of Human Faces," *Canadian Journal of Psychology* 28 (1974): 333–38.

33. Same principles as other mnemonics—Turnure and Lane (5/11). Exception to lack of practicality—Loftus (2/3), 187.

34. First study—P. E. Morris, S. Jones, and P. Hampson, "An Imagery Mnemonic for the Learning of People's Names," *British Journal of Psychology* 69 (1978): 335–36. Second study—McCarty (13/22).

35. Elderly—J. A. Yesavage, T. L. Rose, and G. H. Bower, "Interactive Imagery and Affective Judgments Improve Face-Name Learning in the Elderly," *Journal of Gerontology* 38 (1983): 197–203; J. A. Yesavage and R. Jacob, "Effects of Relaxation and Mnemonics on Memory, Attention, and Anxiety in the Elderly," *Experimental Aging Research* 10 (1984): 211–14. Brain-damaged patients—Richardson et al. (8.19); Moffat, "Strategies of Memory Therapy," in Wilson & Moffat (1/4), 63–88; Wilson (6/45); R. D. Hill, K. D. Evankovich, J. I. Sheikh, and J. A. Yesavage, "Imagery Mnemonic Training in a Patient with Primary Degenerative Dementia," *Psychology & Aging*, 2 (1987), 204–05.

36. Lorayne (13/18).

37. S. S. Smith, "A Method for Teaching Name Mnemonics," *Teaching of Psychology* 12 (1985): 156–58; C. J. Walker, "An Instamatic Way of Learning Who Is in Your Large Classes: A Picture Is Worth a Thousand Names," *Teaching of Psychology* 7 (1980): 62–63.

CHAPTER 14

1. Harris and Morris (2/20); Reason and Mycielska (2/24).

2. Reason and Mycielska (2/24), 243.

3. Baddeley (2/3); Poon (1/4).

4. Cavanaugh et al. (5/9).

5. Bracken (7/3), 115.

6. Cavanaugh et al. (5/9), 113–22.

7. Elderly—Poon (1/4); D. H. Kausler, "Episodic Memory: Memorizing Performance," in *Aging and Human Performance*, ed. N. Charness (Chichester, England:

Wiley, 1985), 101–41. Procrastination—C. H. Lay, "Procrastination and Everyday Memory," in Gruneberg et al. (1/12).

8. J. E. Harris, "Methods of Improving Memory," in Wilson and Moffat (1/4).

9. J. A. Mecham and J. A. Colombo, "External Retrieval Cues Facilitate Prospective Remembering in Children," *The Journal of Educational Research* 73 (1980): 299–301.

10. Richardson et al. (8/19).

11. Thought about doing it—R. E. Anderson, "Did I Do It or Did I Only Imagine Doing It?" *Journal of Experimental Psychology: General* 113 (1984): 594–613; A. Koriat and H. Ben-Zur, "Remembering That I Did It: Processes and Deficits in Output Monitoring," in Gruneberg et al. (1/12); Checkers—Reed (2/23).

12. Harris (7/7).

13. E. Tavon, "Tips to Trigger Memory," *Geriatric Nursing*, (Jan./Feb. 1984), 26–27.

14. *USA Weekend*, October 4–6, 1985.

15. The 1970s quotes are by Allan Paivio, Ernest Hilgard, Gordon Bower, and Laird Cermak can be found in Higbee (7/1). Book—T. G. Devine, *Teaching Study Skills: A Guide for Teachers* (Boston: Allyn and Bacon, 1981), 286. 10 reasons—Levin (7/33).

16. A large part of this research has been done by Joel Levin and Michael Pressley and their associates, and much of it has been cited in chapters 7 and 8. Additional relevant research has been summarized by Higbee (7/1); N. S. Suzuki, "Imagery Research with Children: Implications for Education," in Sheikh and Sheikh (4/25), 179–98; and J. R. Levin, "Educational Applications of Mnemonic Pictures: Possibilities Beyond Your Wildest Imagination," in Sheikh and Sheikh (4/25), 63–87.

17. H. Lorayne, *Good Memory—Good Student* (New York: Stein & Day, 1976); H. Lorayne, *Good Memory—Successful Student* (New York: Stein & Day, 1976); M. Herold, *Memorizing Made Easy* (Chicago: Contemporary Books, 1982).

18. Good students—Levin (14/16). Gifted students—T. E. Scruggs, M. A. Mastropieri, J. Monson, and C. Jorgensen, "Maximizing What Gifted Students Can Learn: Recent Findings of Learning Strategy Research," *Gifted Child Quarterly* 29 (1985): 181–85; T. E. Scruggs and M. A. Mastropieri, "How Gifted Students Learn: Implications from Recent Research," *Roeper Review* 6 (1984): 183–85.

19. U.S. Department of Education, *What Works* (4/20), 37. Teachers' perspective—Devine (14/15), 285–86; C. E. Weinstein and R. E. Mayer, "The Teaching of Learning Strategies," in Wittrock (4/31), 315–27; Wittrock (4/31).

20. The Japanese mnemonics and U.S. fraction mnemonics are described in more detail in K. L. Higbee, "Process Mnemonics: Principles, Prospects, and Problems," in McDaniel and Pressley (3/10), 407–27; and K. L. Higbee and S. Kunihira, "Cross-Cultural Applications of Yodai Mnemonics," *Educational Psychologist* 20 (1985): 57–64. See also K. Machida, "The Effects of a Verbal Mediation Strategy on Mathematics Problem Solving." (Ph.D. diss., University of California at Riverside, 1987). The other mnemonics are also described in K. L. Higbee, "Applied Mnemonics Research Applied" (paper presented at the meeting of the 21st International Congress of Applied Psychology, Jerusalem, July 1986); and K. L. Higbee, "Practical Aspects of Mnemonics," in Gruneberg et al. (1/12). For more information on language-skills mnemonics, contact Leland Michael, MKM, 809 Kansas City Street, Rapid City, S. Dak. 57701; and Nancy Stevenson, Stevenson Language Skills, 85 Upland Road, Attleboro, Mass. 02703. For more information on basic math mnemonics, contact Jan Semple at Stevenson Language Skills.

21. Chipman and Segal (6/2).

22. Texas Christian University—Dansereau (6/28). Texas—Weinstein and Underwood (5/13). Similar programs—Weinstein and Mayer (14/19).

23. Weinstein and Mayer (14/19).

24. Peterson and Swing (8/26); R. M. Plant, "Reading Research: Its Influence on Classroom Practice," *Educational Research* 28 (1986), 126–31.

25. Levin and Pressley (8/34), 168.

26. For example, see J. Kilpatrick, "Doing Mathematics Without Understanding It: A Commentary on Higbee and Kunihira," *Educational Psychologist* 20 (1985): 65–68. Compare K. L. Higbee and S. Kunihira, "Some Questions (and a Few Answers) About Yodai Mnemonics: A Reply to Kilpatrick, Pressley, and Levin," *Educational Psychologist* 20 (1985): 77–81.

27. W. D. Rohwer, Jr., and F. N. Dempster, "Memory Development and Educational Processes," in *Perspectives on the Development of Memory and Cognition,* ed. R. V. Kail, Jr., and J. W. Hagen (Hillsdale, N.J.: Erlbaum, 1977), 407–35.

28. School tasks—Weinstein and Mayer (14/19), 325. Presidents—Lorayne, *Successful Student* (14/17), 14. Loftier educational goals—Bower (9/8), 70.

29. Goals of education—Chipman and Segal (6/2). Process of education—Shuell (4/3).

30. Review of memory research—M. J. A. Howe and S. J. Ceci, "Educational Implications of Memory Research," in *Applied Problems in Memory,* ed. M. M. Gruneberg and P. E. Morris (New York: Academic Press, 1979), 59. Memorization as a precursor to understanding—B. Hayes-Roth and C. Walker, "Configural Effects in Human Memory: The Superiority of Memory Over External Information Sources as a Basis for Inference Verification," *Cognitive Science* 3 (1979): 119–40. Inferences—T. E. Scruggs, M. A. Mostropieri, B. B. McLoone, and J. R. Levin, "Mnemonic Facilitation of Learning Disabled Students' Memory for Expository Prose," *Journal of Educational Psychology* 79 (1987): 27–34.

31. Reasoning and understanding—T. Trabasso, "The Role of Memory as a System in Making Transitive Inferences," in Kail and Hagen (14/27), 333–66. Computer program—M. Lebowitz, "Using Memory in Text Understanding," in *Experience, Memory, and Reasoning,* ed. J. L. Kolodner and C. K. Reisbeck (Hillsdale, N.J.: Erlbaum, 1986). Concepts—Dyer and Meyer (7/30). Clear thinking—R. Flesch, *The Art of Clear Thinking* (New York: Barnes & Noble, 1973), 8.

32. Important role of memory—Stern (2/3), chap. 11; J. L. Kolodner and R. L. Simpson, "Problem Solving and Dynamic Memory," in Kolodner and Riesbeck (14/31). Studies of problem solving—J. Bransford, R. Sherwood, N. Vye, and J. Rieser, "Teaching Thinking and Problem Solving: Research Foundations," *American Psychologist* 41 (1986): 1078–89. Problem-solving techniques—Bransford and Stein (8/38, chap. 3); see also J. B. Belmont, L. Freesman, and D. Mitchell, "Problem Solving and Memory," in Gruneberg et al. (1/12).

33. U.S. Department of Education, *What Works* (4/20), 37.

Index

About the Author

KENNETH L. HIGBEE is a professor of psychology at Brigham Young University, where he teaches on-campus and home-study memory courses. He also conducts research on memory, and has published numerous scientific articles. In addition, he has given hundreds of lectures and workshops, teaching memory skills and reporting his memory research throughout the United States and in several other countries.

GASLIGHTS AND GINGERBREAD

GASLIGHTS

AND

GINGERBREAD

SANDRA DALLAS

SECOND REVISED EDITION

SAGE BOOKS, *Denver*

To Bob . . . who else

Preface

Not so many years ago, the main street of Breckenridge was a dapper boulevard lined with jaunty buildings, some of the best gingerbread architecture in Colorado.

Today, most of the structures are gone, and the few remaining have been refaced. Fortunately for history, they were preserved in print and paint by an enthusiastic chronicler, Muriel Sibell Wolle.

The houses that lived with the buildings? Nobody cared much about them, so they lived their exuberant existences and are crumbling away without even the recognition of a picture on a postcard.

These decorative and lavish homes deserve at least a fleeting note in history. *Gaslights and Gingerbread* has been written to give them their say.

The book was begun with the idea of including only mountain Victorian homes, and most are just that. But others came along, not really Victorian, nor indeed, even built in the nineteenth century, but unusual enough to merit attention. Despite the title's seeming exclusion, they deserve to be included.

Homes in Denver and Colorado Springs were eliminated since there are enough in each city to fill separate books.

Except when noted, all houses are private residences, not open to the public. Many owners are victims of overly enthusiastic sight-seers who punch the doorbell and demand to see inside. So anyone using the book as a tour guide is asked to proceed with courtesy.

(The owner of one particularly interesting home reported coming downstairs dressed in her nightgown early one Sunday morning to find a family peering through the window. They didn't believe anyone "really lived there.")

The colonial houses of New England, the mansions of the South, the adobes of California, all have told their tales. Perhaps through *Gaslights and Gingerbread* Colorado's gay and gaudy homes will tell theirs.

Sandra Dallas

Breckenridge, Colorado

Acknowledgments

So many people made this book — those who collected history in memory and manuscript. From the capable women in the Western History Department of the Denver Public Library and the library of the State Historical Society of Colorado, to the efficient Chamber of Commerce secretaries who answered queries and directed letters to local historians.

Space limits the recognition they should have, but though I list them impersonally and thank them collectively, my appreciation is very great.

Perry Eberhart, author of *Guide to the Colorado Ghost Towns and Mining Camps*. William E. Marshall, State Historical Society of Colorado. Mrs. Grace Warshauer McGregor, Antonito. Mrs. Maumbert Cerise, Mrs. Fred Glidden, Vern Harris, Mrs. Harald Pabst, Aspen. Louis Pircher, Mrs. John I. Smith, Black Hawk. Mr. and Mrs. Donald McInnes, Mrs. Julian Peck, Boulder. Mrs. Bertha Biggins, Mrs. Freda Dodge, Amos Jackson, Mrs. Ambure Otterson, Helen Rich, Belle Turnbull, Breckenridge. Mr. and Mrs. Gus Center, Mr. and Mrs. William M. Tanner, Central City. Norman Meyer,

8

Conifer. Bernice Gardner, Fritz Kochevar, Crested Butte. Mrs. William Ackelbein, Mr. and Mrs. George Blaylock, Mrs. Vivian Richardson, Cripple Creek. Mrs. Cathy McKinny, Fairplay. Mrs. Donald Ahrenholtz, Mrs. Alice Stranton, Betty Woodworth, Fort Collins. Torval Johnson, Mrs. Kathryn Senor, Glenwood Springs. Mrs. Richard Bennett, Mr. and Mrs. Hildreth Frost, Jr., Georgetown. Mrs. Helen Larson, Greeley. Mrs. Leah Hartman Cunius, Mrs. Mil Davis, Gene Grubb, Gunnison. Mrs. Frances Cassidy, Idaho Springs. Robert L. Christy, Lamar. Don and Jean Griswold, Emmett Irwin, Mrs. Marion Poppy Smith, Leadville. Osborn R. Lee, Montrose. Mrs. Benton B. Bailey, Mrs. Mabel L. Franz, Mrs. Frances Johnson, Ouray. Mrs. L. J. Farabaugh, Grace Green, Pueblo. Paula Wolfe, Redstone. Mrs. Frank Chelf, Mrs. Harriet Alexander, Salida. Charles Alfred Johnson, Jr., Mrs. Gordon Rogers, Sedalia. Mr. and Mrs. Claude Deering, William A. Way, Silverton. Clay Monson, Margaret and Lulita Pritchett, Ann Rich, Steamboat Springs. Mrs. William S. Iliff, Trinidad.

No work of mine would be complete without my thanks to Daniel B. Moskowitz, Duane Howell, J. Russell Heitman, and most especially Robert T. Atchison, four friends who unknowingly, perhaps, nursed the seeds that grew into this book.

S.D.

Table of Contents

Table of Illustrations

11

13

Trinidad:

The Bloom Mansion

When Frank G. Bloom left Pennsylvania to make his way in the West, he promised Sarah Thatcher he would come back with enough of a fortune to marry her. Bloom was persistent, Sarah was patient, and three years later Bloom returned for his bride.

He had joined a wagon train headed for Canon City and then had gone to Trinidad where he had opened a trading post with Sarah's brothers. Bloom and his two partners dealt in barter. The Indians traded pelts for coffeepots; for more expensive items the Indians brought cattle.

After a time the three merchants had enough of these bartered animals to sell the store and start what would be one of the biggest cattle operations in the West. Cattle bearing the Diamond A and the Circle Diamond, Bloom's two brands, were to run from the Sangre de Cristos of New Mexico to the Milk River in Montana.

Bloom married Sarah Thatcher in 1869, and took her by train, then stage, to Colorado. She had promised her father she would return for a visit in three years, so the couple waited to begin their family until she had made the trek to Pennsylvania and back to Colorado again.

Bloom Mansion, Trinidad, Colorado.

In 1882 the Blooms started their Victorian home, selected from an architectural journal. They hired a stone mason, turned contractor, to build the house. He constructed it entirely of local materials.

The three-story house, decidedly the most Victorian in Colorado, was built of a natural reddish-pink brick; the corners are accented with sandstone quoins. There is a tower in the center with a cupola. Bright green shutters are at the windows, and grillework etches each story.

Originally, the house had two small porches on either side of the tower which were reached through the parlor and sitting room windows. The lower part of each window was a panel with a slip catch that opened it up to give the entire height of a doorway. Shortly after the house was built, the Blooms decided to enlarge the porches and turned them into a veranda circling three-fourths of the house.

The weathervane cow on top of the cupola today stood for years on the two-story brick barn in the rear of the property. Bloom, always up-to-date on agricultural methods, built a fancy brick chicken house as well.

His daughter Alberta, now Mrs. William S. Iliff, recalls that as a little girl, even before she had learned to read and write, she had a tiny account book in which she kept track of the number of eggs laid each day.

The front doors were handsomely carved with a diamond-in-diamond design and decorated with china knobs and cast-iron hinges. They led into the parlor on the right or the sitting room to the left.

The parlor was furnished with pieces the Blooms had purchased on their honeymoon in St. Louis. Furniture was upholstered in mohair velvet and brocade. There was a grandfather clock in the room that had been in the family over a hundred years. After another eighty, it is still in the family.

Ceilings are sixteen feet high. (When his daughter built a house in Denver in 1900, Bloom thought her ten-and-a-half-foot ceilings very low.)

Both the parlor and sitting room had marble fireplaces and into

Marble-topped washstand in the Bloom bedroom displays antique toilet articles from all over Colorado.

each was fitted a Baltimore heater, quite modern at the time since it heated not only the immediate room but the one above it as well.

The sitting room was the place in which the family usually gathered to read or talk. There was a library table in the middle of the room; and over it hung a gas lamp, its pipes fitted closely together so it could be lowered or raised. Young Alberta Bloom, the only one of the four children to live beyond childhood, studied there and remembers frequently turning to her mother for help in mathematics.

Behind the sitting room is the dining room, the kitchen being behind the parlor. Food had to be carried through a hall to the table.

The home had only a single stairway, and the idea that one could accommodate both family and hired help intrigued the Blooms. Later, however, their daughter tells, they would have preferred two. Apparently the single staircase worked better in the architectural journal.

There are four bedrooms and a bath included in the original house plans for the second floor. Mrs. Bloom had her sewing room in the tower next to her bedroom.

The third floor had four bedrooms for servants. The house was so close to downtown Trinidad where the maids could meet young men that Bloom used to say he was running a "match factory." House maids seldom stayed longer than two years.

A ladder led to the cupola atop the tower, merely a storage area, where little Alberta Bloom, only seven when she moved into the great house, thought she could see the top of the world from its windows.

The house was built on a hill, but when the city put in horse-drawn trolley cars, the hill was cut back, so the Blooms added a four-foot stone embankment in front of the house.

There were always plenty of pets, from a smooth-haired Saint Bernard (later discovered to be a Great Dane) to a tame fawn found by one of the cowboys.

The Blooms had a rat terrier, too, who liked to go to church with the family. He would sit on the wall across the street from the house on Sunday mornings waiting for the family to leave. Then

Longer than floor length curtains with cobweb edging cover a bedroom window.

he would follow along far enough behind so he could not be reprimanded and slip into the church to sleep under a pew.

Though a well-to-do and prominent Trinidad family, the Blooms believed in simple entertainment, usually for family members or church friends.

Several times a year they hosted the presiding elder of the Methodist Church, who usually dropped in unannounced to spend a few days. He inspected the church and accepted the Blooms' unhesitating hospitality.

As staunch Methodists, the Blooms, of course, did not allow dancing in their home. (Mrs. Bloom was shocked to discover her daughter had learned a few steps in college.)

Frank and Sarah Bloom spent nearly fifty years in the house. She died in 1928 and he three years later. After their deaths the house had a succession of owners. One of them painted the place its current bright pink. Another used it as a tea room.

In 1962, the Friends of Historical Trinidad raised funds to purchase the house and present it to the State Historical Society.

After a complete refurbishing, the Bloom home was decorated with period pieces from all over Colorado — from carpet sweeper to cradle, china tie-backs to children's toys.

The Blooms' bedroom holds a scattered collection of embroidered mottos. One tells "The Lord is My Shepherd;" another, "A Merry Heart Maketh a Cheerful Countenance."

Outside, the barn has been torn down and the grape arbor uprooted. In their places is a formal Victorian garden claimed to be one of the most authentic in the country.

The house is known today as the "Bloom Mansion." But that is not quite correct, according to Alberta Bloom Iliff, who spent so many happy years there. "It should have been called," she said, "the 'Bloom Home.'"

21

Aspen:

Pioneer Park

When the wife of Aspen's leading citizen, Henry Webber, died after a short, sudden illness, townspeople began to talk. When they discovered the mysterious illness had been caused by an overdose of strychnine, they insisted the mayor be put on trial.

Local residents said it was murder, Denver and Leadville newspapers reported suicide, but the good jury returned a verdict of accidental death. So Webber was freed to marry the cause of the scandal, a local fancy woman, and Aspenites were so chagrined at their assumption they elected Webber mayor.

The home to which the mayor took his new bride had, apropriately, a mysterious aura. Set back from the street, it stands all alone in the middle of the block and has a high, spiked-iron fence as well as a double row of cottonwood trees stalking it. Because of the cottonwoods bordering the walk, the path along the front of the house was called, incongruously, "lovers' lane."

The house most likely was built in the early 1880's, and for some reason, nobody knows quite why, was dubbed "Pioneer Park." The name is stenciled in old-fashioned lettering on the transom above the front doors.

The first story is Aspen pink brick, now painted bright pink,

Pioneer Park, Aspen, Colorado.

23

the second story with a mansard roof being black clapboard. A symmetrical house, the Webber home has bay windows on either side of the front door.

Originally there were two other bay windows on the east side, but recent owners pushed out the wall to make it even with the end of the bay area to give more room inside.

Both sides of the double front doors bear elaborately flowered "welcome" signs stenciled when Webber built the house.

Though Mayor Webber had gone to great lengths to prove his loyalty to his new wife (he had gotten rid of the old one, hadn't he?), his bride had not been particularly faithful, and Webber was jealous.

Though he had no proof, he suspected his wife had a gentleman friend, and he set out to prove it. One night the mayor told his wife he was going to Leadville and went off on his horse, in proper melodrama fashion, to hide in the trees.

When he returned a short time later, he surprised his wife and her lover, who promptly jumped out of a second story window. Standing at the top of the stairs, the second Mrs. Webber pleaded with him not to harm her. But the enraged husband pulled a gun and shot, first into the banister, then into his wife who crumpled and fell down the stairs at her husband's feet. Legend says Aspen's mayor rode off into the night and never was seen again.

Fact, alas, tells a different tale. The mayor was tried and acquitted of his first wife's murder, but a reliable Colorado historian claims the object of his affection was not a prostitute but his niece, Julia Nevitt, whom he married only four months after the death.

Old-timers say Webber lived on in Aspen for years and lost Pioneer Park in the silver panic.

There is, however, a hole in the banister filled with plastic wood, and a workman in the home several years ago claims to have dug bits of lead out of it. Teenagers who live in the house surmised that if Webber had been standing at the bottom of the stairs and his wife at the top, the bullet would have gone through a partitioning wall to hit the banister, but there is not a mark on the wall. Then they discovered the wall had been added long after the shooting.

Schweitzer Cottage and the newly added swimming pool. Posts in foreground are for a fence now in place.

Gaslight fixture in foyer of Pioneer Park.

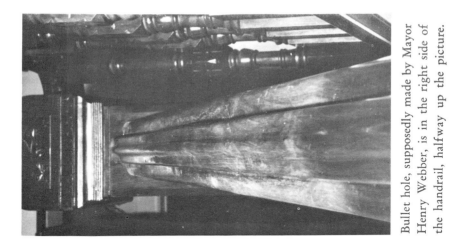

Bullet hole, supposedly made by Mayor Henry Webber, is in the right side of the handrail, halfway up the picture.

Footscraper near the gate.

The first Mrs. Webber is supposed to haunt the house, too. There are strange noises, blamed by the more practical on breezes rustling the transoms, and one guest of recent years claims her bed moved six inches during the night.

Whatever their truth, the stories have not discouraged people from living in the house. During the 1940's, the Walter P. Peepckes, who chiefly are responsible for Aspen's current skiing and cultural booms, purchased the home and renovated it.

They ripped out the wall between two small rooms and moved the east wall of the house to form a large living room. The ceilings were kept at twelve feet, the walnut doors eleven.

The living room ceilings have their original beautiful plaster moldings, and gaslight fixtures have been added. Though the house had gaslights when it was built, the original fixtures were removed.

The house had chimneys for fireplaces, but the Webbers used them for coal stoves only. When the Paepckes purchased the house, they added two fireplaces; the one in the living room is a beautifully carved marble fireplace from the General Grant suite of the Palmer House in Chicago.

Also on the first floor are a library, a bedroom, and a kitchen, part of which was the back porch. The second floor contains three bedrooms and two baths.

Outside there is a simple, round summerhouse at one end of the garden. At the other end is a long stable, now a guest house. Dr. Albert Schweitzer stayed there when he attended Aspen's first music festival, so the renovated stable is called "Schweitzer Cottage." In front of the guest house is a recently added swimming pool.

Despite its infamous, slightly tawdry beginning, Pioneer Park today is one of Aspen's most formal and most dignified homes. Only occasionally, on moonless nights when the storms blow, does one remember its past.

Cripple Creek:

Home of the "Sweet Group"

Most of the men who made their fortunes in Cripple Creek shunned the little gold camp and headed for Wood Avenue in Colorado Springs or Capitol Hill in Denver. Only a few stayed on and built homes on Cripple Creek's posh Carr Avenue. Among them was Charles N. Miller, one of ninety-one lawyers listed at one time in the town's directory.

Miller may have been a lawyer, but he probably made his money in mining. An early day Cripple Creek guide book says that in 1898 he acquired the El Reno, the Comstock, the World's Fair, and the Hilda M. Mines, sometimes called the "sweet group," for $65,000. Miller's picture in an article about the Cripple Creek Mining Stock Exchange Association shows him as a handsome, slightly dapper young man wearing a cravat with a diamond stickpin.

Miller built his Carr Avenue home in 1896, shortly after Cripple Creek's two disastrous fires.

When most of the town's houses were built side by side on narrow twenty-five foot lots, Miller's stood grandly, perhaps wastefully, on two lots. Once a large tan and brown structure, now white and trimmed with gingerbread, it is an imposing home.

Charles N. Miller home, Cripple Creek, Colorado.

There are three gables, each a different size, in front. One of them holds a porch with a triple arch on the second story. The first floor porch, that extends from the front of the house half way around the side, is decorated with lattice work and spindles. There are smartly patterned siding on the second floor and lovely stained and leaded glass windows. (The one in the front of the bay window is not unlike a window at the Imperial Hotel a few blocks away.)

Though built in the last century, the Miller home has features not used in most houses until much later — a spacious entrance hall, large rooms, good-sized closets, a linen closet, an indoor bathroom, and a central heating system with an outlet in each room.

The handsome golden oak staircase in the entrance hall is beautifully paneled, and the lintel is carved. At the first landing is a stained glass window in bright oranges and yellows with jewel-like "marbles" studded in it. Strangely enough, there is no entrance to the sizable area under the stairs, and owners jokingly talk of buried treasure and old skeletons. But farfetched as the idea sounds, it is not really so improbable, as next door neighbors redoing their plumbing found a skeleton buried under their house.

Just off the entrance hall is a coachmen's room in which carriage drivers waited out of the cold for their masters or mistresses who were visiting the Millers. They would shake the snow off their buffalo coats and perhaps warm up a bit with a gulp of something from their pockets. There are benches along the three paneled walls; and at the end of the tiny room, opposite the archway, is a stained glass window in lavender, pink, gold, and green.   ,

The parlor is a large lavish room with one wall a bay window looking out across Cripple Creek in the direction of Victor. On its walls, papered over by some succeeding owner, were hand-painted murals done by a French artist.

The fireplace, though it looks like tile, really is made up of small rectangular pieces of marble streaked with curls of gold, perhaps from some Cripple Creek mine.

The parlor's gaslight fixture, long discarded in the attic, was saved from the dump by the house's present owners when a workman cleaning out the place asked if they wanted "that junk."

There are a sitting room and, through an archway decorted asymmetrically with gingerbread, a dining room. The gingerbread, also found in the attic, was in fifteen pieces when present owners, who restored the house, discovered it. By matching designs, breaks, and screwholes, they put it back together.

Entrance hall with golden oak woodwork, stained glass window.

Stained glass window in the coachmen's room.

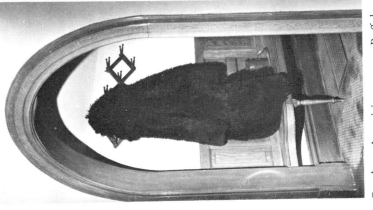

Coachmen's waiting room. Buffalo
coat is an old Cripple Creek relic.

Along one wall is a handsome built-in buffet with drawers and glass doors with a molded border on top. On the opposite wall old lighting fixtures, which once held electric light bulbs as well as gas jets, have been turned upside down to form sconces.

Through the pantry, which displays a large Schepps cake box with the story of Goethe's "The Sorrows of Young Werther" pictured on it, is the kitchen and a maid's room.

Whereas Miller was particularly thoughtful when it came to other people's coachmen, he must have been a hard master with the maid. When the rest of the house was converted to electricity, the maid's room kept its old-fashioned gaslights. Then, too, the call bell switchboard rang not in the kitchen but in her room.

The master bedroom runs the width of the house in front on the second floor. A handsome archway like the one in the coachmen's room downstairs connects it with a tiny sitting room. There also is a door to the second-floor porch.

There are three more bedrooms on the second floor as well as the bath. The bathroom still is equipped with the original porcelain tub and sink, its underside cast in curling designs.

Though woodwork on the first floor is natural wood, that on the second floor has been painted. Local residents accuse present owners of covering up the golden oak. However, some past resident, perhaps even Ed Bell, town sheriff during Cripple Creek's turn-of-the-century labor problems, who once owned the house, had painted the woodwork red. Cost of removing the paint was prohibitive, so the owners painted the woodwork to match the walls.

In each of the bedrooms is a speaking tube to call the maid and a buzzer for the butler. As a cryptic note on the passing of Victorian luxury, the owner says, "You can ring and ring, but the butler doesn't come anymore."

Silverton:

Captain Jack's Waldheim

Most Coloradoans readily can give the name of one state resident who survived the Titanic sinking — Mrs. J. J. Brown — but few have even heard of a second equally astute Colorado woman who lived through the same disaster.

She was the very fashionable, the very social Mrs. Lena Stoiber, but Silverton residents called her "Captain Jack" when she lived in the silver mining town long before shipping magnates had begun building that unsinkable ship.

Sometime in the 1880's, Edward G. Stoiber and his brother Gustav, recent graduates of a school of mines in Freiburg, Germany, discovered the Silver Lakes Mines, which were among Silverton's richest strikes.

The brothers ran the mines together and were particularly close to each other. In fact, Ed's house was just across the street from Gus's. Possibly the handsomest in Silverton at the time, Gus's home was a fancy, three-story residence with "juts" and "pokes" and "pasted-ons," a mysterious, brooding Victorian.

But the brothers' wives did not like each other. Ed had married

Edward Stoiber home, Silver Lakes Mines, Silverton, Colorado.
Photograph courtesy Library, State Historical Society of Colorado.

a pretty little spitfire named Lena. She apparently was married to a Denver & Rio Grande Railroad conductor when she met Stoiber and left her current husband for the greener pastures of the Silver Lakes Mines.

Though Lena was a faithful friend, she "didn't forget her enemies," said one long-time Silverton resident. "She never overlooked a chance to get even." Probably she found a number of chances with Gus's wife, so the brothers split.

Ed took the Silver Lakes property, which reportedly totaled somewhere around 130 mines. Gus got the equally productive Tiger and Iowa Mines in nearby Arastra Gulch.

In 1898, the Stoibers erected their elegant home, not in Silverton but at the Silver Lakes Mines two miles from town. Christened "Waldheim Forest Home," the house's proper name soon was forgotten, and everybody for miles around called it "the mansion."

Nobody remembers how many rooms the house had, but the place was enormous.

A well-built house, it was constructed with two-by-eights, two-by-tens, and even two-by-twelves. The foundation was of stone quarried nearby. The exterior was red brick, supposedly shipped to Silverton from Pennsylvania (Mrs. Stoiber reportedly came from the East), and around the front and two sides was a large pillared veranda.

Inside, the ceilings were twelve feet; and the doors each with a transom, were nearly that tall. The woodwork was put together with square nails. When the interior trim was removed to be re-used, the nails had to be pulled straight out and left gaping holes.

On the main floor were a reception room, parlor, diningroom, kitchen, servants' quarters, and Mrs. Stoiber's office. Stoiber, it seems, preferred to stay at the mine while his wife ran the business, the house, and probably him. Her air of authority seems to have been the reason why Silverton residents nicknamed her "Captain Jack." (One Silverton old-timer who knew her said kindly if understatedly, "She was a 'positive' woman!")

The office had a call-bell system that rang in every room of the house. When the mansion was torn down, a man who purchased much of the building material claimed he got twenty miles of thin bell wiring.

There supposedly was a mirror in the office hung so Mrs. Stoiber could watch the maids working in other parts of the house. Lena Stoiber felt the same way about her servants as she did about other people she knew. She treated them well if they worked hard, but she would not allow any shiftlessness.

The second floor contained bedrooms; there may have been ten, twelve, or sixteen for that matter. No one remembers.

The third floor was the Stoibers' pride, or Lena Stoiber's anyway. There were a game room and a theater with a stage, curtain, and all else that went with it. The Stoibers frequently brought touring acting groups and vaudeville troupes to perform.

Waldheim naturally was the social center of Silverton, and the Stoibers gave fabulous parties and dances. Any famous dignitary visiting the area always stayed at the mansion.

The house reputedly had a burglar alarm system hooked up to every door and window, and there is a story that the property had a tall fence around it, nearly as high as the house, built for spite. Mrs. Stoiber did not like her neighbors and vowed she would "fix it so they can't look into my yard!" So she built the three-story fence.

Mrs. Stoiber was a legend, and a curiosity as well, while she lived in Waldheim. People liked to watch her drive down the street in her fancy buggy drawn by a prancer horse and to wonder where she was headed. Though she was a tough woman to have as an enemy, she would like as not be taking food to some destitute miner's family when she was out for a drive, if she weren't up to some mischief.

Around 1902, the Stoibers sold the Silver Lakes Mines property, which included Waldheim, of course, to the American Smelting and Refining Company for $2,333,000.

The couple moved to Denver where they built an equally sumptuous home known as "Stoiberhof." Not long after that, while in Paris, Stoiber was killed in an atomobile accident, an unusual death in those days.

Mrs. Stoiber remarried, and her third husband went down with the Titanic. Lena, of course, survived and married again. Either the

Gustav Stoiber house, across the street from the site of Edward Stoiber's early home.

38

fourth husband or his immediate predecessor was an Italian count. During that marriage Lena, always fond of pretentious homes, acquired an Italian villa.

Her last husband was a British army officer named Austin. He apparently was the only one to outlive her, though it could be that in Ouray her first, a forgotten railroad conductor, read about her death.

For a number of years managers of the Silver Lakes Mines lived in Waldheim until finally it was deserted with nobody but a watchman to visit it.

Shortly after World War II, the home was torn down for salvage, purchased by its wreckers reportedly for a few thousand dollars.

Parts of the house were removed by a former Silverton resident, Claude Deering, to construct a pretty little farmhouse bungalow near Durango. Lumber available right after the war often was so green that it twisted, and Waldheim's building materials were well aged and quite desirable.

Deering moved the staircase intact; where it once led up to a maze of bedrooms, it now goes down to a simple basement. Doors were cut to fit Deering's house. Windows were trimmed down a third in height and transoms used as basement windows. Fancy gingerbread brackets under Waldheim's cornice have been sized to fit under the roof of the bungalow and that of its garage.

Deering purchased 13,000 bricks to construct the house and estimated he took only a tenth of what was there. "I didn't even get the top layer," he said.

Most of the furnishings in Waldheim had been stolen or wrecked, and the only trinket of the Stoibers which the Deerings have is a pretty silver inkwell engraved with the initials "L.A.S." and given to them by a friend of Mrs. Stoiber.

The Deerings were not the only ones to take away portions of the once magnificent Waldheim. Another chunk went to build a house in Montrose and more to erect a building in Ironton.

Like its mistress, Lena Stoiber, Waldheim has managed a number of marriages.

Gunnison:

Dos Rios

It was a Christmas day in the 1870's when a tall young man, still in his teens, dismounted from his burro — right into Gunnison country history.

He was Alonzo Hartman, a descendant of Daniel Boone, who had been sent from Denver to take care of government cattle for the Los Piños Indian Agency. He reportedly was the first white man to establish permanent residence on the Western Slope.

Young Lon Hartman had lived for several years in Denver, where he had camped on the present site of the Shirley-Savoy Hotel. He also knew the mountains and the Indians, so he was well suited for a job at the agency.

After he had lived on the Western Slope awhile, Hartman became the first postmaster of the small village of Gunnison. He later told his daughter the reason he never smoked was that having to stand behind the small window of the post office and smell the foul breath of the tobacco-chewing miners and trappers cured him of any taste for tobacco.

One of Hartman's close friends was Jake Hinkle who had come

Alonzo Hartman home, Gunnison, Colorado.

to Colorado to seek his fortune. Hinkle told Hartman about his pretty young niece in Kansas, Annie Haigler, a school teacher, and persuaded Hartman to write her. He did, and the two corresponded for quite a while before she came West to meet him. When she left for Kansas, the two were engaged. They were married at her home January 29, 1882.

By that time Hartman, who had spent his wages buying cattle, had built his holdings into the prosperous Don Rios Ranch, where he moved his bride into the first frame house in Gunnison. A mile west of the present-day town, the Dos Rios ranch house is "Union Pacific" yellow with brown trim and has a shingle roof.

Though a plain frame house was elegant enough in Gunnison, Hartman made his home even fancier by varying the direction of the clapboard. For the most part it is horizontal, but under the front gable and the front window the boards are vertical, while above the window they are on a herringbone diagonal.

The gable also sports a handsome bit of gingerbread trim. There is decoration on the porch supports that form pseudo-arches. Though dilapidated, the house still stands in the shadow of the one that replaced it.

The frame house was a pretty fine place, indeed; but Hartman, by now a wealthy rancher, decided an elegant house was not good enough; he wanted a mansion, so he built one. For miles around it was known as just that, "the mansion."

Like any good rancher, Hartman built a new barn and stable before he started the house. The keystone near the top of the barn gable gives the date of completion — 1889. Surprisingly enough, the outside walls are brick, which withstood a fire a number of years ago that gutted the inside and would have demolished any frame barn.

His home, Hartman decided, would be in front of the frame house which could be used for servants' quarters. It was just a short distance from the log post office he had established and was reached by a long circle driveway.

The man Hartman picked to design his show place was the local Methodist minister, a gentleman named Fuller who blended Victorian and Western achitecture with touches of church elegance. He came up with a large, showy, ill-arranged home. When it was finished, it had cost Hartman $45,000.

Constructed of brick which probably was made in Gunnison, natural stone, and wood siding, the house is basically rectangular with a tower, completely out of scale, on the front.

The windows of the tower are set into Italian arches, round-headed at the top. Though the size of the arches is the same, the length of the windows shortens as one ascends the stairs. There are seven windows and eight arches. The third floor of the tower has a conical roof, capped with a metal "dunce" hat and a weather vane.

The entrance hall, by far the most elegant part of the house, has a commanding white oak staircase circling up the tower to the second floor. The balistrades, instead of being straight spindles, entwine to form S-shaped designs winding to the top of the stairs.

On the wall behind the staircase, most likely inspired by Fuller's church background, are long, narrow stained-glass windows, imported from Italy. The top sections of the windows are jewel-colored flowers and owls. The panels below are long strips of colored glass, and underneath them are diamond-shaped pieces of leaded, opaque glass.

Three-fourths of each window is quite conventional, but the bottom panel is a unique piece of abstract art in apple green, turquoise, and orange. Mrs. Hartman must have fallen under the spell of Louis C. Tiffany's new colors and textures of glass. The leaded panes, which seem to be a random sampling of left-over shapes and sizes of glass, allow a Tiffany play of light and color.

The windows are framed with white oak arches, and the keystone area at the top of each is enhanced with a wedge-shaped piece of carved wood.

The fireplace across from the staircase is tile of a pinkish-brown color, and the figures in relief at the top and sides are Italian, purchased at an early Chicago World's Fair.

Hartman's daughter remembers that the hall held two large showcases. Many of their displays were Indian artifacts, most the gifts of Hartman's Indian friends, Chief Ouray and Chipeta.

The staircase is white oak; the windows, designed by the local minister, are a combination of Victorian and abstract designs.

The original Hartman home, just behind the stone house, was the first frame house in Gunnison.

The entrance hall opens into a sitting room with a velvet-draped bay window alcove. The arch to the alcove is decorated with handsome wood filigree to match the oak doors. A leaded, colored glass window looks out onto what is now the kitchen but was originally the butler's pantry. To the right, through an archway decorated with wood filigree work, is the library. Both rooms have tile fireplaces as well as parquet floors.

There is a dining room with fireplace and also a glassed-in playroom and bath, both added later.

The basement originally held the kitchen, and food was brought to the diningroom in a dumb waiter. However, a subsequent owner removed the extravagance and moved the kitchen upstairs.

The basement with its low ceiling is dark and gloomy, but it does have a fireplace and carved white oak staircase connecting with the one in the entrance hall.

Three bedrooms and a bathroom are on the second floor. The bath may have been put into the house when it was built.

The third floor belvedere is a white-washed room with many windows looking out to all parts of Gunnison County. It is reached by a trap door and narrow fold-up staircase. Probably the little room was used just for storage by all owners except Mrs. Hartman, who painted there.

She climbed the steep, narrow stairs in her full skirts, locked the trap door securely so no one could bother her, and painted her proper Victorian pictures. No one remembers whether or not she had talent, but she was prolific, and the house was filled with her work. On the tower wall next to a window, she painted a pretty miniature of a waterfall.

After a number of years, Hartman's ranching business declined, and he started a general store. When that, too, proved unsuccessful, the family sold their home and moved away.

It was worked as a ranch by several owners until a development firm, that fittingly named itself "Dos Rios," purchased the place, parceled off most of its ground for vacation home sites, and left the ranch a gentleman's farm of sixty acres and the home a sort of defrocked manor house.

But three-quarters of a century old and stripped of much of its domain, the Hartman home is as handsome and pretentious as it ever was. It is still every bit "the mansion" of Gunnison.

The fireplace in the foyer is Italian, purchased at a World's Fair.

Waterfall painted by Mrs. Hartman on the tower wall.

Salida:

Steamboat Gothic in a Dry-Land Camp

Salida's "Gray cottage" ("Gray" refers to the house's first owner, not its color) comes closest to being "steamboat gothic" of almost any of the houses in Colorado's dry-land mining camps.

Oh, it's a proper Victorian all right. It has plenty of gables and dormer windows and Italian windows and is iced with lots of gingerbread, but when taken apart, the old house has several Southern features "sneaked" in that make one think its builder or perhaps its designer had had his heart in magnolia blossoms though his hand was among the Western pines.

In the first place, there's the gingerbread. Most Victorian trim looks like stonework done in wood; the delicate wood carvings at the points of the gables and the tops of the dormer windows of Gray's cottage, however, are like cast- or wrought-iron designs traced by a fine carpenter in wood.

Then there are the oversize inverted pineapples, worked in wood, hanging above the front stoop. Of course, most of the miners knew what pineapples were, but not many of them from north of the Mason-Dixon line would have thought to incorporate them into

Gray's cottage, Salida, Colorado.

48

house trim. The pineapple, besides being a warm climate fruit, is a Southern symbol of hospitality.

There is a reminiscence of Greek columns so popular in the South in the pillared porch; and the shutters, nothing new to mining camp Victoria, of course, have a Southern distinction; they look as if they could close to keep out the sun.

The clincher, however, is the front gable; from underneath it looks like the front of a fancy Mississippi steamboat. Looking up, the balcony becomes a deck; the shuttered windows, the entrance to the cabin; and the gingerbread, cast-iron trim. Even the chimney sticking up behind becomes the smokestack.

All that's missing is the captain, and incongruously, it's doubtful that any of the prim Victorian ladies who lived in the old mansion ever resembled even slightly a profane, weathered, old riverboat captain.

They did have an air, however, of Southern gentility and fine manners. Said one long-time Salida resident, "When you went calling at that house, you always went with your gloves on."

When it was built, Gray's cottage was Salida's finest house, and the local newspaper, the *Salida Daily Mountain Mail*, kept a running account of the building progress.

"Timber is on the ground for Gray's new residence." (March 20, 1882)

"Lumber is all on the ground for Gray's new residence..." (April 4, 1882)

"Gray will be in his new residence in two weeks. When completed it will be a daisy." (June 26, 1882)

After the house was finished and the Grays had moved in, the paper carried an impressively long article about the home entitled "A Fine Cottage." The writer called the house the nicest in Chaffee County and claimed the carpenter work was the finest outside Denver, "... first-class in every respect."

Despite its languid Southern look outside, Gray's Cottage was Yankee prim and proper within. No spacious entrance hall and flowing staircase but a slim utilitarian foyer with narrow stairs. The hall was finished in oak and bird's-eye maple and trimmed with black walnut. The sides of the stairs are decorated with a curling design in raised wood.

When built, the house had six rooms on the first floor, but one of them seems to have disappeared. Today there are five.

The parlor is a large room to the right of the foyer and once was formally darkened with louvers (long since moved to the cellar, then to the library.) The twelve-foot ceiling has plaster designs worked in it and two silver and crystal chandeliers. Actually there are five chandeliers in the house. Besides the two in the parlor, there is one each in the diningroom, library, and foyer.

Behind the parlor, separated from it by twelve-foot-high glass-paneled folding doors, is the diningroom. Both parlor and diningroom were originally painted brown, chocolate, black, carmine, and gold. Later owners added flocked wallpaper.

Across the hall from the parlor is the library, probably intended as a bedroom originally. Behind that are a kitchen and a storeroom.

Upstairs are four bedrooms and a bath with a graceful old marble sink. Though the newspaper account of Gray's cottage stated that the celler had waterpipes (clothes presses, too), it's doubtful that the luxury was piped in as far as the bathroom.

From the ground, the house gives a riverboat appearance.

The house, as far as Salida residents can tell, was built by a man named G. R. Gray, who made his money in mining. He worked the Madonna Mine for a time then sold it for $42,000. It later produced millions.

Rumor says that as with the mine, Gray let his sandstone-colored house go for a pittance just a few years after it was built.

Old-timers in Salida tell that Gray gave the home to a little neighbor girl of whom he was fond and name that girl as Rose Craig. Little Rose and her family lived in the house from 1902 to 1918, however, and neither she nor her cousin Mary Craig, who lived there earlier, recall such a generous gift.

Concluding its article on Gray's cottage, the *Salida Mountain Mail* stated, "... Mr. and Mrs. Gray have the neatest home in the country and we hope that they may live in it and be happy during the many long years that their present state of good health forbades."

The article was wrong in one hope; the Grays lived in the home only a few years. But it was correct in the other; Gray's cottage always has been a happy place. Nearly all owners of the house have remarked enthusiastically that it was a pleasant house in which to live. Said Rose Craig remembering back, "It was a charming home, full of happy memories."

Inverted pineapples are worked in wood in the decoration over the

Crystal and silver chandelier in the parlor, one of five in the home.

Tiger-on-the-Swan:

The Dredge King's Nest

Along the valleys of the Swan River lie ugly dumps of water-smooth stones, a silent, grim sort of memorial to Ben Stanley Revett, who brought dredging to French Creek, to the Swan, and to the Blue.

Another remnant of the man, less permanent and less offensive, is the grand house he built overlooking the sweep of the Tenmile Range and the rock piles spewed up by his machines.

Revett, an Englishman, introduced the method of gold dredging to the Breckenridge area in the mid-1890's. The process involved, wrote Revett in a flowery prospectus, consisted "merely" of lifting gravel from bedrock to the surface and washing it into short sluices.

The operation, of course, was not quite as simple as Revett pictured it; but it was an effective way of mining gold, and it was, albeit infrequently, a financially successful one. Too often for Revett, unfortunately, it was just a highly expensive enterprise that cost more gold than it dredged up. Consequently, Revett constantly was in search of financial backing.

"He was always hard put to it to find money for running ex-

Swan's Nest on the Swan River near Tiger-on-the-Swan, Colorado.

penses," said his wenchman. "Probably Revett should not have built such an expensive house as Swan's Nest for his birds."

One of the "birds," undoubtedly, was his wife, Mary Griffith, whom Revett married the first day of 1898. He built Swan's Nest the same year.

The house was constructed near Revett's dredging operations overlooking the Swan where it turns northwest for a time before entering the Blue.

A Breckenridge old-timer who had visited Swan's Nest long ago described the place. A croquet court was on the grounds, and there were pretty walks all neatly lined with dredge rocks.

The house itself is semi-circular, consisting of a large central portion with two small wings. The steeply pitched red roof is broken with sharp dormer windows. A long veranda runs the curve of the front of the house, and it has a peeled log railing in a fancy design.

Outside doors as well as interior doors and archways were made especially wide to accommodate Revett's rotund figure, estimated by one "viewer" at 300 pounds. (Revett was such a large man that a Mexican laborer watching him work in a prospect hole one day reportedly dropped his pick at the sight and exclaimed, "Holy Mother of God! When this hombre meets his death, may it be near the graveyard!")

The hall, as the English Revett called his living room, was, like its lord, good-sized. Across from the front door is a massive fireplace built of stones churned up and discarded by the dredge. Scattered across the stones are tiles with pictures of Indians hand-painted on them by Mary Revett. There was a chair nearby also made of dredge stones.

From the ceiling hung an elaborate crystal chandelier that from the road, recalled a woman who often passed the house at night, looked "just like diamonds."

Dinners in the long diningroom, also in the center portion of the house, were large and lavish, accompanied by a proper course of wines. After dinner the men retired to the library, in the west wing, for Havanas (Breckenridge folks like to recall they cost one dollar each) or to the billiard room for a game.

If the host were in good voice, he would sing for his guests. Once trained for opera, Revett had a mellow tenor voice, and he was as generous with it as he was with his dollar cigars.

When he was ready to perform, he would call the bar at the Denver Hotel in Breckenridge four miles away; the two buildings were among the few in the area to have telephones. The proprietor would announce to his customers, "Gentlemen, Mr. Revett will now sing for you from Swan's Nest," and let the receiver dangle.

The other wing of the house contained a room similar to the library with walls and ceiling of tongue-in-groove siding. Possibly it was Revett's office since just off it is a stone vault once entered through steel double doors. Revett kept nuggets and gold dust from the dredging operations in there.

Each wing had a stairway to a single room above, probably intended for the maid or the Japanese house boy since neither room connected with the rest of the second floor. A third stairway is in back of the living room and leads to the four bedrooms for the family on the second floor.

Revett installed two bathrooms in the house. In one he placed an oversize tub and surrounded it with electric lights to imitate, apparently, a steam bath.

A Breckenridge "historian-in-residence" tells that although Revett was a prodigious eater and enjoyed wines, he was not a heavy drinker. A more skeptical old-timer, however, said that Revett drank as much as he ate and claimed that the steam bath was used to sober him up.

Though Revett loved the Swan River and particularly Swan's Nest, his wife found life there dull and uncultured. She worried that her daughter, born in 1900, would grow up a ruffian.

When the girl was four or five, goes a favorite story around Breckenridge, she and a geologist guest decided to visit a nearby spring for a drink of water.

When they got there, they found the cup had disappeared, and they had no choice but to scoop up the water with their hands. The water was bubbling and cold, and the idea for improvised dippers not very successful.

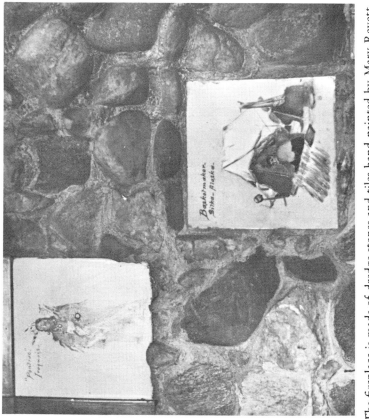

The fireplace is made of dredge stones and tiles hand-painted by Mary Revett.

56

"Did you get any?" asked the little girl.

"Not much, did you?"

"Not one damn drop!" she replied.

The geologist thought the incident funny enough to repeat to the Revetts that night at dinner. Revett laughed, but his wife scowled, thinking it just one more example of the uncivilized life her daughter was encountering on the Swan. It took her ten years longer, however, to finally make up her mind to pack up her daughter and leave Swan's Nest.

About that time, Revett, always plagued with financial problems, found it almost impossible to interest backers in sinking more money into his dredging operations. Not long after his wife left, his fortune dwindled to practically nothing. Revett, too, was forced to leave the "Nest."

He continued to live in high style at clubs and hotels in Denver and San Francisco, partly on the remnants of his fortune, but mostly through the generosity of friends, until his death in 1927.

Swan's Nest was vacant for many years, preyed on by thieves and vandals. Once it was sold for a reported $800 in back taxes. For a time it was the main lodge of a boys' camp.

More grandiose than it ever was elegant, the big barn-of-a-house, unusable and unsalable, is boarded up and decaying. Unlike the stark rock piles that haunt the Swan, Ben Stanley Revett's Swan's Nest is a fleeting reminder of the gold-dusted dredge king.

Conifer:

Circustown

Midway between Denver and Bailey, in a valley gilded in the fall with shimmering leaves of burnished aspen, stands a stately yellow farmhouse with rose-colored shutters. It appears like the serene residence of a gentleman farmer, but its history is a multi-hued as the house itself.

Marauding Indians terrified early settlers; elephants roamed the valley munching mountain meadow grass; open range grazing in the area saw its demise on the property.

The land was homesteaded by Duncan McIntyre, a former seaman. A member of Her Majesty's Navy, McIntyre protested the flogging of a shipmate, struck the punishing officer, and was put into irons. When his ship docked in Montreal, he deserted and roamed the far north as an employee of the Hudson Bay Company.

Four years later, when Queen Victoria pardoned deserters because of widespread brutality on ships, McIntyre returned to civilization — a Colorado homestead. He first homesteaded 160 acres, part of which is now the site of the State Capitol.

Later he acquired the land near Conifer and built his cabin close

Broken Bar M Ranch, Conifer, Colorado.

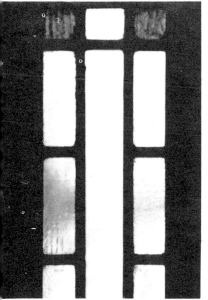

Front door knob was cast with

a daisy design.

Window above the front doors is filled with panes of
colored glass.

to where U. S. 285 passes today. He erected a barn, still standing, of timbers held together with wooden pegs and fashioned a pipeline made of hollowed-out logs from the spring to the house.

Early times were hazardous, and bands of foraging Indians terrified settlers. One party ravaged the valley, burning and plundering; and a brave forced a white woman to sew a button on his shirt, just a few inches below which two fresh scalps dangled from his belt.

Sometime after the Indians left, P. T. Barnum chose the McIntyre homestead as a winter watering spot for his elephants and other circus animals.

Later Conifer residents puzzled that Barnum would choose such a cold place for animals accustomed to a warm climate. They reasoned that, in a time before railroads had reached the area, hauling huge jungle animals in wagons any distance was too expensive, so Barnum wintered his animals near the place that he finished the season. Barnum must have liked the spot because there is evidence that he returned other winters.

Perhaps McIntyre found a combination of Indians and elephants too much for him because he gave up the ranch in the late 1880's and moved away.

The second owner, Louis Ramboz, commissioned the building of the big "Iowa-type" farmhouse in 1889. Sixty years later, in 1950, when owners were installing a heating system, they discovered a board nailed to a joist under the landing of the staircase. Penciled on it was the following history:

Circus-town, October 1889. This house is been built by Joseph Grauffel of the city of Denver for Mr. Louis Ramboz is been commenced in March 1889 and finished in October the same year.
    Joseph Grauffel contractor builder.

Ramboz designed a large house, twelve rooms with six on each floor. The front of the house had a comfortable porch, no doubt with a porch swing, and handsome double doors. Overhead was a window filled with panes of colored glass. There is a decorative iron grillework fence on the roof around the chimney, a weather vane, and lightning rods.

Reported building cost was $2,500, neither a low nor high figure when one considers it was built without water pipes, wiring, or a heating system.

The foyer, the only portion of the house with its original decor, has a well-kept staircase zig-zagging across one wall. The paper, slightly shredded, has been carefully preserved. The pattern is a geometric design in mountain colors — gold, rust, brown, and yellow — embellished with gilt.

Ramboz liked very fancy doors, which are the most attractive feature inside the house. Most of them have china knobs; the front door knob, however, is brass with daisy designs cast into it. Hinges and locks are patterned metal, too. Even door panels are decorative. Some seem as if their varnish were "combed" just before it dried. The deep rust stain on others looks as if a child had finger-painted on them.

Because of its location on the Leadville stage route, the house at Circustown became a stage stop and kind of boardinghouse. One evening in the midst of a snowstorm two women rode up to ask for a night's lodging. The couple turned out to be Helen Hunt Jackson, author of *Ramona*, and an artist friend, and they woke the next morning to find themselves snowbound and forced to spend a week on the ranch. When the weather cleared, the two asked for a bill but were told there was none. The weather had been so unpleasant and the days so drab, their hostess explained, that she wouldn't think of charging them. Besides their company had enlivened the dull winter days. In appreciation for their stay Mrs. Jackson's companion, an accomplished painter, sent the owner an excellent oil of a mountain scene which hung over the fireplace at Circustown for many decades.

A number of years after the house was built a Scotsman, R. W. Kirkpatrick, moved his young family to Circustown and doled out $11,000 for the furnished farmhouse, livestock, and farming equipment. The new owner was something of a progressive and brought the first automobile to the valley, a big EMF convertible now in the Roy Daugherty Antique Museum in Longmont. Kirkpatrick had the automobile shipped to Colorado from Oregon, and railroad officials were so suspicious of it that the owner had to rent an entire freight car so the vehicle could be shipped in solitude.

Kirkpatrick brought another change to the Circustown area; he erected the first fences in the valley. Though a few of the neighbors claim he drilled the postholes with a gun strapped to his hip to protect himself from militant open-range advocates, most recall that Kirkpatrick, a man with decided likes and dislikes, usually settled disputes with words rather than weapons. Kirkpatrick was a smart man who placed the fence posts twenty-five feet inside his property lines to minimize arguments — a cause of litigation today since much of the land has been subdivided.

In 1950 an airline pilot, Norman F. Meyer, and his family purchased the ranch which they named "Broken Bar M," whittled it down in size from Kirkpatrick's 1200 acres to a mere 500, and completely remodeled the farmhouse.

They painted the weathered residence a bright yellow and added rose-colored shutters. They refurbished the grillework and took off part of the porch, eliminated doors and cut new windows.

Inside, the family kept the entrance hall as it was but rearranged other rooms, adding central heating and plumbing. The house was built without fireplaces, so they put in three.

They redecorated and refinished, but despite their changes they kept the original feeling of the house. The home still is a big, comfortable Midwestern farmhouse.

And the Meyers, like the original builder Louis Ramboz, have preserved their own portion of its story. When building the fireplace, they wrote down their part in the house's history and sealed it behind the stones, perhaps to be found in another sixty years by some distant owner.

Original wallpaper, still in the front hall, is in shades of brown.

Greeley:

Go West, Young Man

Journalist Nathan Meeker took seriously the flowery advice of his editor Horace Greeley. After a trip to the Rocky Mountains researching a story on irrigation, Meeker decided to "Go West" permanently.

Meeker was no haphazard wanderer. He approached Greeley about sponsoring a Colorado settlement, and Greeley gave the New York *Tribune's* support. The *Tribune* issued the "call" for settlers in December, 1869. The following spring Meeker and about fifty followers arrived on the bleak prairie site they had chosen for a town.

Meeker knew the barren state of the new-found town, but many of his companions were totally ignorant of it. Convinced the town already had been established and homes and hotels built, they had brought with them their fine possessions. A number were confused and dismayed at the town's conditions.

Meeker, however, was not a man to let others became discouraged. He organized the settlement, laid out the town, and channeled irrigation water for newly planted crops.

Nathan Meeker home, Greeley, Colorado.

He also began construction of his own home; and, to show his faith in the infant community, he built the finest house in the settlement, a home far more expensive than he could afford. Made of adobe bricks, certainly the easiest building material to come by, the home is a tall, symmetrical building painted yellow. The front door is situated in the middle of the first story; there are a window on either side of it flanked by brown shutters and two windows above on the second story.

The brick chimney appears to extend from the exact center of the house, and surrounding it is a pretty grillework fence.

The house inside is as unpretentious and as pleasant as outside. The front door opens directly into the parlor. Behind that is the diningroom-sitting room, farther on the kitchen. From the diningroom is a staircase that leads up to a hall and three bedrooms.

There supposedly was a tunnel from the Meeker house to a location three blocks away, where the family could hide from Indians.

One Greeley man claimed he had been inside it, but the Meekers' niece insisted no such tunnel ever existed.

Actually, if the Meekers had been afraid of Indians, they wouldn't have built such low windows and covered them with shutters that opened and closed only on the outside, nor would they have had doors with glass panes. Most likely the tunnel was some kind of cellar lengthened by imagination.

Though very simple, even slightly primitive, the house was decorated with fine pieces. The Meekers, as most of the settlers, had brought much of their good furniture with them to Greeley.

Just as did the other men, Meeker most likely slept in the freight car with the family belongings during the journey while Arvilla Meeker and the children rode in the day coach. Unlike other pioneers, Greeley's settlers could reach their destination in railroad cars. Consequently, though thoroughly out of place for a time, their furniture could be brought with them.

In addition to their household necessities, the Meekers were able to bring a cherrywood secretary, a parlor set, a diamond dust mirror, a carved black walnut, marble-top sideboard with matching bedroom furniture, and an assortment of fine china, including tea-party dishes that belonged to young Josephine Meeker.

Mrs. Meeker also brought with her a handsome copy of *The Pilgrim's Progress*, illustrated with colored pictures and later to become famous in the history of Colorado's Western Slope.

Located on the corner of Plum and Monroe Streets (later changed to more practical but less euphonious numbered streets), the home was surrounded by trees, some of them exotic species given to the community by Greeley; they did not last long in Colorado.

In 1882 the Meekers extended the house to the south to include several more rooms. The family lived in their home until 1878, when Meeker accepted a temporary position as Ute Indian Agent at the White River Agency located on the Western Slope.

Meeker had borrowed money from Greeley; and, though the lender never intended to collect the amount, the debt, nevertheless, remained on his books. After Greeley died, his estate demanded payment. Meeker did not have the money, so he asked for an appointment as Indian agent to earn it.

Front parlor of the home. Secretary holds books that belonged to the Meeker children.

Since the position was only temporary, the Meekers kept owner-ship of the Greeley house and left it in the care of their daughters, Mary and Rosene. Ther son, Ralph, was living in New York, so they took only the youngest child, Josephine, with them.

The Meekers had the agency less than a year when the Utes went on the rampage and murdered Meeker. Arvilla Meeker and Jose-phine survived the infamous massacre but were held captive for twenty-four days before they were released.

One tale says the reason the two women were not killed was because of the copy of *The Pilgrim's Progress* which Mrs. Meeker had taken with her. The Utes were fascinated with the book, which they called the "spirit book," and attributed holy powers to it.

A more plausible reason, however, is that Greeley residents, pos-sibly even the Meekers, once saved the life of an Indian woman, Shawsheen, and she pleaded with the captors to reciprocate the deed.

After their release the two Meeker women returned to their home in Greeley, Mrs. Meeker living there until just before her death in 1905. Before she died, at ninety years of age, Mrs. Meeker had become enfeebled and had neglected the house so that the yard had grown wild. The house's unkempt look gave rise to rumors that the place was haunted. Rosene Meeker, as she grew older, re-portedly acted somewhat peculiarly, and her actions caused stories of strange goings-on in the old house.

When Rosene Meeker died, the house was sold to a family who added a veranda, extended the house, and removed the shutters and grillework. In 1929 the town of Greeley purchased the home to be operated as a local museum. In 1959 the building was restored, inside and out, as the original Meeker home.

Meeker belongings, scattered after the family died, have been returned. Not only fine pieces of furniture but personal items, also, have been donated to the museum. The children's schoolbooks are in the parlor secretary. Arvilla Meeker's sampler, dated 1827 when she was twelve years old, hangs in the kitchen. (Most fine seam-stresses claim any good sampler has an error. Arvilla Meeker left out the letter *J* in her alphabet.)

In a glass case upstairs is the "spirit book" that may have saved the lives of the Meeker women. Near it is the striped woolen dress Josephine made out of a blanket during her captivity.

The museum chronicles not only the story of the Meekers but that of the town as well. Possessions have been donated by descendants of many of the early pioneers who accompanied Meeker to the desolate town site. The home is a memorial to the men who with Meeker took Horace Greeley's advice to "Go West."

Grandfather clock, manufactured before 1851 in Philadelphia, belonged to the Meekers' niece.

Kitchen has been refurnished with antique pieces.

Black Hawk:

The Lace House

Without a doubt, Colorado's most famous deserted home is the "lace house" in Black Hawk.

Once the proudest, haughtiest, most elaborate home on the mountainside, the lace house is sadly dilapidated, in danger of collapsing altogether.

Facts about the handsome house are lacking. It was built in the 1860's by a family named Osburn. The daughter, old-timers seem to remember, became a stage singer, the son a freight clerk for Union Pacific Railroad in Denver.

Probably the best example of "carpenter gothic" still standing in Colorado, the lace house gets its name from its scroll-sawn bargeboard that extended up and down the front gable, across the house, and around the side gable. There also is elaborate gingerbread carving under the cornice and over the windows and cutout work in the supporting posts of the porch. Reportedly, the carving was done by the German who made the Central City Opera House chairs.

Another equally beautiful feature of the house is its chapel windows in the front and side gables.

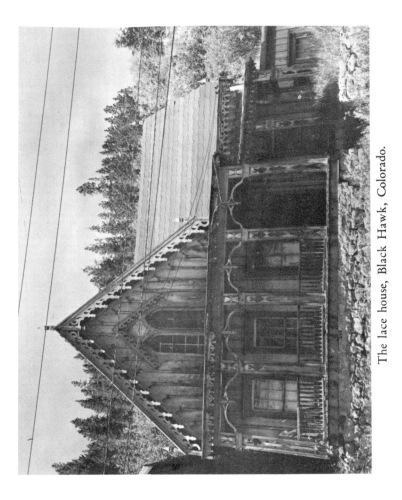

The lace house, Black Hawk, Colorado.

70

Built on a stone foundation, the house was constructed of timbers hauled across the plains by oxcart. Siding is board and batten, and it has held up remarkably well.

Inside, the home was fairly large: a living room, bedroom, kitchen, pantry, diningroom, and storage area on the first floor and three bedrooms on the second.

There was handsome wainscoting in the downstairs rooms, and the house was heated by coal stoves. The kitchen stove was placed in a position to keep water pipes warm.

In 1896, the Osburns sold the home to a family named Pircher for $700, insurance money they had received at Mr. Pircher's death. The Pirchers lived in the house from 1896 to 1913, and during most of that time the son, Lou Pircher, was Gilpin Tramway superintendent.

A few people who had been in the house before it reached its present state of disrepair comment on its once elaborate "original" wallpaper, but that was added by the Pirchers.

After the family left, the house was rented to various tenants who cared little about keeping it up. Vandals broke into the house and destroyed much of its beauty. After a time, the city of Black Hawk obtained title to the property and sold it in 1920, for $20! Stipulation of the sale was that new owners paint the house and keep it in good repair.

The owners, who have kept the house since then, apparently have been little interested in caring for it. Neither do they want to sell the house. Tourists, thinking they're the first to see beauty in the old place, deluge the Gilpin County Court House with requests to buy it for a few dollars in back taxes.

Standing across the ore-strewn creek from the highway, the lace house has a seedy appearance. The weathered, rough boards are bare of even a trace of paint. Glass panes are broken. The trim is falling away. A condemned sign hangs on the door, a warning to trespassing tourists. The porch boards are warped, and moss grows between them.

Windows are covered from the inside with faded newspapers and ragged cloths, and perhaps it's a good thing. Left to the imagination, the interior of the lace house would have embossed wallpaper, rich paneling, and ornate gas jets. Actually, the inside is just like any deserted shack — crumbling plaster, litter-strewn floors, and broken steps.

Colorado historians bemoan the passing of this bit of history, but after all, it has lived a hundred years, longer than most of Gregory Gulch's houses.

These would-be restorers cry at its neglect, but perhaps its air of abandon, its resemblence to the woeful end of a too lavish era, are what make the lace house haunting.

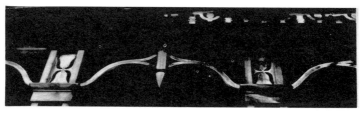

Gingerbread trim across the porch.

Side gable with chapel window.

Idaho Springs:

Yankee Practicality and Southern Embellishments

John Owen was a Confederate, a plantation owner, and a merchant from Crystal Springs, Mississippi, and like a number of his compatriots, he felt the Civil War had ruined the life he loved. So he left the South to start a new kind of life in the West.

About 1870, Owen and his wife, their daughter and son, arrived in Idaho Springs, a raw mining town without a railroad. Owen went into mining, not prospecting but speculating. He bought and sold mines, sometimes making money, other times losing it, and over the years he owned mines with such enticing names as the Sun and Moon, the Bluebird, the Red Elephant, and the Gum Tree.

While he was running the Gum Tree in Freeland, near Idaho Springs, Owen combined his engrained Southern ideals with new found Yankee ingenuity in one of the smartest political maneuvers ever pulled in Clear Creek County.

Just the opposite of our day, ninety years ago the mine owner, Owen, was a Democrat, and his miners (there were 500 to 600 of them) were Republicans. Naturally that many men could swing any election in the county.

John Owen home, Idaho Springs, Colorado.

So on election day, Owen — who believed any citizen, even a Republican, had a right to vote but that any honest trick that kept him from doing so was a smart move — told his miners they could get time off to go to the polls if they wanted to. But, he said, any man who worked all day would get double time. Owen knew his miners well. Patriotic though they might be, they were slightly more mercenary, and not a single one left his job to vote. The Democrats won the election.

Like the man, the house Owen bought was Yankee practicality with Southern embellishments. The architecture was mining camp Victorian, a big rambling house with gingerbread trim, but there were wide porches in front on both the first and second stories, just big enough to be called verandas by any homesick Southerner. And the inside, an organized Victorian maze, was filled with solid mahogany furniture brought from Crystal Springs.

The house, high up Virginia Street on the side of a mountain, was grey clapboard, now white and green, with a stable behind it. (The stable since has been turned into a home.) The outside, less elegant than some, has an air of dignity. There's a lattice-work fence, fancy brackets at the tops of the porch columns. The vertical decorations under the gables appear like dagger sheaths in relief. The windows have just a quirk-of-an-eyebrow tilt at the top, and the veranda balusters look like hand-in-hand cut-out paper dolls.

Like most houses of the time, the Owen home opens onto a long, narrow hall with a staircase hugging one side. The light fixture is an elegant, gilded globe studded with large chunks of colored glass, and it pulled up and down so one could light the candle inside. The newel, the supporting post at the bottom of the stairs, added to the candle-lit softness of the hallway. It had a hole in the top, now covered with a matching piece of wood, to hold a second candle.

Hanging on the wall, still in good working condition, is a German cuckoo clock more than 150 years old.

To the left is the parlor with a tile-inlaid, coal-burning fireplace with mahogany frame. The mahogany settee and chairs were brought from Mississippi, and the needlework and crewelwork pillows scattered about were made by Mrs. Owen and her daughter Mary.

Elaborate archway between the parlor and diningroom.

Glass studded, gilded light
fixture in the hall.

The original wallpaper was a spider-like design that wound its way up one wall, across the ceiling, and down the other. The rug completed the webby enclosure with its massive garlands of bright flowers. Of course, there was a gaslight, a curled brass fixture.

Through a spindlework archway, elaborately draped with rich, dark damask silk, is the diningroom furnished then as now in rich mahogany furniture. Along one wall stands an antique buffet filled with china painted by Mary Owen and a fragile green and white set of Haviland, which Mrs. Owen, a gentle Southern hostess, used for tea.

Next to the diningroom is a warm, cozy sitting room with another elaborately carved archway to the bay window alcove. Now completely redecorated into a bright, sunny room, it originally had dark wallpaper, perhaps a royal blue, with a tiny flower or fleur-de-lis design.

There are a kitchen and bedroom on the first floor, too, and a bath, the first indoor bathroom in Idaho Springs. Originally it had a tin tub that after awhile was painted, and the Owens' granddaughter remembers that whenever she took a bath the paint came off in little flakes and stuck to her skin.

Upstairs are three bedrooms and a bath, that room added sometime after the Owens moved into the house. The bedrooms were filled with good Southern furniture — high bedsteads, mahogany bureaus, and rocking chairs. There was even a tufted-leather fainting couch in the master bedroom.

The Owens were friendly, hospitable people, and over the years they entertained a number of guests. Once when Owen had gone East to interest investors in one of his mines, he returned with a prospect who wanted to look over the property. While he was in Idaho Springs, he stayed, naturally, with the Owens and slept in the upstairs front bedroom. The man was Henry Ford, and he must have liked what he saw because he invested in the mine.

Another guest who spent a summer in the Owen home and stayed in that same guest room was Mrs. Owen's pretty first cousin, Edith Bolling Galt, who not long afterward became Woodrow Wilson's second wife.

The Owens lived in their Idaho Springs home the rest of their lives. She died in 1929; he lived only three years longer. Their daughter inherited the home and lived in it until her death in 1961. The house now is owned by the Owens' granddaughter.

While most Victorian homes have been refurbished many times over the years to suit their owners' whims, the Owen home in Idaho Springs has remained, inside and out, a 19th century abode.

Hot water heat has replaced the old coal stoves, and electricity long since has usurped gas lighting. Gone, too, are light-consuming dark silk drapes and the overpowering wallpaper on the ceilings.

But the present owner has kept the lovely old mahogany furniture gathered around the fireplace. The needlework and crewelwork pillows still are scattered throughout the house, and on the stairs is the handmade carpet Mary Owen hooked many years ago.

The gilded globe in the hall, now lit by a light bulb in place of a candle, still casts a soft glow for guests who walk across the veranda to visit in the atmosphere of another time.

Parlor with tile-inlaid, mahogany-frame fireplace.

Ouray:

Camp Bird

When a group of English investors bought the Camp Bird Mine near Ouray, they must have felt they were sending its superintendent, William J. Cox, out to the colonies to live, for the house they built for Cox and his cohorts was enough to coax any luxury lover to the rugged San Juans.

The home was started by a Denver architect who was so slow that the job was given to a Swiss man. His name is obscure, but his initials on the original blueprints are "E.H.B."

The house was begun in the summer of 1902; the blueprints were completed and dated October, 1902; and Cox and three other executives moved into the finished structure in November. The builder apparently knew what he wanted, and blueprints were just an unnecessary formality.

Though a settlement of just a few houses today, Camp Bird was a thriving community with a store, a school, boarding houses, a reception hall, and a number of homes.

One boarding house built by Camp Bird, Ltd., was particularly fine. It had white maple floors, steam heat, hot and cold running

Superintendent's house, Camp Bird Mine, near Ouray, Colorado.

Water, marble basins, porcelain bath tubs, sewer connections, fire-fighting apparatus, a well-stocked library, and pool and billiard tables.

The recreation hall, too, was well equipped and had a square grand piano of walnut. The piano was obtained for the room through a poker game. One evening two well-known mining promoters, John Hays Hammond and Harry Payne Whitney, got into a stiff poker game in which the high stake was a piano for the recreation hall. Whitney lost and bought the instrument. Hauling charges alone were $1,500.

When the Camp Bird cut down production and the miners went away, the recreation hall was closed and the piano stored on the porch, left to the mercy of pack rats. The sounding board remained good, however, and plans finally were made to store it in a safer place. When the recreation hall was turned into an apartment for miners some time later, however, someone chopped up the piano for firewood.

Two miles farther up the mountain at the mine's third level is the old shack where Thomas Walsh, original manager and promoter of the mine, is supposed to have lived. (Like George Washington, who slept in more places than his years would allow, Tom Walsh is supposed to have lived in a number of Colorado houses.) The only bit of luxury the wealthy Walsh added to his modest shack was a tin-covered walkway from the cabin to the privy. He later sold the Camp Bird for $3,000,000 and his daughter purchased the Hope diamond.

A big square house with a steep roof that fits over it like a bucket, the superintendent's house at the Camp Bird was designed with thirty-two windows and a number of doors.

Local legend says that in certain areas of England, at the time the Camp Bird house was built, residents were taxed for the number of outlets their houses had — windows, doors, chimneys, and so on. When the English firm built its superintendent's house at the Camp Bird and found the government did not care how many openings the building had, the Englishmen just lost control.

The outside of the home was sage green lap-siding though it has

West side of the house. Roof and turret are red.

Mill superintendent's house, designed by the same architect.

been covered with a white composition material. Originally the roof was four-foot shingle strips that formed a design, but the roofing had to be replaced several years ago. Like the tower with its conical turret, the roof is red.

There was tongue-in-groove siding around the tower, under the eaves, across the second story porch, and under the windows, but most of it, too, has been covered with siding.

The house was built with a good deal of tongue-in-groove wainscoting inside, also. The entrance hall has it on the walls and ceiling, and it even curves to fit the underside of the staircase. The grain of the wood was specially matched to take advantage of the curve. The grain started at a point and fanned out. Later owners, however, have had the wood painted.

The hall had a six-foot circular radiator since the house was built with hot-water heat. Electricity was installed when it was constructed. The house and the nearby mill paid five dollars per horsepower each month for the luxury.

To the right of the hall is the living room, its fourteen foot ceilings lowered to twelve. The natural wood fireplace, now painted, has a tongue-in-groove cover to fit across the arched opening since no damper ever was put into the chimney. Behind the living room is the diningroom.

Left of the hall is the library with wainscoting walls, their vertical lines broken part way up by horizontal paneling. Bricks a foot or so high were cemented into either side of the inside of the fireplace to form a simple grate. Until a receit remodeling, the room had a brass chandelier with frosted globes.

A newly-added doorway connects the library with the kitchen directly behind it. Completely modernized, the kitchen still has its "semi-Dutch" door to the porch outside. The top half of the door pushes up, like a window; the bottom half swings open. Winters at the Camp Bird are so severe and snows so deep that one has to climb over the closed bottom part of the door and step onto the drifted snow outside to hang up clothes. Naturally, the clothesline is high off the ground.

The kitchen was equipped with a Majestic coal range, a rack

Camp Bird Mine. Mill superintendent's house is at far right, mine superintendent's next to it.

Purpled bottles in the kitchen, all found around the Camp Bird.

Livingroom fireplace with tongue-in-groove cover.

suspended from the ceiling to hold pots and pans, and a soapstone sink so low, said a woman who lived there, that she practically had to get down on her knees to use it.

For some reason, the kitchen was built without cupboards, and all food and dishes were kept in a pantry, now a bathroom. Camp Bird, Ltd., purchased twelve dozen glasses for the house along with a set of willowware and another of rose-patterned Haviland. There also were four china pitcher-and-basin sets. One set now is on display at Ouray's Beaumont Hotel.

Off the kitchen is a servant's room built for Webster, Cox's servant. There is also a small hallway with a fire hose, used, as far as anybody knows, only once.

A new stovepipe had been attached to the coal stove, and it caught fire. The wife of the superintendent at the time grabbed the hose and put out the flames. Satisfied that the fire was out, she nevertheless went down to the mill office and told what had happened. She asked if someone would check the attic to make sure no sparks had gotten up there.

"That was all those men needed," she said, "to take half a day off." They climbed all over the house, spraying water on everything and ruined her freshly-baked cake.

Upstairs are four good-sized bedrooms (the master bedroom has a tiny sitting room in the tower) and a two-room bath.

The top of the tower is empty. There is a cellar, but it is unfinished and fills with water during spring run offs.

At the same time that Camp Bird, Ltd., built the mine superintendent's house, it had its architect design a house for the mill superintendent and three smaller houses for other employees. Looking like a poorer cousin of the big house, the mill superintendent's home has the same steep-pitched red roof and small veranda in front.

Clustered together at the end of a five-mile shelf road that winds its way high above the swirling Uncompahgre, the little group of houses is all that remains of the busy town that fed one of the world's richest gold producers.

Pueblo:

Wild Lions, Serpents, and Gargoyles

Winged serpents, impish gargoyles, wild lions rendered in stone, stained glass skylight, turret and tower, lavishly carved woodwork — all combined in a happily opulent Victorian house in Pueblo, Colorado.

Erected about 1893, the house was designed by architect George Roe and built by contractor E. W. Shutt. The land first was owned by the Colorado Fuel and Iron Company. Although employees have lived in the house, it is unlikely that the company ordered it built. No one remembers who first owned the house, and records are hazy.

The architect-contractor team of Roe and Shutt built six of the seven houses on the north side of the block, the seventh being added many years later. The group was so elegant that it was featured on picture postcards sold locally.

The north side of the street was so exclusive, in fact, that it was given a special name — Pitkin Place. The most decorative, the gargoyle house on the corner, was number one, the others two through six. The opposite side of the street was the 300 block of West Pitkin Street. In later years, however, because of mix-ups in mail and confused visitors, the block was demoted to just plain West Pitkin.

The gargoyle house, Pueblo, Colorado.

The gargoyle house is made of native pink stone, probably quarried at nearby Stone City, where most of Pueblo got its stone. It features all the pretentious gewgaws which Victorians loved to add to their homes. There are a turret with a steeple top, a tower with carved pillars and battlement. There are enormous archways carved with flowers and leaves, a porch with checkerboard stonework. Impish faces peer from designs in the stone with one saucy elf sticking out his tongue.

Most impressive are the splendid stone lions guarding the steps. Children love them, and owners of the house say not a boy or girl can pass without stopping for a ride. Children of many generations, neighbors recall, loved to mount the beasts. (Some claim they are supposed to roar when a virgin walks by, but no one in the neighborhood reports having heard them. One lion, in fact, has gone to sleep.)

The inside of the gargoyle house is as ornamental as the outside. The entrance hall is lavishly decorated with carved and paneled oak. The stairwell is a carved oak oval; though there have been at least two weddings in the house, neither bride, as far as anyone remembers, walked down the staircase.

The chandelier in the hall is a handsome silver piece with crystal drops and amber jewel-cut glass pieces. Above the door is a brightly colored stained-glass window. The floor was parquet, but the boards were so split and worn by footsteps as well as repeated sandings that the floor had to be carpeted.

The living room, originally front and back parlors has barely a straight wall. It rambles along to fit inside the outside. The tower, which goes from the basement to the third floor, forms a protruding alcove with window glass which is actually rounded. (Glass to replace it cannot be purchased in this country; it has to be ordered from France.)

There were two carved fireplaces, one in each parlor; but, when the rooms were combined, one was removed.

In addition, there are a diningroom and kitchen on the first floor. Later owners added a family room. The second floor had three bedrooms and a nursery. More bedrooms have been added over the family room.

Stonework imps and gremlins.

The third floor is an odd area fitted between the tower and the turret and under the sloping roof. The windows are strangely shaped, some starting at the floor and ending halfway up the wall; although they fit perfectly with the imps and gremlins outside, from within the windows give the room a topsy-turvy appearance.

In the center of the large third-floor room is a skylight of tiny crescent windows. Probably both were stained glass originally though one has been replaced. The colored window has a white fleur de lis in the center with pink, red, gold bits of colored glass around it. The third floor also had a maid's room.

Pretentious but thoroughly original with an impish sense of humor, the gargoyle house is a happy bit of Victoriana.

The carved oak mantel is one of two that were in the livingroom.

Fairplay:

Haunted House on the Hill

Every Western mining town worth its gold dust has a haunted house. Fairplay's stands high on a bluff overlooking the town, and it has all the requirements — rotting exterior, abandoned look, even a mysterious death.

The house was built in 1873 in the best (or worst) of the American Gothic tradition. Big, bulky, high-gabled, disproportionate, it has no handsome mansard or even gay gingerbread. It is the house you notice in Fairplay, and you know despite its unkept appearance that it once was haughty and proud.

The builder of the house was James Marshall Paul, a Leadville mining man originally from South Carolina. His wife, Laura, could not adjust to Leadville's high altitude, so her obliging husband built their home in Fairplay and rode horseback over 13,280-foot Mosquito Pass to work and back.

For his home Paul chose one of Fairplay's high spots from which he could see anywhere in town — or anyone in town could see him. On the site he placed a huge, disdaining two-story structure, complete with stable and even a tennis court. The back of the house

James Marshall Paul home, Fairplay, Colorado.

was on level land, but the front was on a slope. A long staircase went from the small porch down to the street below. Originally, the stone embankment in front was exposed, but present owners have shoveled dirt in front of the house to form a terrace.

In front the house has a double-deck bay window centered under a large gable. A smaller gable covers a flush window on the second floor and the porch below it.

On the east side of the house is a one-story bay window with a little gingerbread rail balcony on top and once-handsome paneling at the bottom. There was a tiny balcony at the second floor window on the other side of the house, too, but it has been taken away.

The front door opens onto a long hall and narrow staircase. A door to the right leads to the parlor and one farther down to the diningroom. The two are connected by a wide archway. Each room has a spacious bay area eight feet high; the ceilings themselves are ten feet. Behind the dining room is the kitchen and to the west a large library, most likely the room where Laura Paul conducted her private school.

The upstairs is a piece of nineteenth-century Americana of the kind described by Booth Tarkington:

> Upstairs were the bedrooms; "mother-and-father's room," the largest; a smaller room for one or two sons, another for one or two daughters; each of these rooms containing a double bed, a "washstand," a "bureau," a wardrobe, a little table, a rocking-chair, and often a chair or two that had been slightly damaged downstairs but not enough to justify either the expense of repair or decisive abandonment in the attic. [1]

Tarkington described the downstairs, too:

> Commonly the family sat more in the library . . . while callers when they came formally, were kept to the "parlour," a place of formidable polish and discomfort. The upholstery of the library furniture was a little shabby, but the hostile chairs and sofa of the "parlour" always looked new. [2]

---

1. From THE MAGNIFICENT AMBERSONS by Booth Tarkington. Copyright 1918 by Doubleday & Company, Inc. Reprinted by permission of the publisher.
2. *Ibid.*

Added to this, the Pauls probably had lace curtains at the bay windows, gossamer curtains to let in the view of South Park with majestic mountains sweeping down to the wide plain but keep out the stares of the riff-raff.

And there was plenty of riff-raff in that tough town of Fairplay. It had been settled fifteen years before by disgruntled miners from Tarryall, who, disgusted at the way they had been treated, dubbed the place "Graball" and started a new settlement to be called "Fair Play" for the treatment any newcomer would receive. One of the men who proposed the name was Jim Reynolds, who shortly afterward became South Park's infamous highwayman.

Reynolds was captured several years before the Pauls moved to Fairplay, but the town still had its share of ruffians.

In 1880, a group of vigilantes was aroused when a Fairplay man accused of murder was allowed to plead guilty to manslaughter and receive what they thought was too light a sentence. They decided to impose their own justice so broke into the jail, kidnapped the prisoner, and hanged him from the courthouse. Next morning the judge and district attorney found a couple of nooses on their desks marked with their names, so they promptly high-tailed it out of town.

Most historical accounts include a 1953 aftermath. When the courthouse was remodeled that year, a workman ripping up the floor found a dust-covered, tagged noose lying under the boards, supposedly evidence against the vigilantes, hidden there by the judge.

A number of Fairplay residents, however, claim the find is a hoax that backfired. A local man is supposed to have hidden it the day before it was found. The rope was not made in 1880, and the tag was a dimestore one. But the man who discovered the noose never believed it a prank, so the story became popular.

It was about the time of the lynching, or perhaps a couple of years earlier, that the Pauls left Fairplay, and the house had a succession of owners including one who used the place as a stagecoach stop.

Over the years it was allowed to rot away until now it contains only vestiges of its former grandeur. The foundation is strong

Most of the gingerbread trim has fallen off; the paneling is rotting away.

The two-story bay window once looked out disdainfully across South Park.

96

enough to last another ninety years, but the rest of the house will have a hard time surviving half that long. The outside, a dull pink, has weathered from lack of paint; the trim long since has fallen away. It is not the fault of owners; repairs would cost many times what the house is worth.

Five times the house has been sold for taxes, and on and off for a number of years it has stood vacant. That is one reason it was dubbed a "haunted house" by Fairplay children, bt there is another reason, too.

A number of years ago a young man killed himself in the tiny bedroom at the top of the stairs. Fairplay residents are close-mouthed about the incident and won't tell anything about the fellow or why he did it, but they do say the man's parents are supposed to have removed his body and locked the door without cleaning the room. They never entered it again. The next owners, to cover the blood stains, painted the floor red.

It may be just a rumor told by children over the years; but there *was* a suicide in the house, and the floor in the room at the top of the stairs *is* red.

The haunted house idea, however, does not seem to spook the little children who live there now and romp through the rooms. To them it is just an old house; there is nothing special about it, and perhaps that is the proud home's *coup de grace*.

Crested Butte:

Ghost in a Hurry

Most ghosts take a long time to die, but Crested Butte's was in a hurry. It died in only twenty-five years or thereabouts.

A relative Johnny-come-lately to the field of crumbling, deserted mining camp houses, the weathered old place was built as late as 1913, but it has stood vacant longer than it has been lived in.

Like most ghosts, Crested Butte's fosters a story. It may not be a completely true one; nobody, even family members, can quite remember what happened, but Crested Butte's old timers say there's at least an element of truth in the tale.

Young Jacob Kochevar built the decorative old home for his parents, Jacob and Maija. Jakie was a good carpenter, the best in Crested Butte. He'd built the house across the street for his sister and ornamented the gable with the year he finished it, "1912," and he'd helped erect the three-story building he owned down the street. That one had been intended as a "sportin' house," but about the time it was completed, Crested Butte got moral and ran all its gilded girls out of town, so Jakie moved in himself, and his wife and son live there still.

Jacob Kochevar's house, Crested Butte, Colorado.

Jakie built the structure of his parents' house and sectioned off the rooms — six downstairs, four upstairs. The entrances (there are three of them) are on the east, and he spaced them evenly along the wall and fitted in the windows symmetrically.

He decided to make the side of the house facing the street the fanciest, most ornamental in town, and from the looks of it today, he succeeded. The first floor, which juts out below the second, was fairly plain: handsome wood siding and a double window in the center decorated around the edges with knobs.

The false-fronted second floor, however, contained enough decoration for the rest of the house. Jakie traced designs along long pieces of wood siding, cut them out with tools he'd made himself, and smothered the side of the second story with them. A few rows were done with scalloped edges, and then he used points. Tired of those, he switched to sharp rick-racked "dog teeth."

When he reached the top, he inverted a big scallop, hooded it with a cornice, and placed inside it the date — "1913."

Jakie even built a wooden sidewalk, a coal shed in back, and an outhouse — a one-story affair, of course. (Local old-timers fume at stories of Crested Butte's two-story outhouses, the second floor to handle winter time traffic. "The only two-story outhouse in this town," said one, "was at the Masonic Hall. One upstairs, one down, both inside, and both the flush kind!")

The Kochevars and their children had come to Crested Butte when young Jacob was about fifteen. The town was the center of a prosperous coal mining area, so Jacob went into the mines. So did his son Jakie until he took up the carpentry trade.

About the time Jakie's fine house was finished, however, Jacob and Maija weren't on speaking terms, so Jacob moved into the new house, and Maija stayed on in the old one, right next door.

Old-timers aren't quite sure just how long Jacob stayed in the house; it may have been only a short time, though one insists he was there until the day he died — nearly twenty years later! But almost anyone who knew them would admit that the two often didn't speak to each other, and for a time one lived downstairs in the old house while the other stayed upstairs.

The old Kochevar home next door.

Scroll-sawn siding done with hand-made tools.

Whatever the arrangement, they apparently died on good terms, within a year of each other, and they are buried side by side beneath the biggest stones in Crested Butte's cemetery.

Their son Jacob kept the house, renting it occasionally or loaning it to family members, but it's been vacant for many years. When he died in 1955, Jakie left the house to his son, the third Jacob Kochevar.

Painted only once, the old house has traces of its bright, bileous yellow. The sides are weathered and falling away; the windows and doors are covered with corrugated iron. The three doors (which open on the side away from Maija's house) still have their shiny china knobs — black, brown, and white — and the "1913," only slightly weathered and appearing more like "1918," still looks down on anyone who glances up to see it.

Next door, the house where Maija lived has fared little better. No one knows when it was built, but it dates back at least as far as 1885. The doors sag open. (There are so many of them opening outside that the old place looks as if it were built as a brothel, but Crested Butte residents say the red-light district was kept strictly across the street.) The walls are caving in, the roof is falling, and it's doubtful anything but a packrat or perhaps a homeless dog has called it home since Maija left.

Side by side, like Jacob and Maija Kochevar, the two houses grow old, and like the old couple, when one goes, the other most likely will pass away shortly.

Decoration on Jakie's sister's house across the street.

102

Carbondale:

The Brick House

"The Brick House" is one of those cumbersome, ill-arranged mansions that lived too long. In fact, it was obsolete almost before it was finished. But it *was* grand!

Called by everyone, even the family, "the brick house," the handsome old structure was built in 1901 by Charles H. Harris. Though it may have vied with another for title of the most ostentatious dwelling in the valley of the Roaring Fork, it was, at least, the biggest — twenty-two rooms, eight of them bedrooms.

Harris, born in 1852, came to Colorado in the early 1880's. For a time he ran a supply house in Aspen — long before the railroads came into the valley. But things didn't look good in town so he and his partner homesteaded ranches in the valley, and in time Harris acquired 900 acres.

Indians had lived on his land until a year or so before Harris moved onto it, and there still were round worn spots in the sod where the tribe had pitched its tepees.

In 1886, he married one of Aspen's first school teachers, Rosetta Noble, and took her to live in a one-room log cabin forty feet long.

The brick house in the Roaring Fork Valley.

Later they moved to a small frame cottage Harris built on the ranch. Then, after four children, Harris decided to build a bigger place, in fact, the biggest house in the valley.

He hired a Glenwood Springs engineer-architect named Rosenberg to draw up the plans, and, according to his son, Vern, he had him "draw until he came up with something Father liked."

What Harris agreed upon was an enormous brick house with a row of tiny gable windows around the second and third stories. Not a man concerned with details, Harris eliminated a great deal of trim, inside and out. But he did like the grand things such as his staircase, wide and spacious, not the cramped darkened stairs crowded into most homes. The entrance hall was ten feet wide, and the stairs six. The banister was the slide-down kind.

On the first floor were a parlor with a tile fireplace, a kitchen and two pantries, a diningroom, and three miscellaneous rooms, one of them a sitting room, the others — just rooms.

The second floor held the eight bedrooms (Harris used one of them for his office.) The third was intended to have three rooms but never was finished.

Though water was piped from a spring to the animals' watering trough, it didn't make it to the house until 1914. A well just outside the back door and a privy, a two-seater, took care of the family.

The furnishings were typical of the day — big "divonas," square diningroom set, clumsy sideboard, bedrooms furnished with a bed, dresser, table, chair, and washstand in each. When the millionaire a few miles up the valley (he owned the only house that could compete with the brick house for elegance) went broke, Harris bought his cherry, walnut, and oak bedroom suites — high bedsteads, marble-topped dressers, the kind with little shelves poking out halfway up the mirrors.

Naturally, since he was anxious to show off his house, which despite its size and ostentation, cost (furnished) only $7,000, Harris gave a house-warming party. Nearly 300 invitations were sent out, and most of them were accepted.

The Glenwood Springs crowd came in a special train chartered for the occasion. (The railroad track was at the front edge of the

Remnants of the kitchen.

property.) There were three different orchestras and the Carbondale band, each playing in a different room. Two rooms had square dancing, the other two "round" dancing — waltzes, two-steps, schottisches. Said Vern Harris, "It was a terrible mob milling around, and they didn't all leave till the next morning."

Despite its title as the grandest house in the valley, the brick house wasn't a very happy place in which to live. There was too much work and not much fun. In the first place, it was much too big, much too over-sized for Mrs. Harris and her three daughters to keep clean.

It was cumbersome; the rooms were arranged in jig-saw order, and they were cold, especially the bedrooms that didn't have coal stoves. The fireplace heated only the parlor (that is, if the doors were closed), and the stoves in the rest of the house kept a person warm only if he stood next to one.

Then, too, the foundation wasn't strong enough to hold the big house, and when the place settled, it was slightly lop-sided.

But though she didn't like it (she'd never been consulted about either the house or the furnishings), Mrs. Harris continued to live in the brick house even after her husband's death in the early 1920's. A few years later she sold it to Mumbert Cerise, and his family didn't like it much better than the house's first mistress did.

The place was so cold and so difficult to heat that the second owners took out the front staircase and roofed over the scar.

The Cerise family, however, lived in the place nearly thirty years before giving up.

The brick house's downfall was its handsomest feature, its gabled windows. The roof had started to rot away, and the price of replacing it, especially around the gables, was far more than the house warranted. The owners considered cutting off the third floor and the attic but decided to build a new home instead and desert the old place.

Now the brick house is crowded with old iron beds, empty cardboard boxes, and a dilapidated doll buggy. But at last, perhaps, its occupants are happy — a bluebird that flutters back and forth in its vast roosting place and several calves that sleep in the shade outside.

Central City:

13 Eureka Street

When sixteen-year-old Gertrude Jenks made up her mind to travel to California in a covered wagon with her favorite brother, her Ohio Quaker family told her, "Gertrude, if thee does this unmaidenly thing, the family will never think the same of thee again."

But Gertrude was young; the year was 1859, and gold was easy to find; and she was an adventurous girl. The pair never made it to California; they settled in Denver where her brother got a job, and Gertrude kept house for him.

One day, alone in the house, Gertrude sat in front of the window rocking. A band of Indians came by, saw her, and pointed to their mouths expectantly. Gertrude, naturally frightened, nevertheless shook her head "no" then turned and began speaking to an empty chair out of sight from outside. The Indians fled thinking someone was with her. Her descendents still have the rocking chair.

In 1863, Gertrude married George Nathan Billings, and they settled on the banks of the South Platte, though Indians had warned settlers to stay away from the seemingly gentle river. Shortly after they moved there, Denver's treacherous flood of 1864 rushed down upon them, and they were forced to flee in the middle of the night.

The Benjamin Prosser Thomas house, Central City, Colorado.

Billings told his young wife to leave everything. "I'll carry you, but you won't be able to take a thing with you," he said. Gertrude pleaded, but he was adamant. It wasn't until years later that he realized why she had been so heavy.

After a time the Billingses moved to Central City. Billings owned the first planing factory in Colorado and apparently did quite well. They had three children, two daughters and a son, and when one of the girls married in early 1895, the Billingses decided to give the couple a home in Central as a wedding present.

The house the Billingses purchased for their daughter and her husband, Benjamin Prosser Thomas, was 13 Eureka Street, just a few doors above the courthouse. It had been built in 1874, by one of the Hendrie brothers of Hendrie and Bolthoff, whose foundry was across the street.

Later the house was sold to Sauer, partner in Sauer-McShane Mercantile. Thomas, too, was involved with Sauer-McShane. He did a bit of grubstaking with the store's groceries as well, but his gambles, unfortunately, were only slightly successful.

The home is a big, yellow, two-story house, slightly colonial looking with its green shutters, but the pink porch is a pure touch of mining camp decor.

The front door of the house, made by Billings's factory, was carved by a Swiss craftsman and set with an oval pane of beveled glass. It had won first prize in a competition; so Billings gave the door to the couple for their home.

A one-story diningroom, kitchen, and storage area "L-ed" out to one side. And in back, high up a steep incline, stood the privy. Said one who had used it, "You could see all over town from up there — and all the town could see you." A sort of drawbridge contraption went from a second floor bedroom to the privy for anyone who didn't want the bother at night of going downstairs then climbing uphill.

The inside of the house has a look of mountain Victorian elegance: velvet furniture, bird cage, scattered bric-a-brac, silk opera programs, brass bed with hand-made quilt, an engraved announcement of the marriage of Baby Doe and H.A.W. Tabor.

110

Sitting room view to the patio. The sofa is covered with a silk and velvet crazy-quilt.

Brass bedstead in the master bedroom.

111

Except in the livingroom, all the wallpaper is original and boldly patterned. The paper in the hall, generously covered with pictures, documents, mirrors, and a deer head, is a gaudy pink, happily faded, with big blue and aqua Indian rug-like designs. Despite its overbearingness, the hall gives a pinkish-warm friendly appearance.

The parlor is furnished with nearly all original furniture and momentia — a velvet love seat and four matching chairs, a table painted to look inlaid with wood, a picture made of colored tinfoil, a motto, "There's No Place Like Home," and a sewing box, a gift to Gertrude Billings from her husband's one-time partner, David Moffat. The original carpet, green background with garlands of yellow and red flowers, still glares up at visitors.

The sitting room behind, dominated by an ornate, old coal stove, has a pretty double window that looks out onto a stone patio cut into the hillside. There's an old sofa in front of the window covered with a silk and velvet crazy-quilt, its pieces caught together with neat feather stitches. Above swings a bird cage.

Off the sitting room is a little office that holds a "lady's chair," a seat with a back and one arm. One side is left open so the lady's hoop skirt could fall gracefully over it. The drapes hung in the doorway were made out of old strips of fabric sewn together. Mrs. Billings had had them made, and when they were small, her two daughters were expected to spend a certain amount of time each day tearing old dresses into strips.

The diningroom, besides its large table, buffet, and coal stove, holds an old wooden soda pop cooler from the Sauer-McShane store, a Regina music box that played big metal perforated discs, and an Edison Home Phonograph.

The room it filled with mementoes of the time — the silver cup Billings won for his door, a beer tray printed with the likeness of Baby Doe, a white-fringed silk program embroidered with purple violets from the first opening night at the Central City Opera House. (The bustled dress Mrs. Billings wore, green silk with black lace and jet, hangs in an upstairs closet.)

The kitchen still has its highly-ornamented cookstove, old bread-box, antique kitchen equipment including a turbine-powered egg-

Diningroom bric-a-brac: cut glass, Red Ridinghood, and
Baby Doe.

beater. The appliance screwed onto the water faucet (the house had
cold running water), and the force of the water going through it
powered the beater.

Hanging in the kitchen is a pretty orange-and-brown-striped
calico dress, Mrs. Billings's wedding dress. Gertrude's brother bet
her she wouldn't dare be married in a calico gown. Gertrude took
the dare and said her vows in the striped cotton dress, but immediately after the ceremony, she stripped off the calico and stepped out of
it in a formal white wedding gown.

Called "Saint's Rest" because of an old print by that name hanging there, the bathroom, added later of course, is decorated with old
"girlie" calendars from Sauer-McShane. Over 100 were stored in the
old house. Once slightly risqué, the calendars are more charming
than tempting today.

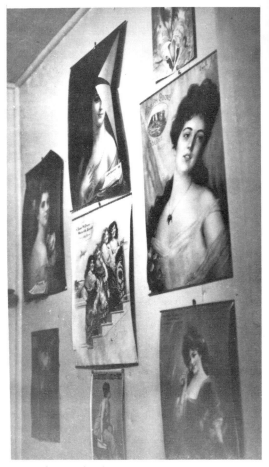

"Girlie" calendars from Sauer-McShane in the "Saints' Rest."

Green and white painted window to the storage area.

Throughout the house are paintings done by Mrs. Thomas. Though some are out of proportion and others horribly sentimental, they were painted in all seriousness by the artist. They're hung today, however, with a sense of humor.

Upstairs are three bedrooms; one (appropriately the room with the drawbridge) has been turned into a bathroom. Its medicine cabinet is a rectangular clock with the workings taken out and replaced with a tiny shelf. The little door that once opened onto the clock's innards now shows off tubes of toothpaste and razor blades.

At one time, the old house contained seventeen clocks. Some were fine old pieces. Others were sent to the Sauer-McShane merchants to be used as premiums. A few, like the orange one in the kitchen in the shape of a piece of fruit, were intended to be used in the store. Most still keep good time.

The master bedroom was indeed elegant — an ornate brass bed in the center covered with a blue and white star-pattern quilt pieced by Mrs. Thomas. Most likely she never intended that it should be used since it never was until after her death.

The pillow covers (these are not "cases" that are slipped over the pillows but flat squares of material that are placed over them during the daytime) are embroidered with "Good Night" and "Good Morning" in pink.

When Central declined, the Thomases moved to Denver, about 1912, and the old house was closed for nearly twenty-five years. In 1935, Mrs. Thomas' sister, who lived in the East, inherited the home. She thought of selling it but told her daughter, "This is the last thing we have in the West, and I don't want to let it go." So it has been used since by her daughter, the Billingses' granddaughter, as a summer residence. She has kept the home just as it was when Mrs. Thomas came to it as a bride in 1895.

Gaudy and elegant, tempered with a sense of humor, the old house is mountain Victorian as it was intended to be.

Montrose:

Mountain Mayfair

T. B. Townsend was a misplaced Englishman who did not much like the United Sates, particularly the rugged Western Slope. Since he made his money there, he had to live there, and so he made the best of it. He built his home as far away as possible from his mining properties in rough Ouray and Silverton; he chose a slightly more genteel, pretty town up the river — Montrose.

Surprisingly enough, instead of an English-Tudor style mansion, he chose American Victorian. It was a stylized Eastern architecture to be sure, not the raw, gaudy hit-or-miss type of the mining camps. It had more of a Mayfair flair but was nevertheless American.

Townsend, who co-founded the first bank in Montrose and dealt in mining property farther south, built his house in the mid-1880's on a former homestead. Most likely Townsend did not file on the land himself but purchased it from someone who did.

The exterior of the house is a brownish-pink brick made by Townsend's brickworks. He founded the factory on his property near the Uncompahgre River, and bricks were made from the river clay. Most likely the plant was set up just to accommodate the house since it closed shortly after the home was completed.

T. B. Townsend home, Montrose, Colorado.

The house has natural stone trim as well as wood in decorative designs. It is built with two gables in front and others on the sides. There are three porches, one on the first floor near the front door, a second above it, and the third around the side on Townsend Avenue. At the peak of the roof is a metal "hog-back" design.

There is a great deal of land around the house even though most of the homestead was parceled off long ago. The pretty iron fence that surrounds the property was added shortly after the home was completed.

Probably the only touch of English décor in the home is the entrance hall's formal pine paneling along the entire staircase. Once highly polished and shining, it gave the house a cool, dignified air. There are unobtrusive knobs in the panels that open them onto closets. The banisters and railing are walnut, fashioned in a criss-cross design.

The front door is wide and handsome with stained-glass panels of red, gold, and green around both the door and the windows to the sides of it.

Townsend's house was built on a center-hall plan. To the right is the front parlor and behind it the back parlor. Strangely enough, these rooms had wall-to-wall carpeting. Townsend, a proper Englishman, disdained central heating, so the house was warmed by coal-burning fireplaces.

The fireplace in the back parlor is brown and white Italian tile. The pieces across the top of the fireplace are designed with apple blossoms in relief; the side tiles show tall asters growing out of fish bowls. The fireplace frame is oak with carved brackets and shelves. Sunbursts and panels are set with mirrors.

The house was lighted with gas originally, but its gaslight fixtures are gone. Though Montrose had no electric plant when Townsend built his home, he, nevertheless, had the home wired hoping the town would have electricity in a few years. Fortunately, it was brought to Montrose shortly after the house was built.

Across from the front parlor is the dining room with a pretty windowed alcove. Its cherrywood fireplace, similar to the one in the back parlor, has wine-colored tiles decorated with geometric de-

Foyer and paneled staircase.

Fireplace tile friezes.

119

signs. In the upper outside corners of the tiled area are two tiles, one of a man, the other of a woman, in Shakespearean garb.

Through a pantry to the back was the original kitchen, now turned into a dining room. It has two entrances to the outside, one on either side of the room. The doors have windows decorated with panes of glass stained every color of the rainbow. Just off the old kitchen, a new kitchen was added in a former back porch about 1900.

Upstairs there are four bedrooms for the family, while down a few steps is a room for the maid. The house was built with a partial bath with running water drained from the roof into a cistern and then pumped to the bathroom.

Originally the second floor had two fireplaces, but succeeding owners took them out when they installed a central heating system.

Townsend did not live in the house long. About a year after it was completed, he and his wife left the United States. Townsend, like any loyal subject of the Queen, wanted his son born in England.

After the Townsends closed the house, it stood vacant for several years until Townsend's partner in the bank, E. L. Osborn, purchased the home for around $8,000. His family still owns it.

Leadville:

Morning Glory Mansard

Leadville architect George E. King liked mansard roofs. He designed a smart one for the courthouse cupola; he put an elegant one on the Tabor Grand Hotel (**renamed** the **Vendome**).

He liked the roof so well he designed two for his funny little top-heavy house — one on the second floor, one on the cupola.

Nobody knows much about King except that he was a prominent Leadville architect. He must have been a dapper little man for his is a grand house with a definite "Charles Addams" touch and is one of Leadville's fanciest.

Shortly after King finished his home, the *Leadville Weekly Democrat* pictured two Leadville houses on the front page of the January 1, 1881, edition. One of them was King's. The accompanying article told about the home and as much as is known about the builder.

> Among the many new and beautiful residences erected during the year none are more tasteful and elegant than that of Mr. George E. King, the well known architect and builder. This handsome house is on Capitol hill, and gives evidence of the superior skill

121

George E. King home, Leadville, Colorado.

of its owner as an architect. Mr. King drew the plans for nearly all Leadville's best buildings, including the fine new courthouse and schoolhouse. As an architect he has no superior in our city and is well deserving of the prominence he has gained in his profession

Over a third of the front of the house is a tower, and the extra weight of its over-sized cupola seems to be held up with brackets.

The windows sticking out of the second floor mansard are round-head Italian. It looks as if King were so taken with them that he later designed the same windows for the Tabor Grand Hotel.

The original exterior was supposed to have been brick though an early picture makes it appear frame. Later clapboard actually was added, probably for warmth since there is no insulation. Sometime after that composition siding was put on. King added, also, a jaunty iron fence that encircled the house.

Inside, though little remains of the house King designed, one can imagine the way it was originally, handsome and pretentious.

The foyer is long and narrow with the staircase on the right. The mahogany handrail on the stairs once was called the most expensive piece of wood in Leadville because of its millwork.

Paneling at the side of the stairs, now painted, is mahogany, too. Originally the hall, like the rest of the house, had gaslights, and the tiny gas pipes still are in the walls.

The living room still has its high ceiling. It is a surprisingly bright room for such a mysterious-looking Victorian house. King probably shut out the **light,** however, with tasseled, heavy, velvet drapes and overpowering, dark wallpaper.

The diningroom originally was the only other room on the first floor, according to one owner, and probably served as a kitchen. A drawing made when the house was completed, however, pictures some sort of back porch or shed if not an actual room behind the present diningroom where today's kitchen stands. If the kitchen were added on, it was done at least sixty years ago.

Strangely enough, the tiny house has a back staircase, very steep, from the back of the dining room to the bedroom above.

Because of the staircase and the size of the house, one owner speculated that the home was built for a bachelor and his servant,

Windows on the Tabor Grand Hotel appear to be copied after those King designed for his own home.

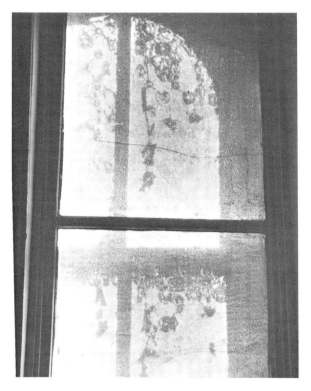

Dormer window at the top of the stairs is etched with morning-glories.

but the property was listed in courthouse records under the name of Harriet as well as George King. The staircase long since has been blocked off and serves as a catch-all.

At the top of the front stairs is one of the dormer windows, and its glass is etched with drooping morning-glories visible only when the morning sun or very bright moonlight hits the glass. One practical resident suspected the inaccessible window was decorated so it would not show dirt and consequently would need to be cleaned less often.

There were three bedrooms upstairs, but the smallest one has been turned into a bath. (The original bathroom was a fancy privy out back.) The small back bedroom was the servant's if there were a servant. The large one was the Kings'.

Off the large bedroom is the tiny room under the cupola, big enough for one bed, but more often used as a closet. A trap door in its ceiling opens into the cupola itself, used only for storage.

Some Leadville residents say the cupola was built as a lookout for Indians, but former owners scoff at the idea saying boys who once lived there made up the story for their friends. It is a believable tale, though; the house is one that invites stories.

An 1879-1880 photograph of Leadville shows King house under construction. *Photograph courtesy Library, State Historical Society of Colorado.*

Georgetown:

Grubstake Odds

Grubstaking was just a little more reliable a way of finding a gold mine than was daydreaming about it. No self-respecting gambler would have taken grubstaking odds, but a few storekeepers thought those same odds just good enough to loan a prospector that small but highly important stake — his grub — for part interest in anything the miner found.

One lucky grubstaker wits H.A.W. Tabor, who parlayed a few dollars worth of food into a strike worth millions. Another fortunate storekeeper was a Georgetown grocer named Potter who staked himself into part interest in the productive Colorado Central Mine.

When Potter struck it rich, he was living high up the mountainside in a crowded two-story house, built in 1867. He decided that such a simple, unpretentious house was not nearly grand enough for a mining magnate, however, so in 1889, he built a $35,000 addition in front. Like the proverbial tail that wags the dog, the addition was so spectacular it made the rear of the house as dull as servants' quarters.

Maxwell House, Georgetown, Colorado. One of the ten outstanding examples of Victorian architecture in the United States.

Like many of the elegant homes of that time, the Potter house was copied by a builder from a magazine. Architects of the day instead of creating homes for individual clients often designed houses and sold the plans to magazines. Builders copied the plans to any degree they wanted, adding or subtracting details, lengthening the porch or pinching in the parlor.

The house could be as simple or as elegant as the owner desired, and Potter chose to be very elaborate — in fact, so spectacular that his home was chosen by an American Institute of Architects' publication of the 1930's as one of the ten outstanding examples of Victorian architecture in the country.

When the silver crash came in 1893, Potter lost his fortune and sold his home to Frank A. Maxwell, who lived there fifty years. Maxwell was a crack mining engineer, but his fame comes from the spectacular Georgetown Loop he designed.

The Loop, a remarkable piece of engineering, was built so trains traveling from Georgetown to Silver Plume, only a mile away but 500 feet higher, could circle around (at one point the engine actually passed over the caboose) and gather enough momentum to climb the steep grade.

Few changes were made in the house during the half-century Maxwell lived there, one reason why the home has kept its Victorian appearance intact. Another is that present owners, keenly aware of Maxwell House's historical importance, have studied old photographs and talked with Georgetown's old-timers about the house's appearance and have decorated it just the way it was originally.

Painted pink, brown, and white, Maxwell House with its jaunty cupola and spire is a happy blend of ostentation and practicality. It combines the architectural features of several countries: the windows are Italian, the mansard roof French, and the spire pure "lightning rod" Americana.

There is a pretty little stoop with railing and pillars and on its roof a balcony decorated with a sunburst in its paneling. The balcony, of course, is pure decoration; no door opens onto it. The cupola with its own private mansard roof has a dormer window poking out on each side. It is topped with a spire that looks like a lightning rod rendered in wood.

The Italian windows in the front of the house protrude slightly, while the bottom one is decorated with pillars in relief. Under the cornice are square designs that stand out like the teeth of a happy gap-tooth grin. The mansard on the sides of Maxwell house is roofed with rows of wooden shingles cut in scalloped and pointed designs.

The glass panels above and to the sides of the front door, like the glass at the top of the parlor window, are encrusted with jewel-like flowers of leaded glass, miraculously unbroken after all these years. The handsome flowers with their diamond-like centers are brilliant red, blue, and green.

Like many houses of the time, Maxwell House opens onto a long hallway with a staircase on one side. It is lighted with the soft pink glow from an acorn-squash-shaped fixture of cranberry-colored Sandwich glass overlaid with milk glass. The fixture once was a gaslight.

To the left is the parlor with its oak door — though not quite oak. If one looks closely (very closely since it is a good job), he discovers the door is not really oak but pine painted to duplicate the grain and coloring of the more expensive wood. The fake is as good a likeness as a fine old tintype.

Still furnished with the original furniture, as is much of the house, the parlor is formal but only slightly stiff. Along one wall is a highly polished fireplace, or at least the shell of one. There is no working fireplace, only a smoke hole. A practical Franklin stove was placed in front of the wood frame since, when Maxwell House was built, working fireplaces were a means of heat, not decoration, and Potter certainly could do better for his family than an open fire.

The original molding is high up on the walls, and hanging from the ceiling is the old gaslight fixture with its morning-glory-shaped globes of pastel Sandwich glass.

In back of the parlor is a study, complete with original fainting couch, and beyond that the diningroom, large and spacious with a huge table. Maxwell kept his collection of rock specimens in this

Parlor door painted to resemble oak.

Fireplace shell in the parlor.

Stained, leaded - glass window next to the front door.

Gaslight with Sandwich glass globes.

130

room since after supper talk normally turned to mining. It was easy to reach over, grab a rock, and say, "Now this piece . . ."

Maxwell's collection of rocks still is kept in the diningroom along with the rock specimens of present owners, another engineer and his family.

Behind the diningroom is a kitchen, now modern. This room probably was the Potter parlor during the grocery days. There are a breakfast room and bath, originally a bedroom, both part of the old house.

The double back porch dates to mining days, too. Maxwell, no matter how prominent, was relegated to the position of any other miner when he came home. He was ordered to shed his dirty mining clothes on the first porch and don cleaner ones on the second. Still sitting on the porch is the carpeted bench Maxwell sat on to take off his shoes.

Upstairs are the master bedroom, two smaller bedrooms in the newer part of the house, and two very small bedrooms in the original part. The master bedroom is an elegant "suite," a small sitting room and bedroom stretching across the front of the house. In one corner, the left front corner of the house, is a pretty little alcove formed by three windows and the mansard roof.

There are two staircases in the house and a bath, not original but most likely added soon after the front part of the house was built. The bath has a big zinc-coated copper tub. The inside of the cupola, ingloriously, is just a storage area.

Battered by the winds of nearly three-fourths of a century, Maxwell House is remarkably preserved, thanks to owners who have loved the house and recognized its historic value. It stands overlooking Georgetown, a remnant of a pretentious era, a monument to a gamble that paid off.

Master bedroom alcove is formed by dormer windows in the mansard roof.

Aspen:

Luke Short's Hideout

Without a doubt, more desperadoes have tasted dust in a snappy, seemingly-innocent little house in Aspen than ever were gunned down on the streets during the town's wild past.

These infamous men come, however, from the famous pen of Luke Short, owner of the house, who estimated in 1964, that he had written nearly half of his thirty-two brawling Westerns while living there.

Though his office is downtown, on summer days he sometimes writes in the side yard behind the up-and-down white picket fence.

One of the prettiest, certainly the most coquettish of Aspen's gingerbread houses, the Glidden home (in humdrum life Luke Short is known as Fred Glidden) is painted white and grey and has shiny black doors with lace curtains.

No den of double-dealing badmen or haunt of fast-talking fancy ladies, the house has a happy, carefree air; in fact, during Aspen's first boom, it was known as a house of gay parties.

The quaint home was built, probably in 1882, by a druggist, D. M. Van Hovenberg, who began his Aspen career as a cashier in

Luke Short's house, Aspen, Colorado.

the Jerome B. Wheeler Bank on the first floor of the Wheeler Opera House.

Shortly after Van Hovenberg built it, the house was sold to a mine manager named Heatherly. After a series of owners, it was purchased by world-famous skiing figure Friedl Pfeifer, who sold it to its present owners in 1948.

The house was very well built and unusual for the time, since it was insulated. Like a Victorian lady losing her ribboned petticoats, when the owners removed a few of the siding boards to make repairs, the sawdust insulation inside tumbled out.

The black star-crowned mansard roof has seven dormer windows poking out of it; the tops are scalloped, and each window is decorated with a white wooden star.

Topping the mansard is a fancy little ironwork "catwalk." (It's too small for a widow's walk," say the owners.) Part of the grill-work was knocked off the front of the roof during a storm, so a portion in the back was moved around to replace it. Matching the seams in the roof are vertical spokes in the catwalk, each with a star on top.

The little front porch (like most front porches in Aspen it's decorated from December to April with skis in one corner) has white wooden columns topped with gingerbread brackets. The porch light is not a remnant of Christmas but a Mexican star. In fact, much of the house is decorated with Southwestern art acquired by the Gliddens when they lived near Santa Fe.

The satin-black doors are decorated with lace curtains. There is a bell in one door, but, sadly, it does not work. Instead, the owners have put up a set of decorative bells at the side which seems to jangle loudly enough to bring someone to answer. The house number, "232," on the glass above the doors is the original decorative type.

If the outside of the house is faithfully preserved Victoriana, the inside has been made modern and comfortable, a characteristic not always found in Victorian homes.

Through the double doors is a cheery entrance hall with an old-fashioned hat rack. Whereas most Victorian stairs crouched along

Carved panel in the fireplace

Gossamer embroidered curtains with glass flower tie-back.

135

a side wall, this staircase, after a twist containing a couple of steps, climbs brazenly up the back wall.

The living room, to the right of the foyer, was once two small rooms. The sectioning wall has been torn out, however, and the result is a good-sized living area with twelve-foot ceilings.

The archways to two bay windows are painted white and gold, and the windows themselves are hung with sheer, embroidered organdy curtains, held with glass flower tie-backs.

The fireplace, once yellow tile, is black, and its carved wood decoration is white. One entire wall is bookshelves containing plenty of "Luke Shorts" as well as some mining era guns. Behind the room is a bedroom and bath.

In back of the foyer is the diningroom, called the "chapel" by Glidden because of its many *retablos* hanging on the walls. Beyond that are a pantry, kitchen, and back porch.

Upstairs are three bedrooms, surprisingly large, and a bath.

Like most Victorian homes, the house has no basement, few closets, and no extra storage space, so its owners have built a shed in back and painted it to resemble the house.

Inside and out, the home has been happily, cheerfully decorated. Like a spry Victorian who has refused to grow old, the little house has acquired a snappy new wardrobe, a few touches of lace, and put up a successful fight to stay dated but debonair.

Common Aspen front porch décor, skis.

Ouray:

Camp Town Jig-Saw

For the most part, mining town homes were an ungainly lot, a sort of camp town jig-saw.

They were one-room log structures with rooms added here and there when they were needed. Sometimes more windows were put in or extra doors were cut. Maybe a second story would be stuck on, or if the miner struck a promising vein, perhaps he'd hide the entire place under a coat of new siding.

Most of the time these add-on structures were cumbersome. Occasionally they were quaint. Only rarely were they charming, and one of these unusually beautiful homes, literally "scarred" with Ouray history, stands gracefully under the towering cliffs that line Ouray.

The first part of the house was built in the early 1880's by an Indian agent named Wheeler, and he chose a spot on the cliff made by the roaring Uncompahgre.

The railroad ran next to the river, and Wheeler was smart enough to use railroad ties — discarded by the railroad, perhaps purchased from it, or maybe ever purloined on a dark night. Two walls of the

137

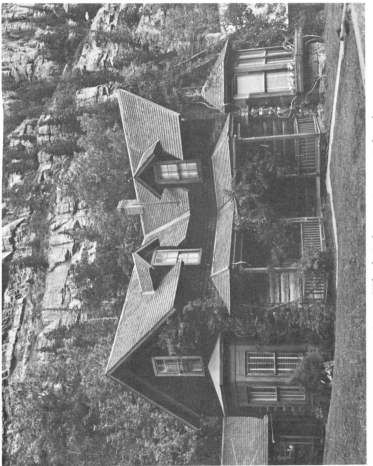

Agent Wheeler's house, Ouray, Colorado.

cabin are made of nearly-square ties chinked together. The other walls are hand-hewn logs.

Wheeler put in a tall chimney of red hand-cast brick and coated the inside walls with canvas. The original house was built on a stone foundation, later portions directly on the ground.

Shortly after he built the house, Wheeler, as Indian agent, arrested Chief Ouray and put him into jail. Ouray's braves, incensed with the action, supposedly attacked Wheeler's house, shot arrows into it, and generally tore it up inside.

Sometime later, Walter Wheeler, a brother of the agent, purchased the house and began the add-on process. Most likely he was the one who built the second story with its two dormer windows in front. Then he added a room onto the back. Next he built a shack behind the house for the cook and put a fireplace inside.

To add a touch of elegance, Wheeler or a later owner removed the flush windows in the front and side of the house and put bay windows into their places.

By the 1890's, the house must have been one of the town's nicest because when George Westinghouse came to Ouray to install the Beaumont Hotel's electrical system, he reportedly wired the log house. Though the original wiring has been added onto, it never has been replaced.

Added on with reason but little intended rhyme, the log cabin, nevertheless, has a pleasing rhythm today. It's in the shape of a couple of "L's" linked together.

The front L is chinked natural log on the first story, stained shingles on the second. Trim on the porch, windows, and the door is green, and there are red and white petunias, orange bittersweet, and red climbing roses growing on the windows and porch.

The back one-story L is wood siding with stained shingles.

Inside, for all its hit-or-miss construction, the house is surprisingly well-arranged. There are a living room, diningroom, kitchen, and four bedrooms, one of them turned into a bathroom.

Though decorated in a fairly modern tone, the home has a Shaker appearance with its white-washed canvas walls which resemble rough plaster more than a finished wall covering. The bay windows give the rooms a soft, diffused lighting.

The cook's cottage.

Cherrywood fireplace; tile is mustard-colored.

The fireplace in the living room is almost out of place with the room's simplicity. Its highly polished carved cherrywood with mustard-colored tile facing probably was added long after the house was constructed, though the house was built with a fireplace.

The only "primitive" sign of the house's humble beginnings is the low archway from the stairway to the diningroom. Cabins often were built with low doorways to the outside, perhaps for heat, perhaps because it was easier, and this might have been the cabin's original back door.

Present owners think perhaps some kind of supporting beam was laid into the wall, and when a builder cut into the wall for the doorway, he could go only as high as the beam.

Spartan and simple but with a decided charm, Ouray's log house is a happy escape from the ostentatious, sometimes frighteningly gaudy houses of the Colorado mining towns.

Chapel window
door with china knob.

141

Breckenridge:

A Common, Ordinary, Everyday House

Life was hard in Breckenridge, just as it was in other mountain mining towns. When men struck it rich, they usually moved someplace where the living was lush — Georgetown, for instance, or glittering, sophisticated Denver.

Until that "inevitable" strike, the miners plodded along sleeping in dirty shanties and tents. The houses were built by more realistic people, those who had come to the mountains to take jobs in the courthouse or the country store; they were the ones who came to establish homes.

Such a man was William Forman, for many years Summit County's clerk and recorder. Forman was "common, ordinary, everyday" according to Breckenridge old-timers. The house he constructed in 1890, neither simple nor elaborate, was typical of prosperous houses in any Colorado mining town.

Forman built his home at the foot of Nickel Hill. (Local legend, unsubstantiated, of course, has it that the mountain got its name from the girls who lived in a shanty up the road and sold their favors for as little as five cents.) He chose a spot from which he could see over the town to lofty Peak Eight of the Tenmile Range.

142

William Forman home, Breckenridge, Colorado.

Forman's house, though not grand in any sense, was among Breckenridge's finest, a pretty two-story yellow structure with white trim. The property is surrounded by a dainty iron fence and low gate with a plate bearing the name "Forman."

In front of the house protrudes a rectangular bay-window alcove decorated with panels below the windows and diamond designs above.

There are latticework, scrollwork, and fancy cornices across the front porch. The back porch, serviceably glassed in, is made of tongue-in-groove siding.

The outside appearance is cheerful and sunny, perhaps to offset the dark and formal interior.

Inside is a maze of rooms — sitting room, conservatory (the front room that despite its small size once held a grand piano), dining-room, bedroom, maid's room, kitchen, and bath all on the first floor with three bedrooms above.

Though the rest of the house has been repapered many times, the maid's room, long used for storage, has its original wall covering — striped paper with gold-bedecked tulips and a lavish border of green-ish-blue flowers.

Walls in the kitchen are oilcloth above tongue-in-groove wainscoting.

Furniture was "heavy and nice," according to a woman who worked for the Formans. In the kitchen Mrs. Forman kept a three-chambered steel cabinet with a kettle in each compartment. She put food into each pot with a heated round stone beneath and closed the cabinet lid. The effect was an early-day steam table.

Mrs. Forman was a pleasant woman, recalled two long-time Breckenridge residents who worked for her after school and on Saturdays for a couple of dollars a week. But she was "hostile if you broke a dish."

Her day's work was lined up years in advance — Monday, wash; Tuesday, ironing; Friday, polish silver, and the silver was "swell stuff." So were the dishes, and Mrs. Forman had "genowine" cut-glass. The Formans kept cows, and the hired girls were expected to scrub the kitchen floor once a week with milk.

Like most of their contemporaries, the Formans lived quiet, obscure lives. Few people remember them though the mark they left was more permanent than that of the miners.

The prospectors and promoters came for what they could take from the land. The Formans and their ilk made a more lasting contribution. They planted flowers on the bleak hills; they built houses on the harsh slopes; they turned the desolate mountains into a homeland.

Latticework trim on the front porch screens the view of Peak Eight.

Wallpaper in the maid's room has a bright border of greensh-blue and brown.

145

Cripple Creek:

Finn's Folly

The Towers in Cripple Creek never would have been built if it had not been for an overly-enthusiastic promise given by J. Maurice Finn to Vice-President Theodore Roosevelt.

Before a crowd of thousands gathered to see the Vice-President, who was making his first official trip to the area, Finn proclaimed, "Someday, Colonel, I hope you will revisit this great District and give Mrs. Finn and me the honor of entertaining the Vice-President of the United States at our home, The Towers!" Roosevelt promised Finn he could expect him the following spring.

Somewhat abashed, Finn realized Teddy meant it, but Finn had not even selected a site for his home as yet. In fact, it never had been more than an enthusiastic idea.

J. Maurice Finn had been a staunch Democrat and a perennial office seeker in his home state of Michigan though he never had been elected to office, when he picked up roots and headed for the Cripple Creek gold fields.

He was a slick lawyer and before long had been engaged as legal council for W. S. Stratton, wealthy owner of Cripple Creek's Independence Mine.

146

A birthday party at The Towers during its brief heyday. *Photo courtesy of Vivian Richardson.*

147

He had also acquired a bride, his third, and encouraged her to indulge her taste for tapestries and oriental rugs in preparation for a mansion he wanted to build. In the meantime, he enlarged his library of rare and costly law books and added to his collection of marble and bronze busts of American patriots.

The Finns were living high when suddenly the unpredictable Stratton fired Finn without notice, so nobody was too surprised when rumors began circulating that Finn was broke. Said author Mabel Barbee Lee's father, "He spent too much on tomfoolery. The only sensible thing he's got to show for his money is a couple dozen cases of Kentucky bourbon."

His dream of a house was forgotten until early in the winter of 1901, when Finn read a newspaper story telling that Roosevelt planned to visit Colorado the following April and hoped to renew his friendship with "that distinguished Democrat, J. Maurice Finn."

Jolted, Finn remembered his magnanimous and easily given promise. He and his wife, Elsie Belle, dauntlessly set out to select a spot for their home.

They decided on a site at the corner of Placer Street and the west slope of Church Hill, despite the fact that the enormous price set by the owner of the land, the city of Cripple Creek, was $3,000, a sum impossible for the Finns to pay.

Finn was resourceful, however, and he proposed to the city council that the land be donated to him free of taxes. (Finn, a champion of the underdog, declared taxes were unfair and never paid them.) He argued that the sort of mansion he planned to build would be a credit to Cripple Creek, a fine place to entertain the town's distinguished visitors. The city fathers liked the idea; in fact, they liked it so much they gave him the land along with $2,000 to pay for grading the foundation.

Finn claimed the house would cost $25,000; but unseen expenses, such as the Michigan lumber that cost the Finns Elsie Belle's $8,000 savings (no other lumber was sturdy enough), nearly doubled that price. After Finn had managed to get most of the house built, resolutely he approached the tight-fisted, unsentimental president of the First National Bank, Bert Carlton, who, to everyone's surprised but Finn's, loaned him money to complete the mansion.

When it was finished, The Towers was by far the finest house in the District. It stood three stories high and had twenty-six rooms.

Its towers, one at each corner of the house, were each topped with an American flag. The entrances, one on each side, were exactly alike. There was a magnificent fountain in the center of the two-story rotunda with a marble rim.

On the second floor there were fourteen bedrooms, each opening onto the balcony around the rotunda. The third floor was an enormous gambling room. The main rooms were named after Finn's favorite historical characters. For instance, the library with its excellent collection of tlaw books was named the Abraham Lincoln Room. The trophy room was the Thomas Jefferson Room.

Since Finn had built the house in Theodore Roosevelt's honor, he decided to have the hero of San Juan Hill chirsten it at the magnificent reception he had planned in Roosevelt's honor.

Nearly everyone in the District had been invited to pay his respects to the Vice-President, and the house was decorated grandly, despite the fact that the grey paint outside was still wet, and carpenters' tools and scraps of building materials had been hidden under the front steps.

There was a string orchestra hidden behind a screen of potted palms in the rotunda; and, along the wall near the semi-circular staircase, Finn had rigged up a giant fresco of the Mount of the Holy Cross with stream of water cascading down into an aquarium of mountain trout. Mabel Barbee Lee recalls that she heard Roosevelt exclaim to Finn when he saw it, "I say, Maurice, this is phenomenal. You deserve a Congressional medal for your ingenuity."

Roosevelt never got around to christening The Towers, but perhaps that was fitting. Before long everybody had forgotten the proper name and was calling the mortgaged manor "Finn's Folly."

Shortly after Teddy's visit, Finn, hounded by creditors, moved his law practice to Denver. Elsie Belle stayed on and managed to meet payments for a time by renting rooms to school teachers.

During the 1920's, when discouraged residents were calling the town "Lame-water Creek," the great house was sold for a few dollars and torn down for salvage. Part of the house was toted away — some say to Canon City, others to north Denver, Colorado Springs, Lake City, or Boulder — to be used as a less elegant but, nevertheless, completely paid-for home.

In the mid-1950's the $3,000 lot Finn had beguiled the city into giving him was sold for back taxes — $26.

The foundation is all that remains of "Finn's Folly."

Georgetown:

Kingmaker's Castle

An early *Rocky Mountain News* article about William A. Hamill called the powerful Georgetown Republican "a Warwick whose specialty was senators, not kings." The party might well like to have Hamill in the Senate, said the writer, but he preferred to manipulate in the background.

Hamill was a strong man with decided tastes, and he had the sort of personality that made him well-liked or hated. Like the man, the house he chose to live in was well-built, lavish, and at times regal. (The highly-ornamental six-seat privy, for instance, has a crown-like top.)

Born in England, Hamill had lived in Philadelphia for many years before coming to Colorado. He was a mine manager and ran some of Georgetown's most productive strikes. In 1877, he formed a partnership in the Terrible Mine with Jerome B. Chaffee, head of the Colorado Republican Party, and though the association undoubtedly spurred his interest in politics, it did not start it.

The year before, in 1876, he had been elected to the State Senate, despite his increasing political power the only elected office

Hamill House, Georgetown, Colorado

he ever obtained. Later he replaced Chaffee as Republican leader in the state. Since he had made his fortune in silver, Hamill quite naturally was interested in the silver question; and, when the country went onto a gold standard, Hamill, who lost his entire fortune, dropped out of politics.

"General" Hamill, as he was called (Governor Pitkin once had appointed him Brigadier-General of the state militia and sent him to Middle Park to quell rebellious Utes), never had had legal training although he represented his mines in legal suits. He was considered an outstanding authority on mining law in Colorado though he was not a member of the Colorado Bar Association.

Hamill did not build his fine Georgetown house. It was constructed in 1867, for $15,000 by his brother-in-law Joseph W. Watson. The two men did much of the labor; and a paper, hand-written by Hamill and included with the abstract, says he helped Watson saw most of the lumber used to build the home.

Watson, himself, was an interesting man, a speculator and a gambler who made and lost three fortunes—in Denver, Georgetown, and Leadville. He reportedly built and lived in the elegant home in Denver that later belonged to H.A.W. and Baby Doe Tabor.

A publication of the time said that in 1863 Watson received $100,000 for the first mine sold in Colorado. In two years he went broke through dissipation. In 1882, he sold his interest in the Evening Star Mines in Leadville for $700,000, but in less than a year he was not worth a cent. One Leadville man said that the omission of the letter "T" in a telegram cost Watson the title of millionaire.

Not long after the Georgetown house was completed, Watson borrowed money on the property. When he defaulted on payment, the bank foreclosed and sold the home for the amount of the loan plus interest — $3,882.50. James Clark, apparently a friend of Hamill's, bought the house and immediately sold it to Hamill for $4,308.84.

The Hamill family owned the home until 1914, when it came into the possession of a bank, which in 1916 turned it into the Alpine Lodge. The lodge advertised fifteen rooms at $2.50 per person per day, room and board.

153

Hamill's office, left, and the stable. Turret on top of the stable was a roost for squab.

Servants' entrance to the six-seat privy.

154

During the Second World War, the home was purchased with the intent of reopening it as a hotel. New owners delving into its background recognized its historical value and opened the house as a museum instead.

When Hamill acquired the house, it was a relatively simple two-story home with a central gable in front. He added first floor rooms in the back as well as a third story to be used as servants' quarters and a schoolroom. The latter had dormer windows, small and high up.

He built a solarium onto the side of the home and used specially-made curved glass for one wall and the ceiling. The room housed some of the rarest and most beautiful plants in Colorado. One Georgetown old-timer remembers walking to school past the house and seeing Hamill eating his breakfast in the solarium. In 1881 Hamill added an iron fountain with cast metal lilies and rams' heads just outside the room.

In 1880, he began an office in back of the house. The building was constructed of granite brought from Hamill's Silver Plume quarries. Inside are elaborately-carved walnut door frames and a suspended staircase that winds up three flights. Hamill lost his money before he finished his office, however, and the staircase from the second floor to the third never was completed. There are grooves in the handrail for decoration, for instance, but the ornamentation never was put into place.

Hamill also erected a stable behind the house with living quarters on the second floor for male employees. The turret on top of the stable was a roost for squab.

Inside, the Hamill home was truly elegant. There was central heating; probably the house was the first in the area to boast of it. The furnace, located in the basement, is cast iron with two feet of soft red brick around it. It shot heat through outlets in the hall, parlor, and diningroom. The second and third floors were heated by fireplaces.

Hamill also had gas lights long before the rest of Georgetown's residents, and he maintained his own carbide gas plant to light them.

Materials in the house were exquisite — flocked camel-hair wall-

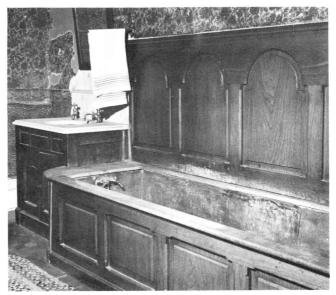

The wood-paneled bathroom with zinc tub.

Decorative lintel
in Hamill's office.

Solarium. The figure
of the boy is pewter.

paper from Paris in the parlor, embossed paper in the library. The chandeliers are gold-washed, and the one in the parlor has French cut-glass globes. Door knobs were plated with gold and window catches with silver. The parquet floors are striped with polished strips of walnut or maple, and the doors and frames are Missouri walnut, hauled across the plains by oxen.

The first floor contains the parlor dominated by an Italian tile fireplace and a lovely old piano. (Mrs. Hamill, a Philadelphia Quaker, was an accomplished musician.) Across from the parlor is the library with formal pieces of walnut furniture and an autographed picture of President William McKinley sent to Hamill's son. Present owners found it discarded in the stable.

Behind the library is the solarium with its rare plants and pewter statue of a small boy. The solarium connects with the dining-room. There are additional first-floor rooms, the kitchen and servants' quarters, reserve by current owners for their private use.

Upstairs are a master bedroom, two smaller bedrooms, and a nursery. The Hamill children were not allowed on the first floor. They were required to stay in their nursery or in the third floor schoolroom.

Another luxury in Hamill House is the indoor bathroom with a marble sink and zinc bathtub. Water was kept in a tank on the roof and heated by the sun so at the end of a hot day one could have a warm bath. Cold baths, unfortunately, were more common during the winter.

Though part of the bathroom was on the second floor, the rest, alas, was outside. The privy had two entrances — the one nearest the house with its three different size walnut seats was for the family. Servants were required to walk around to the other side where there were three pine seats.

The house was a gay place, at least while Hamill was wealthy. There were many parties, and the Hamills were quite socially prominent. The Hamills had four sons and a daughter. Their daughter, Lillian, reportedly was the first American woman presented at the Court of St. James.

After the silver crash in 1893, the Hamills lived quietly. The

157

General died of blood-poisoning in Denver in 1904. His wife, Priscilla, stayed on in the Georgetown home until her death two years later. She died peacefully in the master bedroom on the same night that, just a door down the hall in Lillian's old bedroom, her son's wife gave birth to a child.

First floor staircase in Hamill's office.

Cut-glass light fixture in the foyer.

Glenwood Springs:

The Congressman's Corner

There is a story in Glenwood Springs that when each of Congressman Edward Taylor's three children was born, a rancher friend presented him with a fine blue spruce and planted it in Taylor's yard.

Although Taylor's children most likely were born long before the family built on the site, there are, nevertheless, three blue spruces towering above the three-story house on the corner Taylor built a few years before he went to Washington.

One-time chairman of the powerful House Appropriations Committee, Taylor served in Congress from 1909 until his death in 1941, one of the longest terms in history.

The Taylor Grazing Act, requiring ranchers to own land in proportion to the number of cattle they grazed on the public domain and preventing cattlemen from owning cattle but no land, was one of the most important bills Taylor sponsored.

An educator and lawyer, Taylor had gone to Leadville, where he became superintendent of schools in the early 1880's and later moved to Glenwood. Taylor had made a good deal of money over the years, so he and his wife, Etta, decided to build the most elegant house in Glenwood.

Congressmon Edward Taylor's home, Glenwood Springs, Colorado

Taylor built his home around 1904. (During a remodeling, workmen found inside a wall a Star Plug Chewing Tobacco coupon good for one free plug of tobacco shaped to fit the hip, reclaimable up to 1905.)

The original building cost esimate was $8,000, but Mrs. Taylor made so many changes in the plans during construction that the Congressman confided to a friend he was afraid his wife would ruin him.

Slightly Southern in its appearance, the house is large and symmetrical with a wide veranda supported by white columns.

The front door is centered beneath a tiny gable on the porch roof. The windows to the sides of the door are leaded in geometric designs, somewhat like the patterns a school child makes with a compass. Above the door the glass is leaded in a simple stylized sunburst.

Originally the home had wood-shingle siding, but that since has been covered with asbestos shingles. Though Taylor did not include a stable in his building plans (possibly he already owned an automobile), he did have big stone carriage steps in front and on the side for his horse-drawn friends.

The home had many of the same features of John Cleveland Osgood's "Cleveholm" at Redstone just a few miles away. Local residents claim building materials, such as the mahogany shipped from the Philippines, were brought in the same boat. Cleveholm, however, was built several years before Taylor's home though it is possible, of course, that the Congressman used materials left over from the Redstone home.

The big porch was a friendly place, and the neighbors waited eagerly for the Senator to come home from Congress and sit on the porch swing. That was a signal for anyone nearby to come up onto he porch to hear Taylor tell stories about the Government and about the city of Washington.

Mrs. Taylor was equally as hospitable. Each day she gave the maid three dimes to be given to bums who came to the door. Word must have gotten around among Glenwood panhandlers because the quota and more showed up every day for the dimes.

161

The entrance hall is heavily decorated with mahogany trim cut-in pillars, brackets, spindles, and egg-and-dart designs. All had to be dusted once a day. There was a picture, still hanging there, of Taylor's daughter Etta with her cat, entitled "My Pussy."

To the left of the foyer, through a sliding door, is the dining room with mahogany trim around the fireplace and the arched china cupboard next to it. The cupboard was filled with large, lovely pieces of silver which Mrs. Taylor, a former boarding house helper, liked to display.

Kathryn Senor, a young girl employed by the Taylors during the depression (she worked sixteen hours for a dollar a day plus room and board and thought herself lucky) recalls that the silver had to be taken out and laboriously polished in May and repacked in September.

The diningroom table, an oversize circular piece, matched the mahogany trim. Above it was an expensive crystal chandelier. Since the Taylors dined late, around eight p.m., the help seldom finished cleaning up before ten.

There were two parlors, one for the family, the other, separated from the first by sliding doors, for formal occasions or for callers.

The kitchen was a large room with plenty of space to prepare for elaborate entertaining. There was a large pantry and back porch that held the ice box, while between the kitchen and dining room was a butler's pantry lined with shelves for fine china. Only slightly changed, the butler's pantry now is an economy kitchen.

A spacious staircase off the foyer was for the family; a plainer one just behind it for the help. At the foot of the back stairs was a servants'' call board.

Buzzers were placed in different areas of the house. There was one hanging over the Congressman's desk, for instance, and another on the dining room floor. Instead of stepping out into the hall and calling the maid, Taylor would press the buzzer, and she would look at the board to see where he was.

It was a simple device and not uncommon in large homes, but to some suspicious Glenwood Springs residents not used to electricity, the board was an ominous thing. One confided that the

Congressman was a "smart old guy" who had all the rooms wired so he could listen and "find out where everybody was and what they were saying."

The second floor contained four bedrooms, a sitting room, and the Congressman's office furnished with his huge desk and two round revolving bookcases. The second floor also had a complete bath, and the Taylors boasted theirs was the first house in Glenwood to have one-and-a-half baths.

The third floor contained more bedrooms, while the basement was a recreation room.

The Congressman lived in his home until his death. Shortly afterward the home was offered to Glenwood Springs for use as a library or possibly a museum. The asking price was a token one dollar, but the city turned down the offer.

Later the home, literally a white elephant because of its size when help charged more than a dollar a day in later years and maintenance costs were high, was turned into an apartment house containing eleven units.

Though Glenwood residents might not have liked the idea of changing the fine old mansion, doubtlessly that is the only thing that has kept the once-elegant home from destruction.

Carved woodwork in the Taylor foyer
had to be dusted every day.

Capitol City:

Mansion for the Governor

George S. Lee was an ambitious man, and he was a dreamer, but he couldn't seem to make the two work together for him.

His biggest dream, and his biggest ambition, too, was to make his city capital of the state, and he built the fanciest house in southern Colorado to be the governor's mansion. But by the time he finished the home (most likely even when he started) Colorado already was a state with its headquarters in Denver.

Lee never introduced any sort of legislation to have the capital changed, and his ambitions didn't even make this town county seat. None of this, however, stopped Lee from naming the place "Capitol City."

Perhaps it was a pun, maybe Lee didn't know the fine points of grammar, or probably he was just a poor speller, but even the town's name was a mistake. "Capitol" means a building; "capital," that's the city.

But if Lee failed to have his town made capital city, he was compensated for it by his position as "king of the mountain" in Capitol. He owned the Henson Creek Smelter, a mile below the town, a mill

164

George S. Lee's "Governor's Mansion," Capitol City, Colorado. *Photograph courtesy Denver Public Library Western Collection.*

165

on the other side of town, and the saw and planing mill in the middle; and if he didn't own everything else in Capitol, he had quite a say in running it.

Inspired by Lee's enthusiasm, local residents planned an over-ambitious city — saloons, stores, hotels, restaurants, smelters, sawmill, post office, numerous homes, and a $1500 school — all for a town that never saw more than 800 residents, if that many.

Lee's governor's mansion naturally was the post pretentious building in Capitol, and it was every bit as elegant as the current official residence in Denver, and perhaps even more elaborate.

Set in the midst of the majestic San Juans, on the bank of rushing Henson Creek, the spot, admittedly quite out of the way, would nevertheless have been an inspiring place for the chief executive.

The mansion was constructed of brick supposedly *mailed* to Capitol since freighting costs would have been higher than post office charges. Surrounded by fences and a number of outbuildings, the home faced Henson Creek.

To show he still was patriotic, despite his failure to make his town Colorado's capital, Lee flew a flag from the pole on top of his house. (No one seems to remember, however, if it were a Colorado or a United States flag.)

Naturally, Lee's mansion was the center of Capitol City social life and Lee's wife its mistress.

A publication of the time, Frank Fossett's *Colorado,* printed in 1880, said the Lees were "distinguished for their hospitality."

Nearby Lake City's newspaper, the *Lake City Mining Register,* April 7, 1882, carried a social item about the Lees' hosting a post election celebration.

"The new town officers spread an elegant lunch at Lee's, fascinatingly presided over by Mrs. Lee. Treasurer Lee closed the festivities with a speech on the future of Capitol City." (Lee wasn't the only hospitable one, however, . . . "President Messler pronounced the benediction and set 'em up at the Creek.")

One of the most interesting social events at the Lee mansion was a telephone concert written up in another Lake City newspaper, *The Silver World.*

Ruins of the Governor's Mansion.

Fallen timbers and crumbling walls.

167

Telephone Concert

Interesting experiment with telephone made last Sunday evening. Mr. Bates was at the Lake City instruments and Mrs. Lee at those of her residence in Capitol City. They sang several duets.

Far gone are the days, however, when the Lees entertained in Capitol City or Mrs. Lee sang over the telephone. Their mansion, with only a few walls standing, is a crumble of bricks and broken timbers. It hasn't even been allowed to wear away by itself. Tourists have taken souvenirs; campers have borrowed bricks to build hearths; nearby residents have hauled away building materials for their own use.

No trace remains of the handsome outbuildings that surrounded the home, and only a door or two and a few windows tell that what remains was a house, not a barn.

High winds and the cold have helped demolish the fine old place, too, and even Henson Creek has turned against it. The rushing stream that once flowed at the edge of Lee's yard, gradually has eaten its way up to the ruins of the governor's mansion and someday may undermine what's left of the dream and sweep away its remains.

Fort Collins:

Fairy Tale Cottage

Franklin C. Avery was one of the ambitious young men who answered Horace Greeley's call to join Union Colony, a group of settlers headed for Colorado.

With Nathan Meeker and some fifty other pioneers, young Avery, barely thirty-one years old, arrived in the newly-founded town of Greeley in 1870. A civil engineer, he helped Meeker survey the townsite and lay out its streets.

A year later a group of Greeley men formed Agricultural Colony to settle Fort Collins, thirty miles away. Avery was a member of the new colony, and he was elected to survey and lay out the new town.

Once asked why he planned such wide streets in both Greeley and Fort Collins, Avery replied, "People need wide streets, and land's cheap, so I give 'em to them."

A few years later Avery married, and in 1879 he built his handsome home on Fort Collins's Mountain Avenue.

By that time F. C. Avery was a wealthy man who could afford a fine home. As one of the town's founding fathers, Avery had

Franklin C. Avery home, Fort Collins, Colorado.

170

obtained a good bit of land and had built the Avery Block, a build ing containing a bank, ten stores, and office space.

He had been elected county surveyor, served on the town council, and had a financial interest in the opera house and the Northern Hotel.

In 1880 he would found the Larimer County Bank, later the First National Bank, with a capital of $30,000 and would serve as its president until his retirement in 1910. It was only natural that a man as prominent as Avery would build an imposing house.

Constructed of native stone quarried at nearby Bellevue, and decorated with red sandstone, the Avery home has the look of a fairy-tale cottage.

In front is a large central gable, and accenting the roof with its appearance of thatch are numerous dormer windows, irregular corners, and crevices.

The corners of the house and the windows are etched with dark sandstone. Trim is painted a loden green, while a tiny red wooden border outlines the glass in the windows.

The evergreen trees surrounding the house, planted by Avery and grown to massive size now, add to the storybook look. So do the pretty bird bath made of matching sandstone, the stone porch posts, the gabled stable. There is even a trim little gazebo with a rustic roof in the side yard.

Although the outside looks like "Hansel and Gretel," the inside is conventional Victorian.

The front hall, a large room occupying nearly two-thirds of the front of the house, has a prominent oak staircase, beautifully carved.

Avery, who designed the house, specified that both the outside and the inside walls were to be a foot thick, so the window sills are wide enough for window seats.

A wide archway decorated with pillars at the sides and an oak pediment at the top separates the hall and diningroom with its built-in china cupboard. The fine brass gaslight fixture in the diningroom has two pretty globes, buttercup-shaped, of yellow overlay glass. Next to the diningroom is the kitchen which had waist-high wainscoting and "barn door" cupboards. Behind it was a room for the hired girl.

Like any really good Victorian house, the Averys' home has both a front and a back parlor, larger than most. Avery, it seems, liked the rooms in his home to be as spacious as the streets he laid out surrounding it.

The front parlor has a carved cherrywood and marble-inlaid fireplace. The marble, a veined black, has insets of streaked white marble. The room was furnished with cherrywood pieces from New York.

Picnics were held in the gazebo in the yard.

Keystone over the front door tells that the house was built in 1879.

Curled brass fixture in the diningroom has delicate yellow shades.

173

In the back parlor, the tower on the east side of the house forms an attractive round-windowed alcove. The house has a ribbed radiator that fits neatly around the half-circle wall of the tower. In addition to the hot water heat, the home has a forced air system connected with the fireplace.

There are five bedrooms upstairs — complicated, strangely-shaped rooms fitted under the eaves. Though the Averys had only three children, the rooms could accommodate a good many more people and usually did. There were often elderly relatives living with the family. One of them, Mrs. Avery's Aunt Philomena Edison, spent her time weaving blankets and making paisley shawls for the Avery girls.

The master bedroom is a double-room with a round alcove above the back parlor. It has a private bathroom. Another bedroom is a double room zig-zagging in and out under the roof and the dormer windows.

A third has a sun porch and two tiny rooms adjoining it, in one of which is a huge bathtub but no heat. Several rooms have lavatories, probably added later since the pipes are exposed along the walls. One tiny room with a skylight contains only a commode

Children who lived in the house remember it as a pleasant place. There was a cave in the back yard and a tree house, and the family had picnics near the gazebo. The Averys' grand-daughter recalls that the grownups sat in the shade of the summerhouse while the children romped in the yard.

One long-time Fort Collins resident remembers watching Shetland ponies prancing in the yard among the fruit trees. The family had a St. Bernard dog as well.

The Averys lived in the home for many years, and their children made it their home after them. Only recently has the house been sold for the first time. Its present owners, two local doctors, paint a cloudy future as the Avery house probably will be torn down because of its valuable land.

Redstone:

John Cleveland Osgood's Utopia

John Cleveland Osgood was a turn-of-the-century financial titan who lived like one. He built a mining empire and controlled hundreds of men. He clashed with John D. Rockefeller, and hunted with Theodore Roosevelt.

Like the East Coast magnates, he designed a palatial home; but he built his not along the shores of the Atlantic but in the majestic mountains of Colorado.

Unlike the men of his time, however, Osgood was an idealist. In the years before unionism, he believed in fair wages and good working conditions and established for his coal miners a workers' Utopia.

Osgood, born in 1851 and orphaned only a few years later, went to work as a bookkeeper for the Union Coal Company of Ottumwa, Iowa, when he was nineteen. Convinced by the tally sheets and bank statements with which he worked that the coal business had a good future, he decided to go into coal mining for himself.

In the early 1880's, Osgood surveyed Colorado coal fields, thought them promising, and for a few hundred dollars purchased

"Cleveholm," residence of John Cleveland Osgood, Redstone, Colorado.

the rich land on the Coal Creek, a branch of the Crystal River. In fewer than twenty years, he had mushroomed his holdings into a financial empire.

By the late 1890's, Osgood headed the mighty Colorado Fuel Company. Later he would acquire the Colorado Coal and Iron Company and merge the two into one, the Colorado Fuel and Iron Company. He decided that the time had come to carry out his dream of establishing a model workmen's village. Osgood built Redstone, a town with forty workmen's cottages, each styled and painted differently and surrounded with flower and vegetable gardens.

He constructed two club houses, the Redstone Club for employees and the Bighorn Lodge for company officials and their guests; the Redstone Inn, a residence for bachelor employees; a church, a school, a library, and a bandstand.

Shortly after he completed the town, Osgood married a titled English woman and built for her a grandiose English mansion copied after her family home. He called his estate "Cleveholm," after his middle name.

Built at a cost of two-and-a-half million dollars (construction cost today would be nearly five times that figure), Cleveholm is a rambling castle about a mile from Redstone. Behind it were formal gardens, claimed to be the most elegant in Colorado. In front was a rolling expanse of lawn with a gazebo, that Victorian scene of love trysts, at its edge.

Osgood also established a game preserve with elk, bear, and deer, as much for his famous hunting friend, Teddy Roosevelt, as for himself. Fence posts with the dates 1901 and 1902 stamped on them still mark the edges of the estate.

Though basically an English castle, Cleveholm has touches of Italian, French, Spanish, American, and even German. The towers and big clock in the courtyard have an unmistakable castle-on-the-Rhine appearance.

The exterior of the first two floors is stone, and the third and fourth stories are grey clapboard. There are many touches of Tudor trim under the eaves and around the tower on the terrace side.

The main entrance is off the courtyard. The long entrance hall has linen-covered walls, hand-stenciled in yellow, orange, and green by a craftsman brought from Italy. There are light fixtures from Tiffany's in New York, a leather chair with Mrs. Osgood's family coat of arms tooled on it, and Battenberg lace shading the window in the door.

The two-story living room, oft-times the ballroom, has a massive, hand-hewn sandstone fireplace with the Osgood coat of arms carved above the mantel. The demi-lion rampant holding the sheaf of wheat denotes the "free-born landed gentry." The fleur, counter-fleur, and the demi-lion rampant are of the Scottish Arms. The coat of arms was granted to Osgood's family for military valor during the Border Wars between Scotland and England.

The enormous electric light fixtures in the living room are from Tiffany's and match the gilded fireplace set. In one corner near the windows that look out across the valley of the Crystal River is a Steinway piano, added by a later owner, Mrs. Frank E. Kistler. The piano was dismantled and shipped to France to be hand-painted with cherubs and flowers and then sent back. Mrs. Kistler reputedly had the instrument made electric.

Redstone Lodge, formerly the Redstone Inn, residence for bachelor employees.

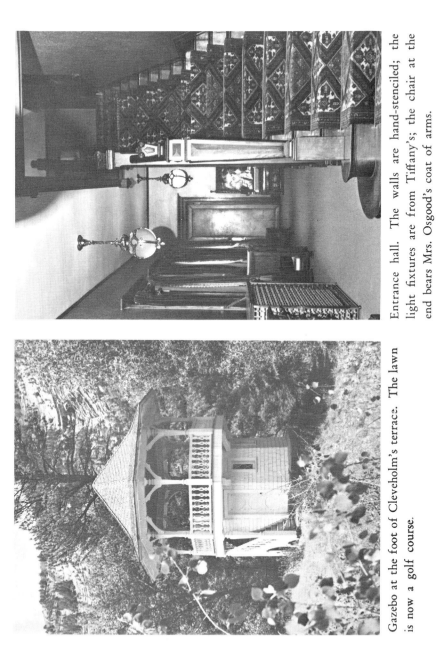

Entrance hall. The walls are hand-stenciled; the light fixtures are from Tiffany's; the chair at the end bears Mrs. Osgood's coat of arms.

Gazebo at the foot of Cleveholm's terrace. The lawn is now a golf course.

179

To the south of the living room is the diningroom with ruby red velvet walls, cherry woodwork, and matching red marble fireplace.

The library is to the south, a handsome, bright room. Its walls are covered with green Spanish leather, not elephant hide as is often claimed. Emerald green velvet drapes match the walls. The bronze light fixtures, beautifully tarnished, are a contrasting green. The ceiling, done by Tiffany, is gold and silver inlay, and the fireplace is Italian marble.

There are many valuable books including a Mark Twain first edition inscribed, "This is the authorized uniform edition of my books."

Called the 'honeymoon suite" today because it is often rented to newly-weds, the music room has pale green brocade walls with matching drapes. The ceiling is molded plaster and has an enormous crystal chandelier worth $25,000. The fireplace is white marble.

Though Osgood had no children, the house was designed with a number of bedrooms, most of them in suites. There is the comfortable, man-sized Teddy Roosevelt Suite on the second floor and the John D. Rockefeller Suite, slightly smaller, up a steep staircase on the third. (Osgood did not much like Rockefeller.)

Mrs. Osgood's suite has a marble fireplace, the only one with stone from Marble, Colorado. A tiny Battenberg lace-covered window looks down onto the living room. Mrs. Osgood apparently was a snob. When parties or balls were held, she liked to look down on the guests and wait until a sufficient number arrived before she made her grand entrance.

Mrs. Osgood also had her own linen closet since no one else was allowed to use her bed linens. There is a private bathroom with a marble mosaic floor and sterling silver fixtures. She also had an enormous wardrobe room with separate closets for shoes and for her riding habit.

Undoubtedly the most charming room in the mansion is Mrs. Osgood's personal maid's room adjoining the mistress's chambers. It has beige and pink flowered, linen-covered walls with tiny paired lamps, their shades covered with the same material. There is a pretty, high-domed ceiling, and the floors are parquet.

Osgood's suite is nearly as elegant as his wife's with a handsome mustard-color, tile fireplace, wardrobe room, bathroom, and smoking room.

The basement, like a classic English structure, has a maze of dungeon-like rooms. A game room is complete with billard table and stuffed animal heads. The oriental carpet on the floor is the only original floor covering left in the house. The floor itself is marble.

Adjoining the house are servants' quarters. The grounds also contain a gatehouse, a carriage house, and an enormous wrought-iron entrance gate with rearing lions on the pillars.

Though Osgood built his bride a grand home, it is rumored that the effort was to no avail. She left him not long after their marriage, and no one seems to know what happened to her. Probably she found life in the American West too hard and went home to England.

A few years later, in 1910, Redstone's coal mines were closed and placed in reserve because of the economic situation. Overnight Redstone became a ghost town and Cleveholm a deserted castle. Osgood closed the home and did not reopen it until April, 1925. He lived there until his death less than a year later.

Osgood's third wife (the English woman had been his second) was forced to sell all but one of the oriental rugs as well as much of the mansion's furniture and decoration in order to meet taxes.

In later years the property was parceled off. Cleveholm and the inn were sold to be used as a resort. The school, club house, Bighorn Lodge, and many of the residences were dismantled either for salvage or to be rebuilt elsewhere. The greenhouse was moved to a location on Highway 6 and 24 west of Glenwood Springs.

In 1957 oil millionaire and businessman Frank E. Kistler purchased the home and inn and most of Osgood's original 4,300 acres around Redstone. He turned the property into a highly successful resort.

Perhaps in the game of competition that turn-of-the-century

financial tycoons played so competently, Osgood has scored a round. While others' once proud homes are fighting a hard battle to survive the sickle of demolition, Osgood's Cleveholm has entered a second life.

A future as one of the most popular resorts in Colorado assures Cleveholm it will long outlast its Eastern counterparts.

Library. The walls are Spanish leather inlaid with gold and silver.

Cherubic design on Steinway piano was handpainted in France.

182

Boulder:

Mansion on Mapleton Avenue

Lumberman John McInnes had slept in enough forest beds. When he retired and married a young woman twenty-two years his junior, he did not care if he ever camped out again.

To bring home his point, he built the finest house in Boulder, and the heartiest activity he performed from then on was riding the "interurban" to Denver to watch stock market returns.

A Canadian by birth but a United States citizen by naturalization, McInnes had come to this country during the Civil War. After sampling a few jobs, he became an estimator for a Michigan lumber company. He could survey a forest, make a few calculations, and estimate just how much lumber it would produce. Sometimes he was out in the timber as long as two weeks without seeing another person.

When he married the daughter of a friend, a girl he had watched grow up, he was ready to settle down in a house in a city. Already retired, McInnes and his bride chose Boulder, Colorado, for their home and moved there shortly after their marriage in 1897.

In 1905, the McInneses completed their fine house on Mapleton

John McInnes home, Boulder, Colorado.

Avenue. They selected the plans for the enormous brick house with rambling verandas from an architectural book. (A daughter-in-law recalls seeing the same home in a Texas town.) Erected at a cost of $22,500, the house was built by a Boulder contractor named Jenkins.

The brick is speckled brown, the trim white, and the roof green porcelain tile. In front are a number of Corinthian pillars acting as roof supports and porch posts. The Southern style home has verandas on both the first and second stories. These extend around the sides, enlarging the appearance of the house.

The three McInnes children, all of whom attended the University of Colorado, used to wax the porch for fraternity dances. On less hectic evenings, John and Georgine McInnes liked to sit there and talk.

On either side of the front steps are lions' heads that are functional as well as decorative. Their mouths are drains used when the porch is washed. McInnes seems to have liked lions' heads and used them inside as well as out.

The house has a central hall plan, the front door opening onto a spacious foyer papered originally in grasscloth. At its end is a curved oak stairway. Young Gertrude McInnes was married in the home. She swept down the staircase in a long white gown for the ceremony performed near the front door.

Wood for the staircase was hand-picked by McInnes, who selected woods for the entire house. The living room is curly birch, the library sycamore, the diningroom fumed oak, the parlor Philippine birch, and the bedrooms maple.

The wooden rings that held the heavy green, blue, or maroon draperies in the doorways matched the woods in the corresponding rooms.

Lining the hall and the staircase were excellent oil paintings, many large and massively framed, some specially lighted. McInnes did not collect any one type of art; he purchased what he liked.

Georgina McInnes's reception room near the front door was a pleasant, formal room in which she received guests who came to her "at homes." Her son Donald remembers that there always was a silver plate in the hall next to the door for the ladies' calling cards.

On other days she would hire a hack and visit her friends. The McInneses owned no horses though they did build high carriage steps at the side of the house for hired hacks and carriages of friends.

The little reception room was papered in panels of white satin wallpaper embossed with figures and had parquet floors. The room was furnished with dainty mahogany pieces — inlaid chairs and settees upholstered in patterned French velvet.

Across the hall is the sitting room with an elaborate fireplace, its corners carved lions' heads. Mrs. McInnes thought the room was too dark and always had a fire burning to brighten it from midday on.

Next to it is an oval room, the library. The window alcove with its rounded glass had a window seat covered with green velvet cushions. There were green velvet drapes and thin lace curtains. Against the walls were mahogany bookcases, and a piano stood at one end.

Staircase is made of oak chosen by McInnes. His daughter Gertrude was married in the hall.

186

The diningroom, at the rear of the house, has a built-in buffet of fumed oak to match the walls, and each drawer is opened with a different key. The matching oak table, with its corners of carved lions' heads, seats twenty. Over it, suspended by chains, is a red and green Tiffany-type shade.

The house was wired for electricity when it was built. In fact, to be sure the wiring was absolutely fireproof, McInnes hired an electrician from Denver at fifty dollars a day to inspect it. Electricity in the early part of the century was so temperamental, however, that the Tiffany fixture as well as others in the house had gas gets.

On the first floor as well are a kitchen, butler's pantry, and office alcove next to the side door. McInnes, who dealt in stocks and served on the board of directors of the First National Bank, kept his big roll-top desk there.

The second floor contained the bedrooms, simple in comparison with the rooms below. One had furniture again with the carved lions' heads.

On the third floor was a ballroom; but since the McInneses preferred simpler entertainment than elaborate dances, the children used it as a playroom. There was a shuffleboard court, and the children liked to roller skate back and forth across the wood floors. Later they held school dances there.

The days of the covered wagon definitely were past by the time the family built the house. Not only could they afford fine furnishings for their home, but they did not have to send to the East for them. The paintings came from Denver galleries. The oriental rugs were purchased from an Armenian dealer in Denver. (There were enough fine orientals in the big house to furnish the homes of the three McInnes children.)

For all its elegance and many servants, the McInnes home on Mapleton Avenue was a friendly, warm place. Mrs. McInnes, who had been a kindergarten teacher, loved children, who always were welcome in the big house. Though her receptions were formal, they were enjoyable and very popular among Boulder's women, as were the club luncheons and church suppers she gave.

The McInneses themselves never seemed too impressed with their fine home. Mrs. McInnes once confided to a friend, in fact, that she enjoyed the big house on Mapleton Avenue but wished sometimes they had settled for just a little bungalow.

The red and green Tiffany lamp in the diningroom was lighted by both electricity and gas.

Carved Lion's head on the corner of the sitting room fireplace. McInnes used lions' heads on furniture and on drain spouts as well.

Leadville:

Healy House

In 1878, August R. Meyer, one of Leadville's most respectable residents, married Miss Emma Hixon in the home of two equally upstanding citizens, a storekeeper and his wife, H. A. W. and Augusta Tabor.

After the ceremony, Meyer took his bride to the elegant home he had built for her on the hill, and the couple began what, unlike that of their wedding hosts the Tabors, would be a quiet, uneventful life.

Meyer had started his August R. Meyer & Company Sampling Works in Leadville just the year before. Anxious to marry but dubious about asking a bride to accept the unruly conditions that existed in Leadville, Meyer decided an elegant home with every luxury Leadville had to offer, along with a few he freighted in, would make up for some of the unpleasantness.

Therefore, he designed his imposing green and white two-story house with all the necessities to make a bride happy and the luxuries to make her friends envious. He loved the mountains and chose a site on top of a hill where no building could obscure his view of the Sawatch Range.

189

Healy House, Leadville, Colorado.

The house Meyer built is nostalgically Midwestern — white clapboard with green shutters and white picket fence. Its relative simplicity (by mining town standards, that is) made it stand out against the decorative, turreted, gingerbread houses surrounding it.

Though the house is simple outside, it is Victorian elegence in its prime inside. The parlor, by far the finest room in the house, features an enormous green fireplace painted with fine lines to resemble the tiny veins in marble. At first glance, it is a fake; at second, a work of art. Because the room, like most parlors, was so seldom used, its rug is in excellent condition — a formal though exuberantly flowered piece.

Across the hall from the parlor is the formal diningroom and off that a smoking room where Meyer entertained his gentleman friends. Behind the dining room is the kitchen, spacious and sunny.

At the top of the narrow staircase, spacious then but nearly claustrophobic now, are French doors opening onto a porch. The second floor contains two sitting room-bedroom combinations and (Emma Meyer's friends were justly awed at such a luxury for a mining camp) her own private drawing room. Just above the parlor, the long drawing room runs the length of the house. A beautiful polished fireplace stands along one wall, and the room was furnished in velveted pieces.

The paper on the wall is pure Victorian elegance — a deep blue accented with red and black and lavishly covered with gilt designs.

The Meyers lived in their house on the hill only a few years, until they sold it in 1881 to the First Methodist Episcopal Church of Leadville. In 1886 it became the property of Patrick A. Kelly. After the Kellys had lived there only a short time, Kelly deserted his wife and daughters, in the fashion of the melodramas popular at the recently-opened Tabor Opera House down the street; and Mrs. Kelly was forced to make a living the only way she could, by turning the big residence into a boarding house.

Mrs. Kelly's home was no mean boarding house, however. Residents were carefully selected, and the home at 912 Harrison Avenue became a fashionable address. It was also a very popular address. Mrs. Kelly had the stable moved against the back of the house and

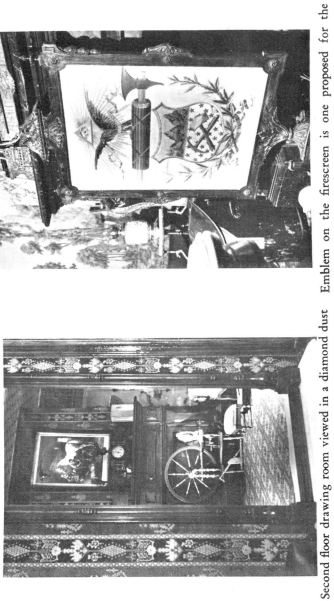

Emblem on the firescreen is one proposed for the Colorado State Seal. Fireplace is wood painted to look like marble. Wallpaper is a prize-winning French design.

Second floor drawing room viewed in a diamond dust mirror.

rearranged the rooms to accommodate the boarders who wanted to live there.

In 1888, the house was deeded to Mrs. Kelly's brother. He leased it to a couple who continued to rent rooms. Ten years later a third story containing four additional bedrooms was added. That remodeling gives Healy House its strange, somewhat out-of-proportion appearance. The house becomes much better looking when one blocks out the third floor in the picture to see what it looked like originally.

In 1912, Miss Nellie A. Healy, a teacher from Michigan who had taught in the Leadville schools for twenty years, inherited her cousin's house. In 1936, she gave it to the Leadville Historical Association. Later the house passed on to the State Historical Society which currently runs it as a museum.

Though Healy House in itself is a stately old mansion, the furnishings gathered from all over the Leadville area make it an especially elegant representative of mining camp Victoriana. Today's furnishings, the pick of a number of old homes, are much like the pieces August R. Meyer chose for his bride.

In the parlor are a velvet love seat and maching chairs that were hauled to Leadville in a covered wagon from the Atlantic Coast; a handsome stained-glass triple window fits into the bay window area; a piano, appropriately fire-scarred, that allegedly survived the Meeker massacre, occupies one end of the room.

In the smoking room is the secretary of another young bride who came West, Augusta Tabor, who brought it with her from Maine. Inside are mementoes of the woman who replaced her — Baby Doe's tiny kid gloves and dance program and doll furniture that belonged to ill-fated Silver Dollar Tabor and her sister.

Throughout the house are lovely pieces of carved black walnut, antique lamps, figurines and dishes, beautiful French dolls, diamond dust mirrors, and even an ornate fold-away bathtub. But by far the most elegant feature of the Healy House is its lavish wallpaper.

Stored for years in a warehouse, the sample rolls of paper, beautifully preserved, were given to the museum by the son of a Leadville paper hanger. They are bright, sometimes gaudy and overbearing

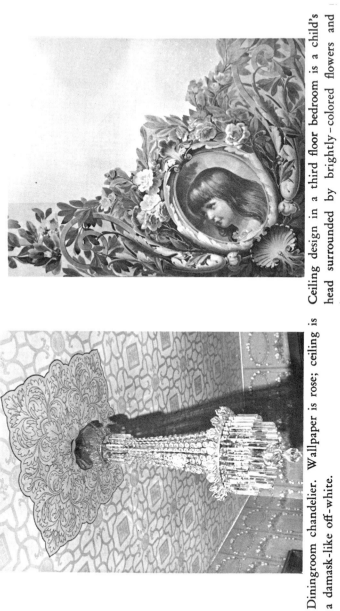

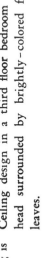

Ceiling design in a third floor bedroom is a child's head surrounded by brightly-colored flowers and leaves.

Diningroom chandelier. Wallpaper is rose; ceiling is a damask-like off-white.

patterns. Designs are similar to the ones that covered the walls originally.

The parlor is decorated with a French wallpaper that took first prize at the 1876 Philadelphia Centennial. The paper has a floor-to-ceiling scene of trees, ferns, and flowers. Its border at the top is figured with mountains and mysterious castles. The smoking room and diningroom paper are in formal panels, the design being flower-garlanded arches.

Even the ceilings are papered much the way they were when Healy House was built, with damask-like rich papers. Many of the chandeliers feature a "patch" of wallpaper in an elaborate square at their bases.

Prettiest of all the wallpapers is on the ceiling of a third floor bedroom. At each corner of the ceiling is the painted head of a child with a design of brightly-colored flowers and leaves trailing from it along the walls.

Healy House with its combination of old and renovated old is a piece of Victoriana revisited.

Steamboat Springs:

The Mansion at Medicine Springs

American tradition likes to believe the West was settled by honest, brave men, not by greedy, grubbing miners as it often was, but by men with a vision, pioneers with a dream. Steamboat Springs was founded by just such a man, James H. Crawford.

With his wife and children, Crawford settled in Steamboat in the mid-1870's, made friends with the Indians, founded a town, and established his home as a sort of hostel for trappers, pioneers, and any other travelers. His story is chronicled beautifully by his granddaughter, Lulita Crawford Pritchett, in a children's book, *The Cabin at Medicine Springs*.

Crawford moved into an old trapper's cabin when he arrived in Steamboat in 1874. He then built a four-room, chinked-log home for his family who came a year later.

Not long after Crawford arrived in Steamboat, he was appointed postmaster of the area. Fed up with traveling so far for a few letters or waiting weeks for a traveler to bring them, Crawford made a trip to complain to Governor Routt. When he returned home, he

James H. Crawford home, Steamboat Springs, Colorado.

197

found a mail sack and key on his doorstep. Inside were a few provisions and his commission as postmaster.

Sometime after Crawford erected the log cabin, he built a white frame house on the hill above it. Then in the mid-1890's, after he had raised enough horses to pay for it, Crawford constructed his fine stone house on the top of Crawford Hill.

Like its predecessors, the stone house was a warm, friendly place open to any traveler. Visiting dignitaries stayed at the stone house, but just as welcome to the Crawford hospitality was old Frank Ding, the trapper.

The three-story home was constructed of native stone quarried on Woodchuck Hill, a quarter of a mile west of the house, and hauled to the building site by teams of animals. Crawford loved the house and said he handled every stone that went into it.

Stonework was done by a mason named Briggs, who worked in Steamboat only a short time. The Crawfords, it seemed, were the only people who could afford a stone house.

The house is a big square with a mansard-like roof at the sides and dormer windows. The front door is set in a large stone archway of which Crawford was especially fond. The wide front porch was added sometime later.

The inside of the arch is traced in wood, and to either side is a narrow window set with panes of colored glass — purple, gold, and opaque white, as well as a red and white star-like design.

The entrance hall is spacious and friendly, big enough for guests to mingle and chat coming and going. Along one wall is a handsomely paneled staircase with a built-in seat next to it. Across from it is the fireplace and bookshelves, but by far the most important object in the hall was the immense deer head with its odd drop horns, a record spread, over the mantel. Crawford always liked to recount how he had shot the buck with a Colt .44 and how Legs, his greyhound, had helped capture it.

The living room has a pretty cherrywood fireplace. In the evenings the Crawfords and their friends liked to sit around the crackling fire and song or listen to tales of early-day Steamboat. Next to it, the dining room is big enough to seat many people, and the built-in cupboards large enough to hold a good sized china service with enough pieces to serve many guests.

The kitchen is another large, cheery room, and guests gathered there, too, to chat while Mrs. Crawford fried young sage chicken or prepared strawberry shortcake, much as the Indian women had gathered to gossip in the log cabin while Mrs. Crawford poured molasses over biscuits for them.

Upstairs are a master bedroom — a double room — and three smaller bedrooms. Curving from the master bedroom to the third floor is a pretty staircase, paneled in tongue-in-groove siding.

Guests who panted up the stairs were warned not to knock their heads on the massive mountain sheep horns beside the third floor door or trip over the prongs of the elk horn chair. The third floor was the Crawford "den" where the family kept Indian relics: guns; grizzly, fox, and wolverine pelts, and a mountain lion, mounted standing.

Besides acting as a museum, the third floor served as a lookout station. Whenever the fire siren blew, someone ran to the front windows to spot the fire and report to the others where it was.

Since the cabin days, the Crawfords had been known for their hospitality. Their granddaughter tells that even then beds were made up in all parts of the house when travelers stopped. Anyone passing through Steamboat was welcome to stay with the family, and people always dropped in.

It was only natural that the new Crawford home would be the social center of Steamboat. The house was the scene of literary guilds, socials, and discussion groups. While the grownups chatted inside, the children braided chains of pink and white alsike clover that grew rank in the yard, or roamed the spacious barn to hunt eggs or fondle the kittens.

At night Crawford liked to turn on all the lights in the house from top to bottom so that every window blazed forth hospitality.

The Crawfords freighted in the first organ to Steamboat so their home was the first to have music. One Steamboat resident whose family owned the first piano in town said people would come from miles around to hear the strains of music and were so entranced they

Paneled staircase in the entry.

Colored glass panes in the front door.

200

sometimes stayed for days. Undoubtedly the same sort of visits took place at the Crawford home.

The house at the top of Crawford Hill was a happy place, and the family were good, generous people. Crawford, it is rumored, would have died a much wealthier man if he had not been so open-handed. Said one loyal Crawford friend when asked if anything scandalous ever took place in the Crawford home, "Lord! If it was the Crawfords, there wouldn't have been a scandal!"

Perhaps the most memorable event the big stone house ever knew, tells Lulita Crawford Pritchett, was the golden wedding anniversary of James and Margaret Crawford, May 25, 1915. From all over northwestern Colorado friends came to pay tribute to the couple who in pioneer days had weathered many hardships but who through the years never had failed to befriend travelers up and down the valley.

Central City:

Crazy-Quilt House

The best Victorian homes today are those that were lavishly overdecorated and have been only slightly desecrated, but the Gus Center home in Central City is just the opposite.

A funny, misshapen little house high up Eureka Street when the Centers bought it, the home has been turned into one of the most delightful examples of unabashedly opulent Victorian décor in Colorado.

Built in the 1870's or eighties, possibly by Hans Jacob Kruse, Central's mayor, the place was the George McFarlane family home from 1905 to 1909. But its real history begins in 1944 when the Centers purchased it.

They pulled out doors, turned windows right side up, added a lawn in front, a grotto in back. In an old photograph the house looks as though it were white clapboard with dark-colored trim. The Centers have changed to color to a deep rose with red trim and black wrought-iron accents.

Walls, and ceilings, too, were covered with the best copies of mid-Victorian wallpaper available. A fancy, iron, coal stove was

Gus Center home, Central City, Colorado.

added to the living room and an iron and porcelain cook stove to the kitchen. Its burners have been wired for electricity.

Says Mrs. Center, "This house belongs to everybody because everybody has made it what it is. Anything that anybody didn't want came here."

Some furnishings are family heirlooms — Cousin Perry's *The Pilgrim's Progress* printed around 1800, for instance. Others are gifts from friends; the handsome kerosene lamp hanging in the kitchen came from the William Tanners who own 13 Eureka. Many were purchased by the Centers, indomitable collectors.

The front door opens directly into the little parlor, so neat and tidy. On the floor is a handwoven ingrain carpet, which, though it is at least 100 years old, looks barely used. The curtains are delicate lace and have mercury-luster tie-backs.

The upright piano, covered with a fringed throw, is an heirloom. Mrs. Center's father, Lincoln Markham, gave the instrument to his wife when their first daughter was born. Its top is covered with Victorian mementoes, and the three books there — "Mrs." Browning's poetry, a Methodist hymnal, and a Bible full of family clippings — were on the piano when Mrs. Center was a little girl.

The only original furnishings still in the house are the settee and matching chairs in the parlor. Above them is a charming American primitive of a curly-haired girl with Renoir eyes who is twisting a moonflower vine through her fingers.

The tiny library off the parlor has a small melodeon, and hanging over it is a picture of Mrs. Center's Grandfather Markward. The bookshelves are filled with leather-bound volumes, including an 1804 edition of *A Lady's Advice to Her Children*. Along one wall is the couch on which Lincoln Markham courted his wife.

The diningroom would have won the heart of any Victorian lady, especially the women of the gold towns who had left their lovely things behind them and had come fortune-hunting with only the ugliest and most utilitarian equipment. There are silver teapots, sugars and creamers, salt dishes, fruit stand, and spoon holders.

The table is covered with a chenille "between meal" cloth since real ladies used tablecloths only during meals. There is a beautifully

Lincoln Markham's "friendship" quilt.

The scarlet lamp reportedly came from an early Central City brothel.

Victorian kitchen clutter.

The parlor is a reproduction of a nineteenth-century sitting room.

carved black walnut buffet with marble top, a fainting couch, and a sewing box with beaded pincushion in the shape of a high-top shoe. There are Gody prints, watercolors by an aunt, oils by another aunt, and pastels by Mrs. Center's mother. In front of the window framed by lace curtains held with Tiffany tie-backs, is the height of Victorian luxury — a scarlet "Gone-With-the-Wind" lamp. Reportedly it came from an early Central City brothel.

On a wooden door, symmetrically arranged, is a collection of iron things — a key to King John's castle in Ireland, H-L hinges from Boston, a Central City railroad spike, and bridle pieces.

Up a flight of incredibly steep stairs, decorated with old prints including one by Charles Dana Gibson, are two bedrooms. Though all too many Victorian sleeping rooms were decorated with leftovers, these are furnished with handsome bedroom pieces — spool beds and walnut and marble dressers.

There is a child's rocker and the rocking chair in which Aunt Susan rocked all her babies, Lincoln Markham's Masonic papers, a decorative marriage certificate lettered in Spencerian tracery, two hand-worked pillow covers embroidered with "A Glorious Morning Unto You" and "Go to Sleep Like the Flowers."

The Victorian Age was a time when women were proud of their folk arts, when handwork was cherished and given proudly. One of the nicest customs of the last century was the "friendship" quilt. These handsome spreads were made for neighbors in distress, for families moving West, sometimes to honor a minister or teacher or hero, for a betrothed girl. Each woman embroidered a block; then the group met to "set" the top and do the "putting in."

Sometimes young women made quilts for men they liked, and Lincoln Markham's girlfriends embroidered one for him. His is an especially handsome quilt, a crazy-quilt made with brilliantly colored scraps of silk and velvet held together with a hundred different types of delicate, feathery stitches. Each girl pieced a square, embroidered it with her initials, and sometimes embellished it with ribbon or chenille flowers, the date, 1884, or special little designs.

Like the coverlet, the Center home is a crazy-quilt of brilliant pieces of Victoriana, pieced together with unbounded enthusiasm.

Antonito:

A Melancholy House

Amid the earth-colored homes that cluster together in the sun-swept towns of Southern Colorado is a ponderous brown brick mansion, its gables tipped with bright oriental design.

Though by far the grandest home in the Antonito area, its history is a sad, melancholy one.

The house was erected well into the twentieth century, in 1913, but it has the opulent feel of the Victorian past. It was built by an Antonito banker and rancher, Fred Warshauer, a Polish immigrant who came to the United States around 1880.

When his previous home, nearly as elegant as the later one, burned down in 1911, Warshauer decided to build the imposing brick one.

The grounds covered an entire block and once were elaborately landscaped and carefully cared for. Behind the house is what appears to have been a tennis court.

The house itself is H-shaped with the entrance in the center off a wide, open porch, and with wings on either side of it. The gables have an oriental tilt at the edges and are decorated on the sides with

Fred Warshauer home, Antonito, Colorado.

bright Chinese red designs and little balconies. The tile roof is the same red.

The French front doors open directly onto a wide corridor or what was the downstairs living room where there are a big English fireplace and dark oak paneling on the walls and staircase. Just below the ceiling is a red and yellow mosaic border of shields and coats of arms.

Behind the staircase a mural was painted by Yens Erickson, a graduate of Paris and Copenhagen schools of art. Erickson had also painted enormous canvases for Warshauer's first house and was commissioned to decorate the second one.

The stairway was lined with bronze statutes purchased by Warshauer on his frequent trips to Europe. He never traveled without bringing something back for his home.

To the left, in the south wing, the library was designed in a grand manner. Though self-educated, Warshauer was a well-read man, a scholar, and on the walls he wanted scenes from the books he loved and portraits of the great scholars and philosophers he admired.

Erickson illustrated pastoral, mythological, and historical works. He painted portraits of statesmen Benjamin Franklin, Thomas Jefferson, Abraham Lincoln, and Benjamin Disraeli; writers Charles Dickens, Dante, Ralph Waldo Emerson, and Voltaire; scientists Thomas Edison, Charles Darwin, and Copernicus. In addition he used elaborate stylized green and orange borders of laurel leaves.

Below the pictures, which were painted directly on the plaster walls, is dark oak paneling; the painting themselves are "framed" with wooden borders hand-carved in an egg-and-dart design.

At one side of the room is a fireplace alcove made of heavy oak and sandstone-colored bricks. Matching wood seats were built in next to the fireplace, and above one is a tiny window, its pane a rectangle of bottle glass.

Some of the furniture from the library is on display in the Colorado room of Constitution Hall, the Daughters of the American Revolution building in Washington, D.C. The library furniture is

Gables tilt at the edges and feature an oriental design
in Chinese red.

Paintings, done directly on the plaster walls,
were executed by Yens Erickson, a graduate
of the Paris and Copenhagen schools of art.

hand-carved mahogany which was part of the prize-winning Florentine display at the 1904 St. Louis Exposition.

The north wing was a combination diningroom and music room with a fireplace alcove similar to the one in the library. Less scholarly in décor than the south wing, the walls were covered with paintings of peacocks, flowers, grapes, and twining vines. There is a border of beer steins around the fireplace alcove, and on the ceiling are music notes and cupids.

The second-floor livingroom, the size of the one below it, is decorated with a painted border near the ceiling. There also are eight immense bedrooms on the second floor and half that many baths. Like the rest of the house, the bathrooms, too, were elegant. They had white tile floors and walls striped with tiles of delft blue.

Warshauer had little time to enjoy the beautiful home he had created. Only a few months after it was completed, he contracted influenzza. When he died, said his daughter, the house died, too. Though Mrs. Warshauer lived in the place until her own death in the early 1940's, the house with its elaborate painting and paneling never seemed to be the home Warshauer had intended.

More an institution than a house, the property was purchased some time after Mrs. Warshauer's death by Our Lady of Guadalupe Parish in Antonito. For a while it served as living quarters for nuns. Occasionally it is used for religion classes, parish activities, or church retreats.

The spirit of melancholia that seemed to descend at Warshauer's death, however, still lingers over the old home. Children have developed stories of mysterious deaths and ghosts, none based on fact. The grounds are ill-kept, and dead leaves drift across the walks. The fine house, intended as a place for music and literature, is a sad, forbidding block.

Stylized borders of leaves in green and orange and hand-carved wood designs "framed" the paintings.

Sedalia:

Cherokee Ranch

A Scottish castle, quite naturally, is not built exactly the same today as it would have been in 1450. Such a pretentious building has to be altered with the fads and changes of 500 years. Between the watch towers it has plaster and half-timber work, added in the sixteenth century when it was safe to live there. Around 1550, oriels replaced slits in the walls used by bowmen.

Vaulted plaster ceilings embellished with tudor roses were added during the reign of Elizabeth I. As the Dutch, French, and Portuguese influence came into Great Britain, manor lords adorned their castles with foreign touches.

In later years fine chandeliers replaced crude wall sconces. Naturally, when it became available, indoor plumbing was installed. A few even put in central heating.

The same concept, a fifteenth-century Scottish hunting lodge with the changes and embellishments that took place over the years, was used in a castle built on top of a Colorado mountain. The only difference is that the architect completed the work of 500 years in two.

Cherokee Ranch, formerly Charlford, Sedalia, Colorado.

213

The castle was built by Denver real estate man Charles Alfred Johnson on a mountain near Sedalia. He originally had selected a higher peak for the estate; but its owners would not sell, so he settled on the lower one nearby.

Neither a rancher nor a farmer, he nevertheless purchased 2400 acres surrounding his mountain in order to protect his view. He commissioned Burnham Hoyt, who later designed the Red Rocks amphitheater, to draw plans for the hunting lodge, originally intended as a vacation home.

Both Hoyt and Johnson were sticklers for detail; they wanted the home to be an accurate representation. Hoyt designed a small Scottish castle with numerous outbuildings and a cobblestone courtyard and added a bastion, a crenellated battlement, and a rampart.

Stone for Charlford, named after Johnson's son and step-son, Charles and Gifford, was quarried on the site. The pink, gray, and yellow-toned volcanic rock was hand-hewn and then hand-chiselled by Welsh craftsmen who lived on the grounds during the two-year construction period. The builder included sedimentary stone, also quarried on the property, as an accent. Roofs are Vermont slate.

Through a long gallery is the castle drawing room. Five hundred years ago it would have been the "great hall" with a massive cross-shape table running its length. The lord and his guests would have sat at the cross-piece with their backs to the fire for warmth. There might have been a roasted ox and huge dogs to gnaw the bones.

The room has a high, vaulted oak ceiling with carved wooden cross-pieces. Walls, which are thick, hand-carved rock, are a series of Romanesque arches with stone cornices holding roof supports.

At one end is a massive stone fireplace hand-carved with an English design of squirrels, oak leaves, and acorns. A craftsman was hired especially to carve the fireplace and the eight cornices around the room. After completing only the mantel and one cornice, however, he reportedly went on a bender and returned three weeks later to complete the job. The architect and craftsman had such a row over the spree that the artisan quit, and seven cornices remain uncarved.

Hoyt designed the iron fireplace screen. It represents history through a much different period than any ever depicted in the decoration of a castle in Scotland. There are evergreen forests, Indians with captured Spanish horses, and prairie schooners.

At the other end of the great room is a smaller, simpler fireplace. Above it is a gracefully carved minstrels' gallery, its back wall Elizabethan plaster and half-timber work.

Continuing the length of the drawing room is the dining hall, its architecture more refined than in the larger room. The plaster ceiling is vaulted with ribbing and Tudor rose designs. Walls are plaster, and the doorways are outlined in stone. A blue and white tile fireplace was designed for the room. Johnson chose the pattern, and each tile was marked at the factory for its particular place.

At the other end of the drawing room is the library, its ceiling crossed with rough-hewn beams. Nearby is the "Rocky Mountain Room," a small tower sitting room with a vast view of the mountains.

Floors in the drawing room are pegged random strips of wood. There are a honeycomb-tile floor in the diningroom and square tiles in the gallery. The Rocky Mountain Room has a stone floor.

There are two bedroom suites on the main floor as well as various rooms for staff.

The second floor would have been the battlement with watch towers, reached by steep, narrow, curling staircases. The towers have

The drawing room has a vaulted ceiling, a seventeenth-century brass chandelier, and a carved minstrels' gallery.

215

Only one of the eight cornices in the drawing room is carved, as a result of a craftsman's bender.

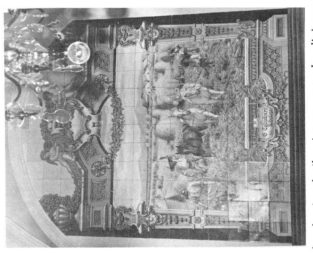

The hand-painted tile picture over the diningroom fireplace was especially made for Charlford.

been turned into bedrooms, and a narrow walk along the battlement has been enclosed to form a passageway.

The high tower, above the Rocky Mountain Room, has been made into a tiny library, and above is a battlement, an excellent place from which to watch the sun set behind the rugged Colorado mountains.

Outside are various utilitarian buildings, constructed of the same volcanic stone and sedimentary rock. The garage has an incongruously flat roof, the result of a contractor's misreading of the architect's specifications and building the peaked roof higher than planned. Johnson, abroad during construction, returned to find the garage roof higher than the house, so he ordered it sliced off.

Johnson and his wife lived in Charlford, with intermittent stays in their Denver town house, until 1949. The castle stood vacant for five years until it was purchased by a family who renamed it "Cherokee Ranch." Like the Indians, the new owners had migrated West from Tennessee and thought the name appropriate.

They named not only the ranch but various sections of it as well. The twisting trail that cuts across the mountain from U.S. 85 is called "Rattlesnake Road." The family enlarged the property to 6200 acres, including the high bluff on which Johnson had wanted to build the house originally. They named the peak "Cherokee Mountain."

Happily, the present owners have carried out the spirit and feeling in which Burnham Hoyt designed the house. Furnishings, most of which are antique pieces, represent various periods of history, and instead of being segregated by era, they have been placed together harmoniously.

Even the working ranch carries out the mixture of centuries. Santa Gertrudis cattle, a 100-year-old Texas blend of two much older breeds, were bred and raised for the first time in the Rocky Mountain states at Cherokee Ranch.

The old Charlford, now Cherokee Ranch, has continued the idea that spurred its architect. There is a definite love of the old combined with a smart respect for progress which, after all, is what an authentic Scottish castle really is.

217

Bibliography

Bancroft, Caroline, *Famous Aspen*. Bancroft Booklets. Boulder, Johnson Publishing Co., 1951.

Bancroft, Caroline, *Unique Ghost Towns and Mountain Spots*. Bancroft Booklets. Boulder, Johnson Publishing Co., 1961.

De Pew, Kathryn, "W. A. Hamill and The Hamill House." Denver, *The Colorado Magazine*, October, 1955.

Eberhart, Perry, *Guide to the Colorado Ghost Towns and Mining Camps*. Denver, Sage Books, 1959.

Fossett, Frank, *Colorado*. New York, C. G. Crawford Printer, 1880.

Griswold, Don and Jean, *A Carbonate Camp Called Leadville*. Denver, University of Denver Press, 1951.

Hollenback, Frank R., *Central City and Black Hawk, Colorado: Then and Now*. Denver, Sage Books, 1961.

Koch, Robert, *Louis C. Tiffany, Rebel in Glass*. New York, Crown Publishers, Inc., 1964.

Lane, Rose Wilder, *Woman's Day Book of American Needlework*. New York, Simon and Schuster, 1963.

Lee, Mabel Barbee, *Cripple Creek Days*. Garden City, Doubleday & Co., Inc., 1958.

Maass, John, *The Gingerbread Age*. New York, Bramhall House, 1957.

Peery, Bill, "Hartman and His Ranch — Showplace of Gunnison." Gunnison, *Western Slope Prospector*, August 19, 1963.

Pritchett, Lulita Crawford, *The Cabin at Medicine Springs*. New York, Franklin Watts, Inc., 1958.

Rocky Mountain Motorists, Inc., *Glidden Tour Triptik*. Denver, 1964.

Tarkington, Booth, *The Magnificent Ambersons*. New York, Doubleday & Co., Inc., 1918.

Turnbull, Belle, "Gold Boats on the Swan." *The Colorado Magazine*, October, 1962.

Wolle, Muriel Sibell, *Stampede to Timberline*. Denver, Sage Books, 1949.

Wood, Myron and Nancy, *Central City: A Ballad of the West*. Colorado Springs, Chaparral Press, 1963.